A *Resource Guide to*
Asian American
Literature

A Resource Guide to

Asian American Literature

Edited by

Sau-ling Cynthia Wong and
Stephen H. Sumida

The Modern Language Association of America
New York   2001

For information about obtaining permission to reprint material from MLA book publications, send your request by mail (see address below), e-mail (permissions@mla.org), or fax (646 458-0030).

Library of Congress Cataloging-in-Publication Data

A resource guide to Asian American literature / edited by Sau-ling Cynthia Wong and
Stephen H. Sumida.
    p. cm.
    Includes bibliographical references and index.
    ISBN 0-87352-271-0 (cloth)—ISBN 0-87352-272-9 (pbk.)
    1. American literature—Asian American authors—Handbooks, manuals, etc. 2. American literature—
Asian American authors—Bio-bibliography. 3. Asian Americans in literature—Handbooks, manuals, etc.
4. Asian Americans in literature—Bio-bibliography. I. Wong, Sau-ling Cynthia. II. Sumida, Stephen H.

PS153.A84 R47 2000
810.9′895—dc21   00-040223

Printed on recycled paper

Published by The Modern Language Association of America
26 Broadway, New York, New York 10004-1789
www.mla.org

Contents

Introduction

Stephen H. Sumida and
Sau-ling Cynthia Wong

This volume is made up of twenty-one units on different book-length works of literature and four review essays on genres other than prose narratives and drama.

Each unit is written by an individual contributor and typically includes the following parts: Publication Information (and, for dramatic works, Production Information as well), Overview, Reception, Author's Biographical Background, Historical Context for the Narratives in the Text, Historical Context for the Writing of the Text (this section is sometimes combined with the previous one, or else omitted when another, contemporaneous title in this *Resource Guide* already provides relevant information), Major Themes, Critical Issues, Pedagogical Issues and Suggestions, Intertextual Linkages (indicating texts both Asian American and other than Asian American with which a given title can be compared), Bibliographic Resources, Other Resources (e.g., films and videos and, in one case, Web sites), and Bibliography (of works consulted in the writing of the unit). In selecting works to discuss for this volume, we decided to feature book-length prose narratives most heavily, since they provide the most ready access to the literature of Asian Americans and their varied experiences and since instructors often assemble syllabi on the basis of this genre. Six units, nonetheless, are devoted to drama. Within each genre, works are listed alphabetically by author.

In the section "Other Genres," four extensive essays cover anthologies, short fiction, and poetry. Sau-ling Wong's essay on anthologies concentrates on panethnic Asian American literary anthologies. For short stories and poetry, teaching suggestions for specific authors and individual pieces are relatively more difficult to make. Rachel Lee's essay on short fiction focuses on twelve titles, indicating themes and approaches that may be generalized from them. There are two essays on Asian American poetry, a vast and wonderfully unruly subject: Sunn Shelley Wong's essay offers a theoretical consideration of the difficulties of reading Asian American poetry, as well as an account of the critical debates poets and their poetry have generated, while George Uba's essay provides a history of the tradition and suggestions for teaching.

Over the course of ten years we have constructed, and the contributors have filled, a manageable table of contents through a difficult questioning and juggling of the following criteria (which, we emphasize, are *not* listed in order of rank and are *not* applicable in all cases): aesthetic interest; commercial availability; current usage among college instructors; gender and ethnic subgroup variations; historical interest; role in the development of Asian American literature; "track record" of responses by readers, critics, and teachers; potential for generating intertextual linkages and encouraging comparative study; productivity in raising certain critical issues commonly debated in Asian American scholarship; and an elusive quality we call "teachability," the reality of which we can attest to only by telling anecdotes.

This sketch explains what the *Resource Guide* contains and why. We are mindful, however, that the sketch and this volume assume understandings of concepts basic to this work but not yet recognized by many of its users. From its inception in 1989–90 this project has been meant to invite newcomers to Asian American literature to really use it. Nowadays even specialists in Asian American studies are themselves asking anew, What do we mean by Asian American studies? When experts need to ask and to ask repeatedly, in order to rake the field and keep it vigorous, newcomers must certainly have questions too. What is Asian American literature?

It used to be, through the 1970s, 1980s, and no doubt more recently on occasion, that the term *Asian American literature* conjured for the uninitiated thoughts about the study of haiku and Chinese classics, little tastes of which one perhaps acquired in a world literature course in one's general education. In the 1970s, however, writers and scholars in Asian American literature emphatically corrected the mistaking of the emerging category Asian American studies for the already established category Asian studies, whether in academia or in popular culture. In opposition to the confusion, a definite understanding of what constitutes Asian American literature was asserted. It is literature written by people of Asian descent in the United States, individuals and a racialized group who have histories distinctive to their presence in and relations to the United States; most often it is literature written originally in English, the educational and literary language of many Asian Americans. While this definition has been questioned since then and at the time was already contradicted by Asian American literary interests that did not fit into the definition, it still marks a point of departure for the processes of understanding an extraordinarily dynamic question, What is Asian American literature?[1]

Here is a material response. Confronting a similar question asked by a reporter in Philadelphia in 1987 on the eve of a conference there on Asian American poetry, Lawson Fusao Inada replied by writing his poem "From Live Do."[2] The reporter had asked, "What is Asian American poetry?" Inada answered:

Asia is where
my people
are *from*.

2

America is where
I *live*.

Poetry is what
I *do*.

So there it is:

Asian American poetry:

From Live Do. (238)

Because of the way Inada is situated in Asian American literary history, he could state with a high degree of certainty—not only for himself but also for Asian American writers generally—that his playful formulation "From Live Do" defines writers and their works in regard to the category of Asian American poetry or literature. Inada's ability to be playful shows a suppleness and implies an authority that come from long experience and memory. He is of a generation of artists and scholars in Asian American literature who established, with considerable struggle and contestation, a version of the very concept that goes by that name.

By the late 1980s, however, the concept of Asian American literature had become established in academia in the United States at least enough that newcomers to the field perceived it as the prescription of a reified identity called "Asian American" and constituted somehow out of the heterogeneity of ethnicities in "Asian America."[3] To newcomers, the term prescribed a hybrid identity rather than posited a political, analytic category, as the term *Third World* used to in the 1970s or the terms *Latina* and *Latino* nowadays do in discourses constructed to deal with internally heterogeneous groups. But where, if anywhere, did this hybrid Asian American identity exist?[4] Inada's poem is clearly not itself Asian American in the sense of being polyethnically Asian. The poem is very specifically Japanese American in being about his grandparents' fish market in Fresno, California, and about his receiving their words and through their words their influences on his poetry. There is no hybrid Asian American identity in the poem, but Inada wrote and introduced his poem by invoking the analytic category called Asian American.[5]

Inada's certainty about what Asian American poetry is in "From Live Do" strikes a pose, the current subtexts of which are richly complicated. Consider the notion of coming "from Asia," whether the arrivee is the Asian American writer her- or himself or is a forebear, with the writer being a second-generation, third-generation, or other descendant yet further distant from the actual experience of immigration. Where is "Asia"? What is it? As an Americanist from Japan quipped, "Asia is a Western geographer's invention" (Aruga). It is an orientalist conceit, in Edward Said's famous term, where "Asia" is a category devised for dividing the globe into regions for the purpose of mapping strategies to take advantage of those regions. In the category called Asian American, where does Asia begin and end? Some scholars and writers consider the indigenous peoples of the Pacific Islands of the United States empire—for instance,

Hawai'i, Guam, and American Samoa—to be part of or at least to be related discursively to Asian Americans.[6] So for some the term implies another questioned term, *Asian/Pacific American*, and in this construction, Asia encompasses the Pacific Ocean as well as the continents and islands to the west of the international date line. In 1994, the Annual Conference of the Association for Asian American Studies included a paper by Moustafa Bayoumi, "Is There an 'A' in Asian American for Arabs?" Where at the western reaches of Asia does the region end, and might the category Asian American be applied to analyzing Arab American literature? The question is not far-fetched. Said's *Orientalism* and studies that preceded and have directly followed it are applicable to the entire hemisphere that in common Europe-centered terminology stretches from the "Near" through the "Middle" to the "far East."

Questioning of the term *Asian American* extends as well, at present, to the questioning of what America is and may yet be. This indeed is one of the preeminent accomplishments of the Asian American literature of immigration that dominated the field up to the mid-1980s. From Sui Sin Far and her late-nineteenth- and early-twentiety-century contemporaries and predecessors—writers of North America who opposed anti-immigrant nativists—to writers such as Joy Kogawa and Philip Kan Gotanda and, in their works of the 1990s, Gish Jen, Shawn Wong, and Frank Chin, the Asian American literature of immigration often challenges any conceptions of America that exclude or alienate Asian Americans from America. It is a literature of inclusion rather than exclusion, a literature that seeks to change homogenizing definitions of America into categories capable of taking all peoples and cultures of the United States into account. Although this literature, numerous examples of which are discussed in this *Resource Guide*, has been used in many ways to study Asian American identity or culturally specific identities, the literature profoundly does not *represent* identity, culture, and groups of Asian American peoples. But it does *present* strategic, fictive bases for apprehending and analyzing historical constructions of American culture in relation to Asian American histories, cultures, and racialization.

In the 1990s the boundaries of Asian America came to include, in ways more assertive than previously, South Asian and Southeast Asian Americans.[7] In that decade, too, new questions produced knowledge about already included groups. For instance, Filipino American writers and their distinctive relation to the category Asian American have been reread and reconsidered in the context of the colonization of the Philippines in 1898, the status of Filipinos as American wards but "noncitizens" from 1898 to 1946, and a literature of exile and of postcolonialism that engages in this history.[8] The occasion of the 1998 centennial of the colonization not only of the Philippines but also of Hawai'i and Guam brought new attention to the literatures of Pacific Islander subjects of the United States and to the long-standing imperial designs of this nation. So Inada's playful and definitive response to the reporter—"*America is where / I live*"—dramatically masks active questions about the meanings of *America* and *Asian America* alike.

"*Poetry is what / I do*," writes Inada. Since the time when he joined Frank Chin,

Jeffery Paul Chan, and Shawn Hsu Wong in the project of literary research and recovery, *Aiiieeeee! An Anthology of Asian-American Writers* (1974), generic boundaries and the values formerly attached to genres have changed markedly. These changes, however, may not always or even often be reflected in the way uninformed readers of Asian American literature read and judge the works of various genres described in this *Resource Guide*. In 1974 and for a few years afterward, Chin and other writers central to the acts of recovery and creation of Asian American literature could prescribe differences among literature, nonfiction, and journalism and rank them thus in descending order. The publication and reception of Maxine Hong Kingston's *The Woman Warrior: Memoirs of a Girlhood among Ghosts* in 1976 affected this certainty about generic boundaries, as can be seen in the article on that work in this volume. "Poetry" (and by extension literature) is "what I do," Inada writes plainly. But what is "literature"?

These questions that "From Live Do" evokes are not performed to confuse the understanding we aim to instill in the articles on individual works and authors and on genres. Rather, we suggest that the reporter's question "What is Asian American poetry?" is as open to inquiry and response as the question "What is American literature?" We who contribute to this volume assume from our individual and collective years of the practices of writing, making art, conducting research, writing up our scholarship, and teaching in Asian American literature that the Asian American cultures interpreted and presented in the literature are living, dynamic, changing, conflictual, and dialogic rather than simplistically preserved ones. In sum, Asian American literature is the very process, a vigorously dialogic one, of asking and addressing the question of what it is. And why not? This process is what empowers, for it sooner or later exposes the structures that make Asian Americans into perpetual aliens or castaways whose cultures tumble nicely and helplessly in history's broad wake. The process enables literature not to be trapped within beliefs of cultural determinism but to be involved in changing the structures of culture that people have made.

Many people have contributed to this project, especially the anonymous readers of the proposals submitted to the MLA's office of book publications and the Publications Committee. We are most grateful to the readers for their insights and critiques. The responsibility for the final shape taken by this volume, however, remains ours.

We also wish to express our deepest gratitude to the members of the Committee on the Literatures and Languages of America and to the members of the Publications Committee, as well as to the MLA colleagues too numerous to name here who helped in many ways during the course of the project. Special thanks go to Martha Evans, director of book publications, for her guidance and her trust, and to Michael Kandel, our copyeditor at the MLA; to all the contributors, for their enthusiasm, fine work, and extreme patience with the numerous delays between conception and delivery of the volume; to Chris Domingo Pocock and D. G. Park, who copyedited the manuscript under often frustrating circumstances; and to Michael Oishi, for his help with researching and checking sources. Like a bibliography of current literature, a work such as this is never finished. We offer our thanks to those who have brought it this far.

Notes

1. It is not our purpose to demonstrate the slipperiness of the term *Asian American* through demographic and sociological analyses. Readers interested in demographic overviews are referred to studies such as Barringer, Gardner, and Levin; Ong and Hee; Min; and Lee.

2. Inada was responding to the question posed by Leonard Boasberg in the *Philadelphia Inquirer* (Inada 236). Inada is noted for his long poems, often occasional ones—in this case, the occasion of the conference on Asian American poetry. The quoted excerpt is one of several punch lines that punctuate the poem, all of them addressing the question in lively, creative ways.

3. Asian American panethnicity, as Espiritu notes, results from both the conflating racialization of Asian Americans by the dominant group and their own self-affirming, self-creating responses to such a construction (*Panethnicity* [1992]). For an update on this research and theory, see Espiritu, *Panethnicity* (1996). Referring to a political alliance as well as a sense of shared association, the term attempts to counter the fragmentation caused by the heterogeneity of "Asian Americans." But the term has always been fraught with tensions, not the least because changing immigration and settlement patterns and concomitant shifts in political forces have, historically, caused the boundaries of the Asian American community to fluctuate quite wildly. In fact, even a group often referred to as a single ethnicity, such as South Asian Americans, is itself coalitional and arguably panethnic (see, e.g., Women of South Asian Descent Collective; Maira and Srikanth) and often beset by internal divisions (see, e.g., Islam). When applied to literature, the term *Asian American* also connotes an uneasy conglomeration of diverse texts—what Sau-ling C. Wong calls a "textual coalition" (9). This strategy for dealing with heterogeneity is by no means unique to Asian Americans. The categories called by such names as Latino/Latina, Native American, and African American are also heterogeneous internally. Indeed, the contemporary concept of pluralism in and of the United States is supposedly an explicit recognition that every group, including European Americans, is made up of constituent parts, none of which constitutes a majority by itself.

4. In her introduction to *The Forbidden Stitch: An Asian American Women's Anthology*, Shirley Geok-lin Lim states, "I knew there was no such thing as an 'Asian American woman'" (Lim and Tsutakawa 10). In his introduction to *Dissident Song: A Contemporary Asian American Anthology*, David Wong Louie notes, "Measured against the diversity in literary styles and political concerns represented here, the term 'Asian American' (except for the sake of political expediency) is rendered all but obsolete" (Chin, Louie, and Weisner). Jessica Hagedorn introduces *Charlie Chan Is Dead: An Anthology of Contemporary Asian American Fiction* with a catalog of the "exhilarating" differences among the authors she includes, and she asks rhetorically, "Asian American literature? Too confining a term, maybe. World literature? Absolutely" (xxx). Garrett Hongo's introductions to his two anthologies, *The Open Boat: Poems from Asian America* and *Under Western Eyes: Personal Essays from Asian America*, attack the identity politics of so-called cultural nationalism as confining and silencing. Though Walter Lew's afterword to *Premonitions: The Kaya Anthology of New Asian North American Poetry* does not directly address the theoretical issues associated with panethnicity, one reviewer calls the volume "a significant gesture toward what we might consider a post-identity politics anthology" (Bascara 6).

5. On "Asian American" as an analytic category rather than as a category of identity, see also Sumida ("Centers"). Since the titles and conceptions of all the anthologies named in the preceding note, like the title of this *Resource Guide*, use the term *Asian American* even while their editors strenuously question it, the term thus names an analytic category. Questions are being usefully and productively raised even about terms of "identity" that still appear to be ethnically specific. For example, the widely used term *Chinese American*, accepted in the United States as "natural," may prove unstable: as Taiwanese identity gains ground in the island state, Taiwanese Americans are differentiating themselves from Chinese Americans (see Ng).

6. Since anthologies are most conspicuously the sites where a coalitional sense of Asian American identity is put to use, some anthologers (e.g., Chung, Kim, and Lemeshewsky; Lim-Hing) have attempted to be maximally inclusive by insisting on using the categories of Asian Pacific American, Asian Pacific Islander, and Pacific/Asian (which have been recognized as bureaucratic categories in state and federal offices) instead of Asian American. Nevertheless, the "Pacific" component is a highly charged one. For example, the Asian American writings of Hawai'i straddle categories of Asian American literature and local literature, each discursive location making its own claims and demands and both in tension with native Hawai'ian discourse (Sumida, *View* and "Postcolonialism"; Fujikane).

7. Shankar and Srikanth devote their entire volume to exploring the complex relations between the categories South Asian American and Asian American. "South Asia" refers to India, Pakistan, Nepal, Bhutan, Bangladesh, Sri Lanka, and the Maldives (ix).

8. Some have argued that, for writers commonly referred to as Filipino Americans, the colonial history peculiar to the Philippines renders ill-fitting the United States nation-based models for identity prevalent in Asian American literary criticism (see Campomanes; San Juan; Gonzalez and Campomanes). In a similar vein, a vision of Asian America based on immigration may be inappropriate for understanding the literature produced by Vietnamese Americans and certain other Southeast Asian Americans (Laotian, Cambodian, Hmong) who came to the United States largely as exiles and refugees (Truong).

Bibliography

Aruga, Tadashi. Personal interview. Jan. 1993.

Barringer, Herbert R., Robert W. Gardner, and Michael J. Levin. *Asians and Pacific Islanders in the United States*. New York: Russell Sage Foundation, 1993.

Bascara, Victor. Rev. of *Premonitions*, by Walter Lew. *ExplanASIAN: The Newsletter of the Asian American Writers Workshop* 3.3 (1995): 5–6.

Bayoumi, Moustafa. "Is There an 'A' in Asian American for Arabs?" Annual Conf. of the Assn. for Asian Amer. Studies. U of Michigan, Ann Arbor. 1994.

Campomanes, Oscar V. "Filipinos in the United States and Their Literature of Exile." *Reading the Literature of Asian America*. Ed. Shirley Geok-lin Lim and Amy Ling. Philadelphia: Temple UP, 1992. 49–78.

Cheung, King-Kok, ed. *An Interethnic Companion to Asian American Literature*. New York: Cambridge UP, 1997.

Chin, Frank, et al., eds. *Aiiieeeee! An Anthology of Asian-American Writers*. Washington: Howard UP, 1974.

Chin, Marilyn, David Wong Louie, and Ken Weisner, eds. *Dissident Song: A Contemporary Asian American Anthology*. Spec. issue of *Quarry West* 29–30 (1991): 1–168.

Chung, Cristy, Alison Kim, and A. Kaweah Lemeshewsky, eds. *Between the Lines: An Anthology by Pacific-Asian Lesbians of Santa Cruz, California*. Santa Cruz: Dancing Bird, 1987.

Espiritu, Yen Le, ed. *Asian American Panethnicity*. Spec. issue of *Amerasia Journal* 22.2 (1996): i–186.

———. *Asian American Panethnicity: Bridging Institutions and Identities*. Philadelphia: Temple UP, 1992.

Fujikane, Candace Lei. "Archipelagos of Resistance: Narrating Nation in Asian American, Native Hawaiian, and Hawaii's Local Literatures." Diss. U of California, Berkeley, 1996.

Gonzalez, N. V. M., and Oscar V. Campomanes. "Filipino American Literature." Cheung 62–124.

Hagedorn, Jessica, ed. *Charlie Chan Is Dead: An Anthology of Contemporary Asian American Fiction*. New York: Penguin, 1993.

Hongo, Garrett, ed. *The Open Boat: Poems from Asian America*. New York: Anchor-Doubleday, 1993.

———, ed. *Under Western Eyes: Personal Essays from Asian America*. New York: Anchor-Doubleday, 1995.

Inada, Lawson. "From Live Do." Nomura, Endo, Sumida, and Leong 236–47.

Islam, Naheed. "In the Belly of the Multicultural Beast I Am Named South Asian." Women of South Asian Descent Collective 242–45.

Lee, Sharon M. *Asian Americans: Diverse and Growing*. Washington: Population Reference Bureau, 1998.

Lew, Walter K., ed. *Premonitions: The Kaya Anthology of New Asian North American Poetry.* New York: Kaya, 1995.

Lim, Shirley Geok-lin, and Mayumi Tsutakawa, eds. *The Forbidden Stitch: An Asian American Women's Anthology*. Corvallis: Calyx, 1989.

Lim-Hing, Sharon, ed. *The Very Inside: An Anthology of Writing by Asian and Pacific Islander Lesbian and Bisexual Women*. Toronto: Sister Vision, 1994.

Maira, Sunaina, and Rajini Srikanth, eds. *Contours of the Heart: South Asians Map North America*. New York: Asian Amer. Writers' Workshop, 1996.

Min, Pyong Gap, ed. *Asian Americans: Contemporary Trends and Issues*. Thousand Oaks: Sage, 1995.

Nomura, Gail M., Russell Endo, Stephen H. Sumida, and Russell C. Leong. *Frontiers of Asian American Studies: Writing, Research, and Commentary*. Pullman: Washington State UP, 1989.

Ng, Franklin. *Taiwanese Americans*. Westport: Greenwood, 1998.

Ong, Paul, and Suzanne J. Hee. "The Growth of the Asian Pacific American Population: Twenty Million in 2020." *The State of Asian Pacific America: Policy Issues to the Year 2000*. Los Angeles: LEAP Asian Pacific Amer. Public Policy Inst. and UCLA Asian Amer. Studies Center, 1993. 11–23.

Said, Edward. *Orientalism*. New York: Vintage, 1979.

San Juan, E., Jr. "In Search of Filipino Writing: Reclaiming Whose 'America'?" *The Ethnic Canon: Histories, Institutions, and Interventions.* Ed. David Palumbo-Liu. Minneapolis: U of Minnesota P, 1995. 213–40.

Shankar, Lavina Dhingra, and Rajini Srikanth, eds. *A Part, yet Apart: South Asians in Asian America.* Philadelphia: Temple UP, 1998.

Sumida, Stephen H. *And the View from the Shore: Literary Traditions of Hawai'i.* Seattle: U of Washington P, 1991.

———. "Centers without Margins: Responses to Centrism in Asian American Literature." *American Literature* 66 (1994): 803–15.

———. "Postcolonialism, Nationalism, and the Emergence of Asian/Pacific American Literatures." Cheung 274–88.

Truong, Monique T. D. "Vietnamese American Literature." Cheung 219–46.

Women of South Asian Descent Collective, eds. *Our Feet Walk the Sky: Women of the South Asian Diaspora.* San Francisco: Aunt Lute, 1993.

Wong, Sau-ling Cynthia. *Reading Asian American Literature: From Necessity to Extravagance.* Princeton: Princeton UP, 1993.

Book-Length
Prose Narratives

Nampally Road
by Meena Alexander

Shilpa Davé

Publication Information

First published in the United States in 1991 by Mercury House, San Francisco, in hardcover and softcover. Distributed by Consortium Book Sales and Distribution, Inc., Saint Paul.

Overview

In *Nampally Road* Meena Alexander tells the semiautobiographical story of a teacher returning to India after being educated abroad in England. The main character, Mira Kannadical, is an English literature instructor at a local college in Hyderabad, a city in South India. Set during the time of Indian martial law in the 1970s, the novel describes Mira's struggle to define her role and identity in relation to an India that is undergoing civil and social upheaval. As the novel opens, Mira witnesses the beginnings of a peaceful protest against new taxes that is violently put down by government troops. This incident sets off the background context of the novel, the unlawful imprisonment of an innocent village bystander, Rameeza, who ultimately is tortured and beaten. This woman becomes the touchstone for the activists, one of whom is Mira's boyfriend, Ramu. Also a teacher at the Central University of Hyderabad, Ramu calls for open protests against the government. Mira's mentor, Durgabai (also called "little mother"), works at a women's health shelter and resists government oppression by ministering to women who are victims of the culture and the system. She represents the alternative side of activism as Mira grapples with her own role as a teacher of English Romantic poetry and wonders whether her position can be seen as a type of activism in its own right. Ultimately, Mira abandons her classroom and fights to free Rameeza from both the government prison and the opportunistic national activists who see the woman only as an object to be used rather than as an individual. The intertwining of identity and the history that forms an individual becomes the major theme that the women's collective of Mira, Durgabai, and Rameeza strives to identify. Cutting across class, educational, and cultural boundaries, the women bind themselves together and support each other through their presence.

Reception

Nampally Road is Alexander's first novel, but before this publication Alexander was a well-known poet. *Nampally Road* is a somewhat controversial novel because the central setting of India and the presence of a Western-educated narrator seem to label Alexander as a postcolonial writer rather than as an Asian American writer. However, Alexander's work has been devoted to defining how identity relates to education and place. Currently, she is a prominent advocate for the importance of a South Asian voice in the Asian American canon. Her work contributes to the expansion of the term *postcolonial* and the relation between America, Britain, and India. More important, her novel focuses on the tension that a woman of color faces in teaching Western classics and on Western stereotypes of the East that are often at odds with her own history and the environment in which she is teaching these narratives. The narrator tries to reconcile herself to the teaching of Wordsworth in the middle of a civil upheaval in Hyderabad. Even though *Nampally Road* is set in India, the issues of immigration, history, representation of multiple viewpoints, and identity that Alexander addresses are shared by Asian American writers and critics.

In her memoir, *Fault Lines*, Alexander explicitly discusses the role of the postcolonial in America. Her vigorous examination of the role she plays as a writer and as a South Asian American teaching in America focuses on issues similar to the ones she raises in her novel. She looks at the relation of personal and institutionalized history to the construction of individual identity. Alexander attempts to resolve the contradictions between Western tropes of the East, such as the docile, educated native, and her own identity as a woman of color who is an educator in an American college. Her work brings together the theorized postcolonial subject and the Asian American immigrant and opens up a new arena of investigation in both Asian American and postcolonial circles, the intersection and interrogation of postcolonialism in America.

South Asian American publications have proliferated in the past several years. Writers such as Vikram Seth, Chitra Banerjee Divakaruni, and Jhumpa Lahiri have been received with popular and critical acclaim, and many new critical anthologies as well as Asian American anthologies routinely include Alexander and Bharati Mukherjee in their collections. The discussion of South Asian American issues and themes in literature courses posits Alexander as an additional or alternative point of view to Mukherjee, who is the more well known South Asian American author. While Mukherjee's characters often seem to be in transit, blinded by the lure of a frontierlike America, Alexander's characters tend to be proactive individuals who wrestle with their identity through the exploration of writing and language. The inclusion of multiple viewpoints provides a more rounded picture of the South Asian experience in Asian American literature and avoids stereotyping an ethnic group on the basis of one writer's portrayal. Alexander and other talented South Asian American writers, by representing various aspects of the South Asian American experience, greatly enhance the body of works that make up Asian American literature.

Nampally Road has received critical acclaim. It was an editor's choice in the Village Voice (Francia) and was favorably reviewed in the Los Angeles Times Book Review (Rubin), in Publishers Weekly and in the Seattle Times (Chait).

Author's Biographical Background

Meena Alexander was born on 17 February 1951 in Allahabad, India. She was the eldest of three children of George and Mary Alexander. When she was five, Alexander's family moved to North Africa, and from that time on she moved back and forth between India and Africa. At eighteen, Alexander went to the University of Nottingham, in England, where she was awarded a scholarship to pursue a doctorate. Six years later, she returned to India, where she taught (from 1974 to 1979) at several Indian universities, including the University of Delhi and the University of Hyderabad. Nampally Road is a semiautobiographical account of some of her experiences in Hyderabad. She published her first volume of poetry, The Bird's Bright Ring, in 1976. Three years later, in 1979, she arrived in New York City.

In the United States Alexander has taught writing and literature and focused on her work as a poet. She has taught at Fordham University and the University of Minnesota and has been the writer-in-residence at the Center for American Culture Studies at Columbia University. Currently, she is a professor of creative writing and English at Hunter College and the Graduate Center, City University of New York.

Historical Context for the Narratives in *Nampally Road*

The novel revolves around a notorious 1978 court case in India in which a Muslim woman was assaulted and raped by several policemen in the city of Hyderabad in the state of Andhra Pradesh. The ensuing uproar over the woman's treatment resulted in riots and the burning of the police station. The book takes place during the 1970s, a time of tremendous political corruption in India's history. The prime minister, Indira Gandhi, declared a state of emergency in June 1975 and suspended all civil rights for Indian citizens. All forms of media required government approval, and those who did not agree with public policy were imprisoned. In particular Gandhi's actions led to a wide interpretation of the law and a flagrant misuse of power. The presence in the novel of Limca Gowda, the corrupt political official, and his "Everready Men" clearly points to the state of India in the 1970s.

Major Themes

the relation of history to self-identity

the relation between Western education and community activism

the exploration of class politics and the status of Indian women

the alienation and isolation of the Muslim minority in the Hindu-dominated
South

the development of a women's community and lines of communication outside
language

the female body and the body politic

geography and displacement

the relation between postcolonial narratives and Asian American narratives

political upheaval and the differences in the roles men and women play in
activism

dream imagery

writing and language

English Romanticism versus Indian geography

Critical Issues

Ketu Katrak characterizes Alexander as a writer who "voices a deep concern for the survival of the female imagination in different spaces [and whose] poetic voice seeks an accountability to a history of migration and dislocation" (206). In *Nampally Road* Alexander questions her identity in relation to the past by addressing both her relationship and her main character's relationship to cultural history and writing. She concentrates on the themes of cultural stereotyping and identity.

As I have noted elsewhere, "Identity is measured by language in this novel" (Davé 108). Mira's inability to articulate her position arises from the events around her. Since the novel is set in India, Mira is a member of the dominant society. And yet Indian culture has been modified by Western culture: the government communicates in English, Western schools are considered the best educational opportunities, and America is the land where success is possible. But instead of abandoning her cultural heritage and burying herself in her Western education, Mira seeks to relate her knowledge of Romanticism to the politically explosive situation in Hyderabad. Thus, the ideas she teaches and writes are pressed by both Indian and English cultures and influence her expression of her identity.

From the onset of the novel, Mira's identity is etched in difference:

> Though I tried I really could not write my story. I could not figure out a line
> or a theme for myself. The life that made sense was all around me in Little

Mother and Ramu and the young students, the orange sellers and the violent and wretched, ourselves included. No one needed my writing. It could make no difference [. . .]. I had no clear picture of what unified it all, what our history might mean. We were in it, all together, that's all I knew.   (28)

Her inability to write reflects her difficulty in reconciling the historical past and the present in a language of her own making.

Mira's search for a universal language translates into a vision with multiple possibilities and opens up identity and culture to various influences, not just to a monolithic Western culture. Alexander depicts concepts of difference in her novel and supports pluralism as a means of reconciling an individual to a community. Although some may argue that dream imagery is not a realistic form of communication, I argue that dreams offer a hope for change, a chance to see a vision other than what is present. In "Real Places; or, How Sense Fragments: Thoughts on Ethnicity and the Making of Poetry," Alexander says, "My job is to evoke [my idea], all of it, altogether. For that is what my ethnicity requires, that is what America with its hot-shot present tense compels me to" (75). Writing becomes a way of weaving her past and present into a presentable form that enacts her identity. Alexander's questioning of her past and her writing opens up the definitions of imperialism, postcolonialism, and culture. The influence of environment or culture is integrated into the vision of the individual with the intent of modifying the worldview into an all-encompassing cultural society. In essence, identity becomes multicultural instead of unicultural.

By asking the question in her novel, How does history make us?, Alexander leads the way to a breaking down of hegemonic barriers. To expand our understanding of identity in relation to culture, we need to explore how the past influences our actions in the present and in the future. Asian American literature incorporates the traditions of two continents; to forgo the one in favor of the other is to become another victim of Western imperialism. But linking the traditions and questioning our relationship to our past help us to forge ahead toward the restructuring of conventional Western narratives and the Asian American canon. Asian American literature is part of a postcolonial diasporic condition because Western expansionism and imperialism are parts of Asian American history.

Pedagogical Issues and Suggestions

Nampally Road is a readable novel that students find easy to discuss once the historical context of the book is set up. Alexander's primary work as a poet clearly comes through in her vivid descriptions of the sights, sounds, and feelings of India. The most frequent question that arises when teaching this book is, How does the book fit into Asian American literature? It is important for teachers to talk about the multiple categories of literature that the work could fit into (postcolonial, Indian diasporic, immigrant,

Asian American, etc.) and to discuss the genealogy of South Asians in America and in literature. Just as the historical circumstances of Western expansion and the internment of Japanese Americans influence Chinese and Japanese American literature, so do the rise of Western educated Indians and the displacement of this educated elite in America influence South Asian Americans. British imperialism also figures strongly into the development of South Asian American identity, and so it is important to discuss the circumstances in India in relation to the immigration history of South Asians to America. The instructor might prepare, or have students prepare, a short history of South Asian immigration and discuss similarities to and differences from the immigration histories of other Asian American ethnic groups.

A discussion of American imperialism and its relation to Asian American immigration at the turn of the century might be useful as a comparative technique. The American presence in the Philippines is a particularly cogent avenue for teachers to pursue because the issues that Alexander brings up in her book relate to issues that Jessica Hagedorn discusses in her novel *Dogeaters*. The historical background is important in the discussion of these novels and provides interesting assignments for students. The relation between history and narrative (both private and public) creates stimulating discussions.

Intertextual Linkages

With Inderpal Grewal's essay "The Post-colonial, Ethnic Studies, and the Diaspora": Discuss relations between postcolonial and Asian American literature.

With a short story in Bharati Mukherjee's collection *"The Middleman" and Other Stories*: Two stories that work particularly well are "Buried Lives" and "A Wife's Tale." The first story focuses on an Indian teacher of English literature in India, and the second story concentrates on a doctoral student who finds herself displaced in America just as Alexander's Mira is displaced in Hyderabad.

With Mukherjee's *Jasmine*: Compare and contrast the treatment of class and the title character of Jasmine and Rameeza in *Nampally Road*.

With Maxine Hong Kingston's *Woman Warrior*: Two themes to focus on are education and women and the relationships between women.

With Kingston's *China Men*: Examine the relation between history and narrative.

With Jessica Hagedorn's *Dogeaters*: Discuss political corruption and American commercialism and consumerism.

With Sonia Shah's *Dragon Ladies: Asian American Feminists Breathe Fire*: Discuss Asian American issues of women and activism.

Bibliography

Alexander, Meena. *The Bird's Bright Ring*. Calcutta: Writer's Workshop, 1976.

———. *Fault Lines*. New York: Feminist, 1992.

———. *House of a Thousand Doors*. Washington: Three Continents, 1988.

———. *In the Middle Earth*. New Delhi: Enact, 1977.

———. Introduction. *Truth Tales: Contemporary Stories by Women Writers of India*. Ed. Kali for Women. New York: Feminist, 1990. 11–24.

———. *Manhattan Music*. San Francisco: Mercury House, 1997.

———. *Nampally Road*. San Francisco: Mercury House, 1991.

———. *Night Scene: The Garden*. New York: Red Dust, 1991.

———. *The Poetic Self: Towards a Phenomenology of Romanticism*. New Delhi: Arnold-Heinemann, 1979.

———. "Real Places; or, How Sense Fragments: Thoughts on Ethnicity and the Making of Poetry." *Asian Americans: Collages of Identities*. Ed. Lee C. Lee. Ithaca: Cornell U Asian Amer. Studies Program, 1992. 71–83.

———. *River and Bridge: Poems*. Toronto: TSAR, 1996.

———. *Root My Name*. Calcutta: United Writers, 1977.

———. *The Shock of Arrival: Reflections on Postcolonial Experience*. Boston: South End, 1996.

———. *Stone Roots*. New Delhi: Arnold-Heinemann, 1980.

———. *The Storm: A Poem in Five Parts*. New York: Red Dust, 1989.

———. *Without Place*. Calcutta: Writer's Workshop, 1977.

———. *Women in Romanticism: Mary Wollstonecraft, Dorothy Wordsworth, Mary Shelley*. Totowa: Barnes, 1989.

Chait, Sandra. Rev. of *Nampally Road*, by Meena Alexander. *Seattle Times* 24 Mar. 1991: K7.

Davé, Shilpa. "The Doors to Home and History: Post-colonial Identities in Meena Alexander and Bharati Mukherjee." *Amerasia Journal* 19.3 (1993): 103–13.

Francia, Luis. "India Ink: *Nampally Road*." Rev. of *Nampally Road*, by Meena Alexander. *Village Voice* 26 Mar. 1991: 74.

Grewal, Inderpal. "The Post-colonial, Ethnic Studies, and the Diaspora: The Contexts of Ethnic Immigrant/Migrant Cultural Studies in the U.S." *Socialist Review* 24.4 (1994): 45–74.

Hagedorn, Jessica. *Dogeaters*. New York: Penguin, 1991.

Katrak, Ketu H. "South Asian American Literature." *An Interethnic Companion to Asian American Literature*. Ed. King-Kok Cheung. New York: Cambridge UP, 1997. 192–218.

Kingston, Maxine Hong. *China Men*. New York: Knopf, 1980.

———. *The Woman Warrior: Memoirs of a Girlhood among Ghosts*. New York: Knopf, 1976.

Knight, Denise. "Meena Alexander." *Writers of the Indian Diaspora: A Bio-bibliographical Critical Sourcebook*. Ed. Emmanuel S. Nelson. Westport: Greenwood, 1993.

Mukherjee, Bharati. *Jasmine*. New York: Grove, 1989.

———. *"The Middleman" and Other Stories*. New York: Grove, 1988.

Rev. of *Nampally Road*, by Meena Alexander. *Publishers Weekly* 14 Dec. 1990: 62.

Rubin, Merle. "A Romantic Faces Reality." Rev. of *Nampally Road*, by Meena Alexander. *Los Angeles Times Book Review* 27 Jan. 1991: 7.

Shah, Sonia, ed. *Dragon Ladies: Asian American Feminists Breathe Fire*. Boston: South End, 1997.

America Is in the Heart
by Carlos Bulosan

Tim Libretti

Publication Information

First published in 1946 by Harcourt, Brace, and Company, Inc. Reprinted in 1973 by the University of Washington Press; has been in print, for the most part, ever since.

Overview

Generally classified as an autobiographical novel, *America Is in the Heart* charts the life of its narrator, Allos (Bulosan's persona), and his family around the end of World War I. Part 1, set in the Philippines, opens with the return of Allos's brother Leon from the war. This opening is symptomatic of the first part as a whole, because Bulosan represents the tragic history of his family and of the dispossessed peasantry overall as entwined with and resulting from the larger historical and economic processes of United States colonialism, absentee landlordism, and industrialization. These events are narrated through the childhood consciousness of Allos, who does not fully comprehend the significance and causality of the developments he witnesses, which include peasant revolts, mass migrations from the country to the city, family dislocations, the breakdown of traditions along generational lines because of the imposition of United States cultural norms in the schools, and increased poverty. The young Allos understands these larger operations of capitalism and imperialism only in terms of the effect they have on his family's welfare. Yet at times in these early moments, the voice of a more mature Allos, speaking from a postimmigration perspective, intrudes to reflect on the importance of these events in shaping his consciousness and on his later view of those events as an experienced man of heightened political and class consciousness. Again, this narrative strategy is symptomatic of the work as a whole, which is structured as a pattern of constant return and reevaluation—in both space and time—in which each return yields a heightened race and class consciousness.

In part 1 of the novel, Allos's experiences, such as going to market with his mother, give him a sense of the dynamics of class society, setting the stage for his later political development. Part 2, which begins with his immigration to the United States in the 1930s as he leaves behind a Philippines and a family life in ruins, focuses largely on the racial discrimination and violent persecution Filipinos and other minorities suffered in the United States. Bulosan describes the West Coast labor migrations of Filipinos who work on farms and in canneries from California to Alaska and frequent gambling dens and bars. Experiencing the typical racial oppression, cultural disorientation, and class exploitation of the Filipino, Allos is victimized by corrupt labor contractors when he arrives in the United States, is later chased by a lynch mob during an anti-Filipino race riot, is beaten severely by two policemen, and has his testicles brutally crushed by white vigilantes. Part 3 details Allos's development of a class consciousness that helps him comprehend his racial and class exploitation from a transnational perspective and participate in the resistance movements of Filipinos in the United States. He becomes involved in organizing workers for UCAPAWA (United Cannery, Agricultural, Packing and Allied Workers of America) and allies himself with the Communist Party as his socialist consciousness grows. Bulosan also describes Allos's intellectual, cultural, and political growth and development into a committed leftist writer, forwarding a socialist agenda of antiracism and working-class liberation in his writing.

Reception

Bulosan was an enormously popular writer in the 1940s in the United States and even abroad. His 1944 collection of short stories, *The Laughter of My Father*, was a bestseller. He was featured on the covers of several major national magazines, and his writings appeared in such magazines and journals as the *New Yorker, Harper's, Arizona Quarterly*, and the *Saturday Evening Post*. *America Is in the Heart* was translated and sold in Sweden, Denmark, Italy, and Yugoslavia. *Look* magazine voted *America Is in the Heart* one of the fifty most important books ever published, and Bulosan himself was considered one of the most prolific authors in the United States. His blacklisting in the 1950s, however, has erased much of his achievement from the pages of United States literary history. The disappearance of Bulosan from dominant renderings of United States literary history can provide students with a concrete example in discussions of literary value, canon formation, and the constructions of literary traditions and their registrations of national consciousness.

Even at the time, however, contemporary reviews tended to misinterpret his work and neutralize or even reverse the radical political content of his writing. Reviews generally viewed Bulosan as a cultural translator or mediator, a goodwill ambassador whose task was to help (white) "Americans" understand Filipino cultural attitudes in order to facilitate Filipinos' assimilation into the dominant United States culture. Some reviews were even more overtly racist, suggesting that Bulosan was educated and made assimilable through his contact with Anglo-Americans. Such reviews neglected both his critique of United States racism and the national and working-class narrative of resistance to United States racial capitalism that his work produces.

America Is in the Heart, however, has become a much used book in courses in a range of disciplines from sociology to literature. In the context of Asian American literature, it is really the only canonical Filipino literary work (though the works of N. V. M. Gonzalez, Bienvenido Santos, Jessica Hagedorn, Ninotchka Rosca, and Peter Bacho get some mention). The danger with the popularity of *America Is in the Heart* and its critical exaltation as Bulosan's key work, even as the definitive account of the first-generation Filipino immigrant experience, however, is that privileging this novel as sociologically "factual" also forwards the political interpretation of the racial and class experience, and by extension the particular strategy of proletarian and Third World resistance embodied in the novel. Bulosan's interpretation and understanding of his racial oppression and class exploitation, as well as his theorization of resistance to those conditions—and his attitudes toward "American" culture—were conditioned by the political and cultural climate of the specific historical moment in which he was writing.

Author's Biographical Background

While *America Is in the Heart* was intended as a collective biography of Filipinos in the United States that would, in Bulosan's words, "give literate voice to the voiceless one hundred thousand Filipinos in the United States, Hawai'i, and Alaska" (Kim 44), many of the details and experiences of the novel are obviously drawn from Bulosan's own life. Because Bulosan was sick much of his life, however, much of the work experience depicted does not represent his personal experience. Born 2 November 1911 in Binalonan, Pangasinan, Bulosan grew up in a Philippines that had been in the colonial grips of United States government and capital since 1898, many of the results and processes of which are represented in part 1 of *America Is in the Heart*. To escape the poverty and feudal oppression at home, Bulosan, along with 100,000 young Filipinos like him who had been recruited from peasant villages to provide labor for Hawai'ian sugar plantations, Alaskan canneries, and West Coast agribusiness, immigrated to the United States in 1931. The colonial education he received inculcated him with illusions of the United States as a democratic society based on individual freedom and equality, where he would be able to pursue his American dream of success through hard work and perseverance.

Bulosan, however, found himself suffering the vicissitudes of migrant labor reserved for people of color, particularly Filipino and Mexican immigrants, as he worked in restaurants and farms during the depression. During this time he met Chris Mensalvas (Jose in *America Is in the Heart*), who gave Bulosan an outlet for his radical sympathies, involving him in the Congress of Industrial Organizations as an organizer and publicist for UCAPAWA. He also became the editor of the *New Tide* in 1934, through which he became acquainted with such authors as Richard Wright, William Saroyan, Sanora Babb, and Carey McWilliams. From 1936 to 1938, Bulosan was confined to Los Angeles County Hospital with tuberculosis. This confinement was a blessing for Bulosan's intellectual growth, giving him the time to read and write with the direction and inspiration of Sanora and Dorothy Babb, the proletarian novelist Ruth McKenney (Alice Odell in the novel), and Harriet Monroe, the editor of *Poetry*.

This moment of confinement sparked a prolific period of writing that lasted unil 1946. *The Laughter of My Father*, a series of tragicomic stories critiquing United States colonial practice in the Philippines while representing Filipinos as culturally resistant, was a best-seller; *America Is in the Heart* was widely popular, and Bulosan also published stories in major national magazines and journals. He remained committed to a working-class anti-imperialist political perspective that supported and advocated the national and working-class liberation struggles of Filipinos and other workers, refusing a sinecure with the exiled government of the Philippines in 1943. Blacklisted after World War II and threatened with imprisonment, he continued to write against capitalist and racial oppression, moving to Seattle in 1950 to edit the yearbook of the International Longshoremen's and Warehousemen's Union, local 37. At this time, he was also writing his extraordinary final novel, *The Cry and the Dedication*, published in 1985 as *The Power of the People* and reprinted in 1995 under its original title by Temple University Press. Portraying the Huk Rebellion against Japanese and then United States imperialist forces after World War II, this novel theorizes national liberation as a stage in the international working-class struggle and represents Bulosan's homecoming of sorts as he turns away from "American" culture as bankrupt and identifies the source of radical struggle and hope in indigenous Third World cultures and anti-imperialist struggles.

Historical Context for the Narratives in *America Is in the Heart*

The informing historical narrative of *America Is in the Heart* involves the related trajectories of United States colonialism in the Philippines and Asian immigration to the United States. The Philippines became a United States colony in 1898 when the United States defeated Spanish forces—which had already been depleted by the Katipunan, a Filipino revolutionary group fighting for national liberation—and reconquered and recolonized the islands. The invasion of United States capital brought industrialization, agribusiness, and absentee landlordism, displacing peasants from their lands, creating the surge of immigration to the United States, and igniting peasant revolts in the Philippines, as we see in part 1 of *America Is in the Heart*. The United States cultural invasion, promulgating in the educational system visions of a United States organized according to the democratic principles of freedom, equality, and opportunity, also encouraged immigration to the United States.

24

Filipino immigration must be understood as a third wave of Asian immigration to the United States. The Chinese had come, or been shanghaied, to build the railroads in the late nineteenth century but faced exclusion by law during the depressions of the 1880s and 1890s. The Japanese then replaced the Chinese in the fields, only to face persecution and finally legal exclusion in 1924, in part because of their success, which brought them into competition with white farmers. To fill the void left by Japanese farmworkers, large numbers of Filipinos poured into the United States in the 1920s and 1930s. Arrivals numbered 5,600 in 1920 and 56,000 in 1931, by which time 150,000 Filipinos were living in the United States. Recruited and hired through contractors at wages less than those other migrant workers received, Filipinos worked in farms along the Pacific coast and in Alaskan canneries. When the depression hit, unemployed white workers suddenly desired these otherwise undesirable jobs, spurring an anti-Filipino backlash manifesting itself in anti-Filipino race riots starting in Washington State in 1928 and continuing in Exeter and Watsonville, California, in 1929 and 1930. Exclusion was legalized, most notably in laws passed in Washington, Nevada, California, and Oregon forbidding marriage between white women and Filipinos—a particular problem for Filipino immigrants who were predominantly male. In 1934, the Tydings-McDuffie Independence Act, which granted the Philippines political independence from the United States, worked as an effective tool for controlling Filipino immigration, limiting immigration to fifty people each year.

Between 1934 and 1937 a series of strikes by Filipino workers broke out in California, events that led to Bulosan's radicalization and that constitute the bulk of part 3 of *America Is in the Heart*, as Bulosan describes his role in unions and with socialist politics in organizing resistance to racial oppression and class exploitation.

Historical Context for the Writing of *America Is in the Heart*

Writing during and after World War II, Bulosan affirmed his support of the war against fascism and aligned himself with the dominant cultural policies of the Communist Party's Popular Front. At the historical moment when Bulosan was writing, his assumption and affirmation of an "American" identity was not by any means a disavowal of socialist values but, rather, an assumption of radical politics. While writing *America Is in the Heart*, Bulosan, uprooted from the Philippines, identified himself with United States culture and history and derived his radical politics from United States cultural and historical traditions and models (which he would later abandon when writing *The Cry and the Dedication*). Searching for roots in "America," Bulosan wrote in 1942, "I was driven back to history. But going back to history was actually a return to the early beginnings of America" (*If You Want* 16). This submersion in United States history and culture, however, needs to be understood as part of the larger historical and political trajectory of the Communist Party, in which Bulosan, if not a member, was certainly involved in a significant way, as we can tell from *America Is in the Heart*.

The ideologies and cultural patterns informing Bulosan's literary practice are certainly partly reflective of those informing the policies of the Communist Party of the United States. In 1935, for example, the Party reformulated its radical proletarian politics in favor of a broader-based antifascist popular democratic front that stressed internationalism in opposition to nationalism and a "people's" outlook in favor of a proletarian perspective. Bulosan's Americanization occurs within the context of this Americanization of the Communist Party during the Popular Front era and its ambitious effort to reformulate United States national consciousness and identity. Read within this context, Bulosan's quest to be American is at the same time his entrance into communism, which the Party's general secretary, Earl Browder, declared "the Americanism of the Twentieth Century." His turn to an American past mirrors the Party's affirmation of the continuity of communism with reform traditions of the United States past, as the Party's constitution figured American communists as carrying "forward today the traditions of Jefferson, Paine, Jackson, Lincoln, and of the Declaration of Independence" (Ottanelli 123). Indeed, Bulosan's recognition that Japanese, Mexican, Filipino, and white workers all shared a faith in the working man and were all fighting a common enemy, fascism, is a paradigmatic assertion and ratification of the Popular Front's internationalism.

Major Themes

the linkage of the development of political commitment and consciousness with the development of Allos as a writer and the discovery and emergence of his literary voice

the destruction of community, family, and culture inflicted by the colonial process and suffered by Filipinos as well as other racialized minorities in both the Philippines and the United States

resistance to oppression and the reestablishment of communal and national identity and consciousness

the role of history and memory in shaping class consciousness

gender, sexual, and racial politics, including the Filipino man's relationship to women of his own culture and to white women

the portrayal of American nationhood and the paradox of America as a country both kind and cruel

proletarianism and the adoption and transformation of the proletarian genre emergent in the 1930s

the immigrant experience

relationship with American culture, including cultural icons like Abraham Lincoln and authors influencing the narrator

violence and cultural degradation

Critical Issues

One persistent issue in the criticism on *America Is in the Heart* is whether the text is autobiographical. Much of the impact of the text derives from the impression of raw immediacy, common in autobiography, that it leaves on the reader, as well as from the concentration of sufferings and persecutions on a single person. The extent of the text's factuality is often an emotionally important issue for students exposed for the first time to Filipino American and working-class history of this period. Elaine Kim, echoing E. San Juan Jr. (*Carlos Bulosan*) and Carey McWilliams, concludes that "Bulosan was primarily a fiction writer, and *America Is in the Heart* is both less and more than a personal history: it is a composite portrait of the Filipino American community" (48).

The generic status of *America Is in the Heart* bears directly on how the text is to be interpreted, especially its controversial ending in which the narrator articulates a desire "to know America, and to become part of her great tradition, and to contribute something toward her final fulfillment" (327), expressed in the face of numerous instances of brutality against Filipino laborers narrated up to that point. Multiple readings of the ending exist. My own interpretation, noted above, places Bulosan's "Americanism" within the context of Popular Front radicalism. In an attempt to resolve the text's internal contradictions and to account for its canonical status within Asian American literature and ethnic studies, Marilyn Alquizola suggests that the narrator is "naive" and that the book's optimistic ending should be understood ironically ("Fictive Narrator" 216). Alquizola's later analysis takes the possibility of authorial ambivalence more seriously and emphasizes the need to remove ad hominem concerns from examination of the text in social contexts past and present ("Subversion"). Kenneth Mostern counters this reading, as well as Sau-ling Wong's notion that the text is formally unmappable (133–36), by arguing that the sections in the book correspond to a Marxist dialectical trajectory of coming into class consciousness; thus the ending must be read against a Marxist teleological vision in which America occupies a culminating place in the march of world history.

A related question is whether *America Is in the Heart* constitutes an example of Third World writing productively grounded in, and internally dramatizing, the historical dynamics of United States–Philippines relations or whether it is continuous with the dominant United States literary tradition. More recently, critical debate has centered on how to categorize Filipino American writing such as Bulosan's. Oscar Campomanes has proposed the rubric of the literature of exile, which may be considered a postcolonial category, while E. San Juan, Jr., since publishing his landmark 1972 study (*Carlos Bulosan*), has repeatedly forwarded Marxist, internal colonial, and Third World models. San Juan worries that the paradigm of exile erases crucial distinctions between migrant workers, émigrés, expatriates, and other Filipinos who might come to the United States with radically varying degrees of mobility and economic potential; in other words, the paradigm would fail "to discriminate the gap between Bulosan's radical project of solidarity with people of color against capital, and the integrationist 'melting pot' tendencies that vitiate the works of [some other Filipino writers]" ("Filipino Writing" 225).

Last but not least, Rachel Lee raises gender issues, which have been obscured in previous readings of *America Is in the Heart* that privilege Bulosan's class and ethnic politics. Lee points out the "gendered limits of fraternity and the tenuousness of brotherly bonds that hinge on the successful regulation of sexuality" (18).

Pedagogical Issues and Suggestions

The Philippines is a complex nation with a variegated population and a convoluted history marked by the influences of multiple cultures, colonizations, and settlements. Students often find it helpful to review the history of the Philippines, of United States–Philippines relations, and of Filipinos in the United States. (A concise and full source would be the UCLA Asian American Studies Center's *Letters in Exile: An Introductory Reader on the History of Pilipinos in America*.) Having this information allows students to understand the unique conditions and experience of Filipino immigration to the United States and to recognize the duplication in the United States of the colonial experience in the Philippines. To emphasize the Filipino immigrant experience as colonial-like or as one of internal colonization, teachers might ask students to think about other immigrant literature they may have read, such as William Bradford's *Of Plymouth Plantation*, Michel Crèvecoeur's *Letters from an American Farmer*, or O. E. Rolvag's *Giants of the Earth*—even Ben Franklin's *Autobiography* would be relevant— or to consider the typical immigrant success story informing the dominant United States culture of capitalism. Students can compare such stories with Bulosan's novel to measure similarities and differences and to register the difference between the experience of people of color in the United States and that of European immigrants.

Unlike many immigrant novels, Bulosan's novel begins in his homeland, not with arrival in the Unites States. Ask students to reflect on the significance of this strategy and on the structure of the novel overall, thinking about what characterizes the content of each of the three parts of the novel and why Bulosan organized the novel in such a way. Comparing Bulosan's representation of peasant life in the Philippines with working-class life in the United States should provoke students to contemplate the transnational perspective of the novel and Bulosan's rendering of racial and class dynamics in the context of capitalism as a global system—of the relation, again, between the colonization of the Philippines and the internal colonization of Filipinos and other peoples of color in the United States.

In reflecting on the title, students can think about why Bulosan figures America as "in the heart." They might make lists of which values for them generally define a United States national identity and set of values and what the defining characteristics of Bulosan's America are. Is the America Bulosan desires the same America we live in now or even the same America idealized in the contemporary dominant cultural imagination?

Intertextual Linkages

With Milton Murayama's *All I Asking for Is My Body*, Louis Chu's *Eat a Bowl of Tea*, and Ronyoung Kim's *Clay Walls*: Examine similarities and differences between the Japanese American, Chinese American, and Korean American male and female working-class and immigrant experiences in the United States.

With Maxine Hong Kingston's *China Men*: Discuss the emasculation of Asian American males and the working-class experience.

With Gish Jen's *Typical American*: Critique American values and the United States racial order, particularly in the context of demythologizing the immigrant success story.

With Jack Conroy's *The Disinherited* or Mike Gold's *Jews without Money*: Compare different uses of the proletarian novel form; discuss the way Bulosan rewrites the master narrative of class struggle through a reinterpretation of the relations between race, nation, and class.

With John Oliver Killens's *And Then We Heard the Thunder*, Richard Wright's *Native Son*, Ann Petry's *The Street*, and Chester Himes's *If He Hollers Let Him Go*: Examine different treatments of the class experience as lived through race and gender by other leftist United States writers working with and rethinking leftist literary paradigms.

With Americo Paredes's *George Washington Gomez*: See how each author deals differently with the role of culture in colonial domination as well as with the Americanization of radicalism in the 1930s.

With Leslie Marmon Silko's *Ceremony*: Compare the mapping of race in global terms and the way each work demonstrates capitalism's uniting of people of color in the global colonial system.

With James Welch's *The Indian Lawyer*: Compare the way each author to some extent de-emphasizes cultural recovery in favor of working within the dominant cultural or political complex for change.

With Rolando Hinojosa's *Klail City*: Compare the representation of the migrant labor experience and the formation of national and transnational identities.

With Carlos Bulosan's *The Cry and the Dedication*: Measure the evolution of his Third World socialist consciousness.

Bibliography

Alquizola, Marilyn. "The Fictive Narrator of *America Is in the Heart*." *Frontiers in Asian American Studies*. Ed. Gail Nomura et al. Pullman: Washington State UP, 1989. 211–17.

———. "Subversion or Affirmation: The Text and Subtext of *America Is in the Heart*."

Asian Americans: Comparative and Global Perspectives. Ed. Shirley Hune et al. Pullman: Washington State UP, 1991. 199–209.

Bulosan, Carlos. *America Is in the Heart*. 1946. Seattle: U of Washington P, 1973.

———. *Bulosan: An Introduction with Selections*. Ed. E. San Juan, Jr. Manila: Natl. Book Store, 1983.

———. *The Cry and the Dedication*. Ed. E. San Juan, Jr. Philadelphia: Temple UP, 1995.

———. *If You Want to Know Who We Are*. Ed. E. San Juan, Jr. Albuquerque: West End, 1983.

———. *The Laughter of My Father*. New York: Harcourt, 1944.

———. *The Philippines Is in the Heart*. Ed. E. San Juan, Jr. Quezon City: New Day, 1978.

———. *The Sound of Falling Light: Letters in Exile*. Ed. Dolores Feria. Quezon City: U of the Philippines P, 1960.

Campomanes, Oscar. "Filipinos in the United States and Their Literature of Exile." *Reading the Literatures of Asian America*. Ed. Shirley Geok-lin Lim and Amy Ling. Philadelphia: Temple UP, 1992. 49–78.

Campomanes, Oscar, and Todd Gernes. "Two Letters from America: Carlos Bulosan and the Act of Writing." *MELUS* 15.3 (1988): 15–46.

Chu, Louis. *Eat a Bowl of Tea*. 1961. Secaucus: Stuart, 1979.

Conroy, Jack. *The Disinherited: A Novel of the 1930s*. Columbia: U of Missouri P, 1991.

Daroy, Petronilo. "Carlos Bulosan: The Politics of Literature." *Saint Louis Quarterly* 6.2 (1968): 193–206.

Evangelista, Susan. *Carlos Bulosan and His Poetry*. Quezon City: Ateneo de Manila UP, 1985.

Gold, Mike. *Jews without Money*. 1930. New York: Carroll, 1996.

Himes, Chester. *If He Hollers Let Him Go*. 1945. New York: Thunder's Mouth, 1995.

Hinojosa, Rolando. *Klail City*. Houston: Arte Publico, 1986.

Jen, Gish. *Typical American*. New York: NAL-Dutton, 1992.

Killens, John Oliver. *And Then We Heard the Thunder*. 1963. Washington: Howard UP, 1984.

Kim, Elaine. *Asian American Literature: An Introduction to the Writings and Their Social Context*. Philadelphia: Temple UP, 1982.

Kim, Ronyoung. *Clay Walls*. Sag Harbor: Permanent, 1986.

Kingston, Maxine Hong. *China Men*. New York: Knopf, 1980.

Lee, Rachel C. *The Americas of Asian American Literature: Gendered Fictions of Nation and Transnation*. Princeton: Princeton UP, 1999.

Letters in Exile: An Introductory Reader on the History of Pilipinos in America. Los Angeles: UCLA, Asian Amer. Studies Center, 1976.

McWilliams, Carey. *Factories in the Field: The Story of Migratory Farm Labor in California*. Boston: Little, 1939. Santa Barbara: Smith, 1971.

Mostern, Kenneth. "Why Is America in the Heart?" *Critical Mass: A Journal of Asian American Cultural Criticism* 2.2 (1995): 35–65.

Murayama, Milton. *All I Asking for Is My Body*. San Francisco: Supa, 1975.

Orendain, Margarita. "Understanding the Dynamics of Third World Writing in Bulosan's *America Is in the Heart*." *Saint Louis Research Journal* 19.2 (1988): 365–75.

Ottanelli, Fraser M. *The Communist Party of the United States: From the Depression to World War II*. New Brunswick, Rutgers UP, 1991.

Paredes, Americo. *George Washington Gomez*. Houston: Arte Publico, 1990.

Petry, Ann. *The Street*. 1946. Boston: Houghton, 1998.

San Juan, E., Jr. *Carlos Bulosan and the Imagination of Class Struggle*. Quezon City: U of the Philippines P, 1972.

———. "Filipino Writing in the United States: Reclaiming Whose America?" *The Ethnic Canon: Histories, Institutions, and Interventions*. Ed. David Palumbo-Liu. Minneapolis: U of Minnesota P, 1995. 213–40.

———. *The Philippine Temptation: Dialectics of Philippines–U.S. Literary Relations*. Philadelphia: Temple UP, 1996.

———. *Reading the West / Writing the East*. New York: Lang, 1993.

Silko, Leslie Marmon. *Ceremony*. 1977. New York: Viking-Penguin, 1986.

Welch, James. *The Indian Lawyer*. New York: Viking-Penguin, 1991.

Wong, Sau-ling Cynthia. *Reading Asian American Literature: From Necessity to Extravagance*. Princeton: Princeton UP, 1993.

Wright, Richard. *Native Son*. 1940. New York: Harper, 1998.

Dictee
by Theresa Hak Kyung Cha

Laura Hyun Yi Kang

Publication Information

First published in 1982 by Tanam Press, New York. Out of print until 1994, when it was published by Third Woman Press, Berkeley, in conjunction with a collection of four critical interpretations, *Writing Self, Writing Nation: A Collection of Essays on Theresa Hak Kyung Cha's* Dictee (Kim and Alarcon).

Overview

Dictee is a layered, multiform text that precludes thematic encapsulation. The book is divided into nine sections, each of which corresponds to one of the nine classical Greek muses and her specific domain of the arts: Clio—History, Calliope—Epic Poetry, Urania—Astronomy, Melpomene—Tragedy, Erato—Love Poetry, Elitere—Epic Poetry, Thalia—Comedy, Terpsichore—Choral Dance, and Polymnia—Sacred Poetry. Multilingually composed of parts in French, English, Greek, Chinese, and Korean, *Dictee* incorporates various elements of found inscriptions such as translation exercises, Catholic religious texts, journalistic accounts, political petitions, and typed and handwritten letters, as well as two full pages of what appears to be a scribbled draft by Cha herself in the process of writing the book. Many visual images are also scattered throughout, including several individual and group portraits of Korean women; historical photographs of Japanese colonial persecution of Koreans, including a mass anticolonial rally; a simple map of the divided Korean peninsula; anatomical diagrams in both English and Chinese; and still images from films.

The heterogeneous composition of the book could be read as accounting for the multicultural, multinational pressures that have wrought the peculiar and crisscrossed contours of a Korean American female subject—an immigrant who has left a multiply dominated and internally divided Korea to live in the United States, a nation-state that has crucially shaped the tragic historical trajectory of her homeland; a student who learns English as a second language while undergoing an extensive education in French Catholicism; a girl-woman who shuttles among differently inflected patriarchal cultures; a diversely located agent of language who is estranged from all the linguistic traditions at her reach; a writer who is actively engaged in film theory and cinematic praxis. Such a manifold yet discontinuous genealogy propels a critical reworking of the fixed terms of both social identification and textual representation, as demonstrated throughout the book.

Dictee interrogates the historical and political grounds for delineating sameness and difference by presenting several instances of distinguished, unequal yet conjoined subject positions: visitor-host, immigrant-native, mother-daughter, husband-wife, colonizer-colonized, student-teacher, performer-audience, addresser-addressee, protester-soldier, penitent-judge. The book references the division of Korea into two adjoining yet hostile nation-states as a particularly striking illustration of the paradox of identity: a distinct "Korean" ethnonationality that has been irrevocably transformed by a history of foreign invasions, colonial reculturations, and transnational migrations even as it has always borne an internal heterogeneity that contains all the binarily opposed identities. The book therefore locates its critique of unified, essential selfhood in an interconnected web of specific sociohistorical contexts rather than in an endless theoretical play of difference and indeterminacy.

Given such a range of situational and overlapping identifications, *Dictee* also works to critically interrogate the logic and methods of discursive representation, both in the sense of an individual articulation that can speak for a social group and as a textual object that can faithfully reproduce external realities. On the first point, the multiple historical and cultural references, ranging from Greek mythology to an avant-garde French film, disturb its categorization as a typical example of Korean, Korean American, or Asian American literature. Although it repeatedly references defining moments of modern Korean history, such as Japanese colonization, the Korean War and the national partition, and the postwar domestic unrest and resulting diasporic migrations of Koreans, the book is not so much a historical remembering as a critical exploration about how that history has been memorialized and written by different authors. Through the incorporation of photographs and film stills, geographical maps and physiological diagrams, the book pushes the conventional limits of what constitutes a text as well as of literary realism.

The book brings together concerns about identification and representation by illuminating the way the authorized forms and methods of linguistic representation serve to legitimate certain social positions over others. The systematic suppression of the native language in favor of the colonizer's language, the patriarchal idealization of female silence, the racist devaluation of "pidgin" English, the religious obligation to make a true confession, and the classroom exercises for inducting students into normative grammar and spelling are all invoked as instances in which language is a formidable medium of social, political, and psychic subjection. While it repeatedly points to the limits of identification and representation, *Dictee* insists on the importance of historical awareness and interpersonal connections even as it brings these matters and their representational methods to the fore of a shared critical discussion.

Reception

Because of its first publication in 1982 with a small press, the initial audience of *Dictee* was both limited in number and scattered in scope. Donald Richie was the first to discuss the book, in 1983, as part of a larger article on Asian literature. Susan Wolf addresses the text along with Cha's live performance and multimedia works in an article for the periodical *Afterimage*. Michael Stephens and Stephen-Paul Martin each devote a chapter to *Dictee* in their book-length literary studies. Trinh T. Minh-ha incorporates several lengthy and significant citations of Cha's book in a chapter on storytelling but does not present any direct critical exegesis. The African American feminist thinker bell hooks praises the book in an essay on language and voice. None of these references to *Dictee* substantively addresses the book in an Asian American context, literary or otherwise.

It was not until a 1991 panel discussion at the meeting of the Association for Asian American Studies that *Dictee* was brought into the center of Asian American literary criticism. The 1994 publication of these four critical readings in *Writing Self, Writing Nation* (Kim and Alarcon) marked the beginning of a significant current interest in the book. We can expect a flowering of critical discourse on *Dictee* in years to come.

The temporal gap between the initial 1982 publication and the current critical interest in the book could be attributed partially to what some readers have perceived as the fragmented and elliptical quality of the book. The difficulty of generic categorization can be noted, for example, in its being placed under "poetry" in *The Forbidden Stitch: An Asian American Women's Anthology* (Lim and Tsutakawa). In general, there has been much more critical work done on novels and autobiographies than on poetry in Asian American literary criticism. Another likely reason may be the book's prominent concern with modern Korean history rather than Asian American history; also its invocations of Greek mythology and French Catholicism may appear to exceed the geographical and cultural boundaries of a narrow Asian American identification. Shelley Sunn Wong attributes the lack of initial critical attention to the book's uneasy fit under the literary and political criteria of representativeness and authenticity that still dominated the Asian American cultural terrain in 1982. Wong notes that significant historical shifts in the late 1980s, such as the growing conversations with semiotics and poststructuralist theories, the emergence of new Asian immigrant communities, and the foregrounding of gender, created a different context of reception in Asian American literary studies more open to experimentation and multiplicity.

Author's Biographical Background

While the book problematizes the categorical boundaries of autobiography, certain sections of *Dictee* draw directly on specific contours of Theresa Hak Kyung Cha's life. (For a detailed chronology of Cha's life and artistic career, see Roth, from which the following biographical synopsis is condensed.) Many aspects of Cha's life are significantly intertwined with the defining moments of the transnational migrations and multicultural displacements of the Korean diaspora in the twentieth century.

Cha's parents were raised in Manchuria as part of the sizable population of Korean exiles who left their homeland to escape the oppressive conditions of Japanese colonial rule. *Dictee* recalls this family and ethnic history by incorporating sections from the journals written at the time by the author's mother, Hyung Soon Huo, that express her sustained love for the Korean homeland and her jubilant return upon liberation in 1945. The author was born in the midst of the Korean War, on 4 March 1951, in the southern Korean coastal city of Pusan. In 1962, the Cha family immigrated to Hawai'i, and then, two years later, they moved to the mainland, settling in San Francisco, where Cha spent the rest of her adolescence immersed in a private Catholic education.

The author went on to study at the University of California, Berkeley, where she obtained two bachelor's degrees, first in comparative literature and then in art. It was at this time that Cha began studying ceramics and performance art, giving several multimedia performances in various locations throughout the San Francisco Bay Area. She also immersed herself in the study of both Korean poetry and European modernist writings as well as French film theory, which she continued to investigate by going to France in 1976 to attend the Centre d'Etudes Américaines du Cinéma à Paris. Cha earned an MA in art in 1977 and an MFA in 1978, both from the University of California, Berkeley. Then, in 1979, Cha traveled back to Korea for the first time since her emigration seventeen years earlier. She returned to Korea two more times between 1979 and 1981. This experience of return, which proved in many ways to be more unsettling and alienating than nostalgically comforting, is centrally referenced in *Dictee* as well as in the audiovisual piece *Exilée*. Cha garnered numerous prestigious awards for her works in film, video, and photography, which continue to be exhibited widely. She sustained her diverse and prolific engagements in textual and visual media until 1982, when she was murdered on 5 November, only a few months after the publication of *Dictee*.

Historical Context for the Narratives in *Dictee*

The history of the Korean peninsula in the twentieth century has been indelibly marked by a series of imperial dominations, internal divisions, and mass emigrations. *Dictee* focuses on this collective ethnic history of severance and scattering as the legacy of multiple displacements inherited by a Korean American female subject. Elaine H. Kim's "Poised on the In-Between" provides important Korean and Korean American historical and cultural contexts for the book.

Instead of drawing clear separations between Korea and the United States, *Dictee* situates Korean immigration to the United States in the mutually implicated trajectory of Korea and the United States in this century. The closing years of the nineteenth century witnessed fierce maneuvering among Japan, China, Russia, France, England, Germany, and the United States for various natural resources and trade rights on the Korean peninsula, escalating into the Russo-Japanese War of 1904–05 that ended with Russia conceding complete domination of the Korean peninsula to victorious Japan. In a petition dated July 1905 and addressed to President Theodore Roosevelt, the Korean immigrant population in Hawai'i asked for recognition of Korea's national sovereignty and intervention against this Japanese military aggression, which went unheeded. *Dictee* "re-presents" this petition in its entirety and sets it against Cha's critical commentary on the diffidence of the United States and other nations in this international conflict. What these earnest immigrant petitioners did not know at the time was that through the secret Taft-Katsura pact, the United States agreed to give Japan free rein over Korea in return for its own unchallenged hegemony in the Philippines. Korea was officially declared a Japanese colony in 1910. The United States government further affirmed the legitimacy of Japanese colonial rule by officially categorizing Koreans as Japanese nationals.

For thirty-five years, the Japanese colonial government systematically enforced the suppression of Korean language, culture, and customs in a drive to transform the colonized Korean people into inferior Japanese subjects. Thousands of Korean men and women, conscripted either forcibly or under false promises of high wages and eventual repatriation, were sent to both Japan and its various distant outposts in Manchuria and the Sakhalin Islands to work as physical laborers and sexual slaves in the service of the expanding Japanese empire. Many Koreans also left their homeland for remote regions of Manchuria, China, and Russia to escape the oppressive Japanese presence. Some also immigrated to the United States. While a few went on to the mainland, mostly as university students, the great majority of early Koreans immigrated to the Hawai'ian Islands to work in the sugarcane fields. Both the Koreans who left and those who stayed behind established and sustained an active struggle for national independence. A mass popular uprising on 1 March 1919 was the most prominent instance of anticolonial Korean resistance. Initially taken aback by this well-guarded but highly organized massive insurgence, the Japanese police eventually responded by wounding and killing many protesters, including many young women who played a central role in staging this event. One of these women, Yu Guan Soon, was executed for her leadership and active participation and continues to be immortalized as a national martyr. A lengthy section of *Dictee* addresses Yu Guan Soon and the near-mythical heroicization of this female figure as patriot-martyr in Korean national lore. The book also briefly invokes Ahn Joong Gun, another highly regarded anticolonial martyr, who was killed for his 1909 assassination of Ito Hirobumi, a key actor in the planning and implementation of the Japanese colonial takeover.

With the defeat of Japan in World War II, Korea was declared to be "liberated" on 15 August 1945. Any hopes of peace and sovereignty were soon dashed, however, by the increasingly contentious struggle between the United States and Russia over influence on and control of the strategically situated peninsula. The conflict, which erupted into a full-scale war on 25 June 1950, lasted for three years and ended in a "stalemate" wherein the intervening superpowers partitioned the country in two at the thirty-eighth parallel, a communist northern half allied with Russia and China and a capitalist southern half allied with the United States. Korea thus became the first pawn in the cold war, and the still-divided peninsula continues to be one of the most heavily militarized regions in the world. Since then, communication and travel between the two sides have been largely impossible. *Dictee* movingly reflects on the tragedy of this antagonistic intranational division at several points.

The immediate postwar era in South Korea was marked by much socioeconomic instability and political repression. In response, the civilian population staged many mass rallies, led in large part by university students, opposing the arbitrary national partition and the economic, political, and military control exerted by the United States. These events culminated in the much memorialized street demonstration of 19 April 1960 in which the United States–backed Korean military killed and injured many of the student protesters. Unlike the colonial context of the 1 March 1919 uprising, the armed police and military officers of 1960 were fellow Koreans acting under orders of the Korean state and military. *Dictee* notes how the author and her family were personally affected by this defining moment that revealed the brutal under-side of the facade of freedom amd democracy projected by the pro–United States regime of President Syng Man Rhee. Then, in 1962, General Park Chung Hee staged a military coup and maintained dictatorial control until his assassination in 1979. The repressive political atmosphere along with the war-induced economic, infrastructural, and familial devastations impelled the immigration of Koreans to other countries.

At around the same time, the easing of a decades-long ban on Asian immigration to the United States, as well as the close political relationship between the United States and Korea, enabled the entry of a small number of Koreans into the United States, including the Cha family, who left for Hawai'i in 1963. Since a restrictive quota on Korean immigration was still in effect, most of the Koreans who came to the United States in the late 1950s and early 1960s gained entry through affiliations with a sponsoring university, a church organization, or the United States military, either as wives of United States servicemen or as employees of the military. A very few with substantial capital gained entry as merchants or businesspeople. It was not until the complete lifting of anti-Asian bans with the Immigration Act of 1965 that a sizable number of Koreans began immigrating to the United States. The continuing political repression and economic instability in the 1970s and 1980s contributed to a significant exodus of Koreans to the United States, Canada, and Australia as well as throughout South America and Europe. These multinational resettlements constitute a truly global Korean diaspora.

Historical Context for the Writing of *Dictee*

There is no singularly definitive historical impetus for the writing of *Dictee*. At the time of its writing and first publication, there was not a broad inclusion or an active participation of Korean Americans in the Asian American literary field. While books by and about Korean American women have been published subsequently, there had not been any prominent works that addressed the specific historical legacies and cultural location of Korean immigrant women before 1982. This literary and historical fact may have influenced the mood of loneliness and isolation that pervades much of the book. That Cha appears to be reaching out to an understanding audience of whose existence she is uncertain, even skeptical, can be discerned in the multiple letters reproduced in *Dictee*, which are never accompanied by corresponding replies.

Another possible historical context for the writing of the book may be the growing civil unrest in South Korea in the period between 1979 and 1981, during which Cha visited the homeland on three separate occasions. With the assassination of the military dictator, General Park Chung Hee, in 1979, there was a glimmer of hope for a true democratization of the country. A series of mass rallies by the Korean citizenry called for an end to the postwar legacy of dictatorial rule. However, through a ruthless military coup, General Chun Doo Hwan took power and declared martial law in early 1980. When the citizens of the southern city Kwangju protested this illegal seizure of power in May 1980, Chun and his lieutenant Roh Tae Woo, with the knowing complicity of the United States army command in Korea, implemented a total blockade and then a full-scale military invasion in which countless women, children, and men were indiscriminately and savagely massacred. Elaine H. Kim notes that Cha paid close attention to these events. *Dictee* contains a long letter, dated 19 April 1980 and written by Cha in Korea to her mother in the United States, that reflects on the tragic irony of uniformed Korean military officers clashing against fellow Korean civilian protesters, with both parties believing they are fighting for the nation's well-being.

The book was produced and disseminated in the context of growing interest in semiotics and poststructuralism in certain artistic and intellectual circles in both American and French arts and cultural criticism. This constituency of artists, filmmakers, and critics would more likely have known about *Dictee* and Tanam Press than an Asian American readership would have.

Major Themes

the significance and the erasure of Korean history, Japanese colonization,
    Korean exiles, the Korean War, national partition, domestic social unrest

the relation between personal memory and collective history, the layering of personal displacement with the collective ethnic displacement of Korea and Koreans

immigration and acculturation, especially the difficult adoption of a new language and the loss of a native language

emigration and repatriation, fragmentation and reconciliation, the desire for homeland and the impossibility of return

the liminality of a Korean American subject position and how it problematizes the demand for singular national allegiance in the logic of citizenship

multiple identifications of ethnicity, nationality, and gender and their shifting delineations of the other

different forms and grades of language: silence versus voice, fluent versus inarticulate, native tongue versus second language

the similarities and distinctions among religion, myth, and history

self-sacrifice, martyrdom, and gender: Joan of Arc, Saint Theresa, Yu Guan Soon

different forms of personal expression, from autobiography to diary to letters to the Catholic confession

the relationships between mother and daughter, Manchurian exile and Korean immigrant, Demeter and Persephone

the cinematic gaze on women and the patriarchal idealization of women's servility and silence

communication and correspondence, letter writing, telephone calls

Critical Issues

The book's multiple and heterogeneous form is an obvious focus of critical and theoretical reflection. On a basic level, the book raises the issue of representation, in the sense both of mirroring back a given reality and of an individual instance that stands in for a larger collectivity. Lisa Lowe argues that the book's "aesthetics of infidelity" resists and unsettles "the core values of aesthetic realism—correspondence, mimesis and equivalence" (36). A second point is that, although the book incorporates some fragments from Cha's personal life, it challenges the individual discreteness of autobiography by multiplying its subjects, which range from mythological figures such as Persephone to historical figures like Yu Guan Soon. At the same time, by persistently pointing to an estrangement from this history in both space and time, the book refuses to be cast as a spokesperson. *Dictee* also raises theoretical questions of language and voice. It challenges the cultural privileging of individual expression in a narrowly regulated syntax, grammar, and accent as an ideological move to diffuse the repressive silencing and delegitimation of many other voices of women, of immigrants, of localized dialects. All these characteristics of the book make it an instructive focus for a critical interrogation of the defining parameters of what counts as Asian American literature and what the relation of this specific literary field is or should be to the broader terrains of literature and literary criticism. A central factor in such an investigation must be the question of audience, which *Dictee* provokes but does not ultimately reconcile.

Other Possible Critical Considerations

literary genres and the logic of generic categorization

the writing of history from official chronicles to individual diaries

individual autobiography versus collective history

translation, whether from speech to writing, as in dictation, or from one distinct language to another (see Lowe)

wholeness versus fragmentation (see Wong)

interstitiality, breakdown of binaries (see E. Kim)

multiplicity, hybridity, heterogeneity

cinematic representation versus linguistic representation

the production of subjects in and through language

Pedagogical Issues and Suggestions

Dictee is likely to provoke bafflement in students, and it may be most productive initially to encourage them to articulate the specifics of their problems with the book. What parts seem most referentially solid to them? Which moments are the most occluded? What are their distinguishing features? Most likely, the students will have different points of entry into the text. From the diversity of their initial reactions to the book, discuss what their interpretations reveal about them as readers, particularly the variations in historical consciousness and textual expectations they bring to the book. At this point, it may be fruitful for teachers to convey that the book is less a clever and intentionally ambiguous exercise in writing than one that seeks to make the reader an active agent in the perception and the making of meaning in the text. Ask students how understanding this concept can further open up their reading of *Dictee* and its multiple references, suggestions, and forms.

Some Other Suggestions

1. Before assigning the book, provide a historical backdrop. Or, if time permits, ask students to conduct collaborative research into the historical events and individual figures invoked in the book.

2. Another good place to start is to ask students to think back to their first memories of attempting to master a language, either in learning to read and write a spoken native language or in acquiring a wholly foreign, second lan-

guage. How does the book evoke that struggle and reveal the ways in which it is infused with unequal social power and awkward physical and mental force? What does it mean if we reconsider language as something other than a natural, intimate, objective, or expressive tool that we control? Finally, the class can discuss the specific resonance of these questions of language for Asian Americans.

3. Break students into groups assigned to research and unravel one of the nine sections. When the class is reconvened, try to recompose the book from their oral presentations of research findings, critical interpretations, and group discussions. Then, as a class, think about the linear ordering of the nine sections and consider the possibility of other arrangements. How would this shift the meaning and the effect of the text? Does this deconstruction of the book shed insights into the logic of the book's organization? Does the fragmented and heterogeneous structure seem appropriate and possibly even necessary in attempting to address the personal and collective histories of dislocation that the book is centrally concerned with?

Intertextual Linkages

With Cha's films *Passages/Paysages* and *Exilée*, which address similar issues of exile, memory, return to homeland: Compare and contrast the textual and visual media.

With Myung Mi Kim's *Under Flag*, a volume of poetry that similarly explores the history of Japanese colonization, United States military domination, and Korean American immigration and acculturation through experimental linguistic techniques.

With Mary Paik Lee's *A Quiet Odyssey* or Ronyoung Kim's *Clay Walls*, which are more accessible instances of autobiography and novel that also reference Japanese colonization and immigration to the United States: Discuss the comparative insights afforded by the very different generic forms of the three texts.

With Elaine H. Kim and Norma Alarcon's *Writing Self, Writing Nation*: Use the four essays as a point of departure for alternative interpretive possibilities.

With Maxine Hong Kingston's *Woman Warrior*: This book addresses common issues of language struggles, bicultural negotiations, the power of myth and mythology, patriarchal oppression, Asian Americans' relationship to Asian homelands, and mother-daughter relationships, but it has been much more widely read and critically discussed in terms of Asian American literature. Explore the politics of canonization as it relates to referentiality, accessibility, and experimental textual practices.

With Audre Lorde's "biomythography," *Zami: A New Spelling of My Name*, and

Gloria Anzaldúa's *Borderlands / La Frontera* in cross-cultural comparisons of multiform texts by United States women of color that work within and against the literary tradition and formal conventions of autobiography.

Bibliographic Resources

Writing Self, Writing Nation (Kim and Alarcon), a full-length book devoted solely to *Dictee*, contains four essays by Elaine H. Kim, Lisa Lowe, Shelley Sunn Wong, and Laura Hyun Yi Kang, as well as artwork by Yong Soon Min. As the first published essays that attempt to place the book in the cultural and political context of Asian American literature, they offer a good starting point for critical and historical illuminations as well as for formulating alternative critical readings.

Both Walter Lew and Juliana Chang have published what could be considered conversational engagements with *Dictee*, which comment on the book's thematic and representational concerns by reproducing its fragmentary structure and elliptical style.

John Cho provides close readings of Cha's evocations of the figure of the female vampire, who is "homeless" and outside time; Anita Choe offers close readings of Cha's reinvention of the Catholic nine-day prayer called the novena.

Those interested in other aspects of Cha's artistic productivity can consult the University Art Museum/Pacific Film Archives at Berkeley, which houses a specially endowed collection of her multimedia works. Her influences and interests in film theory can be seen in a volume of essays she edited in 1980 entitled *Apparatus: Cinematographic Apparatus*. The short preface, which cogently expresses Cha's commitment to active participation by the film viewer, resonates with the challenges imposed on the textual reader in *Dictee*. For a discussion of Cha's live performance works, see Judith Barry.

Other Resources

For further readings into modern Korean history, see Ki-baik Lee's *A New History of Korea*, Bruce Cumings's *The Origins of the Korean War*, and Chungmoo Choi's essay. For background readings into Korean American History, see Wayne Patterson, *The Korean Frontier in America*.

Bibliography

Anzaldúa, Gloria. *Borderlands / La Frontera*. San Francisco: Spinsters–Aunt Lute, 1987.
Barry, Judith. "Women, Representation, and Performance Art: Northern California." *Performance Anthology: A Sourcebook for a Decade of California Performance Art*. Ed. Carl E. Loeffeler and Darlene Tong. San Francisco: Contemporary Arts, 1980. 439–62.

Cha, Theresa Hak Kyung, ed. *Apparatus: Cinematographic Apparatus*. New York: Tanam, 1980.

———. *Dictee*. Berkeley: Third Woman, 1994.

———. *Exilée*. Berkeley Art Museum Pacific Film Archive. 1980.

———. *Passages/Paysages*. Berkeley Art Museum Pacific Film Archive. 1978.

Chang, Juliana. "Transform This Nothingness: Theresa Hak Kyung Cha's *Dictee*." *Critical Mass* 1.1 (1993): 75–82.

Cho, John. "Tracing the Vampire." *Critical Mass: A Journal of Asian American Cultural Criticism* 3.2 (1997): 87–113.

Choe, Anita. "A Novena of Rebirth." *Critical Mass: A Journal of Asian American Cultural Criticism* 3.2 (1997): 74–84.

Choi, Chungmoo. "The Discourse of Decolonization and Popular Memory: South Korea." *Positions* 1.1 (1993): 72–102.

Cumings, Bruce. *The Origins of the Korean War*. Chicago: U of Chicago P, 1987.

hooks, bell. " 'When I was a young soldier for the revolution': Coming to Voice." *Talking Back: Thinking Feminist, Thinking Black*. Boston: South End, 1989.

Kang, Laura Hyun Yi. "The 'Liberatory Voice' of Theresa Hak Kyung Cha's *Dictee*." Kim and Alarcon 73–99.

Kim, Elaine H. "Poised on the In-Between: A Korean American's Reflections on Theresa Hak Kyung Cha's *Dictee*." Kim and Alarcon 3–30.

Kim, Elaine H., and Norma Alarcon, eds. *Writing Self, Writing Nation: A Collection of Essays on Theresa Hak Kyung Cha's* Dictee. Berkeley: Third Woman, 1994.

Kim, Myung Mi. *Under Flag*. Berkeley: Kelsey Street, 1991.

Kim, Ronyoung. *Clay Walls*. Sag Harbor: Permanent, 1986.

Kingston, Maxine Hong. *The Woman Warrior: Memoirs of a Girlhood among Ghosts*. New York: Knopf, 1976.

Lee, Ki-baik. *A New History of Korea*. Trans. Edward W. Wagner. Cambridge: Harvard UP, 1984.

Lee, Mary Paik. *A Quiet Odyssey: A Pioneer Korean American Woman in America*. Seattle: U of Washington P, 1990.

Lew, Walter K. *Excerpts from: Dikth/Diktee for* Dictee. Seoul: Yeul Eum, 1992.

Lim, Geok-lin, and Mayumi Tsutakawa, eds. *The Forbidden Stitch: An Asian American Women's Anthology*. Corvallis: Calyx, 1989.

Lorde, Audre. *Zami: A New Spelling of My Name*. Trumansburg: Crossing, 1982.

Lowe, Lisa. "Unfaithful to the Original: The Subject of *Dictee*." Kim and Alarcon 35–69.

Martin, Stephen-Paul. "Theresa Cha: Creating a Feminine Voice." *Open Form and the Feminine Imagination: The Politics of Reading in Twentieth-Century Innovative Writing*. Washington: Maisonneuve, 1988. 187–205.

Minh-ha, Trinh T. *Woman, Native, Other: Writing Postcoloniality and Feminism*. Bloomington: Indiana UP, 1989.

Patterson, Wayne. *The Korean Frontier in America: Immigration to Hawaii, 1896–1910*. Honolulu: U of Hawaii P, 1988.

Richie, Donald. "The Asian Bookshelf: Transcendent Lives." *Japan Times* 23 July 1983.

Roth, Moira. "Theresa Hak Kyung Cha, 1951–1982: A Narrative Chronology." Kim and Alarcon 151–60.

Stephens, Michael. "Korea: Theresa Hak Kyung Cha." *The Dramaturgy of Style: Voice in Short Fiction*. Carbondale: Southern Illinois UP, 1986. 184–210.

Wolf, Susan. "Theresa Cha: Recalling Telling Retelling." *Afterimage* 14.1 (1986): 11–13.

Wong, Shelley Sunn. "Unnaming the Same: Theresa Hak Kyung Cha's *Dictee*." Kim and Alarcon 103–40.

Eat a Bowl of Tea
by Louis Chu

David Shih

Publication Information

First United States edition published in 1961 by Lyle Stuart, Secaucus. Softcover editions published in 1979 by the University of Washington Press and Lyle Stuart, with a new introduction by Jeffery Paul Chan. Chapters 2 and 13 reprinted in the 1974 anthology *Aiiieeeee!* (Chin et al.); chapters 27 to 34 reprinted in the 1991 anthology *The Big Aiiieeeee!* (Chan et al.). Produced for stage by the Pan Asian Repertory Theater in New York City.

Overview

Eat a Bowl of Tea, a novel set in New York's Chinatown after World War II, revolves around the marriage of Ben Loy and Mei Oi. Ben Loy, a young veteran who served in the United States Army, is the son of Wang Wah Gay, who runs Money Come, a mahjong club for aging Chinatown men like himself. They are members of the "bachelor society" created by racist immigration restrictions, separated for decades from their wives in China or else never married. Wah Gay sends for his son only when Ben Loy is a grown man; father and son have a strained relationship.

Wah Gay arranges to have Ben Loy visit China, marry Mei Oi, the daughter of his old friend Lee Gong, and bring her over as a "war bride." Mei Oi's arrival is of great significance to male-dominated Chinatown, where she is expected to produce an heir to continue the Wang family line (and in the process symbolically renew the entire community). However, Ben Loy's former lifestyle, which included regular visits to prostitutes, has left him impotent. One of the Money Come regulars, Ah Song, seduces Mei Oi, who then continues their affair out of frustration with Ben Loy. Mei Oi eventually becomes pregnant with Ah Song's child.

The Chinatown elders begin their machinations to stop the scandal and save the marriage. Chuck Ting, the president of the Wang Family Association, intervenes to remove the couple to a small town outside New York. When they return, Wah Gay senses the urgency for action and confronts Ah Song, slicing off his ear. The police investigation causes Wah Gay and Lee Gong to "lose face" in the community; they leave for Chicago and Sacramento, respectively, while Ah Song is exiled by the Chinatown elders.

Ben Loy and Mei Oi move to San Francisco, where they hope for a fresh start. Mei Oi gives birth to an "illegitimate" son, Kuo Ming, who is accepted into the family. Ben Loy visits a Chinese herb doctor, who prescribes bitter tea as a cure for his impotence. The novel ends with Ben Loy's regaining his virility and the couple's planning to invite their fathers to the baby's second haircut party.

Reception

Upon its publication in 1961, *Eat a Bowl of Tea* did not enjoy mainstream success, partly because it departed so sharply in style from the novels of Chinatown that had preceded it. The characters have transliterated rather than translated names, and sometimes the vocabulary and syntax of their speech represent near-literal translations from the Sze Yup dialect. Chu faithfully reproduces authentic idioms such as "Wow your mother" and "You dead boy." A *New York Herald Tribune* critic regarded the work as "frequently tasteless and raw" in language and development. Praise was reserved for its documentary quality as an "extended look" into an American Chinatown (Field). *Library Journal* gave a more negative review, remarking that neither the character treatment nor the writing was of "sufficient quality" to recommend purchase (Stucki). The novel was out of print until revived by the University of Washington Press in 1979, largely through the efforts of Jeffery Paul Chan, Frank Chin, Lawson Fusao Inada, and Shawn Hsu Wong, who found the book "in the card catalog of the Oakland Public Library" (Chan et al., "Introduction" 228). The editors included chapters from *Eat a Bowl of Tea* in *Aiiieeeee!* (Chin et al.) and *The Big Aiiieeeee!* (Chan et al.), their anthologies of Asian American literature. *Eat a Bowl of Tea* has received much recent critical attention because of its reputation as one of the first Chinese American novels, and it is used in many college courses today.

Author's Biographical Background

Born on 1 October 1915 in Toishan, China, Louis Hing Chu immigrated to the United States with his family when he was nine. He grew up near Newark, completed high school in New Jersey, and received his AB in English (with a sociology minor) from Upsala College in 1937. He began his graduate training at New York University, where he received his MA in 1940. Like Ben Loy, he served in the Army Signal Corps in

World War II while stationed in Kunming, China, from 1943 to 1945. He returned to New York afterward and continued his graduate studies at the New School for Social Research from 1950 to 1952.

Chu married Kang Wong in 1940 and had four children, a son and three daughters. While best known today for *Eat a Bowl of Tea*, Chu was a popular radio personality and social worker in New York City. For many years he was the city's only Chinese American disk jockey, hosting a ninety-minute weekday program called *Chinese Festival*. The program—produced by Chu and Lyle Stuart, the publisher of *Eat a Bowl of Tea*—included news, interviews, commercials, and Chinese recorded music. Chu believed that the program met the needs of the diasporic Chinese population outside Chinatown: "They are isolated in laundries and restaurants all over the metropolitan area. That's the beauty of our program. It brings them back to China" ("Louis Hing Chu"). *Chinese Festival* ran from 1952 to 1962. Beginning in 1954, Chu served as executive secretary of the Soo Yuen Benevolent Association. He also operated a record store and worked as the director of a day center for the New York Department of Welfare. For the last few years of his life he was the director of the Golden Age Club at the Hamilton-Madison Settlement House. Louis Chu died on 2 March 1970.

Historical Context for the Narratives in *Eat a Bowl of Tea*

Although the narrative takes place near the midpoint of the twentieth century, the novel's American cast is very much a product of the political-cultural climate of the previous century. *Eat a Bowl of Tea* documents a watershed moment in the history of Chinese Americans—the rescinding of exclusionary laws against Chinese immigrants. Many acts of legislation targeted Chinese women in particular; the 1875 Page Law, for instance, forbade any Chinese woman suspected of being a prostitute from entering the country. Since suspicion was the only criterion, many Chinese women fell victim to wholly subjective and biased judgment. The Chinese Exclusion Act, which effectively banned immigration except for a few exempted groups, was passed in 1882 and was extended under other names through 1943. Thus, in the novel Lau Shee, whom Wah Gay married in China in 1923, and Lee Gong's wife are unable to join their husbands in America. In 1940 the ratio of Chinese American men to women was almost three to one. Violence against Chinese Americans in frontier and rural locales forced many of them to migrate to urban areas where they could live in sympathetic communities. There many of the men held occupations—restaurateur and laundryman, namely—historically "allowed" them by the dominant society. For mutual protection, family associations and tongs such as Chuck Ting's Wang Family Association arose within Chinatowns to govern internally and mediate with the outside world. The bachelor societies of American Chinatowns, then, were more indicative of racist exclusionary legislation than of "natural" patriarchal inclinations.

In 1943, as a wartime gesture of goodwill toward China, the United States rescinded past exclusionary legislation, though a quota of 105 Chinese immigrants a year remained in effect. The 1945 War Brides Act initially excluded veterans of Asian ancestry but was amended in 1947 to include them. Thus, Ben Loy in September 1948, ten months discharged from more than three years service, would have been eligible to bring his bride to New York from China on the revised War Brides Act. Chinese wives brought into America in this fashion were not counted against the imposed quota. More than six thousand Chinese women—the main group admitted under the act—entered the country and settled in metropolitan areas.

Historical Context for the Writing of *Eat a Bowl of Tea*

The years between the end of the war and the publication of *Eat a Bowl of Tea* saw relaxed immigration laws and a greater influx of Chinese (and other Asian) immigrants into the United States. In every year of the 1950s Chinese women made up from fifty to ninety percent of all Chinese entries. In addition, the coming to power of the Communists in China convinced many Chinese to leave their home country and those already in the United States to stay. Afterward, a series of refugee acts in 1953, 1957, and 1959 added three thousand immigrants to the five thousand already granted political asylum. By 1960, the ratio of Chinese American men to women had stabilized at 1.3 to 1. By the time *Eat a Bowl of Tea* appeared in 1961, the face of Chinese America had changed dramatically, and the portrait of any fraternal society remained alive only in Chu's narrative. The following years promised even greater change, with John F. Kennedy's 1962 presidential directive and the monumental 1965 Immigration Act that removed "national origin" as a basis for entrance.

Major Themes

individual versus collective parenthood, biological family versus expanded
    definition of family, filiation versus affiliation
immigrant disillusionment and disappointment with the American dream
parents' interference in the lives of their children
the importance of maintaining and saving "face" within one's community
the Chinese diaspora
Chinatown's internal government (family associations, tongs) versus external
    government (city police)
citizenship and legitimacy

Critical Issues

Along with Carlos Bulosan and John Okada, Louis Chu is considered to be one of the pioneers of the Asian American prose narrative. The *Aiiieeeee!* group holds *Eat a Bowl of Tea* in the highest esteem. Excerpts from the novel are anthologized in *Aiiieeeee!* (Chin et al.) and *The Big Aiiieeeee!* (Chan et al.). Jeffery Chan's introduction to the 1979 edition of the novel lauds Chu for his depiction of the lives of Exclusion-era old-timers in a "vision of non-Christian Chinese America" and for his "unerring eye and ear" in accurately expressing idiomatic Cantonese in English (1, 2). Chan reads *Eat a Bowl of Tea* as a comic-satiric parable of community renewal illustrating Chinatown's transition from a bachelor society to a family society. Chan's sentiments are echoed by Elaine Kim in *Asian American Literature*, where she contrasts Chu's authentic picture of Chinatown with the benign and exoticized portrayals in Lin Yu-tang's *Chinatown Family* and C. Y. Lee's *Flower Drum Song* (108).

In the 1980s and 1990s, as Asian American literary study embraced more contemporary writing—especially that by women—these earlier narratives attracted critical attention more for their historical quality than for their aesthetic innovation. Some critics view the older works as problematic anchors, legacies of "dead yellow men" instead of "dead white men." One of the most controversial issues associated with *Eat a Bowl of Tea* is its treatment of a Chinese American patriarchy. Some argue that Ben Loy's "recovery" and the arrival of Kuo Ming, the son, symbolize the emergence of a Chinese American identity released from filial obligation. Others such as Ruth Hsiao regard the ending as nothing more than a rebirth of Chinese American patriarchy, one to be established in San Francisco instead of New York. The significance of Kuo Ming's status as the novel's only native-born American citizen should not be overlooked in any discussion of patriarchy since he represents the best chance for legitimate participation within the American system. Also noteworthy is the simultaneous support and subversion of Confucian patriarchy characterized by the parents' and grandparents' embrace of the "illegitimate" son, Kuo Ming. Ambiguous moments like this one demonstrate the effects of exclusionary legislation on the shaping of cultural practices and values—that is, patriarchy—otherwise interpreted as obdurate and ahistorical.

Any conclusions about the viability of Chinese American patriarchy must take into consideration the character of Mei Oi. An obvious reading of her character would be one informed by stereotypes of Asian (American) women: sensuous, oversexed, and lacking in any meaningful agency. Her relationship with Ah Song begins as either a seduction or a rape—another discussion point—but continues as much because of her desire as because of his. Mei Oi's hope for a privileged lifestyle as the wife of a *gimshun-hok* (a Chinese immigrant to America) is lost amid the banality of her station as a neglected housewife. As Jinqi Ling argues ("Reading"), the scandal of her affair is exaggerated because Mei Oi disrupts the old bachelors' idea of "wife"—itself a construct of their historically marginalized condition. As the overseas wife, Lau Shee is a nonthreatening, agreeable memory that can be evoked at Wah Gay's pleasure. Mei Oi is an interloper to be reckoned with: a vibrant young woman with needs. She is also a harbinger. The adjustments these old men must make to historical change generate the novel's satire, which is made sad only by the exclusionary legislation that produced the multiple readings of "wife" in the first place. Thus the old bachelors' criticism of Mei Oi can also be read as a protest against the masculinization of Chinese American society effected by American immigration restrictions.

Pedagogical Issues and Suggestions

Some contemporary readers of *Eat a Bowl of Tea* may encounter the same difficulty with the language as did its reviewers in 1961. The rough and spirited language of the men is a convincing countertext to the silence or reticence of the Chinaman of white popular culture. Compare the narrative's "authentic" idioms to the "fake" maxims of a Charlie Chan. Ask why Chu's prose was seen as "tasteless and raw" by white reviewers. To encourage participation, an instructor familiar with Cantonese might pronounce all the untranslated names and terms before the first discussion and ask students to record their own phonetic transcriptions in the margins.

Eat a Bowl of Tea is a text that rewards readers familiar with its historical context. Conversely, those new to Asian American studies might find the Chinatown bachelor society foreign and off-putting, perhaps content in its position vis-à-vis the dominant society. Some may not interpret the narrative as a satire of manners or see the behavior of the old men as the result of the anxiety brought on by an impending social transformation. The significance of apparently random dates—1923, 1948—becomes evident when the book is read alongside a historical work such as Sucheng Chan's *Asian Americans*. Before beginning study of the novel, the instructor should introduce students to the series of legislative acts that have checked Asian immigration since the mid-nineteenth century. Still, the instructor should avoid the temptation of approaching the novel as a social document instead of as a work of fiction.

Since a film version of *Eat a Bowl of Tea* is available, the instructor may want to incorporate the film into an analysis of the novel by comparing and contrasting treatments of the characters and events, taking into account issues like artistic medium and intended audience.

Intertextual Linkages

With Sui Sin Far's *Mrs. Spring Fragrance*: Compare prewar and postwar Chinatowns and discuss the complex subjectivities of Chinese women within early immigrant communities.

With John Okada's *No-No Boy*: Examine differences in the postwar experiences of Japanese Americans and Chinese Americans; contrast the filial obligations of Ben Loy and Ichiro.

With Maxine Hong Kingston's *China Men*: Discuss the fraternal society of early Chinese immigrants and the problematic romantic relationships between immigrant men and (white) women.

With Amy Tan's *The Joy Luck Club*: Explore the shift of narrative focus onto matriarchal family systems and the differences between mother-daughter and father-son conflicts of expectation.

With Frank Chin's *Donald Duk*: Compare portraits of modern New York Chinatown and Donald Duk's and Ben Loy's contrasting attitudes toward their fathers' tradition and heritage.

With Fae Myenne Ng's *Bone*: Describe the effect of the absent father figure. Discuss Chinatown family life and the desire of children to leave Chinatown and parents.

Bibliographic Resources

Readers needing background on Chinese Americans during the exclusionary and post–World War II periods can consult the relevant sections in histories of Chinese Americans by Sucheng Chan ("Exclusion"); Shih-Shan Tsai; Roger Daniels; and K. Scott Wong and Sucheng Chan. Peter Kwong writes specifically about New York Chinatown from 1930 to 1950. While her focus is on San Francisco, Judy Yung gives previously neglected perspectives on Chinese American women, including "war brides" like Mei Oi.

Ling-chi Wang's typology of Chinese American identity, mapped onto major events in immigration history, provides a good introduction to a historicized reading of Chu's novel.

Those interested in reading the character of Mei Oi may want to look up *Jin Ping Mei* (also transliterated as *Chin Ping Mei* or *Gim Peng Moy* and translated in English as *The Golden Lotus*; see Hsiao Hsiao Sheng), a classical Chinese novel from the Ming Dynasty. The heroine, whose name has come to stand for excessive, immoral female sexuality, is a housewife who seduces her husband's brother. However, some recent Chinese writers and filmmakers have created revisionist, feminist versions of the story. (In *Eat a Bowl of Tea*, the old bachelors in the Wah Que barbershop are listening to the operatic version of the traditional story when Ben Loy enters; they compare faithless modern women with the heroine, arousing Ben Loy's suspicions of his wife.)

Other Resources

The 1989 film version of *Eat a Bowl of Tea* was directed by Wayne Wang, produced by Tom Sternberg, and written by Judith Rascoe. The movie, partially funded by the PBS American Playhouse production staff, stars Russell Wong as Ben Loy and Cora Miao as Mei Oi. The film version makes explicit some of the historical contexts implied in Chu's novel, incorporating directly into the dramatic action the effects of immigration laws on the Chinese American community.

Bibliography

Chan, Jeffery Paul. Introduction. Chu 1–5.

Chan, Jeffery Paul, et al., eds. *The Big Aiiieeeee! An Anthology of Chinese American and Japanese American Literature*. New York: Meridian, 1991.

Chan, Jeffery Paul, et al. "An Introduction to Chinese-American and Japanese-American Literatures." *Three American Literatures: Essays in Chicano, Native American, and Asian-American Literature for Teachers of American Literature*. Ed. Houston A. Baker, Jr. New York: MLA, 1982. 197–228.

Chan, Sucheng. *Asian Americans: An Interpretive History*. Boston: Twayne, 1991.

———. "The Exclusion of Chinese Women, 1870–1943." *Entry Denied: Exclusion and the Chinese Community in America, 1882–1943*. Ed. Chan. Philadelphia: Temple UP, 1991. 94–146.

Chin, Frank. *Donald Duk*. Minneapolis: Coffee House, 1991.

Chin, Frank, et al., eds. *Aiiieeeee! An Anthology of Asian-American Writers*. Washington: Howard UP, 1974.

Chu, Louis. *Eat a Bowl of Tea*. Secaucus: Stuart, 1961. Seattle: U of Washington P, 1979.

Chua, Cheng Lok. "Golden Mountain: Chinese Versions of the American Dream in Lin Yutang, Louis Chu, and Maxine Hong Kingston." *Ethnic Groups* 4.1–2 (1982): 33–59.

Daniels, Roger. *Asian America: Chinese and Japanese in the United States since 1850*. Seattle: U of Washington P, 1988.

Field, Carol. "Locale: A Chinatown." Rev. of *Eat a Bowl of Tea*, by Louis Chu. *New York Herald Tribune* 19 Feb. 1961, Lively Arts and Book Review: 33.

Hsiao, Ruth. "Facing the Incurable: Patriarchy in *Eat a Bowl of Tea*." *Reading the Literatures of Asian America*. Ed. Shirley Geok-lin Lim and Amy Ling. Philadelphia: Temple UP, 1992. 151–62.

Hsiao Hsiao Sheng. *The Golden Lotus: A Translation from the Chinese Original of the Novel Chin Ping Mei*. Trans. Clement Egerton. London: Kegan Paul, 1995.

Kim, Elaine H. *Asian American Literature: An Introduction to the Writings and Their Social Context*. Philadelphia: Temple UP, 1982.

———. Preface. *Charlie Chan Is Dead: An Anthology of Contemporary Asian American Fiction*. Ed. Jessica Hagedorn. New York: Putnam, 1993.

Kingston, Maxine Hong. *China Men*. New York: Knopf, 1980.

Kwong, Peter. *Chinatown, New York: Labor and Politics, 1930–1950*. New York: Monthly Review, 1979.

Ling, Jinqi. *Narrating Nationalisms: Ideology and Form in Asian American Literature*. New York: Oxford UP, 1998.

———. "Reading for Historical Specificities: Gender Negotiations in Louis Chu's *Eat a Bowl of Tea*." *MELUS* 20.1 (1995): 35–51.

"Louis Hing Chu, a Broadcaster and Social Worker, Dies at Fifty-six." *New York Times* 2 Mar. 1970: 37.

Lowe, Lisa. "Heterogeneity, Hybridity, Multiplicity: Marking Asian American Differences." *Diaspora* 1.1 (1991): 22–44.

Ng, Fae Myenne. *Bone*. New York: Hyperion, 1993.

Okada, John. *No-No Boy*. Seattle: U of Washington P, 1979.

Stucki, Curtis W. Rev. of *Eat a Bowl of Tea*, by Louis Chu. *Library Journal* 15 Mar. 1961: 1156.

Sui Sin Far [Edith Eaton]. *Mrs. Spring Fragrance*. Chicago: McClurg, 1912.

Tan, Amy. *The Joy Luck Club*. New York: Putnam, 1989.

Tsai, Shih-Shan Henry. *The Chinese Experience in America*. Bloomington: Indiana UP, 1986.

Wang, L. Ling-chi. "Roots and the Changing Identity of the Chinese in the United States." *The Living Tree: The Changing Meaning of Being Chinese Today*. Ed. Tu Wei-ming. Stanford: Stanford UP, 1994. 185–212.

Wong, K. Scott, and Sucheng Chan, eds. *Claiming America: Constructing Chinese American Identities during the Exclusion Era*. Philadelphia: Temple UP, 1998.

Yung, Judy. *Unbound Feet: A Social History of Chinese Women in San Francisco*. Berkeley: U of California P, 1995.

Dogeaters

by Jessica Hagedorn

Nerissa S. Balce

Publication Information

First published in the United States by Pantheon Books in 1990. Paperback edition published by Penguin Books in 1991. Received a National Book Award nomination in 1990.

Overview

A novel with more than forty vignette-like chapters set mostly in the Philippines, Jessica Hagedorn's *Dogeaters* challenges the norms of reading with its stylized, non-traditional form. The novel's structure includes different linguistic and stylistic registers that signal shifts in the narratives, giving the effect of a collage of lives or stories. The novel, then, can be read as a text without a single central narrator, since it consistently changes points of view and voice. The episodic scenes in the novel suggest a montage with a dreamlike textuality. The text also includes fictionalized and factual quotations from news accounts and historical sources on the Philippines, Hagedorn's former home. This feature of *Dogeaters* is important when we consider that illusion and reality, symbolized in artifacts such as news reports, gossip, and Hollywood movies, are major themes of the novel.

The novel's characters come from various socioeconomic backgrounds, and they lead disparate lives that are unwittingly linked and even mirror one another. The novel spans the late 1950s and ends in the mid-1980s, an important chapter in contemporary Philippine history capped by the fall of Ferdinand Marcos's twenty-year regime (1965–86). Marcos and his wife, Imelda, are fictionalized here in the novel as the unnamed President and the First Lady. The opposition leader Benigno Aquino, a Marcos critic from an elite family until he was assassinated in 1983, is fictionalized as Senator Domingo Avila.

The novel begins in Manila in 1956 as the country continues to rebuild from the ashes of World War II. The reader is first introduced to Rio, a young mestiza who comes from a wealthy Filipino family. Rio's father is half Spanish; her mother, half American—a heritage symbolic of the colonization of the Philippines by two empires, Spain and the United States (Campomanes, Afterword 146–47). The native elite collaborated with the colonizers, often marrying colonial officials to maintain their wealth and power (Anderson). Rio, as a product of these colonial-historical ties, represents the generations of mestizo ruling elites. The other mestizo characters in the novel, such as the Gonzagas and the Alacrans, symbolize the carnivorous relationship of the elite to the poor—that is, the rich as the eaters of the underdog. Indeed, Rio observes that the Gonzagas are "a carnivorous family" (Hagedorn, *Dogeaters* 91). The title of the novel, a pejorative used by Americans for Filipinos during the early 1900s, refers both to the elites who oppress the poor and to the poor themselves who have no recourse but to eat dog, considered a poor person's meal. The novel's title, then, implies both the contemporary and the historical representations of Filipinos. On the one hand, the elites and the poor are both dogeaters. On the other hand, the novel's reinscription of Philippine history recalls the racialized stereotype of the Filipino as backward and savage (Rydell 154–83).

The first chapter introduces Rio and her cousin Pucha (whose name is a Tagalog euphemism for the Spanish word *puta* or whore), both starstruck by Hollywood idols and the modern American life they represent. Later we encounter another important character, Joey Sands, who is also from a multiracial background but who is the antithesis of Rio in terms of access to privilege: Joey, a prostitute-junkie born of an unknown African American serviceman and a Filipino prostitute, is symbolic of the Philippines colonial history, "what is actually meant by 'special Filipino-American relations'" (San Juan 125; Nguyen, "Writing" 220; Rachel Lee 76, 85–86).

Other characters in the novel include the powerful businessman Severo Alacran, who is a crony of the dictator; his homely and nervous daughter, Baby Alacran; the unlucky Romeo Rosales, who is framed for the death of Senator Avila near the end of the novel; and General Nicasio Ledesma and his fanatically religious wife, Leonor. These mininarratives are often very brief, and readers may wonder what has happened to some characters, such as the mestizo gay club owner Andres Alacran, the Igorot janitor Pedro, the starlet-junkie Lolita Luna, or the fortune-teller La Sultana. The novel is replete with inclusions and digressions that resist a linear or chronological storytelling. The interwoven narratives of disparate characters are Hagedorn's attempt to simulate the "chaos-order" paradox of a city under a military dictatorship. The novel ends with a bittersweet coda "played" for the suffering and insufferable homeland, a country invoked by the unnamed persona through myth and memory. The imagined city of Manila, the central character of the novel (Hagedorn, "Homesick" 327), is the site of memory and neocolonial history.

Reception

Hagedorn's *Dogeaters* was warmly received by the print media and by scholars of American and ethnic literature. It has the distinction of being the first novel written by a Filipino American to be nominated for the National Book Award (1990). While it was lionized in popular reviews by the *New York Times Book Review* (D'Alpuget), the *Times Literary Supplement* (Hussein), the *American Book Review* (Gordon), *Amerasia Journal* (Gonzalez), and *MELUS* (Evangelista), the novel received some negative criticism from both Filipino and American critics (Casper; Hau; San Juan; San Juan qtd. in Wong 15). Like Maxine Hong Kingston's critically acclaimed *Woman Warrior*, Hagedorn's *Dogeaters* is a novel that touches on issues of authenticity, histories, and cultures. Criticisms of the novel include its exoticization of Philippine culture (Balce-Cortes) and its celebration of an upper-class, apolitical, cosmopolitan identity (San Juan qtd. in Wong 15). Despite the mixed responses to the novel, it remains a popular text in college courses on multicultural literature, women's studies, and ethnic studies. Numerous papers at conferences on Asian American studies, ethnic studies, and women's literatures have studied the novel's focus on gender, memory, colonial history, feminism, postmodernism, postcolonialism, and other issues. Critical essays on the novel have been published in academic journals (see Evangelista; Robert Lee 277–79; Nguyen, "Postcolonial State" 88–90; Balce-Cortes; Doyle). Hagedorn's novel, along with Carlos Bulosan's *America Is in the Heart*, is a significant contribution to the growing field of Filipino American writing.

Author's Biographical Background

Jessica Tarahata Hagedorn was born in the Philippines in 1949 and moved to San Francisco at age thirteen. Her poems were first published when she was twenty-four, in an anthology edited by the poet Kenneth Rexroth entitled *Four Young Women* (1973). Her early writings were influenced by the 1970s ethnic consciousness movements. Moved by the political spirit of the times, her poetry, playwriting, and short fiction "employed the psychedelic and rebellious idioms" particular to the moment (Campomanes, "Hagedorn" 370) and are anthologized in *Mountain Moving Day* (Gill), *Third World Women*, and *Time to Greez!* (Mirikitani et al.). She published her first collection of poetry and fiction, *Dangerous Music*, in 1975. Since then, Hagedorn's writings have been included in sixteen anthologies of women's, ethnic, and Third World writing. She moved to New York in 1978.

An accomplished actress, musician, and performance and multimedia artist, Hagedorn has collaborated with American artists and writers such as Thulani Davis and Ntozake Shange. In 1977, Joseph Papp produced *Where Mississippi Meets the Amazon*, her collaborative work with Davis and Shange. In 1978, Papp produced her first solo play, *Mango Tango*. Her subsequent theater works, staged in New York, include

Tenement Lover (1981) and *Holy Food* (1988; radio version, 1989). She staged *Teeny-town* in San Francisco in 1990.

In 1981, Hagedorn's experimental novella, *Pet Food and Tropical Apparitions*, won the American Book Award. Hagedorn received a two-year MacDowell writing fellowship in 1985 and 1986. A third MacDowell fellowship in 1988 allowed her to finish the manuscript of her first novel, *Dogeaters*. In a radio interview, Hagedorn mentioned that her novel explores her "own" past and culture. The novel germinated from the one hundred pages of notes on "the contradictions and elements" of Filipino society that she kept while visiting Manila in the late 1970s (Lipson). In "Homesick" Hagedorn writes that *Dogeaters*, set in the "contemporary Philippines," had been an "obsession" for her for over ten years (328, 327). Since the publication of *Dogeaters*, Hagedorn continues to read her poetry and perform her theater pieces in San Francisco and New York. She has edited a collection of Asian American fiction, *Charlie Chan Is Dead* (1993), and published a second novel, *The Gangster of Love* (1996).

For more information, see Oscar Campomanes's useful biographical profile ("Hagedorn"), from which this account is drawn.

Historical Context for the Narratives in *Dogeaters*

The novel *Dogeaters* spans the period from the late 1950s to the mid-1980s. The setting of the novel is Manila, the capital city of the Philippines. The 1950s was a decade marked by efforts to rebuild the country in the aftermath of World War II. The United States increased military and economic support for the Philippines in exchange for American military bases. With the growing communist threat in Asia, it was crucial for the United States to maintain military bases in the region to ensure United States dominance (Schirmer and Shalom 87). The military bases and the mushrooming of American transnational corporations that followed became symbols of American domination in the Philippines during the 1950s and the succeeding decades (Schirmer and Shalom 87–103). To date, the effects of the presence of American military bases continue to be felt. Prostitution, drugs, environmental hazards such as toxic nuclear waste (see *Toxic Sunset*), and the plight of "Amerasian" children born to "bar girls" (prostitutes impregnated by American servicemen) are among the many legacies of the United States bases.

In the mid-1950s, some elite Filipino families, like the fictional Alacran and Gonzaga families, grew richer from their dealings with American and foreign investors. These families celebrated their revived wealth by throwing extravagant parties not unlike those described in the novel (Manapat 71). The disparities between the lives of the rich and the poor were underscored by the growing agrarian unrest in the countryside led by the Hukbalahap. The Huks, as they were called, were a peasant-based organization at the forefront in the struggle against the Japanese during World War II. After the war, the Huks continued their armed struggle by going against rich landlords and later the Philippine government. In Hagedorn's novel, we encounter the figure of Severo Alacran, a "wheeler dealer" who has done business with "Japs, GI's, guerrillas in the jungle" (20). The chapters in the novel set after the 1960s fictionalize the Marcos years and the period of military dictatorship. Alacran is portrayed as a crony of the unnamed President and First Lady, and later the novel details his close ties with the dictator, his wife, and military officials of the regime.

Dogeaters may be read as a retelling of martial law history. In 1972, Ferdinand Marcos declared martial law to avoid the end of his second term as president and to combat growing resistance to his rule. He masked the power grab with the rhetoric of reform and promises of a "new society." In truth, the Marcoses and their cronies plundered the nation's coffers (Manapat 83–96). Opponents of the corrupt regime were arrested, tortured, "disappeared," and assassinated (Schirmer and Shalom 187–91, 221–23). The Marcoses were billionaire rulers of an impoverished country until they were brought down in a popular revolt in 1986.

Hagedorn's novel draws from this history through allusion and parody. Allusions to famous and infamous celebrities, historical persons, factual and fictive news clippings, disasters, murders, and other national spectacles are narrated in a seriocomic tone. The details in the novel take on surreal effects. A chapter in the novel that reports the discovery of corpses floating on a river, the bodies bearing the marks of torture, parodies a common occurrence during martial law: extrajudicial murders, commonly called "salvagings," that were committed to silence the opposition (Schirmer and Shalom 298). The character of Lolita Luna is an allusion to the popularity of bomba or soft-core pornographic movies during the 1970s (see Rachel Lee 82–85). In *Dogeaters*, rumors of torture camps run by the military and gossip on the foibles of the rich and powerful circulate throughout the city, just as rumors were a principal source of "unofficial" (hence uncensored and credible) information during the martial law years and led to the debunking of the authority and credibility of the Marcoses during their final years (Rafael). The opening of an international film festival sponsored by the First Lady and the collapse of the film festival venue that buries alive numerous construction workers mirror the macabre disaster of the Manila Film Palace in 1984 (*Dogeaters* 130, 134–35; Manapat 51). The figure of Daisy Avila, the beauty queen who becomes an activist, may be read as a representation of the Filipina beauty queen Nelia Sancho, who later joined the anti-Marcos movement (Evangelista 47). The assassination of the nationalist senator Domingo Avila and the false arrest of an innocent man framed for the murder fictionalize the most famous "salvaging" committed by the regime: the assassination of Benigno Aquino. Hagedorn's novel thus reinscribes history by re-creating the famous, infamous, and anonymous citizens of a city under military rule.

Historical Context for the Writing of *Dogeaters*

Popular accounts of the fall of the Marcos dictatorship were published in the United States after 1986, the year Ferdinand Marcos and his family fled to Hawaiʻi to live in exile and Corazon (Cory) Aquino, the widow of Benigno Aquino, was brought to power. Various books, along with documentaries and news features shown on American television, examined the corruption of the Marcoses and the triumph of the "People Power" revolution (see Bonner; Burton; Buss; Ellison; Lyons and Wilson; Manapat; Rempel; Rosca, *Endgame*; and Seagrave). However, many such accounts, which attempt to write "history" through a journalist's lens, must be read critically. For example, Stanley Karnow's Pulitzer Prize–winning book, *In Our Image: America's Empire in the Philippines*, attributes the successful revolt against Marcos to American democratic principles taught to Filipinos but overlooks the history of violence in the United States' colonial rule over the Philippines (see Campomanes, "1898"; Miller; Drinnon; Paulet; Williams).

In the United States, the large Filipino American community closely followed events in the Philippines. Articles on the Philippines were printed in major United States dailies. The euphoria following the 1986 People Power revolt was especially felt by anti-Marcos activists based in the United States. Many were educated professionals who had fled to the United States after the declaration of martial law and who continued to advocate an end to United States support for Marcos (Schirmer and Shalom 267–71). By the time Hagedorn's novel was published in 1990, Marcos and Aquino were recognizable names to the American public. Hagedorn's novel continues to fuel debates in various communities. Filipino immigrants and exiles, as well as a new generation of Filipino Americans, have either cheered or criticized the novel's stylized re-creation of a turbulent period in Philippine history.

Major Themes

memory and authenticity

corruption and innocence

blurring the lines between fiction and historical fact

the paradox of disparity and the similarities between the rich and the poor in a
     Third World city (separated by money yet united by the national
     condition of underdevelopment)

rumor and gossip as means of demystifying and challenging the rich and the
     powerful

Hollywood fantasies and Third World realities

megalomania and arrogance of the elite

"colonial mentality" or the racial stereotypes of Filipinos as a product of their
     colonial history

the city ("Manila") as the site of memory and history

the travails of living under a dictatorship for the rich and the poor

colonialism and Catholicism

repression and resistance

nightmares and fantasies
ethnicity, sexuality, and colonialism
the hybrid culture of Filipinos and their colonial history

Critical Issues

The novel's title recalls the pejorative used against Filipinos during the 1900s. The stereotype of Filipinos as "dogeaters" came into currency after a live exhibition of indigenous Filipino peoples at the 1904 Louisiana Purchase Exposition in Saint Louis. A federally supported spectacle, the Saint Louis exposition presented the triumphs of manifest destiny and validated American overseas expansion, including the "acquisition" of the Philippine Islands and its so-called primitive peoples (Rydell 154–83, 195–96). By presenting the Filipinos as primitives incapable of self-government, the display supplied more justification for the cause of annexation and institutionalization of American colonial rule in the islands (Rydell 170).

The novel's multiple narratives are another focus of study. Critical essays on *Dogeaters* have pointed to the text's "antiform" structure and the nonlinear narration of the various subplots. The text's "formlessness" has been attributed to the dreams and nightmares that are the central metaphors of the novel (D'Alpuget 1; Casper). The nightmarish quality of the imagined city is significant when we consider "Manila" as a postmodern city where the psychic and physical traumas of late-twentieth-century life are relived (West; see also Balce-Cortes). Another critic describes the novel as "the cinematext of a Third World scenario that might be the Philippines" (San Juan 118). The cinematic metaphors are especially relevant here when we consider that Hollywood movies, along with other objects of American or popular culture, invade the "real" and the "reel" life of the characters. The overlapping boundaries of the real and the make-believe, and consequently of fact and fiction, are among the many themes of the novel.

It is also important to note that while the novel begins with the life of Rio, a young mestiza who migrates to America, very little information is given of her immigrant life and her years in the United States. Interestingly, many American readers often identify Rio as the central narrator even though the novel consistently changes points of view, voice, and plot. Rio's story cannot be the central narrative in a novel that has none. Her story and the stories featuring other characters—the prostitute Joey Sands, the beauty queen Daisy Avila, the aspiring actor Romeo Rosales, the flirty cousin Pucha, and so on—are really counternarratives. The different narratives compete for the reader's belief in the "truth," in the authentic voice narrating the events. The novel ends with a *kundiman*, or love song, for the motherland. The song is bittersweet. The images of the motherland, both the secular and the religious, the sacred and the profane, mimic the ambivalence of the author toward her former home.

Lisa Lowe reads *Dogeaters* in terms of how official history writing is disrupted by the novel's competing, sometimes contradictory, narratives and by the circulation of *tsismis*, or gossip, among the marginalized inhabitants of Manila (112–20). Given its formal pastiches, cultural hybridity, epistemological instability, and multiplicity of perspectives, *Dogeaters* is often labeled postmodernist. (For debates surrounding the significance of postmodernist elements, see Hau and San Juan.)

Pedagogical Issues and Suggestions

Dogeaters is a novel that elicits different responses from students. For some, the novel's untraditional form may be confusing and difficult to read. Others, however, may have no difficulty following the various narratives and are drawn to the novel's experimental form. Teachers should address the form, or formlessness, of the novel at the onset. They may discuss the aesthetic of the contemporary novel and the way traditional and modernist ideas of realism, plot, chronology, and other structural forms of the novel have been challenged by contemporary writers.

Before assigning *Dogeaters*, teachers may find it helpful to discuss the concepts of memory, history, and fiction. The articles by Toni Morrison and Ketu Katrak are fine for this purpose.

Because America's role in the colonization of the Philippines is often suppressed or euphemistically presented in hegemonic accounts of American history, it is important for teachers to provide an adequate historical context for *Dogeaters* (see the suggested readings and videos given below).

Intertextual Linkages

With Maxine Hong Kingston's *Woman Warrior*: history and authenticity, the importance of memory, silence and telling, unraveling secrets, the motifs of food and eating.

With Theresa Hak Kyung Cha's *Dictee*: colonial history and personal history, violence and colonization, filmic textuality and fiction, official and repressed histories, vignette or episodic chapters and the function of the "fragment" aesthetic.

With Ninotchka Rosca's *State of War*: the legacies of colonialism and a dictatorship; colonial history and personal history; dreams, nightmares, and Third World realities; the Philippines as "other" of the United States; "Manila" as a Third World city where pervasive violence and American domination are symbolized in subtle forms and artifacts.

With Isabel Allende's *House of the Spirits*: fantasy, colonial history, and personal history; the importance of memory and telling; violence by the colonizer and the elite; the legacies of violence.

With Eric Gamalinda's *Empire of Memory*: official and repressed histories; violence, state repression, and resistance; the burden of memory; silence, censorship, and memory; the invisible and visible legacies of American colonization.

Bibliographic Resources

On American colonization of the Philippines at the turn of the century, see Oscar V. Campomanes's essays ("Filipinos," Afterword, and "1898") and the works by Gareth Jones, Walter Williams, Stuart Miller, and Kristin Hoganson. Robert Rydell covers the Philippine exhibit at the 1904 Saint Louis World's Fair. On American colonization, see Richard Drinnon; Daniel Schirmer and Stephen Shalom; and Amy Kaplan and Donald Pease. Ricardo Manapat gives a lively journalistic account of the excesses of the Marcos regime. The first two chapters can serve as an introduction to the martial law period, and there are useful endnotes on American news coverage of the Marcoses. On the fall of the Marcos regime, see Ninotchka Rosca, *Endgame*, and Vicente Rafael.

Readers who wish to study Hagedorn's poetry and fiction may read her earlier works, some of which have been compiled and republished under the title *Danger and Beauty* (1993). Hagedorn discusses *Dogeaters* and the notions of memory and history in "Homesick" and issues of identity in "The Exile Within / The Question of Identity." Campomanes gives a useful biographical history of Hagedorn ("Hagedorn").

Other Resources

Useful videos include *Bontoc Eulogy*, which contains archival footage on the Philippine Reservation at the Saint Louis World's Fair and deals with the themes of memory, history, and fiction, and *Savage Acts*, which concisely covers American expansion, especially the annexation of the Philippines and the Philippine-American War (1899–1902).

Bibliography

Allende, Isabel. *The House of the Spirits*. New York: Knopf, 1985.

Anderson, Benedict. "Cacique Democracy in the Philippines: Origins and Dreams." *New Left Review* 169 (1988): 3–31.

Balce-Cortes, Nerissa. "Imagining the Neocolony." *Critical Mass: A Journal of Asian American Cultural Criticism* 2.2 (1995): 95–120.

Bonner, Raymond. *Waltzing with a Dictator: The Marcoses and the Making of American Policy*. New York: Times, 1987.

Bontoc Eulogy. Dir. Marlon Fuentes. Perf. Marlon Fuentes and cast. Natl. Asian Amer. Telecommunications Assn. (NAATA), 1996.

Burton, Sandra. *Impossible Dream: The Marcoses, the Aquinos, and the Unfinished Revolution.* New York: Warner, 1989.

Buss, Claude A. *Cory Aquino and the People of the Philippines.* Stanford: Stanford Alumni Assn., 1987.

Campomanes, Oscar V. Afterword. "The New Empire's Forgetful and Forgotten Citizens: Unrepresentability and Unassimilability in Filipino-American Postcolonialities." *Critical Mass: A Journal of Asian American Cultural Criticism* 2.2 (1995): 145–200.

———. "1898 and the Nature of the New Empire." Spec. issue of *Radical History Review* 73.1 (1999): 130–46.

———. "Filipinos in the United States and Their Literature of Exile." *Reading the Literatures of Asian America.* Ed. Shirley Geok-lin Lim and Amy Ling. Philadelphia: Temple UP, 1992. 49–78.

———. "Hagedorn, Jessica Tarahata." *The Oxford Companion to Women's Writing in the United States.* Ed. Cathy N. Davidson and Linda Wagner-Martin. New York: Oxford UP, 1995. 370–71.

Casper, Leonard. "Bangungot and the Philippine Dream in Hagedorn." *Solidarity: Current Affairs, Ideas and the Arts* 127 (1990): 152–57.

Cha, Theresa Hak Kyung. *Dictee.* Berkeley: Third Woman, 1994.

D'Alpuget, Blanche. "Philippine Dream Feast." *New York Times Book Review* 25 Mar. 1990: 1+.

Doyle, Jacqueline. "'A Love Letter to My Motherland': Jessica Hagedorn's *Dogeaters*." *Hitting Critical Mass: A Journal of Asian American Cultural Criticism* 4.2 (1999): 1–26.

Drinnon, Richard. *Facing West: The Metaphysics of Indian Hating and Empire Building.* New York: Schocken, 1990.

Elliott, Emory, ed. *The Columbia History of the American Novel.* New York: Columbia UP, 1991.

Ellison, Katherine. *Imelda: Steel Butterfly of the Philippines.* New York: McGraw, 1988.

Evangelista, Susan. "Jessica Hagedorn and Manila Magic." *MELUS* 18.4 (1993): 41–52.

Gamalinda, Eric. *The Empire of Memory.* Manila: Anvil, 1992.

Gill, Elaine G., ed. *Mountain Moving Day: An Anthology of Women's Poetry.* Watsonville: Crossing, 1973.

Gonzalez, N. V. M. "*Dogeaters*." *Amerasia Journal* 17.1 (1991): 189–92.

Gordon, Jaimy. "Frantic Entertainments." *American Book Review* 12.5 (1990): 16+.

Hagedorn, Jessica, ed. *Charlie Chan Is Dead: An Anthology of Contemporary Asian American Fiction.* New York: Penguin, 1993.

———. *Danger and Beauty.* New York: Penguin, 1993.

———. *Dangerous Music: The Poetry and Prose of Jessica Hagedorn.* San Francisco: Momo's, 1975.

———. *Dogeaters.* New York: Penguin, 1991.

———. "The Exile Within / The Question of Identity." *The State of Asian America.* Ed. Karin Aguilar–San Juan. Boston: South End, 1994. 173–82.

———. *The Gangster of Love.* Boston: Houghton, 1996.

———. "Homesick." *Visions of America: Personal Narratives from the Promised Land.* Ed. Wesley Brown and Amy Ling. New York: Persea, 1993. 326–28.

————. Interview. *Moveable Feast*. Natl. Public Radio. New York, 1990.

————. *Pet Food and Tropical Apparitions*. San Francisco: Momo's, 1981.

Hau, Caroline S. "*Dogeaters*, Postmodernism, and the 'Worlding' of the Philippines." *Philippine Post-colonial Studies: Essays on Language and Literature*. Ed. Cristina Pantoja-Hidalgo and Priscelina Patajo-Legasto. Quezon City: U of the Philippines, 1993. 113–27.

Hoganson, Kristin L. *Fighting for American Manhood: How Gender Politics Provoked the Spanish-American and Philippine-American Wars*. New Haven: Yale UP, 1998.

Hussein, Aamer. "Dogeaters." *Times Literary Supplement* 27 Sept. 1991: 26.

————. *In Search of Marcos Millions*. PBS. 26 May 1990.

Jones, Gareth Stedman. "The Specificity of U.S. Imperialism." *New Left Review* 60 (1970): 59–86.

Kaplan, Amy, and Donald E. Pease, eds. *Cultures of United States Imperialism*. Durham: Duke UP, 1993.

Karnow, Stanley. *In Our Image: America's Empire in the Philippines*. New York: Random, 1989.

Katrak, Ketu H. "Colonialism, Imperialism, and Imagined Homes." Elliott 649–78.

Kingston, Maxine Hong. *The Woman Warrior: Memoirs of a Girlhood among Ghosts*. New York: Knopf, 1976.

Lee, Rachel. *The Americas of Asian American Literature: Gendered Fictions of Nation and Transnation*. Princeton: Princeton UP, 1999.

Lee, A. Robert. "*Eat a Bowl of Tea*: Asian America in the Novels of Gish Jen, Cynthia Kadohata, Kim Ronyoung, Jessica Hagedorn, and Tran Van Dinh." *Ethnicity and Representation in American Literature*. Spec. issue of *Yearbook of English Studies* 24 (1994): 263–80.

Lipson, Eden Ross. "Real Life, Imaginary Dictators." *New York Times Book Review* 25 Mar. 1990: 38.

Lowe, Lisa. *Immigrant Acts*. Durham: Duke UP, 1996.

Lyons, John, and Karl Wilson. *Marcos and Beyond: The Philippines Revolution*. Kenthurst: Kangaroo, 1987.

Manapat, Ricardo. *Some Are Smarter than Others: The History of Marcos' Crony Capitalism*. New York: Aletheia, 1991.

Miller, Stuart Creighton. *"Benevolent Assimilation": The American Conquest of the Philippines, 1899–1903*. New Haven: Yale UP, 1982.

Mirikitani, Janice, et al., eds. *Time to Greez! Incantations from the Third World*. San Francisco: Glide–Third World, 1975.

Morrison, Toni. "The Site of Memory." *Out There: Marginalization and Contemporary Cultures*. Ed. Russel Ferguson, Martha Gever, Trinh T. Minh-ha, and Cornel West. New York: New Museum of Contemporary Art and MIT, 1990. 299–305.

Nguyen, Viet. "The Postcolonial State of Desire: Homosexuality and Transvestitism in Ninotchka Rosca's *State of War*." *Critical Mass: A Journal of Asian American Cultural Criticism* 2.2 (1995): 67–93.

————. "Writing the Body Politic: Asian American Subjects and the American Nation." Diss. U of California, Berkeley, 1997.

Paulet, Anne. "'The Only Good Indian Is a Dead Indian': The Use of U.S. Indian Policy as a Guide for the Conquest and Occupation of the Philippines, 1898–1905." Diss. Rutgers U, 1995.

Rafael, Vicente L. "Fishing, Underwear, and Hunchbacks: Humor and Politics in the Philippines, 1896 and 1983." Association for Asian Studies Annual Meeting. Chicago, 1986.

Rempel, William C. *Delusions of a Dictator: The Mind of Marcos as Revealed in His Secret Diaries*. Boston: Little, 1993.

Rexroth, Kenneth, ed. *Four Young Women: Poems by Jessica Tarahata Hagedorn, Alice Karle, Barbara Szerlip, and Carol Tinker*. New York: McGraw, 1973.

Rosca, Ninotchka. *Endgame: The Fall of Marcos*. New York: Watts, 1987.

———. *State of War*. New York: Norton, 1988.

Rydell, Robert W. *All the World's a Fair: Visions of Empire at American International Expositions, 1876–1916*. Chicago: U of Chicago P, 1984.

San Juan, Epifanio, Jr. "Mapping the Boundaries: The Filipino Writer in the U.S.A." *Journal of Ethnic Studies* 19.1 (1991): 117–31.

Savage Acts: Wars, Fairs, and Empire. Dir. Pennee Bender, Joshua Brown, and Andrea Ades Vasquez. Amer. Social History Project, 1995.

Schirmer, Daniel B., and Stephen Rosskamm Shalom. *The Philippines Reader: A History of Colonialism, Neocolonialism, Dictatorship, and Resistance*. Boston: South End, 1987.

Seagrave, Sterling. *The Marcos Dynasty*. New York: Harper, 1988.

Third World Women. Ed. Third World Women. San Francisco: Third World Communications, 1972.

Toxic Sunset: On the Trail of Toxic Wastes in Clark and Subic. Dir. Benjamin Pimentel and Louella Lasola. Natl. Asian Amer. Telecommunications Assn. (NAATA), 1993.

West, Cornel. "Postmodern Culture." Elliott 515–20.

Williams, Walter A. "United States Indian Policy and the Debate over Philippine Annexation: Implications for the Origins of American Imperialism." *Journal of American History* 66 (1980): 810–31.

Wong, Sau-ling C. "Denationalization Reconsidered: Asian American Cultural Criticism at a Theoretical Crossroads." *Amerasia Journal* 21.1-2 (1995): 1–27.

When Heaven and Earth Changed Places and Child of War, Woman of Peace

by Le Ly Hayslip

Viet Thanh Nguyen

Publication Information

When Heaven and Earth Changed Places first published by Doubleday in hardcover in 1989 and in softcover in 1990. *Child of War, Woman of Peace* first published by Doubleday in hardcover and softcover in 1993.

Overview

Le Ly Hayslip's two autobiographical volumes, *When Heaven and Earth Changed Places* and *Child of War, Woman of Peace*, were both cowritten, the former with the professional writer Jay Wurts and the latter with Hayslip's eldest son, James. The different cowriters probably account for the radical differences in narrative style that characterize the two volumes.

 When Heaven and Earth Changed Places covers two separate periods in Hayslip's life: there is an account of her childhood in her home village of Ky La and her young adulthood in Saigon and another account of her eventual return home to Viet Nam in 1986. The two accounts are interwoven, so that a narrative tension is created as we read alternating chapters that show Phung Thi Le Ly (her given name) growing up and facing extraordinary challenges caused by war, poverty, racism, and sexual exploitation and then Le Ly Hayslip's return to an uncertain welcome as a Viet Kieu, an overseas Vietnamese. Hayslip's memories start with loving accounts of family and rural life, which are marred by the intrusions of French and Moroccan soldiers (this places her early childhood before 1954, when the French were defeated at Dien Bien Phu and eventually forced to leave Viet Nam). After 1954, Hayslip and all the peasants find themselves in a civil war whose causes and ideologies are difficult for them to identify; the most material element of the civil war that the young Hayslip understands is that the Army of the Republic of Viet Nam (ARVN, the army of South Viet Nam) controls the village by day, while the National Liberation Front (the NLF or, as they were pejoratively called by the South Vietnamese government and the American military, the Viet Cong) controls the village by night. Hayslip becomes a "revolutionary heroine" by warning NLF soldiers of an imminent ARVN assault. She is then imprisoned and tortured by the ARVN, but when a relative in the police intervenes and has her released, she finds herself under suspicion by the NLF as a traitor. Eventually her mother takes her to Da Nang and later Saigon to help her escape her probable fate, execution by either the ARVN or the NLF. In Saigon, she becomes impregnated by a rich employer, works in the black market to support her family, and in one notorious incident, prostitutes herself. She later marries Ed Hayslip, an American civilian worker, and leaves for the United States in 1973; she returns in 1986, during a period when it was still risky for civilians, especially overseas Vietnamese, to return to a country with which the United States had no diplomatic relations (and against whom the United States was actively enforcing a crippling embargo). She is reunited with her mother and decides to establish a humanitarian foundation.

Child of War, Woman of Peace is a more straightforward narrative with simpler language than *When Heaven and Earth Changed Places*. The second volume in Hayslip's autobiography documents her years in the United States as an immigrant wife and her multiple returns to Viet Nam after the initial return that is highlighted in *When Heaven and Earth Changed Places*. Hayslip's American life is a dramatic one (or, as some critics have described it, a melodramatic one). She has complicated relationships with several men: Ed, her first husband; Dan, an American officer with whom she has an affair; Dennis Munro, her second and abusive husband; and Cliff Parry, a con man who may have been a Green Beret. (In Oliver Stone's film adaptation of her two books, *Heaven and Earth*, all these men are condensed into one character, played by Tommy Lee Jones.) Eventually, Hayslip renounces her complicated romantic life in favor of a devotion to spiritual and philanthropic causes focused on healing Viet Nam and the survivors of the war, both Americans and Vietnamese. *Child of War, Woman of Peace* also recounts the development of Hayslip's writing interests and the writing process of her first book and discusses the necessary work of economic survival as undergone by an immigrant woman and sometimes single mother. Eventually, the book climaxes with Hayslip's return to Viet Nam, where she builds a health clinic and reestablishes relationships with her family.

Reception

The reception of the two books differed markedly. Specifically, the American reception of the books was highly mediated by the history of American involvement in Viet Nam; the effect of that involvement on American culture, both during the war and after; a lingering sense of guilt felt by some Americans; and a general awareness of a lack of knowledge concerning Viet Nam and the Vietnamese.

When Heaven and Earth Changed Places received widespread favorable reviews, including one in the *New York Times Book Review* (Shipler). In general, critics lauded the book for its dramatic power, its story of tragedy, survival, and redemption, and its insight into "the" Vietnamese experience, which, as many critics noted, was particularly compelling because of the relative dearth of Vietnamese perspectives in English on the war and its aftermath. (There are some other self-written autobiographical narratives and novels, but they are not widely available; this excludes the category of oral histories.)

The Vietnamese American reception of the book and of Hayslip herself, however, was not favorable; Hayslip was castigated for her involvement with the Viet Cong, her prostitution, her perceived self-promotion, and her reluctance to criticize Viet Nam's human rights abuses. In other words, public Vietnamese reception focused as much on Hayslip's personality and perceived motives as on her autobiographical narrative itself.

The non–Vietnamese American reception of *Child of War, Woman of Peace* was less enthusiastic than it was for the first volume. Again, the book was reviewed in the *New York Times Book Review*. Critics who had hailed the drama and tragedy of the first volume found this one to be melodramatic and verging on soap opera because of Hayslip's active and complex love life. The chronological style of the narrative, compounded by the high number of tragedies, contributed to this perception of melodrama.

The two books have not been the subject of widespread discussion in Asian American studies, and it is unknown to what extent they have been taught in Asian American studies courses in the nation. This omission is regrettable, and the lack of recognition of Hayslip's books is probably attributable to the lack of critical material written about them, as well as to the general marginalization of Vietnamese Americans as subjects in Asian American studies.

Author's Biographical Background

Although much of Hayslip's biographical background can be found in her books, readers may also want to know about Hayslip's life since then. Hayslip heads a nonprofit organization called the East Meets West Foundation, which raises funds for its various medical clinics in Viet Nam. The books themselves include brief accounts of East

Meets West's work, and Hayslip continually publicizes her foundation at public appearances. Her use of her books and her own public appearances to raise money adds to the difficulty readers normally have in distinguishing between "truth" and "performance" in autobiographical self-representations.

Historical Context for Hayslip's Autobiographies

The historical context for Hayslip's work is extremely complicated, both for reasons of Vietnamese history and because of Americans' reactions to United States involvement in Viet Nam. Viet Nam was colonized by the French from the late 1800s until 1954, when the French were defeated by the Viet Minh at Dien Bien Phu. The United States was already financially involved in supporting the French before 1954; after 1954, American involvement became more direct, including increased military and political support. By 1965, although war was never declared, the United States had large numbers of ground troops in Viet Nam and aerial bombing had begun in earnest. American involvement officially ended in 1973. The various effects or contributions of American involvement are all treated in Hayslip's first book; some of the most prominent changes induced by the American intervention include a high presence of American troops, an inflationary urban economy, an increase in the black market and the types of businesses, sexual and otherwise, that catered to American troops, the rural devastation caused by counterinsurgency warfare and bombing, the upsetting of cultural mores, the creation of communities of displaced peasants, the fragmentation of families, and the atmosphere of economic and personal exploitation.

The American military failure in Viet Nam, both in sustaining the South Vietnamese government and in "containing communism," was intertwined with widespread domestic political unrest and cultural changes. The United States went through an identity crisis as a result of its involvement in Viet Nam; the high idealism of the Kennedy years and the related sense of democratic mission were destroyed for the "hawks" by military and political failure and for the "doves" by American atrocities in Viet Nam. Much of American foreign policy in the 1980s and early 1990s, beginning with Panama and Grenada and culminating in the Gulf War, was aimed partially at reconstructing American military will and self-esteem. The idea of Viet Nam as a mistake that should not be repeated also haunted American political discussions, especially in the context of El Salvador. For American veterans who became writers and filmmakers and who dwelled on their war experiences, part of the problem of dealing with the war became the fact that any representation of the war eventually seemed incomplete without the Vietnamese perspective. Part of the excitement caused by Hayslip's first book, then, resulted from this sudden opportunity to compensate for a lack of knowledge.

For the Vietnamese American community, the war resulted in a different set of concerns. The most politically powerful elements of the community come from the military and political elites of South Viet Nam, who represent most of the first wave of Vietnamese refugees who came in 1975. (The most economically powerful elements of the community, however, come from the Chinese Vietnamese community, who were harassed and driven out by the communist government during the late 1970s.) These elites remain staunchly anticommunist in their politics and concerns. Any hints of rapprochement with the communist government of Viet Nam by Vietnamese Americans are treated with great hostility; political discourse in the Vietnamese American community is volatile and occasionally violent. In contrast to Hayslip's reception by non–Vietnamese Americans, who welcome her message of reconciliation and healing, Hayslip's reception in the Vietnamese American community has been cold. Although recently much of the Vietnamese American community has become reconciled to such things as visiting Viet Nam and doing business there, the political tone is still strongly anticommunist, and it is still difficult to mention reconciliation publicly as Hayslip does. Hayslip's second book deals with both the Vietnamese and the American reception of her work.

Major Themes

agrarian, communitarian values versus urban, capitalist values
the difficult life of peasants faced with social forces beyond their control
the nature of the Vietnamese family, which for Hayslip includes fragmentation, conflict, and permanent ties
male and female gender roles, in both Vietnamese and American contexts
the strength of the individual, especially the individual woman
the masculine connection between military violence and domestic violence
the global spread of militarism and its relation to capitalism
the never-ending cycle of violence, both personal and political
the possibility of individual intervention in that cycle
the nature of karma, or soul debt, and the possibility of redemption
reconciliation and healing, both for individuals and for Viet Nam and the United States
the difficulties of being an immigrant woman and the immigrant's comic perspective on American culture
the process of writing and publishing and the possibility of speech for a cultural outsider in the United States, especially one who comes from a peasant background

Critical Issues

It would be difficult to address Hayslip's books outside their historical context. Although the books can be read for their deployment of certain images and metaphors (e.g., a masculine-feminine binary is easily detectable in her portrayals of the United States and Viet Nam, violence and healing, and technology and nature), these images are constantly complicated by the textual histories of the two books. One of the most crucial issues that must be addressed with her work, then, is the problem of authorship, mediation, and critical reception and exploitation. This problem is one that is historically inextricable from the genre of cowritten autobiography, especially for people of color. Hayslip acknowledges, both personally and in print, the roles of her two co-authors; what remains unclear is the extent to which her coauthors influenced the writing, particularly in the use of language and its intersection with the nuances of political and cultural expression. For example, distinctions can clearly be made between the two books' choices of images for the Vietnamese, with the first book being dependent on many stereotypically animalistic images. The use of the term *woman warrior* in the first book's opening pages might also be suspect. (Although Viet Nam has a long tradition of warrior women, the term in the context of Maxine Hong Kingston's popularity inevitably recalls her novel of the same name and some of the problems in its orientalized reception. In addition, see Trinh T. Minh-ha's film *Surname Viet Given Name Nam* for an analysis of the ambivalent heroization of women found in the warrior women tradition.) It would be helpful to compare Hayslip's position in this respect with the historical problem faced by writers who are not perceived by the publishing industry and critical reviewers as proficient in writing or speaking standard English: a prime example would be Harriet Jacobs's *Incidents in the Life of a Slave Girl*. A more telling scenario, however, is that embodied in the history of *Black Elk Speaks*, edited by John G. Neihardt, a narrated autobiography that was a countercultural spiritual text of the 1960s. Scholars ultimately showed that the portions of the book that countercultural readers found most "spiritual" were actually written by Neihardt (De-Mallie). Although nothing conclusive has yet been established about Hayslip's writings, readers and teachers of her work should keep in mind the possibilities of distortions and manipulations by the cowriters and use the opportunity to raise questions about the generic possibilities and constraints of cowritten autobiography for people of color in the United States.

Also important to keep in mind are possible distortions and manipulations by Hayslip herself. Anyone who has seen Hayslip speak in person, especially multiple times, is aware of Hayslip's performative abilities; she usually affects her audience greatly with her deployment of tears and traumatic stories. Hayslip can be seen in the category of the trickster, someone who manipulates mainstream perceptions and needs for her own purposes; of course, these purposes may be a combination of selfish and selfless. The trickster, in relation to mainstream culture, occupies a position of both resistance and self-exploitation; part of Hayslip's strategy is her self-shaping to fit certain American expectations of the victim who forgives. Hayslip's memoirs also fit into the literature of witness, but again her writings have special resonance within the context of American postwar discourse over the Viet Nam War and American responsibility and failures—military, political, moral, and otherwise. In short, Hayslip's textual strategies should be historically contextualized to stress the ways American and

Vietnamese American readers take away different things from her works according to their own situations.

Thus, reader response is another crucial element to explore in discussing Hayslip's work, especially if an instructor chooses to teach both books or one book in full and another in excerpt or summary. The books usually generate a predictable reader response: generally, the first book is more favorably received than the second. This effect is due, at least in part, to differences in narrative structure as well as to differences in subject matter, since the first book is more explicitly concerned with the war and its attendant tragedy and possible guilt for American readers, while the second one is concerned with domestic issues in all senses of the word: immigration, assimilation, marriage, domestic abuse, New Age spirituality, and homeland nostalgia. Readers should ask why the first set of concerns might be more appealing than the second set; certainly, the critical response that the first book is tragic and affirming while the second book is melodramatic and soap operatic is partially overdetermined by gendered and political expectations (to put it crudely: war in a foreign country is exciting, domestic violence here is boring).

Hayslip's book is also deeply concerned with issues of spirituality. Instructors can stress the version of Buddhism that is found here, the notion of karma or soul debt that is related to populist notions of justice, and the links to American New Age spirituality as well.

Pedagogical Issues and Suggestions

Autobiographies, cowritten or otherwise, and the literature of witness inevitably implicate the reader in their textual strategies in a more crucial way than the reader is implicated in reading literature that is marketed as fiction. That is, the reader of a cowritten autobiography is challenged to believe in the authenticity of the primary subject's voice; likewise, in the literature of witness, the issue of the author or subject's veracity concerning the facts of oppression is fundamental to the moral and political effect of the literature. Hayslip's book raises issues of both authenticity and veracity, and these issues can be particularly compelling in relation to the demographics of a class reading her books. For example, Asian American readers, especially Vietnamese American ones, tend to be much more skeptical of Hayslip's veracity and motives than non-Vietnamese or non–Asian American readers, such as American veterans of the war or antiwar protesters who approach Hayslip's message of reconciliation with very different understandings of what, if anything, needs to be reconciled. Instructors should stress the readers' reactions to the books, help the students analyze their responses in the general historical context and in the context of their own personal histories, and highlight any differences in reader response that arise in class.

Because of the relatively marginalized position of Vietnamese Americans within Asian American studies, students may have a limited awareness of Vietnamese American history and culture and the particular ways they manifest themselves in community concerns and literary formation. Instructors might therefore find it useful to give lectures that address both the specific historical context of Vietnamese Americans and the differences between this historical context and those of dominant groups like Japanese and Chinese Americans. For example, as Oscar Campomanes has pointed out in the Filipino context, the literature of Japanese and Chinese Americans tends to fit an immigrant model that is settlement-focused; this model may not work very well in considering certain elements of the Filipino population in the United States who see themselves as exiles.

Vietnamese Americans also differ in many ways from the immigrant model. Vietnamese Americans of the military and political elites are concerned with loss, exile, displacement, and homeland nostalgia—in short, they tend to look backward much more than they look forward. This was especially true in the 1970s and 1980s. Chinese Vietnamese, who never had much political stake in Viet Nam, tend to be more concerned with economic survival, as are working-class Vietnamese Americans who come from rural and working-class backgrounds in Viet Nam and who were refugees in the late 1970s and 1980s. In most examples of Vietnamese American literature, issues of racial discrimination and identity, which prevail in early Japanese and Chinese American literature, are relatively muted; instead, the dominant issues are labor, family fragmentation or alienation, nostalgia, the problem of memory and historical reconstruction, exile, loss, postwar trauma, and so on. Stressing the historical conditions for the emergence of these themes can help readers understand the ways in which Asian American literatures differ from one another thematically and formally.

Intertextual Linkages

Hayslip's books offer potentially rich sources of cross-disciplinary as well as cross-cultural links:

With the work of Trinh T. Minh-ha: Some of Trinh's work has been
    concerned with representations of the Vietnamese in Western discourse, as
    well as with the representation of women within Vietnamese discourse.
    Her film *Surname Viet Given Name Nam* questions both the heroization
    and marginalization of women in Vietnamese history and the mechanism
    of documentary representation that can exploit these women. Her film *A
    Tale of Love*, loosely based on Viet Nam's national poem, *The Tale of Kieu*,
    examines the lives of Vietnamese working-class immigrant women in
    California; it differs radically in formal style from Hayslip's work and may
    make a productive comparison. Instructors can combine Hayslip's books
    with either of Trinh's films, as well as with supplementary material found
    in Trinh's collection of interviews, *Framer Framed*, and her essay on
    the "meaning" of Viet Nam in Western discourse, "All-Owning
    Spectatorship."

With Jade Snow Wong's *Fifth Chinese Daughter*: Wong's autobiography was prized in the 1950s as an early account of Chinese immigrant success. As Elaine Kim has documented, Wong was sponsored by the United States State Department for overseas goodwill tours (60). Comparing Wong's work with Hayslip's can raise questions about the nature of autobiography, especially in the use of political discourse over Americanization, the perceived patriarchal backwardness of Asian cultures, and the role of women in being witnesses for and against these cultures.

With Harriet Jacobs's *Incidents in the Life of a Slave Girl* and with John Neihardt's edition of *Black Elk Speaks*: See the section on critical issues. The three books could be taught together in a course on autobiography, stressing the collaborative aspects of the minority traditions.

With Nguyen Du's *The Tale of Kieu*, for courses interested in the intersection of Asian and Asian American studies: *The Tale of Kieu*, the story of a daughter who must prostitute herself to save her family, is Viet Nam's national poem; it is available in a bilingual edition. Even though it is a nineteenth-century poem, many overseas Vietnamese see it as an apt political and moral allegory for their own postwar situation. It resonates in possibly ironic ways with Hayslip's own story; it is certainly ironic that overseas Vietnamese identify with a prostitute-heroine but cannot forgive one of their own for her allegedly immoral acts. See my "Representing Reconciliation" for an elaboration of the parallels between Hayslip's autobiography and *The Tale of Kieu*.

With Oliver Stone's *Heaven and Earth*: Stone's film is for the most part a faithful adaptation of Hayslip's memoirs, except for the decision to collapse all her lovers into one character. The film decides to follow the chronological style of the second book, resulting in a rather long and overwhelming narrative, but if the instructor cannot teach both books, Stone's film can be used to supplement either chosen text. In addition, using Stone would be a good way to introduce the issue of American perspectives on the Viet Nam War, especially as they center on the roles and identities of the Vietnamese themselves. Stone's *Platoon* would be another supplementary film, this time stressing the American soldier's perspective, racism, solipsism, and all.

With other recent, critically interesting literature and films by Vietnamese Americans: One entertaining and teachable film that contrasts well with Hayslip's and Trinh T. Minh-ha's works is Tiana's *From Hollywood to Hanoi*, which documents the filmmaker-actress's return to Viet Nam. Tiana (her actual name is Du Thi Thanh Nga) surveys the geography, people, and cultures of the northern, central, and southern regions of Viet Nam and includes a discussion of Vietnamese American identity. Her work provides the perspective of a younger generation that is more acculturated to American mores; her film is also more accessible than Trinh's work.

Once upon a Dream, edited by De Tran, Andrew Lam, and Hai Dai Nguyen, is a collection of fiction, poetry, memoirs, artwork, and photographs by Vietnamese Americans. Although the quality of the content varies, a significant amount of the material is teachable (depending on one's interests); from a literary perspective, the poems of Truong Tran, Bao-Long Chu, and Mong Lan are notable, as are the short stories of Andre de Bac Lieu (a pseudonym for Andrew Lam), Nguyen Qui Duc, and Laithanh Ha. Ha's and Lam's short fiction is also available in *The Other Side of Heaven*, edited by Wayne Karlin, Le Minh Khue, and Truong Vu. They are the only Vietnamese Americans writing in English in this valuable collection of fiction, which features many notable Vietnamese and Americans writing about the war. Lam's and Nguyen Qui Duc's short fiction is also available in *Vietnam: A Traveler's Literary Companion*, edited by John Balaban and Nguyen Qui Duc. With the war as a focal point, teachers could also use Nguyen Qui Duc's and Jade Ngoc Quang Huynh's memoirs, although neither is available in paperback and neither received the same critical or popular attention as Hayslip's works. The Asian American Writers' Workshop has published an anthology of new Vietnamese American literature entitled *Watermark* (Tran, Truong, and Khoi). Besides these accessible book-length works, numerous examples of fiction, poetry, and memoirs have been published in a variety of journals and collections, including *Manoa, Pequod, Threepenny Review, North American Review*, ZYZZYVA, *APA Journal, Amerasia Journal, On a Bed of Rice, Massachusetts Review, Harper's* and *Best American Erotica 1995*. It is hoped that they can one day be cataloged or anthologized.

Bibliographic Resources

Vietnam: The Struggle for National Identity, by D. R. SarDesai, is a brief and readable introduction to Vietnamese history, with its emphasis on the French, American, and postwar periods. *Vietnam Documents*, edited by George Katsiaficas, provides some key documents, Vietnamese and American, concerning the war. Additional historical information that is less accessible but very useful is found in Nha-Trang's dissertation on Vietnamese women and gender roles. *The Viet Nam War / The American War*, by Renny Christopher, addresses the literature about the war in English; her comments on other Vietnamese exile literature provide a contrast with Hayslip's work. Qui-Phiet Tran's essay on writings by other Vietnamese American women summarizes other writers' concerns; in addition, Monique Thuy-Dung Truong's insightful essay discusses the limits of collaborative writing for other Vietnamese Americans. Thomas DuBois's summary of the ways in which Southeast Asians have been depicted in academic and popular discourse as "emblematic victims" (4) provides a useful context for understanding how Hayslip's work is often read.

Bibliography

Balaban, John, and Nguyen Qui Duc, eds. *Vietnam: A Traveler's Literary Companion*. San Francisco: Whereabouts, 1996.

Campomanes, Oscar. "Filipinos in the United States and Their Literature of Exile." Lim and Ling 49–78.

Christopher, Renny. *The Viet Nam War / The American War: Images and Representations in Euro-American and Vietnamese Exile Narratives*. Amherst: U of Massachusetts P, 1995.

DeMallie, Raymond J., ed. *The Sixth Grandfather: Black Elk's Teachings Given to John G. Neihardt*. Lincoln: U of Nebraska P, 1984.

Du, Nguyen. *The Tale of Kieu*. Trans. Huynh Sanh Thong. New Haven: Yale UP, 1983.

DuBois, Thomas A. "Constructions Construed: The Representation of Southeast Asian Refugees in Academic, Popular, and Adolescent Discourse." *Amerasia Journal* 19.3 (1993): 1–25.

Hayslip, Le Ly. *Child of War, Woman of Peace*. New York: Doubleday, 1993.

———. *When Heaven and Earth Changed Places*. New York: Doubleday, 1990.

Huynh, Jade Ngoc Quang. *South Wind Changing*. Saint Paul: Graywolf, 1994.

Jacobs, Harriet. *Incidents in the Life of a Slave Girl*. Ed. Jean Fagan Yellin. Cambridge: Harvard UP, 1987.

Karlin, Wayne, Le Minh Khue, and Truong Vu, eds. *The Other Side of Heaven: Post-war Fiction by Vietnamese and American Writers*. Willimantic: Curbstone, 1995.

Katsiaficas, George, ed. *Vietnam Documents: American and Vietnamese Views of the War*. Armonk: Sharpe, 1992.

Kim, Elaine. *Asian American Literature: An Introduction to the Writings and Their Social Context*. Philadelphia: Temple UP, 1982.

Lim, Shirley Geok-lin, and Amy Ling, eds. *Reading the Literatures of Asian America*. Philadelphia: Temple UP, 1992.

Neihardt, John G., ed. *Black Elk Speaks*. Lincoln: U of Nebraska P, 1988.

Nha-Trang Cong-Huyen-Ton-Nu-Thi. "The Traditional Roles of Women as Reflected in Oral and Written Vietnamese Literature." Diss. U of California, Berkeley, 1973.

Nguyen, Viet Thanh. "Representing Reconciliation: Le Ly Hayslip and the Victimized Body." *Positions: East Asia Cultures Critique* 5 (1997): 605–42.

Nguyen Qui Duc. *Where the Ashes Are*. New York: Addison, 1993.

SarDesai, D. R. *Vietnam: The Struggle for National Identity*. Boulder: Westview, 1992.

Shipler, David K. "A Child's Tour of Duty." Rev. of *When Heaven and Earth Changed Places*, by Le Ly Hayslip. *New York Times Book Review* 25 June 1990: 1+.

Stone, Oliver, dir. *Heaven and Earth*. Warner Brothers, 1994.

———, dir. *Platoon*. Hemdale, 1986.

Tiana, dir. *From Hollywood to Hanoi*. Indochina Film Arts Foundation, 1994.

Tran, Barbara, Monique T. Truong, and Luu T. Khoi, eds. *Watermark*. New York: Asian Amer. Writers' Workshop, 1998.

Tran, De, Andrew Lam, and Hai Dai Nguyen, eds. *Once upon a Dream: The Vietnamese American Experience*. Kansas City: Andrews, 1995.

Tran, Qui-Phiet. "From Isolation to Integration: Vietnamese Americans in Tran Dieu Hang's Fiction." Lim and Ling 271–84.

Trinh, T. Minh-ha. "All-Owning Spectatorship." *When the Moon Waxes Red*. New York: Routledge, 1991. 81–105.

———. *Framer Framed*. New York: Routledge, 1992.

———, dir. *Surname Viet Given Name Nam*. Women Make Movies, 1989.

———, dir. *A Tale of Love*. Women Make Movies, 1996.

Truong, Monique Thuy-Dung. "The Emergence of Voices: Vietnamese American Literature 1975–1990." *Amerasia Journal* 19.3 (1993): 27–50.

Wong, Jade Snow. *Fifth Chinese Daughter*. 1950. Seattle: U of Washington P, 1989.

Clay Walls
by Ronyoung Kim

Chung-Hei Yun

Publication Information

First published in 1986 by the Permanent Press, Sag Harbor; softcover published in 1990 by the University of Washington Press.

Overview

Clay Walls is the saga of a Korean American family. It is composed of three parts, each named after a main character: Haesu, an immigrant woman from a *yangban*, or aristocratic, background; Chun, Haesu's husband, who is from a farming family in Korea and becomes a produce merchant in America; and Faye, their American-born daughter. The novel details the first generation's struggles as immigrants and the second generation's coming of age in the 1940s. The first two parts are told from a third-person point of view; the third, from Faye's first-person point of view.

Except for flashbacks from Chun's memories in part 2, the narrative moves in a straightforward manner. Not long after the Japanese annexation of Korea in 1910, Chun, mistaken for a student protester wanted by the police, escapes to America with the help of the missionary for whom he has been working as a houseboy. Haesu, then betrothed to Chun, follows him to Los Angeles. The couple struggles to make a living and raise a family, but differences in class background and temperament between Haesu and Chun, as well as harsh economic realities compounded by racial discrimination, put great strain on the marriage. Haesu finds Chun indifferent or even hostile to her activities, from learning English to being involved in the Korean independence movement; she greatly resents his patriarchal values. Chun finds Haesu snobbish and overbearing, unable to adjust to her diminished circumstances and unsympathetic to his struggles to support the family.

Exhausted, disenchanted, and homesick, Haesu returns to Korea with her children for a visit but finds her homeland shrouded in fear and anxiety under Japanese rule. Haesu and the children return to America only to discover that Chun has been cheated out of the contract he signed for his wholesale produce business. Chun becomes addicted to gambling, leaves his family and his business, and eventually dies alone and homeless in Reno, Nevada. Haesu struggles to bring up the children on her own, working as a seamstress. Eventually, she lets go of a piece of land in Qwaksan (in what is now North Korea), which she bought on her visit to assure herself that her home and heart are still in Korea and onto which she has tenaciously held.

Faye grows up as part of a second generation of American-born Koreans whose only home is America. Her male friends and brothers join the United States military after Pearl Harbor. At the end of the novel, Faye is courted by a Korean young man from Connecticut, a future doctor studying at Yale; a happy future is hinted at.

Reception

Giving a noble and compelling voice to the Korean American experience, Clay Walls appeals to readers in both academe and the popular market and has earned recognition among the canons of ethnic literature as the first Korean American novel. It was translated into Korean in 1989 as Todam (literally, "earthen walls"). Since its first publication in 1986, Clay Walls has continued to be a paradigmatic title in Korean American literature. A common thread in book reviews is the novel's significance as a pioneering work and an authentic record of a vanishing generation of Korean Americans. Until recently, when a number of literary works by Korean American writers were published to critical acclaim (e.g., Chang-rae Lee's Native Speaker; Nora Okja Keller's Comfort Woman), Clay Walls was the only text of its kind.

Critical assessments of Clay Walls are mostly positive. Amy Engeler of the New York Times, who calls it "one of the first [novels] about the plight of Korean Americans," finds it aesthetically somewhat lacking but historically interesting: "[The] political-historical moments are the pearls in the novel, for the writing tends to get flat-footed and overexplanatory, and the tensions not peculiar to Koreans—such as adolescent sexual confusion—are treated routinely. Still, one is grateful for being invited into that closed but lively world."

A number of reviewers familiar with Korea and the Korean American community have been highly enthusiastic. The author Richard E. Kim (The Martyred and Lost Names) writes that the novel "is told with a crisp and confident voice, a lucid and assured style, and with much love for her people who [. . .] gently whisper, 'We are here also, but we have been here all along'" (from the dust jacket of the 1986 hardcover edition). Sam Solberg calls Clay Walls "the first novel in fifty years to examine what it means to be Korean in America, and, to my knowledge, the first to consider what it is to be Korean-American." He adds, "This is a germinal novel that will stand beside the works of John Okada and Louis Chu. [. . .] It is *must* reading for anyone interested in American ethnic history." Michael Robinson writes that "with *Clay Walls*, the experiences, feelings and attitudes of the first Korean-American community [have] found a voice [. . .]. It will stand as required reading for a new generation of Koreans as well as a source for the general readership interested in knowing more about this important and rapidly growing ethnic community" (the quotes from Solberg and from Robinson are also from the dust jacket).

Author's Biographical Background

Ronyoung Kim, also known as Gloria Kim, was born in 1926 in the small original Koreatown of Los Angeles, California.[1] Her parents were among the first few thousand exiled "first-wave" Korean immigrants at the turn of the nineteenth century before and during the oppressive Japanese occupation of Korea. Despite being raised and educated in America, except for a delightful two-year visit with her extended *yangban* family in Sun Chun, North Korea, she retained strong emotional, linguistic, and cultural ties with her Korean peers in America until the age of nineteen. Her marriage to Richard Hahn, a young Korean American medical student, in Chicago in 1945 resulted in an abrupt and prolonged departure from the protective comfort of family and friends in the ethnic enclave. For the rest of her life, following her husband's pioneering career in heart surgery, she resided and raised four children in the white, isolated suburbs of many cities in America.

Although she adapted readily, there is little doubt that she retained strong emotional and intellectual ties with her Korean identity. In midlife, after her three daughters and one son had graduated from college, she began her own serious study of Asian art, Asian art history, and Asian languages. She was an original docent of the former Avery Brundage Asian Art Museum and subsequently returned to college to earn a baccalaureate degree in Far Eastern art and culture from San Francisco State University. She studied Chinese calligraphy under the tutelage of a master in the San Francisco Bay Area. In 1976, a diagnosis of breast cancer radically altered the course of her activities for the next ten years. She immediately began to study the craft of writing by attending classes and workshops and reading volumes of literature while simultaneously writing *Clay Walls*. She had a more urgent task than that of simply writing an autobiographical novel, and time was running out:

> While America sings with voices from many lands, her literature speaks in monotones, with a sound that springs from an established tradition of Western literature. From this polyglot nation, I wanted to bring the voice of an American born of two cultures, East and West, in order to take the reader into the world of people living in the United States who have been rarely portrayed: people who have been characterized superficially and, oftentimes, erroneously. A whole generation of Korean immigrants and their American born children

could have lived and died in the United States without anyone knowing they had been here. I could not let that happen.

(*Clay Walls*, dust jacket)

Kim was at work on her second novel when the cancer returned in 1986. She lived eight painful months, long enough to see the first hardback edition of *Clay Walls* but too debilitated even for book signing. She was nominated, however, for the Pulitzer and learned of this honor before she died on 3 February 1987.

Clay Walls has accomplished Ronyoung Kim's purpose. It is estimated that more than one million Koreans now reside in the United States. Kim would not have been surprised to learn that very few of the post-1965 arrivals knew that any Koreans had been in America as early as the turn of the century. Few knew that the exiles had organized political parties; smuggled food, clothing, and money to their suffering relatives through China and Manchuria; and trained a fledgling Korean Independence Air Force and guerrilla militias in anticipation of their long hoped for freedom and repatriation. Very few knew the history of the Korean independence movement in America, which had been the lifeblood of Kim's parents' generation for more than thirty-five years. Kim was correct in assuming that without her book few would know that Koreans had lived and died in America. She did not fail in her promise.

Historical Context for the Narratives in *Clay Walls*

The time period covered in *Clay Walls*, roughly between 1920 and 1945, begins with the aftermath of the Japanese annexation of Korea and ends with World War II. The first wave of significant Korean immigrants consisted of laborers who went to work on Hawai'i's sugar plantations (1903–05). They were followed by political refugees (including students), many of whom had to escape from Korea after the March First Movement of 1919 in which the Korean Declaration of Independence was made. In the novel, although Chun is not a participant in the anti-Japanese movement, his immigration to the United States is an effect of Japanese police surveillance and persecution of dissidents. The patriots' zeal continued in the United States, and many Korean immigrants supported them either by joining their organizations or by donating money to the cause. In the novel, Haesu attends meetings of pro-independence organizations and gets into a conflict with Chun over pledges. Japanese colonization is also reflected in the intrigue and espionage on the ship *Taiyo Maru* and in the episode about Haesu's uncle being a political fugitive in Korea.

Asian immigration in general was banned in 1924. Haesu's children represent the American-born generation that grew up increasingly distanced from their parents' immigrant culture and interacting more with other American-born Asians (including Chinese and Japanese) and with young people of other ethnicities, such as African Americans. The novel reflects this distancing in the accounts of Faye's social life in Los Angeles.

After Pearl Harbor, Koreans in America, "Orientals" sharing the Japanese skin color, were often mistaken for Japanese; even the United States government, which considered Koreans officially Japanese, almost sent them to the internment camps until a community member went to Washington to explain Korea's colonial status. First-generation immigrants strongly supported the United States war effort against Japan, Korea's colonizer, in spite of continued racism against Asians—as seen in the episode in *Clay Walls* where Harold, Haesu's elder son, tries to join the Air Force but is told by the recruiting officer that "Orientals are not allowed in officers' training" (270).

Major Themes

personal, social, and cultural liminality

immigrants' dreams: realized, deferred, ruptured, revisioned

nostalgia, homesickness, ambivalent desire

the psychology and struggles of the displaced

gender relations in immigrant families: changes in gender roles, intensification of gender conflict due to uprooting, resettlement

the meaning of *home*: Where is home? How does one make a home? When does the "alien land" become home?

patriotism and loyalty: To which land does one owe allegiance?

cultural conflict: philosophical and generational differences

the making of a multicultural community, Asian American panethnicity

Critical Issues

Clay Walls, with its linear narrative structure, easy diction and sentence flow, and relatively simple character as well as plot development, is not the kind of novel that leaves room for ambiguity or invites close readings. The closest one comes to a controlling metaphor in the novel is the image of clay walls, which evokes a particular kind of wall that surrounds Korean village houses. Both Haesu and Chun haul invisible "clay walls" with them when they emigrate from Korea, but each views the walls in different ways. For Chun, the clay walls stand for the familiar, the known, the shield that protects him from the alien and hostile world. For Haesu, however, they represent the oppressive forces emanating from her culture, especially toward Korean women. Chun wants to build walls around the house they bought; Haesu wants to annihilate walls altogether.

Although *Clay Walls* is the title of the novel, Kim does not elaborate on the trope of clay walls or carry it through sufficiently to admit multilayered readings. But it does compel readers to contemplate the other "clay walls" that the second generation could be facing. In some ways, the contours of *Clay Walls* conform to a kind of American master narrative, the immigrant family saga of struggles in a new land and eventual triumph. Yet the novel also shows many realistic details that would cast doubt on the immigrant success story. It would be useful to analyze the novel in this light.

Another issue to consider is that, although Chun is the focus of one of the three sections, the novel is essentially Haesu's story—a woman's story. Thus we find in *Clay Walls* portrayals of daily domestic interactions, male authority over the household, female friendships, and so on from the point of view of a spirited, decidedly unsubmissive woman. Whether *Clay Walls* is a feminist, or at least protofeminist, work would be an interesting question to explore.

Pedagogical Issues and Suggestions

The strength of *Clay Walls* lies in its accessibility (even junior high school students can enjoy it), its easy-to-identify-with characters, and its vividly rendered scenes, not in formal complexities that call for inventive interpretations. Besides providing background information on Korean Americans, teachers would do well to focus on selected encounters described in the novel and conduct discussions on their significance. One such example is the opening scene, in which Haesu is bent over, cleaning a toilet for the wealthy Mrs. Randolph, who watches for missed spots like a hawk, leading Haesu to quit her job in outrage. Haesu's rebellion constitutes her initiation rite into her new land, but she phrases this in terms not of awareness of social inequality but of personal honor as a *yangban*. (The worst term of insult she hurls at Mrs. Randolph is *sangnyun*, "low woman," a class-based term.) This brief scene, barely two pages long, brings out a wealth of issues—differing cultural or even religious attitudes toward work and manual labor in particular, hierarchical social and economic organization, the interaction between class and race, the gendered nature of different types of work— that can be fruitfully discussed in the classroom.

Other situations that would be interesting for class discussion include Chun's "marital rape" of Haesu in the wake of an argument over donations to the Korean independence movement, Clara's botched cosmetic surgery, Haesu's unsuccessful campaign to get her American-born sons into Edwards Military Academy, Haesu's pressure on Chun to buy a piano so that the children could acquire some "culture," Chun's relations with the Reverend McNeil and the latter's role in Chun's marriage and emigration, Faye's fight with Haesu over a pair of three-inch heels, and the ending scene where Faye is about to open a special-delivery letter from Daniel.

Intertextual Linkages

With Younghill Kang's *The Grass Roof* and *East Goes West*: life before and
    after immigration to the United States; the differences between the
    American experiences of men and women, intellectuals and the less-
    educated immigrants.

With Chang-rae Lee's *Native Speaker*: the figure of the Korean greengrocer from different historical periods, father-son and mother-daughter relationships in the immigrant family, American-born children's inability to understand parents, assimilation rewards and costs.

With Theresa Hak Kyung Cha's *Dictee*: the role of memory and language in recovering the past; Japanese colonialism and its effects on the Korean diaspora; maternal legacies; personal, communal, and national identity and history.

With Maxine Hong Kingston's *The Woman Warrior*: matrilineal tradition, the meaning of *home*, first-generation women as "warrior" role models who exorcise the "ghosts" and remake, or forge new, identities.

Note

1. Since published accounts of Ronyoung Kim's life are sketchy and few, Kim's husband, Richard S. Hahn, and Melanie Miran Hahn helped prepare the biographical section. Their assistance is gratefully acknowledged. See also Elaine Kim's essay in *The Oxford Companion to Women's Writing in the United States* for biographical information.

Bibliography

Ashley, Beth. "A Novel Approach to the Korean Experience." *Marin Independent Journal* 2 Dec. 1986: D1+.

Cha, Theresa Hak Kyung. *Dictee*. New York: Tanam, 1982.

Choy, Bong-Youn. *Koreans in America*. Chicago: Nelson, 1979.

Engeler, Amy. Rev. of *Clay Walls*, by Ronyoung Kim. *New York Times* 11 Jan. 1987, sec. 7: 18.

Fenkl, Heinz Insu. *Memories of My Ghost Brother*. New York: Dutton, 1996.

Kang, Younghill. *East Goes West*. New York: Scribner's, 1937.

———. *The Grass Roof*. New York: Scribner's, 1931.

Keller, Nora Okja. *Comfort Woman*. New York: Viking, 1997.

Kim, Elaine H. *Asian American Literature: An Introduction to the Writings and Their Social Context*. Philadelphia: Temple UP, 1982.

———. "Kim, Ronyoung." *The Oxford Companion to Women's Writing in the United States*. Ed. Cathy N. Davidson and Linda Wagner-Martin. New York: Oxford UP, 1995. 457.

Kim, Elaine H., and Eui-Young Yu, eds. *East to America: Korean American Life Stories*. New York: New, 1996.

Kim, Elaine H., et al., eds. *Making More Waves: New Writing by Asian American Women*. Boston: Beacon, 1997.

Kim, Ronyoung. *Clay Walls*. Sag Harbor: Permanent, 1986.

Kingston, Maxine Hong. *The Woman Warrior: Memoirs of a Girlhood among Ghosts*. New York: Knopf, 1976.

Lee, Chang-rae. *A Gesture Life*. New York: Riverhead, 1999.

———. *Native Speaker*. New York: Riverhead, 1995.

Lee, Kyung-won. "Whispers from *Clay Walls* Heard around the World." *Newsreview* 10 Sept. 1988: 30–31. [From an oral history series, Ethnic Concerns Committee of the Sierra Mission Area, Presbyterian Church USA.]

Oh, Seiwoong. "Cross-Cultural Reading versus Textual Accessibility in Multicultural Literature." *MELUS* 18.2 (1993): 3–16.

Okada, John. *No-No Boy*. Seattle: U of Washington P, 1976.

Solberg, S. E. "*Clay Walls*: Korean-American Pioneers." *Korean Culture* Dec. 1986: 30–35.

Takaki, Ronald. "Struggling against Colonialism." *Strangers from a Different Shore: A History of Asian Americans*. New York: Penguin, 1989. 270–93.

Yun, Chung-Hei. "Beyond *Clay Walls*." *Reading the Literatures of Asian America*. Ed. Shirley Geok-lin Lim and Amy Ling. Philadelphia: Temple UP, 1992. 79–95.

The Woman Warrior: Memoirs of a Girlhood among Ghosts
by Maxine Hong Kingston

Patricia P. Chu

Publication Information

First published in the United States by Alfred A. Knopf in 1976; softcover editions published in 1977 and 1989. British editions include those by Allen Lane in 1976, Penguin in 1976, and Pan in 1977. Translations include those published by Crown, Taipei, in 1977; Gallimard, Paris, in 1979; Elsevier Manteau, Amsterdam, in 1980; Norstedt and Soners, Stockholm, in 1978; and Bompiani, Milan, in 1982. A recorded version and a large print edition are available in the United States.

Overview

The Woman Warrior: Memoirs of a Girlhood among Ghosts is a sustained autobiographical essay in which the author imaginatively transforms stories from her personal and family history, Chinese folklore, and Chinese history. Kingston initially conceived the book as fiction but allowed it to be published as a memoir, thereby provoking controversy about its "authenticity" as an ethnic text. Kingston and numerous critics, however, have emphasized the distance between her real self and the book's first-person narrator. Moreover, the book thematically underscores the difficulty of understanding one's cultural heritage, which is presented as the product of numerous verbal constructs (stories, songs, and sayings) throughout the book. The complexity of this process of construction is accentuated by the narrator's double perspective: she "speaks" as an adult recalling, and to some extent reliving, her experiences and perspectives as a girl growing up in Stockton, California, in the 1940s and 1950s.

Each of the book's five chapters illustrates an aspect of the narrator's girlhood search for a viable identity as a working-class Chinese American girl confronting sexism within her immigrant community, and sexism and racism in the mainstream community. In the first chapters, "No Name Woman" and "White Tigers," the narrator retells two of her mother's stories about Chinese women. In the first, an unnamed aunt of the narrator is hazed by her fellow villagers in China for conceiving an illegitimate child; she responds to this disgrace by committing infanticide and suicide after giving birth. Posthumously punished by official erasure from the family memory, this "no name woman" is the first of the titular ghosts haunting the narrator's childhood, ghosts representing all that is repressed but deeply felt in her communications with her mother, family, and community.

The second chapter introduces the woman warrior, a legendary Chinese heroine who proved her worth as a daughter by taking her father's place in war. The narrator's embellishments on the traditional story convey her wish to overcome her community's devaluation of her gender: she envisions herself, as the warrior, receiving martial arts training and then combining martial success with marriage, childbirth, and the punishment of a family oppressor who is also a male chauvinist. As a champion of both her family and her gender, the woman warrior bears her family's grievances literally, through the ritual of having them carved on her back. These "words at her back," an embellishment of Kingston's, then become the metaphor that links the narrator to the legendary warrior: language will be the medium for the narrator's empowerment.

Chapter 3 depicts two faces of the narrator's mother, Brave Orchid, already established as a powerful storyteller, the source of the previous two stories. Her former high status as a doctor-midwife in China contrasts with her low status as laundry worker, wife, and mother in the United States. A scene in which the adult narrator visits her mother in old age introduces the vulnerability underlying Brave Orchid's strength. In chapter 4, Brave Orchid brings her sister Moon Orchid, a sheltered elderly woman, to the United States and forces her to confront her husband, a younger, tougher immigrant who has remarried and achieved professional success in the United States. At first, the chapter seems to caricature both sisters, but when Moon Orchid is rejected by her husband and subsequently loses her sanity, Brave Orchid's grief and powerlessness lend further complexity to the narrator's understanding of her.

In the final chapter, the narrator focuses on her own girlhood struggle to confront the fears and parental expectations that her parents refused to discuss directly with her. Through an incident where the narrator bullies a younger, similar Chinese American girl, a scene where she angrily confronts her mother, and a final story that represents reconciliation between an exiled Chinese poet and her "barbarian" children, the narrator develops the theme of gaining autonomy by creating an art based on the foundation of her mother's stories.

Reception

The Woman Warrior and its companion volume, *China Men*, were both critically acclaimed best-sellers when first published. *The Woman Warrior* received the National Book Critics Circle Award for the best nonfiction in 1976 and was rated one of the decade's top ten nonfiction books by *Time* magazine. *China Men* won the American Book Award and the National Book Award for nonfiction and was nominated for the National Book Critics Circle Award and the Pulitzer Prize. For many years, *The Woman Warrior* was by far the single best-known Asian American text. It is the subject of a volume in the MLA's Approaches to Teaching World Literature series; excerpts have been widely anthologized; and it is said to be the most widely taught book by a living author on American college campuses. The author's numerous honors include honorary doctorates from four American universities and the rare title of Living Treasure of Hawai'i, conferred by a Buddhist group in 1980.

Because of its complexity and early prominence, *The Woman Warrior* aroused immediate controversy. Kingston herself criticized many mainstream reviewers for characterizing the book in terms of stereotypes about oriental exoticness or inscrutability, failing to recognize it as American, or supposing the book pretended to speak for all Chinese Americans. Some early Chinese readers were jarred by the book's adaptations of traditional Chinese stories, her disclosure of family secrets, her criticism of her mother, and the narrator's provocative, often naive generalizations about Chinese. The book's defenders reply to these concerns by stressing Kingston's artistic intentions in reinventing Chinese stories for an American context, the conciliatory resolution of her book, and the author's use of an oft-naive narrative persona to dramatize the process of evaluating seemingly anti-Chinese perceptions. More recently, mainland Chinese writers who feel cut off from their own cultural heritage have hailed Kingston's work as part of the new Chinese "roots literature" in which contemporary writers seek to return to their cultural roots.

Kingston's most hostile critics have been Asian American writers offended by Kingston's feminist alterations to traditional stories; her early emphasis on the patriarchal and misogynist aspects of Chinese American culture; her perceived portrayal of Chinese Americans as alien, difficult to understand, and in some cases unmanly; and the fact that she published *The Woman Warrior* and *China Men* as nonfiction. In particular, Frank Chin has attacked the entire genre of autobiography as based on a Christian tradition of confession, which to him implies conversion, self-exposure, and self-abasement inappropriate for Asian Americans addressing mainstream readers. These criticisms have been seriously considered and ultimately rejected by a host of scholars, as well as by Kingston, in one of the most heated debates in Asian American cultural studies. Meanwhile, over eighty articles, book chapters, and dissertation chapters attest to the interest the book has generated since its publication.

Author's Biographical Background

Maxine Hong Kingston was born on 27 October 1940 in Stockton, California, the daughter of Cantonese immigrants. Her father, Tom Hong, was a teacher and scholar in China but worked as a laundryman and gambling house manager in the United States, after arriving in New York sometime around 1923. Kingston's mother, Ying Lan Chew, was a successful doctor-midwife in China but became a laundry worker and field hand in the United States. According to Kingston, her mother ran a hospital in a cave during the Japanese invasion of China, fled Canton just as the Japanese were about to take the harbor, and joined her father in New York in 1939. The couple then moved to Stockton, California, where Maxine and her five younger siblings were born and raised. After growing up in Stockton's Chinatown, Maxine earned a BA in English literature from the University of California, Berkeley (1962), married the actor Earll Kingston, earned a teaching certificate, and taught English and mathematics in Hayward, California (1965–67). In 1967 the Kingstons moved with their son, Joseph, to Honolulu, where she held various high school and college teaching positions. The couple now live in Oakland, California, and Kingston teaches creative writing at the University of California, Berkeley.

In addition to *The Woman Warrior*, Kingston has published the companion volume *China Men*, which depicts, in mythical and anecdotal form, the history of Chinese men in the United States, using the men of her own family as examples. Kingston's 1989 novel *Tripmaster Monkey*, set in the San Francisco Bay Area in the 1960s, draws on her interest in redefining Asian American culture in the United States and her deep antipathy to the Vietnam War and to war in general. She has also published *Hawai'i One Summer* (1987), a collection of prose sketches; she lost one manuscript in a fire in 1991.

Historical Context for the Narratives in *The Woman Warrior*

The book's critique of the immigrant community's sexism may first be placed in the context of Chinese neo-Confucian ideology, which designated sons as the heirs and future supporters of their parents but daughters' bodies and labor as the property of their future husbands and in-laws. This ideology, combined with severe material hardship, encouraged traditional Chinese to value sons more than daughters, and also to place severe restrictions on women's liberty and education, restrictions often rationalized as protective of their chastity. Though traditional attitudes and gender hierarchies surely persist in modern China, various groups have worked to improve women's lot in China from the nineteenth century onward. Indeed, the protofeminism of the traditional woman warrior story as well as elements of Brave Orchid's medical career point not only to Western influences but also to feminist elements indigenous to Chinese culture and society.

The immigrant villagers' sexism, their secretiveness, and their mistrust of whites must also be understood in the context of anti-Chinese and anti-Asian United States government policies. Although Chinese men were initially welcomed to the United States in the nineteenth century, anti-Chinese feeling developed rapidly, resulting in a series of laws severely restricting Chinese immigration from 1882 until 1943. During this period, Chinese who had lived in the United States, and their children, could enter more easily than other Chinese laborers. Therefore, many Chinese came in with false names and papers, posing as previous immigrants or their offspring. To weed out these "paper sons," American immigration authorities initiated special detention centers where Chinese entrants were subject to minute interrogations designed to gauge the authenticity of their identities, sometimes over a period of many months, before being permitted to set foot on American soil. This history explains why some immigrants in Kingston's stories are reluctant to reveal personal information, especially their real names, to whites. Though the era of Chinese exclusion officially ended in 1943, the threats of deportation and government harassment remained serious in the 1940s and 1950s, as proved both by the example of the Japanese Americans (who were arbitrarily interned and in some cases deported or repatriated during World War II) and by the anticommunist witch hunts of the cold war era.

In discussing the sexism of Kingston's community, one must recall that United States immigration policy was initially designed to admit Chinese males as laborers but to discourage them from settling in the United States or starting families here. Hence, immigrant Chinese were declared "aliens ineligible for citizenship" from 1878 to 1943; the entry of Chinese women was even more restricted than that of men; antimiscegenation laws prevented Chinese from marrying non–Asian Americans in many states; and, from 1922 to 1936, female United States citizens who married aliens ineligible for citizenship lost their own citizenship. So strictly were Chinese women barred from entering that in 1890 the community's male-to-female ratio was 27 to 1. As a result, generations of Chinese laborers lived in "bachelor communities," either unable to marry or indefinitely separated from wives and children left behind in China. As a child born in 1940 into what had historically been a bachelor community, Kingston would have confronted attitudes toward women developed over six decades of enforced sexual segregation.

Historical Context for the Writing of *The Woman Warrior*

The American women's movement of the 1960s and 1970s enabled Kingston to clarify, and to gain an attentive audience for, her critique of patriarchal thinking as well as her examination of female subjectivity. The book was also written near the beginning of a wave of interest in, and institutional support for, Asian American cultural studies on the West Coast. (*The Woman Warrior* bears few direct signs of this ethnic studies movement, but *China Men* clearly draws upon and adds to the cultural and historical research of its time.) Finally, the book is indirectly influenced by the cold war environment of the 1950s and 1960s, which only thawed with Nixon's visit to the People's Republic of China in 1972. The narrator's baffled, almost comically garbled descriptions of Communist Chinese conduct partly reflect the real traumas Chinese suffered in those decades, but they should also be read in the light of cold war restrictions on travel and information between the United States and the People's Republic of China, which made it hard even for sinologists to get a clear picture of Chinese life. By presenting her Chinese American narrator both as a cultural insider and as another American seeking information about Chinese culture, Kingston drew upon, and no doubt contributed to, American readers' interest in and curiosity about the country in the post-Vietnam era.

Major Themes

women as literal and literary warriors
the construction of Chinese American culture and ethnicity, "talking story"
speech, silence, power, madness; voice, authorship, authority
ghosts, memory, history, identity
sexuality, marriage plots, resistance to marriage, gender construction
immigration, assimilation, racism, ethnicity and race
filial duty, mother-daughter ties, coming of age

Critical Issues

The book's distinctive narrative structure, voice, and method of narration are addressed in the overview, above, and in numerous articles. As discussed earlier, the book's use of Chinese sources and the appropriateness of its representations of Chinese and Chinese American culture have formed a second focus of critical attention. Notwithstanding the allusions discussed above, the critical consensus is that the book is about forging an identity as an American woman and that the book's ethnic allusions are clearly mediated through an American perspective. A third set of critical issues pertains to the text's construction of a literary voice that is marked by the author's female, Chinese American subjectivity. In addition to countering discourses that silence and devalue women, the narrator must overcome the silencing and devaluation of her racial and ethnic communities by mainstream society. These issues may be addressed on a material level (by addressing the social history) or on a cultural and linguistic level (by extending feminist theories about the linguistic construction and gendering of the subject to address race and ethnicity).

Pedagogical Issues and Suggestions

Pedagogically this text poses challenges on three levels: formal, informational, and ideological. The text is formally challenging because it eschews a conventional narrative structure in favor of a series of meditative essays, linking multiple stories with meditations about the difficulty of interpreting stories and other texts. The five-chapter schema outlined in the overview above may provide a helpful framework for initial readings. The text also merges "factual" information with stories that are "just stories," thereby challenging readers to replicate the interpretive skills developed by the narrator to understand her mother's stories. Pushed harder, the text asks readers to question the very validity of the distinction between "facts" and "just stories."

The instructor can address this issue by alerting students to the book's internal cues for distinguishing facts from received or self-invented stories. For instance, the "No Name Woman" story is told several times: first ostensibly in Brave Orchid's voice and then in shorter versions as the narrator seeks an interpretation that will be both plausible and personally empowering. Looking closely, we can see that even the mother's version is actually far more literary and artfully crafted in English than the original Chinese "talk-story" probably was. Similar cues are offered within Kingston's feminist revision of the famous woman warrior story, retold in the first person to emphasize its wish-fulfilling function; by the story of Brave Orchid's exorcism of her medical school's ghost, depicted as "true"; and by Kingston's account of the Moon Orchid adventure, which is immediately contrasted with her brother's brief, bare version. In addition, the narrator is unreliable in the sense that she merges two levels of awareness: that of the adolescent girl protagonist and that of the articulate, wise adult looking backward. Students may need to be introduced to the ironic distance between these two levels of awareness, as in the statement, "Brave Orchid's daughters decided fiercely that they would never let men be unfaithful to them. All her children made up their minds to major in science or mathematics" (160).

These interpretive challenges are sharpened by an informational challenge: most students are unfamiliar with Chinese and Chinese American culture and history. In addition to consulting the sources listed below, one may wish to discuss the degree to which the narrator's vision seems deeply subjective, specific to her family, or transformed by her or her mother's imagination. She herself raises this question:

> Chinese Americans, when you try to understand what things in you are Chinese, how do you separate what is peculiar to childhood, to poverty, insanities, one family, your mother who marked your growing with stories, from what is Chinese? What is Chinese tradition and what is the movies? (5)

The ideological challenge is to deal fairly and fully with the narrator's anger at her community's misogyny and her mother's perceived complicity in a cultural and social system that discriminates so pervasively against girls. The danger is that the text may simply confirm Western stereotypes of Chinese culture's backwardness and sexism. One good response is to emphasize the elements of female empowerment and validation to be found in the text, particularly those associated with Brave Orchid, who is caught in a position of negotiating with Chinese and American sexism and who seeks to teach her daughter her survival strategies. It also helps to situate the text historically; to point out parallels between the narrator's grievances and feminist critiques of Euro-

American culture, in which the book is rooted; and to point out how Euro-American sexism also affects the narrator, for instance in expectations of such "American feminine" behavior as speaking softly and desiring dates or in limiting her career aspirations to being a clerk-typist.

Intertextual Linkages

With Fae Myenne Ng's *Bone* and Amy Tan's *The Joy Luck Club*: mother-daughter bonds, Chinese and Chinese American ethnicity and gender, differences in narrative technique and what they imply about "knowing" Chinese culture, healing and reconciliation through acts of memory or narration.

With Toni Morrison's *Beloved* and James Baldwin's *Go Tell It on the Mountain*: generational conflict; sexual disgrace, illegitimacy, infanticide; legacies of oppression; guilt, ghosts, and the recovery of repressed family traumas; oral traditions and literary authorship.

With Marilynne Robinson's *Housekeeping*: coming of age; female marginalization within patriarchy; female play, flight, imagination, and rebellion; longing for the absent mother.

With the titles mentioned in King-kok Cheung, "Don't Tell"; Reed Dasenbrock; Donald Goellnicht; and Shirley Geok-lin Lim, "Tradition."

Bibliographic Resources

Kingston's own *China Men*, focusing on the men in her family and community, is an essential text completing the Hong family portrait. Three excellent texts for instructors at all levels are Lim's *Approaches to Teaching Kingston's* The Woman Warrior, which features an extensive collection of essays and a broad bibliography; Cheung's *Articulate Silences*, which addresses feminist theories pertaining to speech and silence and also provides needed background information; and Sau-ling Cynthia Wong's *Reading Asian American Literature*, which interprets the text in relation to Asian American literature as a whole. An early presentation of ideas used in Wong's book is her "Necessity and Extravagance." Wong's casebook on *The Woman Warrior*, part of the Casebooks in Contemporary Fiction series edited by William L. Andrews for Oxford University Press, presents a variety of critical essays and provides an annotated bibliography.

Kingston comments directly on the critical reception of her early texts in "Cultural Mis-readings" and in a lively recent interview with Marilyn Chin. Among the numerous articles on the "authenticity debate," Frank Chin's "Come All Ye Asian American Writers" voices the key complaints of Kingston's main attacker. Other treatments include those by Cheung ("Chinese-American Critic"), Wong ("Autobiography"), and Deborah Woo. Additional interviews are offered by Paul Skenazy and Tera Martin (Kingston, *Conversations*).

Elisabeth Croll's and Kazuko Ono's works give excellent introductions to women's roles in traditional Chinese society, as well as to feminist movements in modern China. Ono begins her book with a chapter on women warriors. Further perspectives on Chinese women are offered by Margery Wolf's analysis of female suicides in China and Weili Ye's discussion of the careers of the first American-trained women doctors in China. Robert Lee situates *The Woman Warrior* within Chinese American historiography; Sucheng Chan provides a thorough introduction to Asian American history; and Judy Yung gives a detailed social history of Chinese women in San Francisco.

In terms of literary history, Elaine Kim places Kingston within Asian American literary history, while Amy Ling situates her among other women writers of Chinese descent. King-kok Cheung (*Articulate Silences*), Sau-ling Cynthia Wong ("Handling"), and David Lei-wei Li provide useful background on Chinese sources for the book; Patricia P. Chu discusses Kingston's imaginative revisions of marriage plots common to Chinese and Anglo-American narratives; and Gayle Fujita Sato and Reed Way Dasenbrock offer fine readings of the controversial "ghost" motif.

Excellent readings applying feminist theories of language and subjectivity are offered by Donald Goellnicht; Shirley Geok-lin Lim ("Tradition"); Suzanne Juhasz; and Leslie Rabine. In addition, Malini Schueller offers a Bakhtinian reading that emphasizes the tensions between gender and race within the narrator's subjectivity.

Other Resources

Bill Moyers's interview with Maxine Hong Kingston provides a stimulating portrait of the author, who doesn't miss a beat even when Moyers introduces her work as "exotic." Wayne Wang's smart, subtle film *Dim Sum*, about a Cantonese mother and her American daughter, addresses many of the same emotional dynamics as Kingston's book does. Wang's relatively lighthearted film *Eat a Bowl of Tea*, adapted from Louis Chu's novel (see the essay on Chu in this volume), provides an alternative vision of sexual pressures within a Chinatown bachelor community.

Bibliography

Baldwin, James. *Go Tell It on the Mountain*. New York: Random, 1995.

Chan, Sucheng. *Asian Americans: An Interpretive History*. Boston: Twayne, 1991.

Cheung, King-kok. *Articulate Silences: Narrative Strategies in Hisaye Yamamoto, Maxine Hong Kingston, and Joy Kogawa*. Ithaca: Cornell UP, 1993.

———. "'Don't Tell': Imposed Silences in *The Color Purple* and *The Woman Warrior*." *PMLA* 103 (1988): 162–74.

———. "*The Woman Warrior* versus the *Chinaman Pacific*: Must a Chinese-American Critic Choose between Feminism and Heroism?" *Conflicts in Feminism*. Ed. Marianne Hirsch and Evelyn Fox Keller. New York: Routledge, 1990. 234–51.

Chin, Frank. "Come All Ye Asian American Writers of the Real and the Fake." *The Big Aiiieeeee! An Anthology of Chinese American and Japanese American Literature*. Ed. Jeffery Paul Chan et al. New York: Meridian, 1991. 1–92.

Chu, Louis. *Eat a Bowl of Tea*. 1961. Secaucus: Stuart, 1979.

Chu, Patricia. "'The Invisible World the Immigrants Built': Cultural Self-Inscription and the Antiromantic Plots of *The Woman Warrior*." *Diaspora: A Journal of Transnational Studies* 2.1 (1992): 95–115.

Croll, Elisabeth. *Feminism and Socialism in China*. London: Routledge, 1978.

Dasenbrock, Reed Way. "Intelligibility and Meaningfulness in Multicultural Literature in English." *PMLA* 102 (1987): 10–19.

Goellnicht, Donald C. "Father Land and/or Mother Tongue: The Divided Female Subject in Kogawa's *Obasan* and Hong Kingston's *The Woman Warrior*." *Redefining Autobiography in Twentieth-Century Women's Fiction*. Ed. Janice Morgan and Colette T. Hall. New York: Garland, 1991. 119–34.

Juhasz, Suzanne. "Maxine Hong Kingston: Narrative Technique and Female Identity." *Contemporary American Women Writers*. Ed. Catherine Rainwater and William J. Scheick. Lexington: UP of Kentucky, 1985. 173–90.

Kim, Elaine H. *Asian American Literature: An Introduction to the Writings and Their Social Context*. Philadelphia: Temple UP, 1982.

Kingston, Maxine Hong. *China Men*. New York: Knopf, 1980.

———. *Conversations with Maxine Hong Kingston*. Ed. Paul Skenazy and Tera Martin. Jackson: UP of Mississippi, 1998.

———. "Cultural Mis-readings by American Reviewers." *Asian and Western Writers in Dialogue*. Ed. Guy Amirthanayagam. London: Macmillan, 1982. 55–65.

———. *Hawai'i One Summer*. Illus. Deng Ming-Dao. San Francisco: Meadow, 1987.

———. "A MELUS Interview: Maxine Hong Kingston." Interview with Marilyn Chin. *MELUS* 16.4 (1989–90): 57–74.

———. "The Stories of Maxine Hong Kingston." Interview with Bill Moyers. *World of Ideas*. Videocassette. Films for the Humanities, 1994.

———. *Tripmaster Monkey: His Fake Book*. New York: Knopf, 1989.

———. *The Woman Warrior: Memoirs of a Girlhood among Ghosts*. New York: Knopf, 1976.

Lee, Robert G. "*The Woman Warrior* as an Intervention in Asian American Historiography." Lim, *Approaches* 52–63.

Li, David Lei-wei. "The Naming of a Chinese-American 'I': Cross-Cultural Sign/ifications in *The Woman Warrior*." *Criticism* 30 (1988): 497–515.

Lim, Shirley Geok-lin. *Approaches to Teaching Kingston's* The Woman Warrior. New York: MLA, 1991.

———. "The Tradition of Chinese American Women's Life Stories: Thematics of Race and Gender in Jade Snow Wong's *Fifth Chinese Daughter* and Maxine Hong Kingston's *The Woman Warrior*." *American Women's Autobiography: Fea(s)ts of Memory*. Ed. Margo Culley. Madison: U of Wisconsin P, 1992. 252–67.

Ling, Amy. *Between Worlds: Women Writers of Chinese Ancestry*. New York: Pergamon, 1990.

Morrison, Toni. *Beloved*. New York: Knopf, 1987.

Ng, Fae Myenne. *Bone*. New York: Hyperion, 1993.

Ono, Kazuko. *Chinese Women in a Century of Revolution, 1850–1950*. Ed. Joshua A. Fogel. Stanford: Stanford UP, 1989.

Rabine, Leslie W. "No Lost Paradise: Social Gender and Symbolic Gender in the Writings of Maxine Hong Kingston." *Signs* 12 (1987): 471–92.

Robinson, Marilynne. *Housekeeping*. New York: Farrar, 1997.

Sato, Gayle K. Fujita. "Ghosts as Chinese-American Constructs in Maxine Hong Kingston's *The Woman Warrior*." *Haunting the House of Fiction: Feminist Perspectives on Ghost Stories by American Women*. Ed. Lynette Carpenter and Wendy K. Kolmar. Knoxville: U of Tennessee P, 1991. 193–214.

Schueller, Malini. "Questioning Race and Gender Definitions: Dialogic Subversions in *The Woman Warrior*." *Criticism* 31.4 (1989): 421–37.

Tan, Amy. *The Joy Luck Club*. New York: Putnam, 1989.

Wang, Wayne, dir. *Dim Sum: A Little Bit of Heart*. Videocassette. Pacific Arts, 1987.

———, dir. *Eat a Bowl of Tea*. Videocassette. RCA-Columbia, 1989.

Wolf, Margery. "Women and Suicide in China." *Women in Chinese Society*. Ed. Wolf and Roxanne Witke. Stanford: Stanford UP, 1975. 111–41.

Wong, Sau-ling Cynthia. "Kingston's Handling of Traditional Chinese Sources." Lim, *Approaches* 26–36.

———. *Maxine Hong Kingston's* The Woman Warrior: *A Casebook*. Casebooks in Contemporary Fiction. New York: Oxford UP, 1998.

———. "Multicultural Autobiography: American Lives." *American Lives: Essays in Multicultural American Autobiography*. Ed. James Robert Payne. Knoxville: U of Tennessee P, 1992. 248–75.

———. "Necessity and Extravagance in Maxine Hong Kingston's *The Woman Warrior*: Art and the Ethnic Experience." *MELUS* 15 (1988): 3–26.

———. *Reading Asian American Literature: From Necessity to Extravagance*. Princeton: Princeton UP, 1993.

Woo, Deborah. "Maxine Hong Kingston: The Ethnic Woman Writer and the Burden of Dual Authenticity." *Amerasia* 16.1 (1990): 173–200.

Ye, Weili. "'Nui Liuxuesheng': The Story of American-Educated Chinese Women, 1880s–1920." *Modern China* 20.3 (1994): 315–46.

Yung, Judy. *Unbound Feet: A Social History of Chinese Women in San Francisco*. Berkeley: U of California P, 1995.

Obasan
by Joy Kogawa

Marie Lo

Publication Information

First published in Canada in 1981 by Lester and Orpen Dennys, Toronto; softcover edition published in 1982. Penguin (Markham, Ont.) edition published in 1983. Translated into French by Dorothy Howard; published by Quebec-Amerique, Montreal, in 1989. First published in the United States by David R. Godine, Boston, in 1982; softcover edition published in 1984. Subsequent United States editions include Penguin in 1983 and Anchor-Doubleday in 1994. British Penguin (Harmondsworth) edition published in 1983. Translated into Japanese by Nagaoka Sari as *Ushinawareta Sokoku* ("The Lost Native Land"), published by Futami Shobo, Tokyo, in 1983.

Overview

The effect of internment and forced relocation on Japanese Canadians is told from the perspective of Naomi Nakane, an unmarried thirty-six-year-old small-town schoolteacher. Forced to leave the comfort of its Vancouver home in 1942, the tightly knit Nakane family is fragmented and dispersed. Naomi's father, like many men, is sent to interior British Columbia to road gangs, where he contracts tuberculosis and later dies. Naomi's mother, having gone to visit family in Japan shortly before the outbreak of war, is never heard from again. Naomi's mother's side of the family, the Katos, manage to move to Toronto and escape the remote mining towns of British Columbia. However, Naomi, her surrogate parents, Aya Obasan and Uncle Isamu Nakane, and older brother Stephen are not so lucky. They live in a shack in remote Slocan and then, at the end of the war, move to the prairie province of Alberta.

These events leave devastating psychological scars on the family. Stephen throws himself into music, becoming a musician of some renown who travels the world to escape his ancestry and his "too Japanese" family. Naomi, who had always been a quiet and introspective child, grows up a reclusive and emotionally crippled adult. Obasan and Uncle, to the confusion of the children, retreat into silence.

The story opens on the twenty-seventh anniversary of the Nagasaki bombing with Naomi and Uncle Isamu walking along the coulee, a yearly ritual whose significance is lost to Naomi. A month later, Uncle suddenly dies, and Naomi, living in nearby Cecil, is the first to return to the aging Obasan. While they await the arrival of the rest of the family—Stephen and Aunt Emily, an outspoken and untiring activist lobbying for Japanese Canadian rights—Naomi discovers a package from Aunt Emily, filled with letters, Emily's journal, and newspaper articles on the Canadian government's injustices against the Japanese Canadians. The package, which raises as many questions as Obasan's years of silence did, forces Naomi to reexperience the collective and personal traumas long repressed. Aside from the memories of the forced evacuation and dispersal of her family, memories of sexual abuse at the hands of a white neighbor resurface. It is shortly after this abuse that Naomi's mother leaves for Japan, entangling Naomi's feelings of shame and guilt with her mother's mysterious absence.

Only at the end of the novel, when everyone has arrived, do we learn the significance of the ritual visit to the coulee. Naomi's mother, unable to return to Canada, is terribly disfigured by the atomic bombing of Nagasaki and later dies from her wounds. Out of love, she asks Obasan and Uncle to shield her suffering from her children. Although the story ends with Naomi's return to the coulee, perhaps signifying the start of her healing, the novel does not end here. Immediately following this scene is the memorandum sent by the Cooperative Committee on Japanese Canadians decrying the government's intention to deport its citizens. This memorandum undermines a neat closure and suggests that, despite the beginnings of personal healing, collective healing can happen only when the Canadian government addresses the atrocity of its actions.

Reception

Kogawa's *Obasan* was met with instantaneous critical and financial success. Its initial run of three thousand copies quickly sold out, and it has since garnered such prestigious Canadian and American literary awards as the Books in Canada First Novel Award (1981), the Canadian Authors Association Book of the Year Award (1982), the Before Columbus Foundation American Book Award (1982), the American Library Association's Notable Book Award (1982), and the Periodical Distributors of Canada Best Paperback Award (1983). Recognized as an important book, *Obasan* has become a staple in many ethnic literature courses and has been excerpted in many American and Canadian anthologies. A further testimony of *Obasan*'s impact is that, on 22 September 1989, excerpts from *Obasan* were read in the Canadian House of Commons as well as at a press conference later that day to celebrate the settlement finally achieved between the Canadian government and the Committee for Japanese Canadian Redress (Jones 121).

Although *Obasan* deals with Japanese Canadian internment, its popularity in Asian American studies in the United States may be due to similarities in Canadian and United States government policies toward their Japanese citizens during World War II and *Obasan*'s relevance to recurrent themes and issues in Asian American literary and cultural criticism.

The majority of United States scholars tend to frame *Obasan* within discussions of minority writing and racial identity. Some read *Obasan* as a narrative of the immigrant experience, which chronicles and evaluates each successive generation's process of assimilation. In this respect, *Obasan* shares similar concerns with popular Asian American novels like *The Woman Warrior* and *The Joy Luck Club*, in which the generation gap between mother and daughter is widened by cultural differences (Harris, *Kogawa* 10). The multilayered *Obasan* also touches on many issues debated within Asian American studies, particularly the dichotomy between silence and speech. As critics begin to expand the definitions of silence and speech and to question this privileging of speech over silence, many are turning to *Obasan* for its complex portrayal of both the destructive and the redemptive aspects of silence and speech.

In contrast to *Obasan*'s reception in the United States, Canadian scholars generally read *Obasan* as a Canadian novel, subsuming issues of ethnicity and racial identity within debates on national identity and literary traditions. Given Canada's dual French and British colonial legacy, its cultural diversity, and its varied geographic landscape, the search for a unifying "Canadian" identity is still ongoing.

Many Canadian scholars have analyzed *Obasan* in terms of the vision of "Canada" it offers, reading the displacement of the Japanese Canadians as but one example of the kinds of displacements Canadians as a whole feel. More specifically, they have read *Obasan* in relation to Canada's controversial multiculturalism policy, which was instituted to recognize and preserve Canada's cultural diversity. However, the definition of *multiculturalism* and its implementation are still the subjects of heated debates, and *Obasan*'s interconnected themes of personal, communal, and national identity dovetail with these discussions. Frank Davey argues that *Obasan* supports a universalist vision of multiculturalism, while Coral Ann Howells argues that *Obasan* "questions the benevolent Canadian social myth of multiculturalism" and that, as a feminist novel concerned with multiple oppressions, it provides narrative models for a postcolonial nation like Canada (119). For a critique of the primacy of nationalist concerns in *Obasan* scholarship, see Roy Miki.

Author's Biographical Background

Most of the major events in the text are drawn from Kogawa's own life. Kogawa (née Nakayama) was born in Vancouver on 6 June 1935 and spent her early years, like Naomi, in the well-to-do Marpole neighborhood until 1942, when she and her family were forced to the interior British Columbia mining town of Slocan. In 1945, after the war, having had all their Vancouver possessions liquidated and being unable to return to British Columbia, they were forced to move to a beet farm in the town of Coaldale, Alberta. Unlike Naomi's family, however, Kogawa's family remained together. The portrayal of many of the characters in *Obasan* is influenced by family and friends. Her mother, a kindergarten teacher, is the model for both Obasan and Naomi's mother and her father, an Anglican minister, for Nakayama-Sensei.

Kogawa attended the University of Alberta in 1954 and later taught in a Coaldale elementary school for a year. She then left for Toronto, where she studied music at the University of Toronto. From 1956 to 1957, she attended the Anglican Women's Training College. In 1968, she was also a student at the University of Saskatchewan.

In 1958, she married David Kogawa, and after eleven years of marriage, they divorced. After the birth of her two children, when she was living in Grand Forks, British Columbia, she began to pursue writing seriously. In the mid 1970s, Kogawa lived in Ottawa and from 1974 to 1976 worked as a staff writer in the Prime Minister's Office. In 1978, she was a writer in residence at the University of Ottawa. Kogawa is currently living in Vancouver and Toronto.

Kogawa began her writing career as a poet, publishing three collections of poetry before writing *Obasan*. Her disappointment with the reviews of her third book of poetry, *Jericho Road*, led her to focus on prose. Although a private person, Kogawa, with the success of *Obasan*, became seriously involved with the Japanese Canadian Redress Movement in 1983. Her second novel, *Itsuka*, the 1992 sequel to *Obasan*, follows Naomi as she deals with the necessity of a political voice and becomes involved in the redress movement. After *Itsuka* Kogawa published another novel, *The Rain Ascends*, in 1995. Neither *Itsuka* nor *The Rain Ascends* has generated the same acclaim and scholarship that *Obasan* continues to inspire.

Historical Context for the Narratives in *Obasan*

Although the first Japanese immigrant arrived in Canada as early as 1877, by 1941 the approximately 22,000 Japanese Canadians in British Columbia were still considered outsiders and were barred from voting, from entering certain professions (law, pharmacy, etc.), and from holding office. Race relations on the West Coast had always been turbulent. In 1907 in Vancouver, economic resentment and racism boiled over as approximately fifteen hundred white union leaders and store owners looted Chinese and Japanese stores and destroyed property. With the outbreak of World War II, however, the hostilities fostered by the rhetoric of the "yellow peril" converged more specifically on the Japanese Canadians.

In part, the escalating anti-Japanese sentiment in Canada stemmed from the white population's inability to distinguish among the Japanese government, Japanese nationals, and Canadians of Japanese ancestry. Still recovering from the debilitating effects of the depression, white Canada viewed Japanese aggression in Manchuria and China and the threat it posed to British economic interests there as a foreshadowing of what was to come within its own boundaries. By the time Canada declared war on Japan, rumors of sabotage and espionage along the West Coast had already begun circulating.

Immediately after the bombing of Pearl Harbor on 7 December 1941, the Canadian government proclaimed that all civilians of Japanese ancestry, regardless of their citizenship, had to register with the Registrar of Enemy Aliens by 7 February 1942. Since those of German and Italian ancestry also had to register, this action did not come as a surprise to the Japanese Canadians. Unlike other groups, however, Japanese Canadians became the target of unprecedented measures taken in the name of national security. On 17 December the Pacific Coast Security League was formed. Made up of provincial legislators, the league demanded that the federal government evacuate everyone of Japanese ancestry, but the government could not justify this measure. According to Lieutenant General Ken Stuart, Chief of General Staff, "From the Army point of view, I cannot see that they constitute the slightest menace to national security" (Adachi 203).

Despite the army's assessment, the pressure from the British Columbian government and the growing public paranoia led the Canadian government to declare, on 16 January 1942, that all male Japanese "aliens" between eighteen and forty-five years of age be moved from a one-hundred-mile "protected area" along the western coast. Aside from the breakup of families, this measure threatened many families with financial ruin as some seventeen hundred male nationals, many of them breadwinners, were sent to road projects in the interior. In addition to this forced relocation, some twelve hundred fishing boats were impounded, and those who remained within the protected zone were restricted from fishing or holding fishing licenses and were denied their livelihood.

On 25 February 1942, the Order in Council P.C. 1486 declared that the maintenance of this "protected area" necessitated the evacuation of everyone of Japanese ancestry. Before they were moved to ghost towns in interior British Columbia, many Japanese Canadians were sent to the Hastings Park Exhibition Grounds, a "clearing center," while they awaited their fate. They were crowded into converted livestock stalls, and disease ran rampant. Once they arrived at the ghost towns isolated by the harsh wilderness, many lived in accommodations that ranged from canvas tents to wooden shacks. During this time, the property of Japanese Canadians, entrusted to the Custodian of Alien Property, was liquidated without consent to help fund the cost of internment.

Ironically, for many, living conditions grew worse after the war. Following the war, even when it was obvious that the Japanese Canadians were and had never been a military threat, the British Columbian government refused to allow its residents to return. In fact, even Prime Minister Ian Mackenzie openly advocated and implemented a policy of dispersal. As a result, some four thousand Japanese Canadians were deported to a Japan devastated by war and foreign to many, while the rest were forced east of the Rockies. Many were reduced to working on sugar beet farms, a grueling job with inhuman living conditions, just as Naomi and her family were. In 1945, the Japanese

Canadians constituted sixty-five percent of the beet laborers. Not until 1949 were Japanese Canadians allowed to return to the West Coast.

Historical Context for the Writing of *Obasan*

Although the writing of *Obasan* coincided with the rise of a nationwide Japanese Canadian redress movement seeking official apology and compensation from the Canadian government, Kogawa describes herself, a Nisei or second-generation Japanese Canadian, as initially very much like Naomi's brother, Stephen: "I had spent my childhood convinced that the way to live was to be as non-Japanese as possible, to deny it as much as possible. I felt a kind of revulsion at the whole experience of my ethnicity" (Garrod 146). Brought up in the Canadian school system to believe in the ideals of Canadian democracy and equality, the Nisei worked hard to fit in but repeatedly encountered discrimination and marginalization, which led them to take an increasingly activist stance.

In contrast, the Issei, or first generation, tended to maintain their Japanese traditions and outlook, preferring peaceful coexistence rather than assimilation. According to Ken Adachi, the cultural and generation gap "served to give the Issei and Nisei different cultural perspectives through which to interpret their experiences" (169). This contrast is highlighted in Obasan's and Aunt Emily's differing responses to the internment experience. Ironically, despite differing perspectives, the community as a whole offered little resistance to the Canadian government's racist policies in an effort to prove their support and loyalty to Canada and to demonstrate their "Canadianness" (Adachi 226).

The actual writing of *Obasan* took four years. *Obasan* began as a short story, entitled "Obasan," that tells of Naomi's discovery of old letters at the home of her recently widowed Obasan. While in Alberta, Kogawa had a dream telling her to go visit the Public Archives of Canada in Ottawa. There she discovered the wartime letters and journals of Muriel Kitagawa, an activist and champion of Japanese Canadian rights who later became the model for Aunt Emily. In fact, much of chapter 14 of *Obasan* is taken from Kitagawa's journals, with minor editing to fit Kogawa's narrative. Inspired by Kitagawa's works, Kogawa continued to write and eventually produced her first novel, *Obasan*.

Major Themes

collective trauma caused by racism and its effects on the individual
the importance of memory as a means of reconnecting to lost history and
 attaining healing
the creation and fragmentation of community

the price of assimilation
the psychology of the victim (including victims of sexual abuse)
silence and voice
the revelation of family secrets
the relationship between mother (including surrogate mother) and daughter
the quest for the lost or absent parent
learning from older role models
love and forgiveness in a religious sense
generational and cultural differences

Critical Issues

After applauding Kogawa for bringing to light the experiences of the Japanese Canadians and exposing the crimes committed against them during World War II, many literary critics have gone on in the next breath to discuss how Kogawa, through fiction, challenges the constitutive boundaries and authority of history. Indeed, the novel's nonlinear narrative structure, infused with autobiographical elements and historical source materials such as diaries, letters, and newspaper clippings, raises questions about genre distinctions (is *Obasan* autobiography? fiction? other?) and the epistemological process as the reader follows Naomi in her excavation of her past. One influential essay within this postmodern interpretive trend is Donald Goellnicht's "Minority History as Metafiction: Joy Kogawa's *Obasan*," which argues that access and knowledge of past events are always mediated by textualization and that the novel's critique of conventional history writing is made through yet another partial history, from the fictive perspective of Naomi.

In contrast, Rachelle Kanefsky, in "Debunking a Postmodern Conception of History: A Defense of Humanist Values in the Novels of Joy Kogawa," contends that a theory arguing the inability of language to capture empirical reality has within it the seeds for destructive historical misappropriation. Furthermore, if language is denied its power to represent the past truthfully, then history loses its didactic potential for avoiding the mistakes of the past.

The conflict between poststructuralist interpretations like Goellnicht's and Kanefsky's humanist reading of *Obasan* raises important questions about the tensions between ethnic literature and history, personal memory and collective history, as well as the general problem of theory and practice, catching ethnic writers like Kogawa in a double bind: "First, to make a space of articulation for themselves, to carve out an area for revision, they must first dis-place history, and yet such destabilization of the dominant history necessitates a preliminary critique of any history's epistemological claims" (Palumbo-Liu 211). For one attempt to reconcile this tension through the notion of redemptive testimony, see Marilyn Rose.

Another area of debate surrounding *Obasan* is the relation between silence and speech. Many scholars of *Obasan* have tended to dichotomize speech and silence, privileging speech as the channel of resistance and the source of Naomi's and the novel's resolution. However, this dichotomy is oftentimes uncritically mapped onto an East (Obasan) versus West (Emily) conflict, with the implication that Naomi's coming into voice is a victory of Western values over Asian ones. Other interpretations focus on the differing signification of silence before and after internment and dispersal (e.g., Magnusson; Harris, "Broken Generations").

In contrast to these interpretations, which still seem to maintain silence as distinct from speech, is a growing body of work that attempts to explore the different ways in which silence might "speak." Gayle Fujita argues that Naomi's bicultural heritage gives her the ability to attend to her mother's silence as one that speaks of love and sacrifice. Drawing on Fujita, King-Kok Cheung elaborates on the idea of "attentive silence" and suggests that toward the end of the novel, Naomi comes to understand silence and speech as complementary.

Pedagogical Issues and Suggestions

Obasan is a novel that teaches well, and students often respond very positively toward it. Many United States students are surprised to learn that the Canadian government, too, adopted a policy of interning its own citizens. It might be helpful for students unfamiliar with the major events of Japanese Canadian internment to compare and contrast the Japanese Canadian internment with the internment of Japanese Americans. A useful text to consult is Roger Daniels's *Concentration Camps, North America: Japanese in the United States and Canada during World War II*. Students may find their understanding of such a demanding and complex narrative helped by doing a time line so that they can see how Naomi and her family's moves from Vancouver to their final stop in Granton, Alberta, are shaped by political and historical events.

Students may also find it useful to see how Kogawa incorporates historical documents into the text, for many have expressed frustration and the desire to sort out what is "fiction" and what is "real" in *Obasan*. Students can research, for example, Muriel Kitagawa's journals and letters to see how Kogawa shaped these letters to fit within her narrative. They can consult a number of interviews with Joy Kogawa in which she tells of the autobiographical elements in *Obasan*. These exercises might help students grasp the complexity of Kogawa's narrative structure, as well as provide concrete examples from which they can discuss the larger questions of genre disruptions and their rhetorical effects. Another way to approach these questions of genre might be to have students consider Jeanne and James Houston's *Farewell to Manzanar*, a more straightforward autobiographical account of the Japanese American internment experience. Students can compare the rhetorical effect of a fictional account of internment with an account that is more obviously documentary.

Students may also express some frustration toward the religious metaphors and references they sense are in the text but don't know how to approach. For two good essays on the Christian and Buddhist influences on this text see Cheng Lok Chua and Teruyo Ueki.

Intertextual Linkages

With Maxine Hong Kingston's *The Woman Warrior*: mother-daughter relationships; the mystery and silence of one's past; the intersection of racism and patriarchal oppression; the tension between voice and silence; the use of myths and fairy tales; the gendering of cultural ties: mother tongue versus fatherland (see Goellnicht, "Father Land").

With Monica Sone's *Nisei Daughter*: the differences between Japanese Canadian and Japanese American internment; the ways gender affects the protagonists' responses to internment and the mother-daughter relationship; women's poetics and the blurring of genre distinctions; fragmented subjectivity and the pressure and price of assimilation (see Lim).

With Toni Morrison's *Beloved*: collective traumas, personal experiences, memory, and official history; the power of language to define reality and subjectivity; the intersection of the discourses of race and gender; alternative conceptions of "history"; matrilineal heritage; the female body as text (see Turner; Grewal).

With Jamaica Kincaid's *Lucy*: the mother figure as the prelinguistic and cultural "other"; the effects of assimilation on the mother-daughter relationship; the relationship between sexuality and race consciousness (see Ty).

Bibliographic Resources

Muriel Kitagawa's papers, which inspired and were incorporated into *Obasan*, have been published as *This Is My Own: Letters to Wes and Other Writings on Japanese Canadians, 1941–1948*, edited by Roy Miki. Ann Gomer Sunahara's *The Politics of Racism* and Roger Daniels's *Concentration Camps, North America* are good sources of background information on Japanese Canadian internment, with the latter offering a comparison with the Japanese American case. For an extended book-length analysis of *Obasan*, see Arnold Davidson's *Writing against the Silence: Joy Kogawa's* Obasan.

Other Resources

To provide students with historical background and to help sort out the chronology of events in *Obasan*, instructors may want to consider some of the videos available on

Japanese Canadian internment. *Of Japanese Descent*, a 1945 propaganda film made by the Canadian government, depicts Japanese Canadians happily at work in the beet fields of Alberta. *Enemy Alien* is a documentary that looks at the political and economic forces and the bigotry that led to the Japanese Canadian internment.

For more personal perspectives instructors may want to use *Minoru: Memory of Exile*, a short animated film that tells the story of Minoru Fukushima, who was a nine-year-old boy living in Vancouver when the Japanese Canadians were dispatched to internment camps in interior British Columbia. Narrated by Minoru and his son, the director Michael Fukushima, the film weaves personal recollections with archival documents; unlike *Obasan*, the film is chronologically organized. In contrast to Naomi and her family, who remained in Canada after the war, Minoru and his family, along with thousands of other Japanese Canadians, were deported to Japan. For Joy Kogawa's own experiences of internment, instructors may want to use *The Pool: Reflections of the Japanese-Canadian Internment*.

Bibliography

Adachi, Ken. *The Enemy That Never Was: A History of the Japanese Canadians*. Toronto: McClelland, 1976.

Cheung, King-kok. *Articulate Silences: Hisaye Yamamoto, Maxine Hong Kingston, Joy Kogawa*. Ithaca: Cornell UP, 1993.

Chua, Cheng Lok. "Witnessing the Japanese Canadian Experience in World War Two: Processual Structure, Symbolism, and Irony in Joy Kogawa's *Obasan*." *Reading the Literatures of Asian America*. Ed. Shirley Geok-lin Lim and Amy Ling. Philadelphia: Temple UP, 1992. 97–108.

Daniels, Roger. *Concentration Camps, North America: Japanese in the United States and Canada during World War II*. Malabar: Krieger, 1981.

Davey, Frank. *Post-national Arguments: The Politics of the Anglophone-Canadian Novel since 1967*. Toronto: U of Toronto P, 1993.

Davidson, Arnold. *Writing against the Silence: Joy Kogawa's* Obasan. Toronto: ECW, 1993.

Enemy Alien. Dir. Jeanette Lerman. National Film Board of Canada, 1975.

Fujita, Gayle K. "'To Attend the Sound of Stone': The Sensibility of Silence in *Obasan*." *MELUS* 12 (1985): 33–42.

Garrod, Andrew. *Speaking for Myself: Canadian Writers in Interview*. St. John's: Breakwater, 1986.

Goellnicht, Donald C. "Father Land and/or Mother Tongue: The Divided Female Subject in Kogawa's *Obasan* and Hong Kingston's *The Woman Warrior*." *Redefining Autobiography in Twentieth-Century Women's Fiction: An Essay Collection*. Ed. Janice Morgan and Colette T. Hall. New York: Garland, 1991. 119–34.

———. "Minority History as Metafiction: Joy Kogawa's *Obasan*." *Tulsa Studies in Women's Literature* 8 (1989): 287–306.

Grewal, Gurleen. "Memory and the Matrix of History: The Poetics of Loss and Recovery in Joy Kogawa's *Obasan* and Toni Morrison's *Beloved*." Singh, Skerrett, and Hogan 140–74.

Harris, Mason. "Broken Generations in *Obasan*: Inner Conflict and the Destruction of Community." *Canadian Literature* 127 (1990): 41–57.

——. *Joy Kogawa and Her Works*. Toronto: ECW, 1996.

Houston, Jeanne Wakatsuki, and James D. Houston. *Farewell to Manzanar: A True Story of the Japanese American Experience during and after the World War II Internment*. 1973. New York: Bantam, 1979.

Howells, Coral Ann. *Private and Fictional Words: Canadian Women Novelists of the 1970s and 1980s*. New York: Methuen, 1987.

Jones, Manina. *That Art of Difference: "Documentary Collage" and English-Canadian Writing*. Toronto: U of Toronto P, 1993.

Kanefsky, Rachelle. "Debunking a Postmodern Conception of History: A Defense of Humanist Values in the Novels of Joy Kogawa." *Canadian Literature* 148 (1996): 11–36.

Kincaid, Jamaica. *Lucy*. New York: Plume-Penguin, 1991.

Kingston, Maxine Hong. *The Woman Warrior: Memoirs of a Girlhood among Ghosts*. New York: Vintage, 1977.

Kitagawa, Muriel. *This Is My Own: Letters to Wes and Other Writings on Japanese Canadians, 1941–1948*. Ed. Roy Miki. Vancouver: Talon, 1985.

Kogawa, Joy. *Itsuka*. New York: Doubleday, 1993.

——. *Jericho Road*. Toronto: McClelland, 1977.

——. *Obasan*. New York: Anchor-Doubleday, 1994.

——. *The Rain Ascends*. Toronto: Knopf, 1995.

Lim, Shirley Geok-lin. "Japanese American Women's Life Stories: Maternality in Monica Sone's *Nisei Daughter* and Joy Kogawa's *Obasan*." *Feminist Studies* 16.2 (1990): 288–312.

Magnusson, A. Lynne. "Language and Longing in Joy Kogawa's *Obasan*." *Canadian Literature* 116 (1988): 58–66.

Miki, Roy. *Broken Entries: Race, Subjectivity, Writing*. Toronto: Mercury, 1998.

Minoru: Memory of Exile. Dir. Michael Fukushima. National Film Board of Canada, 1992.

Morrison, Toni. *Beloved*. New York: Signet, 1989.

Of Japanese Descent. Prod. Dallas Jones and Leon C. Shelley. National Film Board of Canada, 1945.

Palumbo-Liu, David. "The Politics of Memory: Remembering History in Alice Walker and Joy Kogawa." Singh, Skerrett, and Hogan 211–26.

The Pool: Reflections of the Japanese-Canadian Internment. Dir. Mark de Valk. Falcon, 1992.

Rose, Marilyn Russell. "Politics into Art: Kogawa's *Obasan* and the Rhetoric of Fiction." *Mosaic* 21.3 (1988): 214–26.

Singh, Amritjit, Joseph Skerrett, and Robert Hogan, eds. *Memory and Cultural Politics: New Approaches to American Ethnic Literatures*. Boston: Northeastern UP, 1996.

Sone, Monica. *Nisei Daughter*. 1953. Seattle: U of Washington P, 1979.

Sunahara, Ann Gomer. *The Politics of Racism: The Uprooting of Japanese Canadians during the Second World War*. Toronto: Lorimer, 1981.

Turner, Margaret E. "Power, Language, and Gender: Writing 'History' in *Beloved* and *Obasan*." *Mosaic* 25.4 (1992): 81–97.

Ty, Eleanor. "Struggling with the Powerful (M)Other: Identity and Sexuality in Kogawa's *Obasan* and Kincaid's *Lucy*." *International Fiction Review* 20.2 (1993): 120–26.

Ueki, Teruyo. "*Obasan*: Revelations in a Paradoxical Scheme." *MELUS* 18 (1993): 5–20.

The Coffin Tree
by Wendy Law-Yone

Tamara C. Ho

Publication Information

First published in the United States by Alfred A. Knopf in 1983; published in England by Penguin in 1985. Softcover edition published by Beacon Press in 1987. Both hardcover and softcover versions are now out of print.

Overview

The Coffin Tree is a novel in the form of a memoir being written by an unnamed woman recalling her childhood in Burma[1] and her subsequent immigration to the United States. The narrator's motherless childhood in the capital city of Rangoon is marked by guilt about her mother (who died during the narrator's birth), the death of her oppressive grandmother, her father's revolutionary involvement with dissident minority tribes, her own traumatic schooling at a local English Catholic school, and a military coup that throws the country into chaos. The narrator's half-brother, Shan, her senior by ten years, is her constant companion and in many ways her social opposite. Shan, who spent his early life in a rebel stronghold, vividly remembers his mother as their father's first lover, an ethnic minority "mountain woman" who became deranged and "wild" after the birth of her children. When their father goes underground after the coup to lead the renewed insurrection against the central government, the narrator and Shan are left in the care of various aunts and uncles at their well-fortified house. After three years, the children receive news that their father has ordered them to go to America to avoid the upcoming bloodshed in the country.

The twenty-year-old narrator and Shan land in New York. After six months of trying to survive on their own, Shan falls victim to chronic fatigue and malaria; his constant need for attention causes the narrator to lose her job. The two are forced to seek the help of Benjamin Lane, an American journalist sympathetic to the Burmese rebel cause, who takes in the young immigrants. Grateful to the Lanes, yet afraid and suspicious of their American ways, the narrator and Shan retreat into isolation and paranoia. Shan slips increasingly into xenophobic conspiracy fantasies, but the narrator finds the strength to cope and eventually obtains another job.

Brother and sister travel south to find work and warmer weather. As Shan deteriorates, the narrator feels trapped between concern for him and increasing resentment about his inability to deal with American life. Shan's sudden death brings the narrator relief, then profound grief and a sense of exile. A letter about their father's death in Burma sends her further into a deep, morbid despair. After an unsuccessful suicide attempt, she is interned in 3 East, the mental ward of a hospital. As she befriends the other inmates and undergoes therapy, the narrator gains insight into her past.

In the final chapter, while sorting through Shan's trunk, the narrator finds the book of the coffin tree, a document that she has considered "a fake map leading to bogus treasure" (192). What she discovers is not a guide to material wealth but a story of the spirit of the coffin tree, who guides the dead in the world between death and resurrection to await another life cycle. Reading this myth of otherworldly hope, she comes to realize that her "insane" brother was not as out of touch with reason as she had suspected. Touched by Shan's vision, his ability to find "some story [. . .] some illusion to shape the future, some dream to lighten the days" (192), she experiences an epiphany and finds the inspiration to stubbornly go on living in a world marked by trauma, false hopes, exile, and instability. The narrative concludes some years later with the narrator, having finally found the truth of her own strength, writing the finishing pages of her story.

Reception

The Coffin Tree was favorably reviewed in established publications such as the New York Times Book Review (Milton), America (Breslin), the Atlantic (Adams), the Boston Globe (Monsky), Booklist (Banas), Publishers Weekly (Bannon), and the Nation (Forbes). Because of the reading public's unfamiliarity with the Burma setting, the book had limited sales and is currently out of print. Nevertheless, it is still being taught in various universities with course offerings in Asian American literature.

Because of the scarcity of literature by or about Burmese Americans, The Coffin Tree stands as a rare and remarkable achievement. Considering the growing attention in Asian American studies to previously less vocal groups, it is fitting that The Coffin Tree should be recognized as an integral part of the Asian American canon. Since Aung San Suu Kyi's Nobel Prize in 1991, the American public has become more aware of and curious about Burma; perhaps this development will increase interest in The Coffin Tree and result in its republication.

While the book has been praised by various Euro-American critics for its brilliant mix of the familiar and the bizarre, its convincing depiction of psychic alienation and madness, and the narrator's "triumph" of personal strength and perseverance, some Asian American scholars contend that such universalized and depoliticized readings elide the book's eloquent depiction of postcolonial conditions in Asia and particular kinds of immigrant experiences in America. Law-Yone's articulation of a strong Asian female protagonist and minority-within-minority issues (Shan's hill tribe people within Burma; Burmese and Southeast Asian immigrants within America) adds to the work's relevance to fields such as feminist studies and postcolonial studies. Further, *The Coffin Tree*'s pointed critique of masculinist nationalism, of the supposed benevolence of America, and of institutional authority (familial, governmental, religious, academic, and medical) from marginalized points of view evokes numerous related themes and makes it an important work in Asian American and American literary studies.

Author's Biographical Background

Like the narrator, Wendy Law-Yone grew up in Rangoon and attended a prominent Roman Catholic girls' high school run by Irish nuns. In 1967, having married an American citizen, Law-Yone tried to leave Burma but was arrested and held for interrogation before being permitted to go; this ordeal is detailed in her short story "The Year of the Pigeon." After acquiring United States citizenship the following year, she returned to Southeast Asia and lived briefly in Thailand, Singapore, and Kuala Lumpur. Eventually divorcing her first husband, Law-Yone moved back to the United States in 1973 and attended Eckerd College in Florida, where she received a Special Talent Award in 1974. Since 1975, Law-Yone has been living in Washington, DC, and working as an editor and writer. She is the mother of four children.

The Coffin Tree was Law-Yone's first published novel. She has received writing fellowships from the National Endowment for the Arts and the Carnegie Endowment. In the past decade, she has published a number of nonfiction articles and fictional short stories in magazines, anthologies, and journals. Returning briefly to Burma in 1989, Law-Yone reported on rebel camps along the Thai-Burma border where thousands had fled after the 8 August 1988 uprising. In 1995, she was nominated for the Irish Times Literary Award for her second novel *Irrawaddy Tango*.

Historical Context for the Narratives in *The Coffin Tree*

Bordered by China, Thailand, Laos, and India, Burma is the largest country in Southeast Asia and was once one of its richest and most culturally developed as well. In the past forty years, isolation, economic mismanagement, and massive civil strife have made it "one of the world's most withdrawn and least industrialized countries" (Muller

110

609); it holds one of the most atrocious records for human rights violations in the world. While Law-Yone describes the backdrop for her novel as postwar Burmese politics (E-mail), readers may need some historical details to understand the setting for the narrator's life in Burma.

The history of Burma dates back to approximately 2000 BCE. Waves of emigration from Central Asia, Thailand, and India have resulted in broad ethnic and cultural diversity today. Buddhism and animism are the country's principal religions. The Burmese-speaking Burman (or Bamar) people make up the largest ethnic group; the other major ethnic groups are the Shan, Mon, Karen, Kayah, Chin, Kachin, and Arakanese (the Rakhine). Peoples of Chinese and Indian descent make up approximately five percent of the population.

The country is currently divided into areas called states and divisions; the states are populated mainly by the ethnic minority peoples; the divisions, by Burmans, Chinese, and Indians. Represented in the book by the narrator's half-brother, Shan, and his "hill tribe" mother, the Shan peoples, the third largest ethnic group, live in the hilly northeastern regions of Burma and have a long history of armed struggle with the Burman majority. Shan territories fall within the "Golden Triangle," where Burma, Laos, and Thailand meet, an area known for its production of opium poppies and heroin.

Following over a millennium of Burmese monarchical rule, the country was forcibly annexed by Britain in 1886 after a series of Anglo-Burmese wars. Under the colonial "divide and rule" policy, ethnic divisiveness was encouraged. The Shans in the northern hill areas remained under indirect British control, while Lower Burma was directly ruled as a province of British India. British influence was also strongly felt in education; many missionary schools, like the one attended by the narrator, were established. Protests surged in the 1920s over the establishment of Rangoon University, and nationalist sentiments grew in both the university and Buddhist groups. Aung San emerged as the leader of the anticolonial student movement and with his comrades formed the core of the Burmese Independent Army. Supported by the majority of the Burmese and helped by alliances with the Shans, Chins, and Kachins, Aung San's party (the Anti-Fascist People's Freedom League, or AFPFL) gained power against British rule in a series of armed struggles. In 1947, on the eve of independence, General Aung San was assassinated by a political rival.

In 1948, Burma became an independent republic. U Nu, the most senior member of the AFPFL remaining after Aung San's assassination, was elected the first prime minister. (Law-Yone's father, a friend and supporter of U Nu, started the *Nation* in the same year.) In 1962, following a period of unrest, General Ne Win, one of the original generals of the Burmese Independent Army, took control in a political coup with the military's support. While Ne Win declared Burma to be a socialist republic guided by the Burmese Socialist Programme Party, he maintained central control as party chairman and head of the army and set the country on a course of totalitarianism and isolation.

Historical Context for the Writing of *The Coffin Tree*

During the 1970s, the Burmese Socialist Programme Party attempted to establish a self-sufficient Burma by nationalizing businesses and the media and closing the country to the outside world. Pressured by social unrest, many leading generals resigned from their military posts in 1972, and General Ne Win officially resigned as head of the government in 1981. Most of these men, however, retained government posts as civilians, and many assumed that Ne Win was still in control behind the scenes. Because of martial law, the demonetization of the economy, the financial onus of continued civil war, and ongoing military repression, Burma in the 1980s was characterized by civil unrest, economic instability, and heightened ethnic insurgency. The end of the decade was marked by the 8 August 1988 ("8-8-88") massacre in Rangoon in which thousands of student and civilian protesters were killed or arrested and tortured without trial. The resistance leader Aung San Suu Kyi was placed under house arrest, and the military refused to cede power, establishing instead the State Law and Order Restoration Council (SLORC).

Taking over the government, SLORC severely curtailed civil liberties. In 1989, it officially changed Burma's name to Myanmar on the rationale that *Burma* appeared to represent only the majority Burman ethnic group. Though in official use, the name tends to be associated with the military government and has not been universally accepted either inside or outside the country. Since *The Coffin Tree* is set in a period before the name change, this essay follows Law-Yone's use of *Burma*.

Readers interested in political developments in Burma since the publication of *The Coffin Tree* are referred to the works by Josef Silverstein, Aung San Suu Kyi (listed under Suu Kyi), Martin Smith, Alan Clements, and Anna Allott. There are also numerous Amnesty International reports on Burma. While *The Coffin Tree* is a work of fiction, there are sections of the narrative that seemingly correspond with history. For example, the narrator refers to the punishment schoolchildren receive if they "lapse into pidgin" (9), which was typical of the kinds of discipline enforced in the British school system under colonialism. In chapter 2, the father's student radicalism signals the 1930s period when many Burmese students left their university studies to protest and fight against the colonial system and Rangoon, the "lowland government" (18). Occurring around 1939, Shan's birth is perhaps symbolic of the alliance formed between the young Burmese nationalists and the ethnic tribes against the British rule. The "coo coo" episodes in chapter 3 seem to reflect the chaos that characterized General Ne Win's coup in 1962, including dependence on the black market (31).

Major Themes

banishment and exile
legitimacy and illegitimacy as related to vagrancy, family, asylums, schools,
    laws, and citizenship

insanity, deviance, cultural conditions leading to "dis-ease"

xenophobia, paranoia, and isolation

alternative interpretations of idleness, indolence, and apathy (e.g., the aunts, uncle, and Shan)

emigration from a tumultuous situation in Asia to an apparently hostile American environment

the clash of cultural or religious systems, especially the tensions between Catholicism and Buddhism

the limits and problems of authority; coming to terms with an authority (familial, religious, and institutional)

authoritative father figures (familial and religious)

dreaming, fantasy, and storytelling as a means of healing loss and understanding history and family

loss of culture, home, family members

nostalgia and anger of immigrants or refugees

women's survival abilities compared with men's

Critical Issues

The novel's abundance of themes presents fertile ground for critical analysis. For example, one can consider the narrative's interrogation of madness and reason. Madness and the abandonment of reason can be examined from a number of perspectives, ranging from a personal sense of loss and alienation to larger cultural and historical situations of chaos, trauma, marginality, and exile. The significance of deviant behavior gathers force as the narrative progresses. For example, Shan's mother's apparent wildness and insanity in the jungle present a precursor to Shan's later paranoia and irrational behavior in the United States. The behavior of the aunts after the coup (paranoia, skittishness, psychosomatic disorders, and bizarre mimicry) bears striking similarity to Shan's state after immigration to the United States. Is this proliferation of "insanity" based on some physical or psychological weakness, or is it just a reaction to (perhaps a coping strategy for) a chaotic social situation that treats one as already marginal, suspicious, and flawed? If these characters are indeed performing the worst aspects of the stereotypes that would render them marginal (e.g., weak, crazy women; paranoid immigrants), should readers interpret this behavior as resistant or subversive?

Law-Yone's narrative repeatedly presents notions of social, political, and institutional exteriority and interiority in relation to madness and deviance (e.g., Shan's mother running wild in the hills, the vagrant outside the house in Rangoon, the behavior of the Burmese after the coup, the position of the narrator and Shan in the Lanes' basement, and the inmates of 3 East). The dominance of the center and the "inferiority" of the margins are often subverted and questioned in this narrative (Lee). For example, despite the narrator's apparent rationality throughout and the legitimacy of her parentage, her centrality is offset by the narrative focus on Shan, the irrational bastard son of a crazed, ethnic minority "mountain woman." The view of history and culture as examined from a marginalized perspective is an important critical theme in this text. While one reviewer commented on Law-Yone's depiction of madness as "cosmic" and "beyond the political and the historical" (Milton), the narrative seems to suggest a careful examination of the political and historical conditions that contribute toward certain populations' "dis-ease" with rationality and reason. Since one character in the book describes "dis-ease" as "this aching, throbbing, god-awful incurable pain [. . .] known as life" (134), readers of *The Coffin Tree* should consider how it is that Law-Yone's construction of madness comments on or critiques different cultural conditions that cause the characters to abandon reason in both Asia and the United States.

Another critical issue of importance concerns disruptions of temporality and narrative structure. While the narrative is generally linear, there is a sudden rupture when the narrator enters 3 East. It is not until her internment in the hospital mental ward that the narrator comes to terms with her history, her feeling of exile, and her memories of Burma, Shan, and their father. Only after traveling through the narrator's memories and her experience in the asylum do readers discover what led her to her suicide attempt. Michel Foucault proposes a model of history that focuses on local, discontinuous, disqualified, illegitimate knowledges as an alternative to any claims of a unitary, continuous history. *The Coffin Tree* is certainly a book about national and cultural narratives gone awry, in Burma and in the United States. For both Shan and the narrator, the authority of nation, father, and religion are undermined by chaos, abandonment, and exile. Since narratives of exile and immigration usually struggle with one's place in a disrupted world and interrupted teleology, readers of *The Coffin Tree* might examine the structural trajectory of the narrative; the role of legend, stories, and dreams versus that of official documents and histories; the related implications about official Burmese and American history; and the common elements of marginalization in both the First and Third Worlds.

In the novel's many situations of cultural contact between the West and the East, the narrator describes Western ways as bizarre and unfamiliar, and the faraway, chaotic world of Burma is the site of home, security, and family. This narrative strategy seems an intentional reversal of orientalist notions of Asia and perhaps a critique of the (lack of) benevolence in American society toward immigrants. The one point of overlap between the narrator's Westernized life and her Burmese culture is the powerful role of cultural institutions. While she resents the role of her Catholic education in her life, she recognizes in the figure of the omnipotent and vengeful Catholic God an imaginary, male force of authority much like her father. Because of the common elements of surveillance, interrogation, guilt, and confession, the establishments of school, religion, family, and, later, medicine become conflated as social institutions that can be as alienating, abusive, and repressive as they can be supportive and healing.

Throughout the text, the role of women is contrasted with the role of men. While the men occupy the extremes of the narrative (father as national hero, Shan as disempowered minority and "failed" immigrant), the women (the aunts, the narrator) find themselves subject to the whims of men, culture, and nation, and yet in the end, they are the ones who find the ability to cope and survive in the absence of nation, father, and stability. While this book has been characterized as feminist by some, it is also recognized for its sensitive depiction of flawed male authority, complex gender relations, and the ability of the forgotten to survive in adverse circumstances.

Pedagogical Issues and Suggestions

The Coffin Tree is accessible to readers because of Law-Yone's sophisticated and sensitive rendering of personal displacement, loss, and marginalization and of the narrator's struggle to survive. However, it would be useful for instructors to contextualize the book with cultural and historical information about Burma to provide students with an understanding of the narrator's Asian background. While the narrative stands well on its own without any knowledge of Burmese history or culture, instructors should provide an introductory lecture and perhaps assign students research projects related to the book's context and themes.

Some Suggestions
1. After outlining Burma's history of British colonization, civil war, democracy struggles, and ethnic tensions, ask students to identify allusions to historical events and dates in Law-Yone's story.
2. Ask students to check out Burma-related Web sites or to collect and summarize for the class articles about Burma or Burmese immigrants in the United States, especially works on or by Burmese women (see Bibliographic Resources, below).
3. Before students read the book, show one of the films about Burma suggested below (see Other Resources).
4. In an advanced class or a class dealing with secondary works of a theoretical nature, have students read Michel Foucault's *Discipline and Punish* and discuss the role of institutions in the book. Or read Homi Bhabha's "Dissemination" and discuss issues such as minority discourse, time, and violence in the context of modern nationalism.
5. Contrast the students' first impressions of Burma from their initial reading and the narrator's and Shan's perceptions of life in the United States.

Intertextual Linkages

With Jessica Hagedorn's *Dogeaters*: nostalgia, memory, and displacement in
relation to Southeast Asian culture; a backdrop of civil and political
turmoil in a country of origin; competing religious ideologies (Catholicism
vs. indigenous religious beliefs); the presence of ethnically and culturally

marginalized male figures (e.g., Shan and Joey Sands) paralleling or in contrast to more "legitimate," privileged female protagonists (Rio and the narrator in *The Coffin Tree*); the role of fantasy and alternative narratives; the fragmentation of temporal linearity and narrative form and content; reconstructing the past through stories, memory, and documents; "authenticity" and "falsehood" in history; forgiveness and coming to terms with one's culture, parents, and family; survival.

With Joy Kogawa's *Obasan*: loss of, partial memories of, and guilt about an absent mother; a child narrator naively taking responsibility for the absence of the mother; separation from and death of parents (fathers) due to larger historical circumstances; coming to terms, through memory, fantasy, and dream work, with collective and personal trauma; textual linkages between family dislocation and cultural history; abusive male authority figures; orientalist typologies of Asia.

With Wendy Law-Yone's *Irrawaddy Tango*: history and current political events in Burma; immigration issues and the status of the refugee from Burma; problematizing American benevolence and humanism in relation to Burma and the Third World; the relationship of female protagonists to male-centered authority; civil and ethnic insurgency; ethnic and class tensions among Burmese (both in Burma and abroad); the loss of home and a sense of exile (historical and geographical); madness; surviving collective and personal trauma; the resolution of personal and cultural issues through memory and storytelling.

With Bharati Mukherjee's *Jasmine*: the comparable yet distinct immigration experiences of South and Southeast Asians in America; the questioning of the American "success story" from an immigrant perspective; nostalgia and the isolationist behavior of immigrants; the effect of gender on the protagonists' experience and ability to survive in the United States; differences in the relationships of Asian women to authority figures and institutions.

With Karen Yamashita's *Brazil-Maru*: Asian immigrants in the Americas; the isolation of immigrants from the mainstream culture; the cultural and historical centrality of male figures and the commensurate marginality of women; the effect of abusive father figures on children; immigrant nostalgia; stories from and survival against a backdrop of violence in and destruction of the Asian homeland; insanity and history.

Bibliographic Resources

For sections of *The Coffin Tree* set in the remote northern regions of Burma, Law-Yone consulted the works of Francis Ward and Edmund Leach. The story of the spirit of the coffin tree is actually an excerpt from *The Tibetan Book of the Dead*.

For an excellent introduction to postwar Burma, see Aung San Suu Kyi. Josef Silverstein covers Burma at a time contemporaneous with Law-Yone's novel. The American journalist Bertil Lintner, frequently published in *Far Eastern Economic Review* and elsewhere, has written extensively about Burma.

Burmese gender issues differ significantly from gender issues in other Asian cultures; consult Maureen Aung-Thwin and Yayori Matsui. Tinzar Lwyn offers a comprehensive, feminist, anthropological study of Burmese women and activism. Ma Ma Lay's *Not out of Hate* (translated by Margaret Aung-Thwin), currently the only novel of Burmese fiction translated into English, concerns the life of a Burmese girl during the British colonial period.

Little has been written on Burmese Americans as a group or on Burmese immigration to the West. Autobiographical pieces like those by Sue Arnold and Than Than Win might provide some comparative perspectives. A bimonthly newsletter, *The Burma Debate*, published by the Burma Project (see below), features a regular section entitled "In Their Own Words," with interviews and writings by Burmese students and refugees.

Published criticism on Law-Yone's writing, apart from book reviews, is limited to the articles by Janie Har and Rachel Lee.

Other Resources

Set in 1988 (when a massive prodemocracy demonstration was brutally repressed by the government), John Boorman's film *Beyond Rangoon* (1995) offers a fairly accurate representation of contemporary Burma, although the story is fictional and sometimes questionable in its focus on the heroics of the white American female protagonist. *Lines of Fire* (1990) is a nonfiction account of the forty-year civil war in Burma between the government and the various ethnic groups. Lindsey Merrison's *Our Burmese Days* (1995) documents her voyage into her ancestral culture.

The Burma Project, operating under George Soros's Open Society Institute in New York, is a private organization coordinating a wide variety of programs involving Burmese refugees, students, and scholars in America. The Burma Project Web site (<http://soros.org/burma.html>) provides historical references about Burmese culture, current updates, and multimedia resources about Burma in relation to the world at large and Burmese in the United States.

Some Other Useful Web Sites on Burma

BurmaNet (<http://www.burmanet.org> or subscribe by e-mailing <strider@igc.org>)

Free Burma (<http://metalab.unc.edu/freeburma>)

Myanmar: The Land of Pagodas (<http://triton.ori.u-tokyo.ac.jp/~moe/ myanmar.html>)

Notes

I owe great thanks to the following people for their help with this project: King-Kok Cheung, Wendy Law-Yone, my parents, Saya Ma Than Than Win, Maureen Aung-Thwin, Rachel Lee, and Lindsey Merrison. Special thanks also go to David A. Martinez and Connie Razza.

1. When the military government announced a change in the country's name, some debate and contention occurred. According to the State Law and Order Restoration Council, *Myanmar* (more formally, the Union of Myanmar) was to be used officially as the name of the country and in reference to anything related to the whole country, in order to include all the different ethnic groups living there. Commensurately, many cities' names have also been changed to reflect their Burmese pronunciation more accurately; for example, the narrator's city of birth, Rangoon, is now called Yangon. Traditionally, in English, *Burmese* was used to refer to all the different peoples living in the country, while *Burman* or *Bamar* was used to refer to the dominant ethnic group. The official rationale for the name change was that the previous name of Burma appeared to represent only the Burman ethnic group and was, therefore, not representative of the union. As John Okell writes in his leading textbook on Burmese for nonnative speakers, "The new name has not been taken up universally outside of the country. Some writers [. . .] continue to use 'Burma' on the grounds that many readers won't recognize the name 'Myanmar.' Opponents of the military government defiantly reject the new name as a way of flaunting their opposition. Supporters of the military government use 'Myanmar' assiduously, and it is also used by international agencies like the U.N." (27).

Bibliography

"About Wendy Law-Yone." Press release. New York: Knopf, 1993.

Adams, Phoebe Lou. Rev. of *The Coffin Tree*, by Wendy Law-Yone. *Atlantic* June 1983: 105.

Allott, Anna J. *Inked Over, Ripped Out: Burmese Storytellers and the Censors.* New York: PEN Amer. Center, 1933. Chiang Mai, Thailand: Silkworm, 1994.

Arnold, Sue. *A Burmese Legacy.* London: Hodder, 1996.

Aung-Thwin, Maureen. "Burma: Attitudes towards and Political Activity of Women in Burma." *Ms. Magazine* July–Aug. 1991: 18–21.

Banas, Mary. Rev. of *The Coffin Tree*, by Wendy Law-Yone. *Booklist* 15 Apr. 1983: 1057.

Bannon, Barbara A. Rev. of *The Coffin Tree*, by Wendy Law-Yone. *Publishers Weekly* 4 Mar. 1983. 86.

Bhabha, Homi. "Dissemination: Time, Narrative, and the Margins of the Modern Nation." *Nation and Narration.* Ed. Bhabha. London: Routledge, 1995. 291–322.

Boorman, John, dir. *Beyond Rangoon.* Castle Rock, 1995.

Breslin, John. Rev. of *The Coffin Tree*, by Wendy Law-Yone. *America* 27 Aug. 1983: 97–98.

Clements, Alan. *Burma: The Next Killing Fields?* Foreword by the Dalai Lama. Berkeley: Odonian, 1992.

Forbes, Nancy. "Burmese Days." Rev. of *The Coffin Tree*, by Wendy Law-Yone. *Nation* 30 Apr. 1983: 551.

Foucault, Michel. *Discipline and Punish: The Birth of the Prison.* Trans. Alan Sheridan. New York: Vintage, 1979.

Hagedorn, Jessica. *Dogeaters.* New York: Penguin, 1991.

Hail, John. "Shan Rebels Fight Little-Known War for Independence; Shun Burma Opium War." *Los Angeles Times* 26 Dec. 1983, sec. 7: 7.

Har, Janie C. "Food, Sexuality, and the Pursuit of a Little Attention." *Critical Mass: A Journal of Asian American Cultural Criticism* 1.1 (1993): 83–92.

Horn, Andrew. Rev. of *Our Burmese Days,* dir. Lindsey Merrison. *Moving Pictures Berlinale.* Rpt. in press release, Lindsey Merrison Film, Berlin, 1996.

Kang, K. Connie. "Burmese Press Their Cause Here (Expatriates in Los Angeles)." *Los Angeles Times* 11 Mar. 1996: B1.

Kogawa, Joy. *Obasan.* New York: Anchor-Doubleday, 1994.

Law-Yone, Wendy. "Ankle." *Grand Street* 7.3 (1988): 24.

———. "The Burma Road." *Asian Art and Culture* 9.1 (1996): 4–11.

———. *The Coffin Tree.* Boston: Beacon, 1987.

———. "Drought." *Slow Hand: Women Writing Erotica.* Ed. Michele Slung. New York: Harper, 1992. 27–40.

———. E-mail to the author. 1997.

———. Interview with Tamara Ho and Nancy Yoo. *Words Matter: Conversations with Asian American Writers.* Ed. King-Kok Cheung. Honolulu: U of Hawai'i P, 2000. 283–302.

———. *Irrawaddy Tango.* New York: Knopf, 1993.

———. "Life in the Hills." *Atlantic* Dec. 1989: 4–28.

———. "The Year of the Pigeon." *Without a Guide: Contemporary Women's Travel Adventures.* Ed. Katherine Govier. Toronto: Macfarlane, 1994. 41–60.

Lay, Ma Ma. *Not out of Hate: A Novel of Burma.* Trans. Margaret Aung-Thwin. Introd. Anna Allott. Ed. William H. Frederick. Afterword Robert E. Vore. Monographs in Intl. Studies: Southeast Asia Ser. 88. Athens: Ohio U Center for Internatl. Studies, 1991.

Leach, Edmund R. *Political Systems of Highland Burma: A Study of Kachin Social Structure.* Cambridge: Harvard UP, 1954.

Lee, Rachel. "The Erasure of Places and Re-siting of Empire in Wendy Law-Yone's *The Coffin Tree.*" *Cultural Critique* 35 (1996–97): 149–78.

Lines of Fire. 1990. Videocassette. 62 min. (Available from Wong Audiovisual Center, University of Hawai'i, Manoa.)

Lwyn, Tinzar. "Stories of Gender and Ethnicity: Discourses of Colonialism and Resistance in Burma." *Women's Difference: Sexuality and Maternity in Colonial and Postcolonial Discourses.* Spec. issue of *Australian Journal of Anthropology* 5.1-2 (1994): 60–86.

Matsui, Yayori. *Women's Asia.* [In Japanese] Tokyo: Iwanami Shoten, 1987. [In English] London: Zeds, 1989.

Merrison, Lindsey. *Our Burmese Days.* Lindsey Merrison Film, 1996. 35mm. 90 mins. (Available by mail from Lindsey Merrison Film, Bissingzeile 11, D-10785, Berlin, Germany; by telephone at 49 30 262 13 87; or by e-mail at Merrison@aol.com.)

Milton, Edith. "Newcomers in New York." *New York Times Book Review* 15 May 1983: 12.

Monsky, Susan. Rev. of *The Coffin Tree,* by Wendy Law-Yone. *Boston Globe* 22 May 1983: A11+.

Mukherjee, Bharati. *Jasmine.* New York: Grove, 1989.

Muller, Helen J. "Women in Urban Burma: Social Issues and Political Dilemmas." *Women's Studies International Forum* 17 (1994): 609–20.

Nu, U. *Saturday's Son.* Trans. U Law-Yone. Ed. U Kyaw Win. New Haven: Yale UP, 1975.

Okell, John, with U Saw Tun and Daw Khin Mya Swe. *Burmese: An Introduction to the Script.* Southeast Asian Language Text Ser. DeKalb: Northern Illinois U, 1994.

Said, Edward W. *Orientalism.* New York: Vintage, 1979.

Silverstein, Josef, ed. *Independent Burma at Forty Years: Six Assessments.* Ithaca: Cornell Southeast Asia Program, 1989.

Smith, Martin. *Burma: Insurgency and the Politics of Ethnicity.* London: Zed, 1991.

Suu Kyi, Aung San. *"Freedom from Fear" and Other Writings.* Ed. and introd. Michael Aris. New York: Penguin, 1991.

Ward, Francis. *Burma's Icy Mountains.* London: Cape, 1949.

Win, Than Than. "Going to America: I Always Wear My Longyi (Adventures of a Burmese Woman in the United States)." *Images '93.* Spec. issue of *Asiaweek* 22–29 Dec. 1993: 64–75.

Yamashita, Karen. *Brazil-Maru.* Minneapolis: Coffee House, 1992.

Jasmine
by Bharati Mukherjee

Susan Koshy

Publication Information

First published in Canada by Viking (Markham, Ont.) in 1989; softcover edition published in 1991. First published in the United States by Grove Weidenfeld (New York) in 1989; softcover edition published in 1991.

Overview

The action of Bharati Mukherjee's *Jasmine* unfolds through the voice of the title character, who recounts the multiple transformations through which she has been reborn as Jane Ripplemeyer, a young Indian woman living with and pregnant by a middle-aged American banker. Jasmine begins her life as Jyoti, a Hindu village girl in the Indian state of Punjab, where the Sikh separatist demands for autonomy from a Hindu-majority state have escalated into violence. Jyoti falls in love with and marries Prakash, who renames her Jasmine. But just as they are about to leave for the United States, he is killed in a firebombing by Sukkhi, a Sikh terrorist. Widowed, Jasmine decides to complete Prakash's "mission" of traveling to America and then commit sati by immolating herself at the site of their American destination—a university in Florida. She travels with false papers to Tampa, where she is raped on the first night by Half-Face, a Vietnam veteran who traffics in illegal immigrants. Jasmine, ritually assuming the aspect of the Hindu goddess Kali, murders Half-Face. Her violent rebirth in America transforms her understanding of her mission, and she rejects suicide for a new beginning. She is helped by Linda Gordon, who aids undocumented women; with Linda's help she makes it to New York. After a claustrophobic stay with an Indian family, she begins work as an au pair for a white couple, Taylor and Wylie, taking care of their adopted child, Duff. When their marriage breaks up, Jasmine (now Jase) steps into Wylie's place. The cozy relationship breaks up when Jasmine flees to Iowa after being spotted by Sukkhi in the park. In Iowa, she finds a job in a bank where her boss, Bud Ripplemeyer, ravished by her beauty, abandons his wife of many years and moves in with her. He names her Jane. They adopt a Vietnamese boy named Du, but shortly after, Bud is paralyzed when he is shot by a farmer. Du leaves the Ripplemeyers to join his sister in California. Taylor follows Jasmine to Iowa and asks her to go with him to California, where with her unborn child and Duff, they can make a new life together. Jasmine agrees; she hurtles toward a new unknown.

Reception

Following closely on the publication of *"The Middleman" and Other Stories*, for which Mukherjee won the National Book Critics Circle Award, *Jasmine* has benefited from the acclaim of its predecessor. As a result, it has never been out of print, a fate meted out to *Darkness*, the fine but less well known collection of stories that preceded *"The Middleman."* *Jasmine* grew out of a short story of the same name in *"The Middleman,"* and it shares with that story and the collection an exuberance about assimilation. The novel's favorable reception is crucially linked to its celebration of assimilation, as well as to its American idiom, postmodern techniques, topicality, and glitziness, all of which serve to domesticate the largely unfamiliar ethnic identity represented in the fiction.

Mukherjee's life and career have spanned three countries—India, Canada, and the United States—and her fiction has found an audience in all three areas, although her reception has been quite different in each. Indian audiences have generally been more attentive to her earlier fiction because the setting and characters are based in or begin in India. Reviews of *Jasmine* have been more sporadic and critical and especially have questioned the terms of its American success. The book's Canadian reception remarks the disjunction between Mukherjee's hostility to Canadian multiculturalism and her celebration of United States assimilation and emphasizes the postcolonial provenance of her fiction.

Since Mukherjee has not had the popular success of a writer like Amy Tan, the university remains the primary arena for the interpretation and circulation of her writing. *Jasmine* is widely used in women's literature, American literature, and ethnic literature classes. In courses on Asian American literature, *Jasmine* is included because of its alertness to its American context and its incorporation of the experiences of other minority groups and because its affirmation of assimilation makes it a provocative choice for the syllabus.

Author's Biographical Background

Born in Calcutta in 1940, during the last decade of British rule, Bharati Mukherjee was one of three daughters from an upper-caste Hindu family. Her family was part of the bhadralok (respected or refined people), or the Bengali middle class, who occupied a distinctive and contradictory position under colonial rule, having been profoundly shaped by complex oppositions to and coalitions with colonial authority. Bengali-speaking at home, she received her early education in a missionary school and schools in Switzerland and England and became completely bilingual. On her return to India, she studied in Loreto House, an exclusive convent school run by Irish nuns; the devaluation of Bengali language and culture that was a product of this education led to her declining fluency in Bengali. She graduated with honors in English from Calcutta University in 1959 and completed her MA at Baroda University in 1961. The degree from Baroda offered Mukherjee an opportunity to renew her relationship to aspects of Indian culture within the framework of her literary studies—the master's degree in English required a master's in a regional Indian language or in ancient Indian culture. Mukherjee then left to do further graduate work in the United States, and she has since returned to India only for visits. She earned an MFA at the Iowa Writer's Workshop and a doctorate in English and comparative literature before taking up a teaching position at McGill University in Montreal. She lived in Canada from 1966 to 1978, a period when racist attacks against "visible minorities" were on the increase, an experience that she has written about with scathing irony in essays and short stories. Her major work during this period consists of two novels, *The Tiger's Daughter* (1972) and *Wife* (1975), and her memoirs of a one-year return visit to India, *Days and Nights in Calcutta* (with Clark Blaise, 1977). Two Canadian nonfiction pieces that indict the official policy of multiculturalism, "An Invisible Woman" (1981) and *The Sorrow and the Terror: The Haunting Legacy of the Air India Tragedy* (with Clark Blaise, 1987), an investigative report on the Air India bombing in which 323 people were killed, were written only after she had left Canada for the United States. In the United States, Mukherjee taught literature and creative writing at several colleges and universities before accepting a distinguished professorship at the University of California, Berkeley, where she now works. These years have been remarkably prolific ones for her. After a ten-year gap, Mukherjee returned to fiction with the collection *Darkness* (1985). In the much-quoted introduction to this book, she traces the transformative and enabling effects of her relocation to the United States. This book was followed by *"The Middleman" and Other Stories* (1988), which won her the National Book Critics Circle Award in the very year she became an American citizen; *Jasmine* (1989); *The Holder of the World* (1993); and *Leave It to Me* (1997).

Historical Context for the Narratives in *Jasmine*

While other Asian American novels like Joy Kogawa's *Obasan* and Maxine Hong Kingston's *China Men* reveal the erasures, artifices, and conventions of historical narrative, Mukherjee's *Jasmine* assumes the inscription of historical context to be much less problematic. An intensely compressed style and intercut vignettes situate the events in particular times and places: Punjab and the United States in the 1970s and 1980s.

The historical referentiality of the novel operates through journalistic images (rotting carcasses, terrorists), aphoristic statements, and jargon or insider talk ("non-ag use," "golfing boys" [23, 24]). Discussing the way these modes of discourse evoke a real world to which historical veracity attaches can offer students valuable insights into the genealogies that shape their reading practices.

For a lucid account of the Sikh separatist or Khalistan movement, see the works by Rajiv Kapur and T. N. Madan; Harjot Oberoi's discussion of the development of Sikh tradition in the nineteenth century is critical to understanding the dimensions of the present conflict. For readers unfamiliar with the broader context of Indian history, the selections from Ranajit Guha's *A Subaltern Studies Reader* provide a good starting point.

Major Themes

immigration as a form of reincarnation or rebirth of the self stressing disjuncture, violence, and renewal

assimilation as a two-way transaction between the mainstream and new immigrants

the underside of American immigration: refugees, middlemen, terrorists, undocumented workers

the postmodern geography of America inscribed as fluidity, transformation, and speed

revisions of archetypal American figures and topographies: pioneer, self-maker, conqueror; frontier, ghetto, heartland

the critique of imperialist feminisms: ironizing Jane Eyre; mainstream American feminism and the domestic labor of women of color

female power and the acts of sanctioned suicide (sati) and murder

romance as the idiom of cross-cultural encounter

Critical Issues

Mukherjee's *Jasmine* is the most frequently taught of her texts because it engages multiple intersecting discourses that have a curricular locus: postmodernism, feminism, postcolonialism, and multiculturalism (ethnic, immigrant, and diasporic writing). Moreover, *Jasmine* is a novel, the most accessible genre to students; it celebrates the "infinitely possible geography of America" (Raban 22); it provides a New World feminist heroine or, at least, an idea of the heroic; it translates the Third World through neat, ironic juxtapositions. However, its very assimilability (and this, indeed, is the subject of *Jasmine*) is precisely the problem—the source of the ambivalences in the text and the critical controversies it has generated. The conflicting possibilities contained in the text have their analogue in the representation of the heroine's own emergence—Jyoti/Jasmine/Kali/Jase/Jane is reborn at every stage when she cathects (or inhabits in response to a desire) the place of the "other" of a male fantasy. But Mukherjee represents such positioning as allowing for agency and as effecting a reciprocal transformation. It is important to note here that Jasmine's power is crucially linked to her exotic beauty, her ability to speak English, and the lack of referential density attaching to Indian ethnicity in the United States. Mukherjee's representation of assimilation is, thus, an optimistic one that elides asymmetry of power to celebrate the exceptional fate of a beautiful woman from India who manages without proper papers or much money to make it in America. The genres that support an inscription of this exceptional fate are the fable, fairy tale, romance, and novel, the ideological underpinnings of which offer a productive way to explore the scope and limits of such a fiction of America.

Since Jasmine's story is such an exceptional one from the perspective of the Asian Indian experience in the United States, some sociological information might help forestall the tendency among readers to turn *Jasmine* into a representative Asian Indian narrative. The Asian Indian community, which numbered over 800,000 in the 1990 census, will probably, by the time of the next census, be the third largest Asian American group. Geographically the Asian Indian population is fairly evenly dispersed, although concentrations have emerged in the Northeast (New York, New Jersey) and more recently in California. Most of the immigrants enter the country with, or are soon followed by, family members (this more typical trajectory is explored in *Wife*). The post-1965 Indian immigrants were largely part of the educated, urban, and English-speaking middle class in India and have formed an anomalous minority group that challenges the historic correlation between color and class in the United States (Koshy, "Category Crisis"). Many are highly educated professionals who work in medicine, engineering, and computer science, although there has been a trend since the 1990s toward greater occupational diversity and downward mobility. The changes in the American economy since the 1970s and the lower educational qualifications of sponsored family members partly account for these newer trends. Thus, although seventy to eighty percent of Asian Indian immigrants in the early 1970s were employed as professionals, that figure has dropped to just over forty percent among recent immigrants. Almost a third of the immigrants from India are from Punjab like Jasmine, many of them from families who fled to India when the state was divided between India and Pakistan during Partition in 1947.

The novel's celebration of American self-invention coexists with its critique of American self-reflexiveness, although the tone of celebration predominates. American provincialism, New Age spiritualism, and yuppie self-actualization are gently ironized; nativism and Vietnam-style imperialism are trenchantly anatomized. But the imaginative geography of America is everywhere marked by fluidity, transformation, and openness and newly inhabited by protean migrants (middlemen, refugees, terrorists, undocumented workers). Figured in all these respects as the space of modernity and the transnational, it holds out the seductive promise of new lives and unimagined prospects. However, the representation of America depends on a retrospective inscription of Jasmine's prior life within a counterspace signified as closed, "tradition"-bound, oppressive. To give this space the proper name Punjab and frame it within the opposition between the modern and the "traditional" is problematic, reinforcing as it does orientalist discursive constructions. Extending this discussion to Mukherjee's other uses of tradition in the context of ethnic identity formation also yields insights into the slippage between criticism and complicity in her texts.

Mukherjee's engagement with mainstream feminist versions of liberated female subjectivity in her text usually produces widely divergent readings among students about her critique of imperialist feminisms and Jasmine's status as a feminist heroine. Mukherjee clearly parodies Jane Eyre in casting the Third World woman as the governess and making the crippled Rochester/Ripplemeyer a way station in the Unplain Jane's Progress to better lives. Similarly, the professionalism of Wylie, the middle-class feminist, is shown to be built on the labor of illegal immigrants like Jasmine, however cozy the naming of these arrangements ("caregiver," "day-mummy" [175, 177]). But Jasmine's reincarnations manifest a growing individualism not altogether removed from liberal feminist positions, and her empowerment depends on her exotic sexuality to a degree that makes its feminist claims ambiguous. The most compelling interpretations of Mukherjee's *Jasmine* are able to address the ambivalence in her writing, an element that Mukherjee's own discussions of her texts leave unexamined.

Pedagogical Issues and Suggestions

Jasmine is seductively easy reading for many students, and this ease, in itself, opens up a rich area for investigation. Getting students to analyze how seduction operates as a theme and as a reader response will help them uncover the production of certain fictions of America (opportunity, mobility, transformation) and help them recognize the centrality of romance as a defining idiom of cross-cultural encounter in the text. Seduction also operates through the power of a first-person narrator who solicits identification on a number of levels. There is much less distance between author and narrator in this novel than in other Mukherjee stories; accordingly, *Jasmine* is more frequently the agent of the ironic perspective than it is its object. *Jasmine* also acts as a translator of Jasmine's prior life for her readers, simplifying and assimilating its difference within the framework of her American life.

Student responses to *Jasmine* tend to be polarized between those that praise Mukherjee's celebration of American possibility and those that decry her assimilationist position. As a way of thinking through such polarization, teachers and students might analyze how the text elicits such divergent interpretations and the extent to which such divergences emanate from assumptions about textual correspondence to or location in a "real" world.

It is important to note that Jasmine is neither a refugee nor an immigrant to the United States as is often assumed. Before Prakash's death, the couple planned to enter the United States as economic migrants. After his death, she plans to go to America and immolate herself over her husband's symbolic body (his suit) at the site of their former immigrant dreams. However, the force of the American mythology of immigration and Mukherjee's celebratory account of Jasmine's rebirth in this country lead some readers to cast her as another in a long line of hopeful immigrants. Rather than dismiss such readings, teachers and students may find it valuable to explore what produces them.

Intertextual Linkages

With Mukherjee's short story "Jasmine": seduction as a metaphor for Americanization; mainstream feminism and the politics of caregiving.

With Mukherjee's novel *Wife*: suicide, murder, and female subjectivity; female power and kinship inscriptions; ethnic identity and ghettoization.

With Maxine Hong Kingston's *The Woman Warrior*: the tension between ethnic identity and feminism; assimilation as narrative resolution; the popularity of both texts and the critical controversies over their reception.

With Jamaica Kincaid's *Lucy*: anthropologizing American family relationships; the au pair as inside/outside the home; irony and point of view.

With Charlotte Brontë's *Jane Eyre* and Jean Rhys's *Wide Sargasso Sea*: *Jane Eyre* and its postcolonial renarrations; the female bildungsroman and the ideology of romance; feminism and racial difference.

Bibliographic Resources

Mukherjee has given several interviews in which she discusses her vision of immigration and her positionality as a writer; in one of these she focuses specifically on *Jasmine* ("Interview" [1990]). The introduction to *Darkness* encapsulates many of the ideas that recur in the interviews.

Critical writing on Mukherjee is extensive, and articles on *Jasmine*, in particular, are numerous. The single collection of criticism on Mukherjee's writing is useful, if uneven in quality (Nelson).

Other Resources

See "Conquering America with Bharati Mukherjee," an interview with Bill Moyers for the series *World of Ideas*.

Bibliography

Alam, Fakrul. *Bharati Mukherjee*. New York: Twayne, 1996.

Aneja, Anu. "*Jasmine*, the Sweet Scent of Exile." *Pacific Coast Philology* 28.1 (1993): 72–80.

Brewster, Anne. "A Critique of Bharati Mukherjee's Neo-nationalism." *SPAN* 34-35 (1992–93): 50–59.

Brontë, Charlotte. *Jane Eyre*. New York: Norton, 1987.

Carter-Sanborn, Kristin. "'We Murder Who We Were': *Jasmine* and the Violence of Identity." *American Literature* 66 (1994): 573–93.

Chua, C. L. "Passages from India: Migrating to America in the Fiction of V. S. Naipaul and Bharati Mukherjee." *Reworlding: The Literature of the Indian Diaspora*. Ed. Emmanuel S. Nelson. New York: Greenwood, 1992. 51–62.

Crane, Ralph J. "Of Shattered Pots and Sinkholes: (Female) Identity in Bharati Mukherjee's *Jasmine*." *SPAN* 36 (1993): 122–30.

Davé, Shilpa. "The Doors to Home and History: Post-colonial Identities in Meena Alexander and Bharati Mukherjee." *Amerasia Journal* 19.3 (1993): 103–13.

Grewal, Inderpal. "Reading and Writing the South Asian Diaspora: Feminism and Nationalism in North America." *Our Feet Walk the Sky: Women of the South Asian Diaspora*. Ed. Women of South Asian Descent Collective. San Francisco: Aunt Lute, 1993. 226–36.

Guha, Ranajit, ed. *A Subaltern Studies Reader, 1986–1995*. Minneapolis: U of Minnesota P, 1997.

Hawley, John C. "Assimilation and Resistance in Female Fiction of Immigration: Bharati Mukherjee, Amy Tan, and Christine Bell." *Rediscovering America, 1492–1992: National, Cultural, and Disciplinary Boundaries Re-examined*. Baton Rouge: Louisiana State UP, 1992. 226–34.

Kapur, Rajiv A. *Sikh Separatism: The Politics of Faith*. London: Allen, 1986.

Kehde, Suzanne. "Colonial Discourse and Female Identity: Bharati Mukherjee's *Jasmine*." *International Women's Writing: New Landscapes of Identity*. Ed. Anne E. Brown. Westport: Greenwood, 1995. 70–77.

Kincaid, Jamaica. *Lucy*. New York: Farrar, 1990.

Kingston, Maxine Hong. *The Woman Warrior: Memoirs of a Girlhood among Ghosts*. New York: Knopf, 1976.

Koshy, Susan. "Category Crisis: South Asian Americans and Questions of Race and Ethnicity." *Diaspora* 7.3 (1998): 285–320.

———. "The Geography of Female Subjectivity: Ethnicity, Gender, and Diaspora." *Diaspora* 3.1 (1994): 69–84.

Low, Gail Ching-liang. "In a Free State: Postcolonialism and Postmodernism in Bharati Mukherjee's Fiction." *Women: A Cultural Review* 4.1 (1993): 8–17.

Madan, T. N. "The Double-Edged Sword: Fundamentalism and the Sikh Religious Tradition." *Fundamentalisms Observed*. Ed. Martin E. Marty and R. Scott Appleby. Chicago: U of Chicago P, 1991. 594–627.

Mukherjee, Bharati. "Bharati Mukherjee: An Interview." By Runar Vignisson. *SPAN* 34-35 (1992–93): 153–68.

———. "Conquering America with Bharati Mukherjee." Interview with Bill Moyers. *World of Ideas*. Videocassette. Princeton: Films for the Humanities, 1994.

———. *Darkness*. New York: Penguin, 1985.

———. *The Holder of the World*. New York: Knopf, 1993.

———. "An Interview with Bharati Mukherjee." By Alison B. Carb. *Massachusetts Review* 29 (1988): 645–54.

———. "An Interview with Bharati Mukherjee." By Geoff Hancock. *Canadian Fiction Magazine* 59 (1987): 30–44.

———. "An Interview with Bharati Mukherjee." *Iowa Review* 20.3 (1990): 7–32.

———. "An Invisible Woman." *Saturday Night* Mar. 1981: 36–40.

———. "Jasmine." "*Middleman*" 123–35.

———. *Jasmine*. New York: Grove, 1989.

———. *Leave It to Me*. New York: Knopf, 1997.

———. "*The Middleman*" *and Other Stories*. New York: Grove, 1988.

———. *The Tiger's Daughter*. Boston: Houghton, 1972.

———. *Wife*. Boston: Houghton, 1975.

Mukherjee, Bharati, and Clark Blaise. *Days and Nights in Calcutta*. Garden City: Double-day, 1977. Rev. ed. Markham, Ont.: Viking, 1986.

———. *The Sorrow and the Terror: The Haunting Legacy of the Air India Tragedy*. Markham, Ont.: Viking, 1987.

Nelson, Emmanuel S., ed. *Bharati Mukherjee: Critical Perspectives*. New York: Garland, 1993.

Oberoi, Harjot. *The Construction of Religious Boundaries: Culture, Identity, and Diversity in the Sikh Tradition*. Chicago: U of Chicago P, 1994.

Raban, Jonathan. Rev. of "*The Middleman*" *and Other Stories*, by Bharati Mukherjee. *New York Times Book Review* 19 June 1988: 1+.

Rhys, Jean. *Wide Sargasso Sea*. New York: Penguin, 1968.

Shankar, Lavina Dhingra. "Activism, 'Feminisms,' and Americanization in Bharati Mukherjee's *Wife* and *Jasmine*." *Hitting Critical Mass: A Journal of Asian American Cultural Criticism* 3.1 (1995): 61–84.

Tapping, Craig. "South Asia Writes North America: Prose Fictions and Autobiographies from the Indian Diaspora." *Reading the Literatures of Asian America*. Ed. Shirley Geok-lin Lim and Amy Ling. Philadelphia: Temple UP, 1992. 285–301.

Wickramagamage, Carmen. "Relocation as Positive Act: The Immigrant Experience in Bharati Mukherjee's Novels." *Diaspora* 2.2 (1992): 171–200.

All I Asking for Is My Body

by Milton Murayama

Stephen H. Sumida

Publication Information

Publishers either rejected the three-part manuscript of the novel, the first part of
which, "I'll Crack Your Head Kotsun," had appeared as a short story in the *Arizona
Quarterly* in 1959, or recommended that Murayama correct his English, beginning with
the title, *All I Asking for Is My Body*, to eliminate his uses of pidgin and Hawai'i
creole that he was told would alienate mainstream readers. Murayama and Dawn Pyne
responded by publishing the novel themselves and naming their outfit Supa Press, after
their "super" dog. The first Supa Press printing of two thousand copies in 1975 was
followed by three more, from 1976 to 1981, that produced another eleven thousand
copies. As the pace of orders slowed and the filling of them came to feel burdensome,
Murayama and Pyne began in 1982 to deal only with exceptional requests for copies,
until only a dozen remained. *All I Asking for Is My Body*, however, continued to circulate in the mid-1980s through the used-book trade and other means for supplying
copies to students taking courses that included the text. In 1988 the University of
Hawai'i Press reprinted *All I Asking for Is My Body* with an afterword by Franklin Odo.
The work continues to be available from that press.

Overview

The history of the novel's publication suggests the wry humor as well as the sense of
cultural agency that runs through the work—a sense that Murayama and those he
could count on would produce and disseminate the book themselves, in the languages
of the experiences narrated, even if no one else would. Set in Hawai'i during the 1930s
and early 1940s, *All I Asking for Is My Body* is a comedy that ends in a happy turn of
the plot, even though a good portion of it concerns issues of racial and class oppression

and struggle that remain unresolved beyond the close of the story. Yet it is not an assimilationist work: it neither assumes nor promotes the idea that attaining success and happiness for the American-born Nisei requires submission to the rules and standards of a dominant "American" culture. The dominance of America in the characters' lives is, meanwhile, manifest everywhere. It is present in the physical layout, the social organization, and the economic controls imposed by the Frontier Mill sugar plantation, an American institution that exploits the labor mainly of Japanese and Filipino American laborers of that era. Kiyo, the first-person narrator of All I Asking for Is My Body, moves from childhood obliviousness to an awareness of the injustices of the plantation system. He observes but does not comprehend some of the effects of these injustices on his own family. Later he begins to understand and reject the wrongs that have trapped the workers generally, and his family in particular, within spirals of debt that have forced them to perpetuate the giving of their labor, their bodies, to the plantation.

All I Asking for Is My Body is made up of three sections: two short sketches followed by a novella-length final section. Part 1, "I'll Crack Your Head Kotsun," tells of Kiyo's relationship with an older Japanese boy, Makot (Makoto), whose mother is a prostitute serving the plantation laborers in the "camps." Kiyo's parents disapprove of the friendship, to the bewilderment of the young narrator.

Kiyo narrates part 2, "The Substitute," as an unexamined account of the characters' dialogically diverse religious and spiritual affiliations and skepticisms. While Kiyo at first questions his mother's beliefs, he finds comfort in one of them when a revered elder, Obaban (his "granny," who is actually his great aunt), dies of a stroke and thus "substitutes" for his mother in death.

The first two parts of the novel establish the close bonds among family members, even when they argue. Part 3, "All I Asking for Is My Body," is punctuated by fights between Toshio, who is Kiyo's older brother and the family's chonan or number one son, and their parents. Mother insists that it is Tosh's filial duty to "repay" the still-growing monetary debt they incurred when she and Father "gave" Grandfather all their savings upon his return to Japan in the early 1920s. Tosh counters that the debt is Grandfather's—that Grandfather "stole" the money—and that it is not the children's or grandchildren's duty to "repay" it. Tosh and Kiyo are not allowed to enroll in high school and aim for better-paying jobs; they must work on the plantation to support the family, and they have nursed their mother during a protracted illness. Thus, Tosh argues, they have not received the "piety from the parent to the children" (42) that would theoretically be their parents' basis for asking the children to "repay" the debt.

Despite protests, Tosh acts in a consistently "filial" way. After the United States enters World War II, he marries, settles into the raising of his own family on the plantation, and regularly turns over to his parents all his wife's wages and a third of his own from their manual labor on the plantation. It is the plantation bosses' dream come true, the perpetuation of a labor supply for them. In part 3 Kiyo tries to come to terms with these conflicts and to see them not as intercultural clashes but as problems of justice and injustice; he realizes that he must criticize subservience and not go along with it "no matter how lovingly it was dished." In January 1943, when the United States Army asks for volunteers to form an all-Nisei regiment, Kiyo joins, partly to get away from home and partly to make money to send home. In the last scene, Kiyo wins big in a crap game in the barracks and sends $6,000 to Tosh to pay up the family debt: "Take care of the body. See you after the war" (103).

Reception

Shortly after publishing *All I Asking for Is My Body*, Murayama was invited to deliver readings at book signings in Hawai'i, both at bookstores and at sites associated with the history and communities of the plantations. Thus his peers and contemporaries, Murayama thinks, accounted directly or indirectly for much of the exuberant initial demand for the book (Telephone interview). Interestingly, while the novel is an earthy critique of the plantation system, Murayama's generation (and the next) warmly considered the novel a major recognition rather than a repudiation of their and their forebears' experiences. This reception itself shows how, by the 1970s, the sugar plantations of Hawai'i had become objects of nostalgia for those who had left them for middle-class lives.

But the appeal of the novel was by no means limited to that generation in Hawai'i. In 1976, Murayama participated in the Pacific Northwest Asian American Writers' Conference in Seattle, where he not only read from his novel but also spoke about his strategies for writing in mixed languages. In 1978, he similarly took part in Talk Story: Hawai'i's Ethnic American Writers' Conference in Honolulu, at a time when his novel was one of the most prominent works in print of an Asian American literature of Hawai'i. The book has appeared in American literature courses of various kinds. Murayama recalls that from 1975 to 1982 book orders came from the University of Hawai'i; the University of California, Berkeley; the University of California, Santa Barbara; Washington State University; the University of Washington; and Temple University (Telephone interview). A critic's characterization of *All I Asking for Is My Body* as "an underground classic" is controverted by the work's reception as well as by its stylistic and thematic features (Wilson, Review 2). According to an editor for the University of Hawai'i Press, demand for the novel continues to run high.

Author's Biographical Background

Milton Murayama's early life resembles the life of Kiyo, the narrator in the novel. Murayama grew up in the coastal town of Lahaina (the fictional Pepelau in the novel) and the upcountry plantation "camp," or village, of Pu'ukoli'i (which he calls Kahana in the novel) on the island of Maui. He served in the Military Intelligence Service (MIS) of the United States Army from 1944 to 1946. The intensive training in and use of Japanese that this work called for stirred Murayama's interest in Japanese culture.

He had enrolled at the University of Hawai'i, intending to major in English, in 1941. Using the GI Bill that funded veterans' educations, he emerged from military service and resumed his studies, earning a bachelor's degree in English from the University of Hawai'i and completing a master's degree in Japanese and Chinese at Columbia University from 1948 to 1952.

Murayama states that his writing of fiction was unaffected by the fact that the Nisei veterans of the MIS were classified, forbidden to speak of their service and their unit (until 1975). John Okada, the author of the novel *No-No Boy* (1957), also served in the MIS and, like Murayama, attended Columbia University in the postwar years. The two never met, as far as Murayama can recall (Telephone interview). After moving to San Francisco, Murayama got a job with the United States Customs Service that left him free to read and write at night. He is now retired but continues to write. In 1994 the University of Hawai'i Press published his *Five Years on a Rock*, a novel narrated by Sawa Oyama, the mother in *All I Asking for Is My Body*. His third novel, *Plantation Boy*, narrated by Kiyo's older brother, Tosh, was published in 1998. In the years since the publication of the first book in the series in 1975, Murayama's projects have also included the drama "Yoshitsune" (1977), based on the historic Japanese figure, and a staged version of *All I Asking for Is My Body*.

Historical Context for the Narratives in *All I Asking for Is My Body*

The importation of contract labor from Japan to sugar plantations in Hawai'i commenced in 1885. Under their contracts, the workers were each to give three years of labor to the plantation. Sugar planters managed to forestall the formation of labor unions and to squash strikes through the 1920s and 1930s, the decades of labor unrest to which the novel alludes.

Practices of "divide and rule" are evident from the very beginning of the novel, when Kiyo notes that Makot's Japanese family was the only one to live in "Filipino Camp." He goes on to realize that the organization of housing by ethnicities, the inequalities of pay, and the assignment of status by race serve to divide the exploited.

The polyethnicity of the plantation does not constitute a racial paradise in Murayama's novel. Neither is it idyllic in history. Led by contemporary European theories of race, efforts had been expended in the nineteenth century to find "cognate races" of peoples both to labor on the plantations and to repopulate the islands, since native Hawai'ians were grievously diminished in number by exposure to diseases foreign to them before the arrival of Captain James Cook and his crew in 1778. In *All I Asking for Is My Body* there are allusions to workers, former workers, and field bosses among whom are natives, immigrants, and offspring of native Hawai'ians, Chinese, Japanese, Portuguese, Spanish, Puerto Rican, Korean, and Filipino peoples, while the plantation manager, Mr. Nelson, is an Anglo-American privileged to hold that status along with the Scots and Germans managing other plantations. Integral to *All I Asking for Is My Body* is the immigration of Japanese families rather than males alone. The sugar planters sought to import and then keep families on the plantations so that the children brought to Hawai'i or born there would themselves become laborers. This motive underlying the paternalism of the plantation is important to an understanding of Tosh's—and later Kiyo's—views (Sumida, *View* 290n13).

A second major historical context for and in the novel is the Japanese bombing of Pearl Harbor on 7 December 1941 and its consequences for families such as the Oyamas. While the bombing shocks Kiyo, awareness of Japan's warmongering develops earlier in the story, where we learn that in their respective ways Father and Tosh follow the news of Japan's invasion of China during the 1930s. One of Tosh's responses is to cancel his and Kiyo's dual citizenship with Japan, an arrangement Japanese immigrants made through their consulate to enable their American-born children to assume Japanese citizenship if necessary. This concern reflected the fact that Japanese and other Asian immigrants were prevented by the laws of the United States from becoming naturalized Americans. Given their precarious legal status, the immigrants tried to equip their children with Japanese language skills and dual citizenship in case they had to leave America. By the time of the Japanese attack, however, the second generation of Japanese Americans in Hawai'i had come to recognize their own American citizenship and birthrights. Nowhere does Kiyo question his loyalty to an ideal of America, although he criticizes the practices of the plantation. Unlike Ichiro and others in Okada's *No-No Boy*, Kiyo never sees a need to prove his American citizenship by enlisting, because by birth he is an American citizen. The declaration of war with Japan opens the way for Kiyo to join the United States Army. The plantation cannot stop him and his peers from doing so. By this means Kiyo escapes the plantation that held him and his parents in bondage—in, as he puts it, the "icky shit hole" (98).

Historical Context for the Writing of *All I Asking for Is My Body*

The publication of Asian American literature of Hawai'i in English dates back to the early 1900s. In the 1920s and early 1930s, writers—mainly university students who published their works in yearbooks—occasionally devoted their attention to stories with local Hawai'i settings, themes, histories, and sometimes, pidgin and creole languages. Drama and fiction in the vernaculars of Hawai'i grew in extent through the next four decades (Murayama's "I'll Crack Your Head Kotsun" being an excellent example of an individual contribution to this history). *All I Asking for Is My Body*, while written and published in San Francisco, arrived in Hawai'i and contributed to this literary history. But in 1975 and for three years afterward, neither Murayama nor his readers in Hawai'i knew much if anything at all about that history. Rather, it was *All I Asking for Is My Body* that was among the inspirations for further writing in the vernaculars of Hawai'i and for the research that uncovered a literary history of Asian Americans in Hawai'i. The novel marks a cultural and literary coming of age, so to speak, empowered by a political rise of the Nisei of Hawai'i that surged in the 1950s when veterans educated in law and other professions through the GI Bill of Rights— as presumably could have happened to Kiyo—took steps to effect political and social change.

Major Themes

class struggle in relation to race and ethnicity

relationships among members of an immigrant generation and between that generation and the next

the chonan, or number one son, in Japanese American literature (as well as the jinan, or number two son)

the construction and perpetuation of culture and identity under the influence of the characters' actions, poverty, debt, lack of political power, and nationalisms

education and literacy

vernacular diversity and its functions

the effects of the bombing of Pearl Harbor on residents of Hawai'i

an insider's view of a seemingly common family

devotion to family and to the resolution of its central problems

Critical Issues

Like John Okada's *No-No Boy* and other works of Asian American literature, *All I Asking for Is My Body* depends in its reading on how one applies questions that arise from historical contexts that oftentimes are not known to the general reader. In Murayama's novel, the questions inhere in the novel itself but may be unexpected and thus unasked—unexpected, for example, because a reader may mimic the naive narrator and through most of the novel fail to question what is being told about a childhood prejudged to be idyllic in Hawai'i. Realizing the immaturity and naïveté of the narrator is especially crucial when one reads part 1, where Kiyo perceives but fails to adequately interpret certain realities about camp life, such as the ethnic segregation of plantation workers or the poverty and oppression that ironically make the most affluent member of the camp a prostitute. At critical junctures in parts 2 and 3, Kiyo presents Tosh's version of the Oyama family history and their mother's version of how the family has accumulated a $6,000 debt. These histories, along with the structure of the novel and Tosh's own decision to fulfill family obligations in spite of all his griping, raise questions about filial duty that both Tosh and Kiyo explicitly ask their parents and the teacher of the camp's Japanese language school. Questions that students and teachers ought to ask when reading the novel include the following: Why do the parents insist that

135

filial obedience is owed without question by a "Japanese" child, whereas Mother reveres Obaban, who came in exile to Hawai'i because she was disobedient? Do cultural generalizations about the Issei—a term that literally means the "first Japanese American generation" and not the last Japanese one—hold true in this novel, when not only is Obaban a "black sheep" but Father and Mother have joined the Methodist church? What is "Japanese"? If Tosh and Kiyo were able somehow to proffer the money to fill the hole created when Mother and Father "repaid" their filial debt to Grandfather, then will Mother and Father have "paid" any net sum at all? What does this inheritance of a debt mean in terms of filial piety, and how did it become incurred? Why does Tosh fulfill those filial obligations he can fulfill? Is he a hypocrite? Is his objection specifically against his paying Grandfather's debt to Mother and Father? What does the novel's ending achieve? What issues does it not affect?

Pedagogical Issues and Suggestions

To reach beyond superficial and preconceived responses to *All I Asking for Is My Body* (as enjoyable and indeed important as such initial responses may be in the experience of reading this novel), teachers may find that posing clusters of questions constitutes a useful pedagogical strategy. Begin by examining the way readers are responding to the narrator in part 1. Is the narrator reliable? How can you tell? What limits define the narrative point of view? How does Murayama use these limits? These questions about narrative strategy and character are tied to a question about the plot: What is happening at the end of "I'll Crack Your Head Kotsun" and why? What is "funny about Makot" (1)? Why do some readers initially grasp the subtext beneath the naive narration while others do not? What are some implications of such discrepancies or ironies, not only among characters but also among readers?

In part 2, examine Kiyo's relationship with his parents—especially his mother—and with his mother's and Obaban's beliefs. How do relationships between parents and children in the Oyama family compare with relationships depicted earlier, in part 1, including that between Makot and his parents?

In part 3, many of the questions asked above, under Critical Issues, come into play. Because the concept of filial piety becomes emphatic in part 3, teachers need to clarify this concept either through commentary or questions and responses. Ideally, filial piety is, as Tosh charges, the repayment children make to their parents for the care and upbringing the parents have given them. The concept implies reciprocity (a number of other thematically important principles in this novel are similarly reciprocal or are interventions breaking bad cycles). But what if the parents have not provided for, or have not been able to provide for, the raising of their children? What education have Tosh and Kiyo received? Why? Who cared for Mother and the rest of the family, in part 2, when she was ill for a year? What has been the family's educational history, and how is that history relevant to what the family is undergoing now? How does the plantation affect the parents' assertions about filial piety in the Oyama family? How is the plantation affected by these questions and conflicts—and the debt—within the family?

Intertextual Linkages

With Carlos Bulosan's *America Is in the Heart*: proletarian literature; comparisons of conditions of work in Hawai'i and the American West for two Asian American groups of contract laborers and their societies; narratives of labor strikes and attempts to form unions.

With John Okada's *No-No Boy*: comparisons among characters' views of the effects of World War II and perceived associations of Japanese American characters with Japanese culture and nationalism; comparative treatments of assimilation, resistance, cultural agency, and identity, where the principal characters in *All I Asking for Is My Body* are neither depressed nor driven by an assimilationist view of their lives.

With Hisaye Yamamoto's "Yoneko's Earthquake" and "Seventeen Syllables": especially in the former, the use of a naive narrative point of view to disclose a "mature" subtext; also comparisons with Yamamoto's, Toshio Mori's, and Wakako Yamauchi's narratives of pre–World War II Japanese America.

With Monica Sone's *Nisei Daughter*, John Okada's *No-No Boy*, Louis Chu's *Eat a Bowl of Tea*, Frank Chin's *The Year of the Dragon* and *Donald Duk*, Maxine Hong Kingston's *The Woman Warrior*, Joy Kogawa's *Obasan*, and others: roles, expectations, and aspirations of oldest sons and daughters as interpreted in and through Asian American literature.

With Kazuo Miyamoto's *Hawaii: End of the Rainbow*: comparison between Murayama's rendition of the bildungsroman genre with Miyamoto's use of epic concepts in writing fiction based on plantation histories of Hawai'i.

With Darrell H. Y. Lum's stories and dramas in *Sun: Short Stories and Drama* and *Pass On, No Pass Back!* and Lois-Ann Yamanaka's *Saturday Night at the Pahala Theatre* and *Wild Meat and the Bully Burgers*: uses of pidgin and Hawai'i creole in contemporary literature.

With Juliet S. Kono's *Hilo Rains* and *Tsunami Years*, Sylvia Watanabe's *"Talking to the Dead" and Other Stories*, and Marie Hara's *"Bananaheart" and Other Stories*: uses of pidgin and creole; narratives and lyrics touching on spiritual beliefs and questions about them, in comparison especially to part 2 of Murayama's novel.

Bibliographic Resources

For historical background about Hawai'ian plantations, see the works by Ronald Takaki and Gary Okihiro. Novels on the lives and histories of Japanese contract laborers on sugar plantations of Hawai'i include Shelley Ota's *Upon Their Shoulders* and Margaret Harada's *The Sun Shines on the Immigrant*.

The most extensive critical analysis published to date on *All I Asking for Is My Body* is in Stephen Sumida's *And the View from the Shore: Literary Traditions of Hawai'i*. This analysis takes into consideration criticism by Rob Wilson and Arnold Hiura. See also Murayama's published comments about writing the novel, and see the afterword by Franklin Odo to the current edition of *All I Asking for Is My Body*. Further studies of Murayama's novels are under way in the addressing of such topics as polyethnic cultural contexts of Hawai'i and literary treatments of education, literacy, race, and class. See, for instance, Morris Young's dissertation.

Bibliography

Bulosan, Carlos. *America Is in the Heart*. 1946. Seattle: U of Washington P, 1973.

Chin, Frank. The Chickencoop Chinaman *and* The Year of the Dragon: *Two Plays*. Seattle: U of Washington P, 1981.

———. *Donald Duk*. Minneapolis: Coffee House, 1991.

Chock, Eric, and Jody Manabe, eds. *Writers of Hawai'i: A Focus on Our Literary Heritage*. Honolulu: Bamboo Ridge, 1981.

Chu, Louis. *Eat a Bowl of Tea*. 1961. New York: Stuart, 1986.

Hara, Marie. *"Bananaheart" and Other Stories*. Honolulu: Bamboo Ridge, 1994.

Harada, Margaret N. *The Sun Shines on the Immigrant*. New York: Vantage, 1960.

Hiura, Arnold. "Comments on Milton Murayama." Chock and Manabe 65–67.

Hiura, Arnold T., and Stephen H. Sumida. *Asian American Literature of Hawai'i: An Annotated Bibliography*. Honolulu: Japanese Amer. Research Center and Talk Story, 1979.

Kim, Elaine H. *Asian American Literature: An Introduction to the Writings and Their Social Context*. Philadelphia: Temple UP, 1982.

Kingston, Maxine Hong. *The Woman Warrior: Memoirs of a Girlhood among Ghosts*. New York: Knopf, 1976.

Kogawa, Joy. *Obasan*. Boston: Godine, 1982.

Kono, Juliet S. *Hilo Rains*. Honolulu: Bamboo Ridge, 1988.

———. *Tsunami Years*. Honolulu: Bamboo Ridge, 1995.

Lum, Darrell H. Y. *Pass On, No Pass Back!* Honolulu: Bamboo Ridge, 1991.

———. *Sun: Short Stories and Drama*. Honolulu: Bamboo Ridge, 1979.

Miyamoto, Kazuo. *Hawai'i: The End of the Rainbow*. Rutland: Tuttle, 1964.

Mori, Toshio. *Yokohama, California*. Introd. Lawson Fusao Inada. Seattle: U of Washington P, 1985.

Murayama, Milton. *All I Asking for Is My Body*. San Francisco: Supa, 1975. Afterword Franklin Odo. Honolulu: U of Hawai'i P, 1988.

———. *Five Years on a Rock*. Honolulu: U of Hawai'i P, 1994.

———. "I'll Crack Your Head Kotsun." *Arizona Quarterly* 15 (1959): 137–49. Rpt. in *The Spell of Hawai'i*. Ed. A. Grove Day and Carl Stroven. New York: Meredith, 1968. 323–25.

———. Letter to Darrell H. Y. Lum. *Bamboo Ridge: The Hawai'i Writers' Quarterly* 5 (1979): 6–7.

———. "A Novel, Untitled, Part I: *Five Years on a Rock.*" *Seattle Review: Blue Funnel Line* 9 (1988): 150–55.

———. *Plantation Boy.* Honolulu: U of Hawai'i P, 1998.

———. "Problems of Writing in Dialect and Mixed Languages." *Bamboo Ridge: The Hawai'i Writers' Quarterly* 5 (1979): 8–10.

———. Telephone interview. 22 July 1996.

———. "Yoshitsune." Typescript. 1977.

Okada, John. *No-No Boy.* 1957. Seattle: U of Washington P, 1979.

Okihiro, Gary Y. *Cane Fires: The Anti-Japanese Movement in Hawai'i, 1865–1945.* Philadelphia: Temple UP, 1991.

Ota, Shelley Ayame Nishimura. *Upon Their Shoulders.* New York: Exposition, 1951.

Richie, Donald. "Life as a Japanese-American in Wartime Hawai'i." *Japan Times* 25 Feb. 1989: 14.

———. "Trapped on Distant Shores." *Japan Times* 18 Apr. 1995: 18.

Shinn, Christopher A. "Sawa's Story: An Immigrant Woman in Hawai'i." *International Examiner Literary Supplement* Fall 1995: 2.

Sone, Monica. *Nisei Daughter.* 1953. Seattle: U of Washington P, 1979.

Sumida, Stephen H. *And the View from the Shore: Literary Traditions of Hawai'i.* Seattle: U of Washington P, 1991.

———. "Japanese American Moral Dilemmas in John Okada's *No-No Boy* and Milton Murayama's *All I Asking for Is My Body.*" *Frontiers of Asian American Studies: Writing, Research, and Criticism.* Pullman: Washington State UP, 1989. 222–33.

Takaki, Ronald. *Pau Hana: Plantation Life and Labor in Hawai'i, 1835–1920.* Honolulu: U of Hawai'i P, 1983.

Trask, Haunani-Kay. *From a Native Daughter: Colonialism and Sovereignty in Hawai'i.* Monroe: Common Courage, 1993.

Watanabe, Sylvia. *"Talking to the Dead" and Other Stories.* New York: Doubleday, 1993.

Wilson, Rob. Rev. of *All I Asking for Is My Body*, by Milton Murayama. *Bamboo Ridge: The Hawai'i Writers' Quarterly* 5 (1979–1980): 2–5.

———. "The Language of Confinement and Liberation in Milton Murayama's *All I Asking for Is My Body.*" Chock and Manabe 62–65.

Wong, Sau-ling Cynthia. *Reading Asian American Literature: From Necessity to Extravagance.* Princeton: Princeton UP, 1993.

Yamamoto, Hisaye. "Seventeen Syllables." Yamamoto, *"Seventeen Syllables"* 8–19.

———. *"Seventeen Syllables" and Other Stories.* Albany: Kitchen Table, 1988.

———. "Yoneko's Earthquake." Yamamoto, *"Seventeen Syllables"* 46–56.

Yamanaka, Lois-Ann. *Saturday Night at the Pahala Theatre.* Honolulu: Bamboo Ridge, 1993.

———. *Wild Meat and the Bully Burgers.* New York: Farrar, 1996.

Yamauchi, Wakako. *And the Soul Shall Dance. Between Worlds: Contemporary Asian-American Plays.* Ed. Misha Berson. New York: Theatre Communications, 1990. 128–74.

———. "Songs My Mother Taught Me." *Amerasia Journal* 3.2 (1976): 63–73.

Young, Morris S. H. "Literacy, Legitimacy, and the Composing of Asian American Citizenship." Diss. U of Michigan, 1997.

No-No Boy
by John Okada

Jinqi Ling

Publication Information

First published by Charles E. Tuttle, Rutherford, Vermont, and Tokyo, Japan, in 1957. Out of print in the United States until 1976, when the second edition was issued by the Combined Asian American Resources Project, Seattle and San Francisco, in softcover. Third edition published by the University of Washington Press in 1979 in softcover; eight printings released by 1993. Widely available.

Overview

The plot of *No-No Boy* revolves around the painful search for a Japanese American identity by Ichiro Yamada, a twenty-five-year-old Nisei (American-born, second generation), who was imprisoned for refusing to serve in the United States military during World War II. Before Ichiro's imprisonment, he and his family—both parents and a younger brother—had been interned in a relocation camp under Executive Order 9066 (issued on 19 February 1942). The novel begins with Ichiro's release from the federal penitentiary and his eager return to the Japanese American community in Seattle. But the moment Ichiro arrives home, he is caught between two opposing forces that repeatedly foreground the irresolvable nature of his identity crisis. On the one hand, Nisei who agreed to serve in the United States Army during the war treat him with contempt and hostility, seeing his refusal to fight as a failure to prove himself "American"; on the other, his Issei (first-generation immigrant) mother supports his draft resistance in terms that not only ignore his own feelings but also confirm the misperception that his decision was motivated by his loyalty to Japan. These extreme attitudes in the Japanese American community show that the home Ichiro returns to is no less divided than his split self, a situation that intensifies rather than alleviates his originary identity crisis. In the novel, three characters exert strong influence on Ichiro's search for answers to his moral dilemma: Kenji, a war veteran who is suffering from a terminal case of gangrene in his leg and who is sympathetic with no-no boys; his pro-Japanese mother, who finally commits suicide as a result of her rigid resistance to racial discrimination; and Emi, a Nisei woman abandoned by her husband, who shows compassion for Ichiro through love, understanding, and pragmatic advice. In comparison with Kenji and his mother, both of whom die in the course of the novel's development, Emi is instrumental in shaping Ichiro's perception of his past as a no-no boy, of his "mistake" in resisting the draft, and of his relationship with a society that remains indifferent to Japanese Americans' wartime sufferings. At the end of the novel Ichiro reconciles with his past and gains an ambiguous new hope for a better future.

Reception

Neither the literary establishment nor the postwar Japanese American community welcomed *No-No Boy* when it was published in 1957. By the time Okada died in 1971, the novel's first edition of only fifteen hundred copies had not yet sold out (Chin et al. xxxvi). Several factors may have contributed to the literary establishment's lack of interest in Okada's work. First, critics tend to see Asian American literary writing as sociological documentation of "Japanese" culture, and consequently they are unable to recognize the literary value of Okada's novel. Second, the rhetorical strategies and linguistic innovations in Okada's work enabled it to find a publisher, but its deviation from the prevailing generic assumptions about novel writing lessened its appeal to readers accustomed to autobiographical representations of Asian American experiences. Finally, general readers in the 1950s did not know about the suffering endured by Japanese immigrants and their American-born descendants both historically and during World War II. The Japanese American community's lack of enthusiasm about *No-No Boy*, however, reflects the lasting effects of the internment and the draft process on the Japanese American psyche and consequently the community's moral ambivalence toward the controversial way in which Okada attempted to address the no-no boy issue. A more important reason for Japanese Americans' silence about *No-No Boy* in the immediate postwar era was the dominance, both in the majority society and within the ethnic community, of the new stereotype of Nisei as "loyal" Americans as a result of the wide publicity given to the heroic wartime exploits of Nisei soldiers (Ichioka, "Meaning"). Okada's novel was recovered by Frank Chin and the other editors of *Aiiieeeee!* during the Asian American cultural revival of the 1970s. Thanks to the Combined Asian American Research Project, a second edition of *No-No Boy* was published in 1976, which led to repeated reprintings thereafter.

Author's Biographical Background

Little is known about John Okada's life beyond the information collected by the editors of *Aiiieeeee!* in the aftermath of Okada's death. Okada was born in the old Merchants

Hotel in the Pioneer Square area of Seattle in September 1923. He attended Bailey Gatzert Elementary School, Broadway High School, and Scottsbluff Junior College in Nebraska. But his initial college education at the University of Washington was interrupted by World War II, during which his family was interned along with many other Japanese Americans. Okada volunteered for military service in the United States Army and was discharged as a sergeant in 1946. Some of the details of Okada's experience as an internee and as a United States soldier may be reflected in the novel in the exchange between the Japanese American soldier and the white lieutenant who are flying a reconnaissance mission on a B-24 between Guam and Japan (ix–xi). After the war, Okada graduated with a BA in English from the University of Washington and then received an MA in sociology from Columbia University in 1949. Afterward, he returned to the University of Washington for a BA in library science, and around the time of his completion of that degree, he married Dorothy and started a family. Okada found employment in the business reference department of the Seattle Public Library and then moved to Detroit to take a job at the Detroit Public Library for more money. For a while, he became a technical writer for Chrysler Missile Operations of Sterling Township, Michigan. Despite his constant movement from job to job across the country, he persisted in his work on fiction, a narrative form, he believed, through which "the hopes and fears and joys and sorrows of people [could] be adequately recorded" (qtd. in Chin 257). According to Bill Osuga, Okada worked briefly as the assistant head of the circulation department of the library at the University of California, Los Angeles, in the late 1960s, supervising library clerks, student workers, and a library guard. Osuga, Okada's colleague at the university library during the period, remembers the writer as "a 'clean desk' manager" and "an unpretentious and amiable person." Okada died of a heart attack in 1971. He was never able to finish his second novel—one on the life of Issei—which he started writing on his completion of *No-No Boy* around 1955. Okada was survived by his wife and two children.

Historical Context for the Narratives in *No-No Boy*

Several interrelated historical contexts need to be foregrounded to help readers understand this novel: the internment of Japanese Americans during World War II, the draft process of 1943, and the generational conflict in Japanese American families during the period. The decision to relocate thousands of Japanese Americans was made on 19 February 1942 under Executive Order 9066, which was issued approximately two months after Japan's attack on Pearl Harbor on 7 December 1941. The stated rationale for the decision was "military necessity," namely, to safeguard the national security of the United States against possible Japanese sabotage. Unstated was American policy makers' conviction that persons of Japanese ancestry residing in the United States were engaged in subversive activities on behalf of the Japanese government. Under the terms of the executive order, over 120,000 Japanese Americans were uprooted from their homes throughout the West Coast and confined initially to sixteen assembly centers and later to ten more-permanent relocation camps in desolate interior lands away from strategic locations. The entire removal took place at short notice and without any due process of law: there were no formal charges brought against the "evacuees," nor were hearings or trials conducted to investigate their loyalty.

In February 1943, the United States Army began a recruitment drive in the intern-ment camps in conformity with the War Department's instruction that each camp provide a quota of volunteers for an all-Japanese combat regiment to be made up of Nisei from Hawai'i and from the ten camps. As a security clearance measure, the War Department decided to conduct a registration among the interned Nisei males by way of a questionnaire, known as the "Statement of United States Citizenship of Japanese Ancestry" (Selective Service Form 304A). Central to the questionnaire are questions 27 and 28, which read as follows:

No. 27. Are you willing to serve in the armed forces of the United States on combat duty, wherever ordered?

No. 28. Will you swear unqualified allegiance to the United States of America and faithfully defend the United States from any or all attacks by foreign or domestic forces, and forswear any form of allegiance or obedience to the Japa-nese emperor or any other foreign government, power or organization?

The self-contradictory nature of these questions is obvious: If Nisei were eligible for serving in the United States Army, why had the United States government in-terned them out of "military necessity"? How could Nisei renounce allegiance to the Japanese emperor if they had had no such allegiance in the first place? And wouldn't renouncing such allegiance confirm that they had indeed been loyal to the emperor? (see Sumida, "Moral Dilemmas").

At the same time, the War Relocation Authority (WRA), which collaborated with the War Department in devising the questionnaire and carried out the security clearance, decided to use the questionnaire for administrative purposes—that is, to sort out and segregate the "troublemakers" from the ten camps, which had experienced growing resistance since the second half of 1942. Under such circumstances, the regis-tration not only became compulsory but also extended to all adult internees—male and female Nisei seventeen years old and above and all Issei. Because these questions completely ignored the moral and emotional trauma inflicted on the internees during the initial phase of the relocation, they gave rise to further fear, confusion, and defiance among those forced to answer them (see Emi). According to Ronald Takaki, of the 21,000 Nisei males eligible to register for the draft, some 4,600 answered the two questions with an explicit "No" or with no response (397). Nisei who answered the two questions negatively were immediately separated from other internees and put into the Tule Lake segregation center along with "disloyal" internees classified under other categories. One year after their segregation, these "no-no boys" were charged, tried, and convicted.

One consequence of the internment and the draft process was the near disintegra-tion of the Japanese American community and family, as well as the exacerbation of generational differences in Japanese American families. Before the war, generational conflict between Issei and Nisei was largely shaped by the issue of citizenship. The phenomenon of dual citizenship repeatedly called into question Nisei's American identity because Japanese law made the offspring of a Japanese father, regardless of place of birth, a natural Japanese citizen. In contrast, American law generally recognized anyone born on American soil, regardless of the parents' nationality, as a United States citizen (Chan 112–15). This phenomenon of dual citizenship lasted throughout the war despite a 1924 Japanese act that specified limited conditions under which Nisei were exempt from their Japanese citizenship on the basis of paternal descent (Ichioka, *Issei* 196–210). No Issei could become United States citizens until the passage of the 1952 McCarran-Walter Act. Before this act, United States citizenship had been reserved for white persons through the Naturalization Law of 1790 and through many subsequent anti-Asian immigration restrictions at both federal and state levels (e.g., the 1907 Gentlemen's Agreement, the 1913 Alien Land Law in California, the 1921 Alien Land Law in Washington, and various antimiscegenation laws). As a result, the prewar Japanese American population was characterized by "unique age distributions" and "distinct age peaks." By 1940, for example, the average age of Issei males was between fifty and sixty-four, whereas Issei women were generally ten years younger. Most of their American children were born in the 1910s and 1920s (Nagata 4–5). As Nisei came of age in the 1930s and 1940s, they were seen as Americans by their parents, who self-consciously regarded themselves as "sojourners." But Nisei could not enjoy the rights and privileges that they, as United States citizens, were entitled to, and they found themselves no better off than their parents, socially, economically, and politically. Nisei's identity problems were complicated by parental restrictions on their education, employment, social relations, and marriages. Although conflict between Issei and Nisei had been a constant ingredient in prewar Japanese American family life, such conflict was rarely expressed in purely political terms (see Sumida, "First Generations"). Yet under the stress of the internment of 1942 and the draft order of 1943, this tension in Japanese American family life was exacerbated and transformed into a destructive political struggle, in which Japanese Americans were particularly forced to participate.

Historical Context for the Writing of *No-No Boy*

The writing of *No-No Boy* coincided with official cold war celebrations of American nationalism that characterized the United States as an affluent society free from racial and class conflict. During the period, Japan became America's chief Asian ally in its global contest against communism. With the relationship between the two countries improving, the image of Japanese Americans in the American popular imagination underwent a corresponding change—from that of subversive alien to that of successful, "assimilated" minority, especially in view of African Americans' civil rights agitation in the 1950s. It was under these circumstances that Charles E. Tuttle, a mainstream publisher interested in publishing Japanese materials, began to look for Japanese American writers who could tell stories of friendly cultural encounter and of successful adaptation to American society.

Two intellectual developments in the 1950s, though not directly affecting the writing of *No-No Boy*, need to be recognized as part of the cultural climate under which Okada was contemplating his fictional project. The first was the revival of black literary voices, the achievement of the Jewish American novel, and the experimentation in other literary forms that satirically addressed issues of social inequality or existential dilemmas in an age of political conformity, middle-class suburbia, and mass culture (e.g., the works of Richard Wright, Ralph Ellison, Norman Mailer, Saul Bellow, J. D. Salinger, Arthur Miller, and Tennessee Williams). The second important development was the sociological critique of an alienating culture driven by corporate values (e.g., in the works of C. Wright Mills, David Riesman, Vance O. Packard, William H. Whyte, and John Galbraith). These intellectual and cultural developments ironically contrast with the scarce and subdued Japanese American literary voices of the era while they demonstrate that American society in the 1950s was not as politically uniform or monolithic as it is often made to seem.

Major Themes

exile and homelessness
race and social power
existential dilemmas
inarticulateness, voicelessness, and impotence
the role of family in the Japanese American community
mother-son relationships
nation and the body
generational conflict
cultural ventriloquism
memory and healing
the price of assimilation
the pain of having no available language for articulating historically submerged
    sensibilities
inner versus outer experience (e.g., the rhetorical functions of interior
    monologue)

Critical Issues

Most critical discussions of Okada's novel have emphasized a theme of ethnic recuperation, with a focus on Ichiro's ability to overcome his self-hatred and to complete his quest for a sense of "wholeness." This emphasis reflects the critical community's traditional concern with the social function of literature, a concern manifested, during the ethnic canon formation in the 1970s and the early 1980s, in a privileging of the community's political desires in assessments of Asian American literary works. This approach to *No-No Boy*, however, is problematic for at least two reasons. First, critics who adopt the approach tend to overstate the novel's conceptual coherence within a given ideological continuum while ignoring the novel's internal complexities and differences. By reducing the novel's multiple concerns to preconceived interpretive ideals, this approach thus leaves unexplained important questions about the book's status as a fiction in Asian American literary history—that is, its specific forms of engagement with the social and cultural dynamics in the cold war era; its actual conditions of emergence, disappearance, and belated recognition; and its continued relevance to contemporary Asian American literary and cultural productions. Second, the emphasis on a theme of recovered wholeness in *No-No Boy* often becomes the ground for readers strongly informed by antihumanist theoretical perspectives to dismiss the novel as aesthetically simple and politically naive, an emblem, as it were, of nationalist essentialization. To understand *No-No Boy* in its historical specificities, critics need to resist presentist impulses and to make sense of the novel by situating it among the historical conjunctions within which it took shape. Such critical efforts would necessarily involve an examination of the novel's formal and ideological ambiguities, because these textual features reveal the social power embedded in the novel's production and register the nuances of Okada's symbolic struggle with various external constraints on his literary voice.

Pedagogical Issues and Suggestions

No-No Boy is a text that evokes strong responses from students. One such response is engendered by the novel's effective dramatization of the arbitrary and partial nature of the Euro-American definition of "American," as well as its demonstration of how such a definition is informed by racial assumptions about Asians in American society both in the immediate postwar period and in contemporary American society. Examining *No-No Boy* from this perspective, however, can give rise to two interpretive problems for students: a tendency to see the generational conflict through a culturalist or anthropological lens and, consequently, to blame Issei for being "repressive" toward their American-born children; and a tendency to see the death of Ichiro's mother, Nisei's symbolic breaking away from Issei, as Okada's prescription for Japanese Americans' entry into the mainstream society in postwar America. These perceptions mainly result from an inadequate attention to the role of the internment and the draft process in determining both Ichiro's identity crisis and his conflict with his mother; they are also caused by a failure to recognize that the Ichiro-Ma conflict is essentially a domestic or familial manifestation of the existing racial hierarchy in American society, one that was predicated on Eurocentric assumptions about Americanization.

In dealing with these issues, the instructor must acknowledge, from the outset of discussion, the ambiguity of the immigrant generation's projection of its inherited—and often imagined—Asian cultural values onto its American-born offspring. This ambiguity results because such cultural values are often produced and maintained in contexts of legal exclusion of Asian immigrants and of deep-rooted orientalist assumptions about Asians in American society. On the basis of this recognition, the instructor can remind students that the portrayal of generational conflict in No-No Boy—like that in Louis Chu's Eat a Bowl of Tea (1961) and in Milton Murayama's All I Asking for Is My Body (1975)—does not reflect any "authentic" perspectives on the differences between Japanese and American cultures; rather, this portrayal implies the author's ironic awareness of the devastating social and psychological consequences of internment and its assumptions on the Japanese American community, as well as on the community's social-material foundation—the family. The instructor can then further suggest to students that Okada's depiction of the mother's extreme anti-American stance may not be a direct reflection of the attitude of most first-generation Japanese immigrants in the United States in the period. Rather, it can be seen as an inverted rhetorical construction that aims to parody and thus ironically to critique the stereotypical perception of Japanese Americans as unassimilable, perpetual cultural aliens—a perception that had fueled wartime decisions to intern Japanese Americans in the first place. From this perspective, the generational conflict in Okada's novel can be understood as performing the unique function of revealing both the depth and the complexity of Japanese Americans' experience of race in postwar American society.

Intertextual Linkages

With Monica Sone's Nisei Daughter, Momoko Iko's Gold Watch (play), Hisaye Yamamoto's "The Legend of Miss Sasagawara," Kazuo Miyamoto's Hawai'i: The End of the Rainbow, Joy Kogawa's Obasan, Cynthia Kadohata's In the Heart of the Valley of Love, Karen Tei Yamashita's Brazil-Maru and Tropic of Orange, and Stewart David Ikeda's What the Scarecrow Said: internment as political imagery in Japanese American literary representation; differences among mainland Japanese American, Hawai'ian, Japanese Canadian, and Japanese Brazilian relocation experiences.

With Carlos Bulosan's America Is in the Heart, Shawn Wong's Homebase, Cynthia Kadohata's The Floating World, Peter Bacho's Cebu, and Sara Suleri's Meatless Days: exile, homelessness, diaspora.

With Louis Chu's Eat a Bowl of Tea, Ronyoung Kim's Clay Walls, and Fae Myenne Ng's Bone: literary realism, generational conflict, representation of class and dysfunctional families.

With Gus Lee's China Boy and Honor and Duty: initiation into a male America through violence; racial contradictions precluding or qualifying full membership in such a construct of America; issues of honor and duty; the meaning of national identity.

With Zora Neale Hurston's *Their Eyes Were Watching God*, Toni Morrison's
Song of Solomon, Eudora Welty's *Losing Battles*, Rudolfo Anaya's *Bless Me
Ultima*, and Leslie Marmon Silko's *Ceremony*: orality, countermemory,
identity quests.

With Maxine Hong Kingston's *The Woman Warrior* and Joy Kogawa's *Obasan*:
voicelessness, silence, psychological trauma.

With Sylvia Watanabe's "The Caves of Okinawa": the life of Japanese
American servicemen during World War II.

With Carol Roh-Spaulding's "Waiting for Mr. Kim" and Kolin J. M. Ohi's "A
Backward Glance": interethnic and interracial relations, sexuality.

Bibliographic Resources

For discussions of long-standing hostility toward Japanese immigrants and their Ameri-
can descendants in Hawai'i and the American West, see, for example, Gary Okihiro's
Cane Fires: The Anti-Japanese Movement in Hawai'i, 1865–1945 and relevant chapters
in Sucheng Chan's *Asian Americans: An Interpretive History* and in Ronald Takaki's
Strangers from a Different Shore: A History of Asian Americans. Yuji Ichioka's *The Issei:
The World of the First Generation Japanese Immigrants, 1885–1924* and Eileen Tamura's
Americanization, Acculturation, and Ethnic Identity: The Nisei Generation in Hawai'i offer
thorough studies of Japanese American history from the nineteenth century through
the present. Michi Weglyn's *Years of Infamy: The Untold Story of America's Concentration Camps* remains one of the most comprehensive historical accounts of the circumstances that led to the internment, while Eric Sundquist's "The Japanese American
Internment: A Reappraisal" and Roger Daniels's *Prisoners without Trial: Japanese Americans in World War II* provide detailed analyses of historical and legal factors that surrounded the decision to intern Japanese Americans in 1942. Since the mid-1970s,
several essay-length studies of Okada's novel have been published. Frank Chin offers a
useful biographical study of Okada; Elaine Kim (147–56), Dorothy Ritsuko McDonald,
William Yeh, and Stan Yogi all examine Ichiro's identity quest in terms of his moral
dilemma and desire for reconciliation; Stephen Sumida ("Moral Dilemmas") analyzes
the rhetoricity of Okada's depiction of Ichiro's identity crisis in relation to issues of
race and generational conflict; Gayle Sato discusses the novel's treatment of gender
and the role of the Japanese American family by focusing on the Momotaro story; and
Jinqi Ling historicizes the novel's production and reception in the cold war context.

Other Resources

Robert Nakamura has produced a documentary film, *Something Strong Within: Home
Movies from America's Concentration Camps*, that features rarely seen footage of the
forced removal and incarceration of Japanese Americans during the war.

Bibliography

Anaya, Rudolfo. *Bless Me Ultima*. New York: Warner, 1999.

Bacho, Peter. *Cebu*. Seattle: U of Washington P, 1991.

Bulosan, Carlos. *America Is in the Heart*. Seattle: U of Washington P, 1973.

Chan, Sucheng. *Asian Americans: An Interpretive History*. Boston: Twayne, 1991.

Chin, Frank. "Afterword: In Search of John Okada." Okada 253–60.

Chin, Frank, et al., eds. *Aiiieeeee! An Anthology of Asian-American Writers*. Washington: Howard UP, 1974.

Chu, Louis. *Eat a Bowl of Tea*. Secaucus: Stuart, 1979.

Daniels, Roger. *Prisoners without Trial: Japanese Americans in World War II*. New York: Hill, 1993.

Emi, Frank Seishi. "Draft Resistance at the Heart Mountain Concentration Camp and the Fair Play Committee." Nomura et al. 41–69.

Hurston, Zora Neale. *Their Eyes Were Watching God*. Urbana: U of Illinois P, 1978.

Ichioka, Yuji. *The Issei: The World of the First Generation Japanese Immigrants, 1885–1924*. New York: Free, 1988.

———. "The Meaning of Loyalty: The Case of Kazumaro Buddy Uno." *Amerasia Journal* 23.3 (1998): 45–71.

Ikeda, Stewart David. *What the Scarecrow Said*. New York: Harper, 1996.

Iko, Momoko. *Gold Watch*. *Unbroken Thread: An Anthology of Plays by Asian American Women*. Ed. Roberta Uno. Amherst: U of Massachusetts P, 1993. 111–53.

Inada, Lawson Fusao. Introduction. Okada iii–vi.

Kadohata, Cynthia. *The Floating World*. New York: Ballantine, 1991.

———. *In the Heart of the Valley of Love*. Berkeley: U of California P, 1997.

Kim, Elaine H. *Asian American Literature: An Introduction to Their Writings and Their Social Contexts*. Philadelphia: Temple UP, 1982.

Kim, Ronyoung. *Clay Walls*. Sag Harbor: Permanent, 1986.

Kingston, Maxine Hong. *The Woman Warrior: Memoirs of a Girlhood among Ghosts*. New York: Knopf, 1976.

Kogawa, Joy. *Obasan*. New York: Anchor-Doubleday, 1994.

Lee, Gus. *China Boy*. New York: NAL-Dutton, 1994.

———. *Honor and Duty*. New York: Knopf, 1994.

Ling, Jinqi. "Writing the Novel, Narrating Discontents: Race and Cultural Politics in John Okada's *No-No Boy*." *Narrating Nationalisms: Ideology and Form in Asian American Literature*. New York: Oxford UP, 1998. 31–52.

McDonald, Dorothy Ritsuko. "After Imprisonment: Ichiro's Search for Redemption in *No-No Boy*." *MELUS* 6.3 (1979): 19–26.

Miyamoto, Kazuo. *Hawai'i: The End of the Rainbow*. Rutland: Tuttle, 1964.

Morrison, Toni. *Song of Solomon*. New York: Knopf, 1977.

Murayama, Milton. *All I Asking for Is My Body*. Honolulu: U of Hawai'i P, 1988.

Nagata, Donna K. *Legacy of Injustice: Exploring the Cross-Generational Impact of the Japanese American Internment*. Ann Arbor: U of Michigan P, 1993.

Nakamura, Robert, dir. *Something Strong Within: Home Movies from America's Concentration Camps*. Los Angeles: Media Arts Center of the Japanese Amer. Natl. Museum, 1994.

Ng, Fae Myenne. *Bone*. New York: Hyperion, 1993.

Nomura, Gail, et al., eds. *Frontiers of Asian American Studies: Writing, Research, and Commentary*. Pullman: Washington State UP, 1989.

Ohi, Kolin J. M. "A Backward Glance." *Best American Gay Fiction*. Ed. Brian Bouldrey. Boston: Little, 1997. 72–84.

Okada, John. *No-No Boy*. Seattle: U of Washington P, 1979.

Okihiro, Gary Y. *Cane Fires: The Anti-Japanese Movement in Hawai'i, 1865–1945*. Philadelphia: Temple UP, 1991.

Osuga, Bill. "Notes on My Association with John Okada." Letter. 1996. UCLA Asian Amer. Studies Center Lib., Los Angeles.

Roh-Spaulding, Carol. "Waiting for Mr. Kim." *Ploughshares* 16.2-3 (1990): 245–59.

Sato, Gayle Fujita. "Momotaro's Exile: John Okada's *No-No Boy*." *Reading the Literatures of Asian America*. Ed. Shirley Geok-lin Lim and Amy Ling. Philadelphia: Temple UP, 1992. 259–81.

Silko, Leslie Marmon. *Ceremony*. New York: Viking-Penguin, 1986.

Sone, Monica. *Nisei Daughter*. Seattle: U of Washington P, 1979.

Suleri, Sara. *Meatless Days*. Chicago: U of Chicago P, 1991.

Sumida, Stephen H. "First Generations in Asian American Literature: As Viewed in Some Second Generation Works." *Asian American and Pacific American Education*. Ed. Nobuya Tsuchida. Minneapolis: Asian-Pacific Amer. Learning Center, 1986. 64–70.

———. "Japanese American Moral Dilemmas in John Okada's *No-No Boy* and Milton Murayama's *All I Asking for Is My Body*." Nomura et al. 222–33.

Sundquist, Eric. "The Japanese American Internment: A Reappraisal." *American Scholar* 58 (1988): 529–47.

Takaki, Ronald. *Strangers from a Different Shore: A History of Asian Americans*. New York: Penguin, 1989.

Tamura, Eileen. *Americanization, Acculturation, and Ethnic Identity: The Nisei Generation in Hawai'i*. Champaign: U of Illinois P, 1993.

Watanabe, Sylvia. "The Caves of Okinawa." *Talking to the Dead*. New York: Doubleday, 1992. 24–46.

Weglyn, Michi. *Years of Infamy: The Untold Story of America's Concentration Camps*. New York: Morrow, 1976.

Welty, Eudora. *Losing Battles*. New York: Vintage, 1990.

Wong, Shawn. *Homebase*. New York: Reed, 1979.

Yamamoto, Hisaye. "The Legend of Miss Sasagawara." *"Seventeen Syllables" and Other Stories*. Latham: Kitchen Table, 1988. 20–33.

Yamashita, Karen Tei. *Brazil-Maru*. Minneapolis: Coffee House, 1992.

———. *Tropic of Orange*. Minneapolis: Coffee House, 1997.

Yeh, William. "To Belong or Not to Belong: The Liminality of John Okada's *No-No Boy*." *Amerasia Journal* 19.1 (1993): 121–33.

Yogi, Stan. "'You Had to Be One or the Other': Oppositions and Reconciliation in John Okada's *No-No Boy*." *MELUS* 21.2 (1996): 63–77.

Nisei Daughter
by Monica Sone

Traise Yamamoto

Publication Information

First published in hardcover as an Atlantic Monthly Press book by Little, Brown, and Company in 1953. Reissued in 1979 in paperback by the University of Washington Press with an introduction by S. Frank Miyamoto and a preface by Monica Sone. Chapter 8, "Pearl Harbor Echoes in Seattle," was excerpted in *Northwest Review* (17.2-3 [1977]: 243–58). Chapter 1, "A Shocking Fact of Life," has been anthologized in *The Big Aiiieeeee!* (Chan et al. 222–32).

Overview

Nisei Daughter was the first published autobiography written by a Nisei woman. Sone begins with her childhood in Seattle's Skid Row during the 1920s, when her parents owned and operated the Carrollton Hotel, which catered to the primarily white dock-working community. Much of the first half of *Nisei Daughter* concerns details of every-day family life and the character of the prewar Nikkei (people of Japanese ancestry living in the United States) community, including some accounts of the discrimination they faced. Sone's account of her childhood is framed by her conflicted feelings about her identity, which inform the often humorous descriptions of her home, school, and community.

The latter sections of *Nisei Daughter* focus on the evacuation and internment of Japanese Americans during World War II and the resulting tensions within the Itoi family. After her release to the Midwest in 1943 to work and attend college, Sone returned to visit her still-incarcerated parents.[1] The narrative closes at the end of this visit, the description of which represents Sone as having resolved her identity conflict and successfully assimilated into mainstream American society.

Reception

Sone's autobiography was favorably reviewed when it was published, receiving praise for its straightforwardness, humor, and absence of bitterness. Reviewers wrote approvingly about *Nisei Daughter* as an example of the successful resolution of cultural conflict and the ability to rise above self-pity in the face of prejudice. Reviews declared Sone's book to be "heartening" (Rev. of *Nisei Daughter*), a story told with "frankness but without bitterness" (Scoggin) and "an encouraging reminder of the melting pot at work" (Oka).

Since its reissue in 1979, a year that marked the beginnings of the redress movement, Sone's autobiography has been used in Asian American studies courses not only for its descriptions of the prewar community, the evacuation and internment, and Sone's sense of cultural conflict but also as a narrative characteristic of the assimilationist orientation of the time.

While contemporary critical work on *Nisei Daughter* has not been extensive, scholars have evaluated Sone's text in relation to second-generation Asian American autobiography (Kim), other autobiographies by Nisei women (Rayson), the thematic of the racial shadow (S. Wong), and a feminist poetics of raced maternality (Lim). As a result, *Nisei Daughter* emerges as a much more complicated narrative than it would if taken at face value (see Sumida).

Author's Biographical Background

Kazuko Monica Sone (née Itoi) was born in 1919 in Seattle, Washington. Her father immigrated to the United States in 1904, intending to study law. Her mother, a tanka poet, was the daughter of a Congregational minister who brought his family to the States after having made two previous preaching missions there. In addition to her parents' atypical (for Issei) backgrounds, the young Sone's daily contact with the white boarders in the family's hotel resulted in a childhood somewhat uncharacteristic of the prewar Nisei.

Following the events narrated in her autobiography, Sone graduated from Hanover College in Hanover, Indiana. In 1949, she received a master's degree in clinical psychology from Case Western Reserve University in Cleveland, Ohio. She presently lives in Canton, Ohio, with her husband Geary, a Nisei veteran. They have four children. *Nisei Daughter* remains Sone's only book.

Historical Context for the Narratives in *Nisei Daughter*

Japanese immigration to the United States began in 1868, which marked the beginning of the Meiji restoration in Japan, and continued until 1924, when the National Origins Act severely restricted and all but stopped Japanese immigration to the United States altogether. The majority of Japanese immigrants (Issei, or first-generation) settled along the West Coast of the United States, where most worked in some form of agriculture, gardening, fishing, or domestic service. The success of Japanese farmers contributed to an already existent anti-Asian sentiment and resulted in the passage of the Alien Land Laws of 1913 and 1920 in California and similar laws elsewhere. These laws prohibited aliens ineligible for citizenship from owning or leasing land. Although targeted specifically at the Japanese, these laws affected all Asians, who, as a group, could not become naturalized citizens. It was not until 1952 that the land laws were declared unconstitutional and Asian immigrants could be granted citizenship.

The years between 1924 and 1941 represent a period of settlement, the development of the Nikkei community, and the significant growth of the first American-born generation (Nisei, or second-generation). The Issei strongly urged their children to assimilate into mainstream American society, with the hope that the Nisei could thereby avoid the racism experienced by their parents. Despite these efforts, college-educated Nisei were similarly discriminated against and were often forced into agricultural or service occupations within the Nikkei community.

The bombing of Pearl Harbor on 7 December 1941 brought decades of anti-Japanese sentiment to the level of mass hysteria. The Nikkei were accused of disloyalty and suspected of spying. President Franklin Roosevelt signed Executive Order 9066 on 19 February 1942, which ordered all persons of Japanese ancestry on the West Coast to report to what were euphemistically termed "relocation centers." Often given only a few days to prepare and allowed to bring only what they could carry, evacuees were forced to sell their belongings at prices far below their worth (an estimated $400 million was suffered in material losses). Over 120,000 Nikkei were imprisoned, of whom approximately sixty-five percent were American-born citizens. After temporary incarceration in hastily converted fairgrounds or horse-racing tracks, ten more permanent War Relocation Authority camps were constructed in desolate inland areas.

Conditions in the camps were far from the comfortable accommodations depicted by the mainstream press: internees lived in wooden barracks covered with tar paper (a family of four or more might live in a room approximately eighteen by twenty feet) and insufficiently heated with a single coal-burning stove; meals of often substandard food were served mess-hall style in rotating shifts; and bathroom facilities were inadequate and afforded no privacy. The stress of camp life eroded family relationships, and the Issei often found themselves replaced as community leaders by the younger, English-speaking Nisei. Conflict within the camps was exacerbated by the infamous "loyalty questionnaire," which required both Issei and Nisei, male and female, to state their willingness to serve in the armed forces and disavow any loyalty to Japan (see the unit on Okada's *No-No Boy* in this volume).

Beginning in 1943, college-age Nisei were allowed to leave the camps to continue their education in the Midwest and on the East Coast, provided they had a sponsor. Their departure furthered the postwar dispersal of the Nikkei community, since many Nisei did not return to the West Coast after the war. Instead of illustrating the futility of assimilation, the internment experience reinforced for many Nisei the necessity of a more complete assimilation into white society.

The release of Japanese nationals and Japanese Americans from the camps began in January 1945. They had no homes or jobs to return to, their communities had been decimated, families had sometimes been separated by forced "repatriation" to Japan, and many older Issei were emotionally broken. For some the closure of the camps (completed in mid-1946) and the process of resettlement represented an experience as traumatic as the internment itself. Ironically, the eventual recovery of Japanese Americans after the war led to an exchange of old stereotypes for a new "model minority" stereotype.

In 1979, inspired by the civil rights movement, Sansei (third-generation Japanese Americans) and younger Nisei began the redress and reparations movement, which eventually resulted in the United States government's making a formal apology and paying each living internee $20,000. Perhaps the most important effect of the redress movement was that it opened a dialogue about the internment, a topic that had been smothered in shamed silence for decades.

Historical Context for the Writing of *Nisei Daughter*

Published in 1953, *Nisei Daughter* was written during the immediate postwar period when anti-Japanese sentiment was still high. In addition, the push to assimilate the Nikkei into the white American mainstream came from both within and outside the community. These two facts help explain the stance and tone of Sone's narrative, as well as the book's favorable reception. Written so that what happened to the Nikkei community in 1942 "will not be forgotten and lost to future generations" (xvi), *Nisei Daughter* was reprinted in 1979, during the beginnings of the redress campaign.

Major Themes

cultural and language differences between the Issei and Nisei
"Americanization" and assimilation
gender expectations and gender roles
the effect of racism on generational relationships
the material and psychological effects of white American racism
the effects of the war and internment on Nisei identity
the split or conflict between "American" and "Japanese" aspects of identity
    and the attempt to reconcile them

Critical Issues

From its opening pages, Sone's narrative is clearly concerned with the theme of cultural conflict and with identifying what is "American," "Japanese," and "Japanese American." Informed by her mother that she and her brother have "Japanese blood," six-year-old Kazuko feels like she was "born with two heads" (19). The following chapters describe the differences between white American and Japanese cultural practices but also, through descriptions of the Itoi household and the linguistic blending of Nikkei speech, suggest the ways in which the lines between "American" and "Japanese" are not rigid ones. Nevertheless, Sone often depicts what she identifies as "Japanese" in negative terms: this tendency is particularly clear in her account of the differences between American public school and the after-hours Japanese school, which she associates with conformity, repression, and obedience, as well as in her description of the Japanese cousin she meets during the Itois' trip to Japan. While feeling "like an alien" (108) in Japan, Kazuko also comes to recognize the ways in which her "habits" (142) suggest that her "Americanization" (139) has not been as complete as she had thought.

The issue of identity is inherently connected to the incidence of what Sone refers to as "prejudice," examples of which sprinkle the early chapters of *Nisei Daughter*. The reality of racial discrimination becomes increasingly evident in the latter half of the book, which focuses on the evacuation and internment of the Itoi family and the Seattle Nikkei community. However, the critique implied by such accounts serves primarily to underscore the necessity of assimilation into the dominant culture.

Sone's closing passages, in which she claims to have resolved the sense of duality described throughout the book, have been the focus of recent attention. The somewhat awkward tone of cheery optimism there has prompted several critics to look carefully at the disjunction between event and narrative tone elsewhere in *Nisei Daughter*. Readers might also consider those passages where Sone refers to feelings of anger and rage that are not textually represented but suggest emotions that cannot be completely contained beneath the narrative surface.

Pedagogical Issues and Suggestions

Students tend to respond well to Sone's straightforward writing style and humor, as well as to her nonconfrontational approach to the subject of white American "prejudice." Instructors may find that a useful starting point for discussion is to foreground this response and connect it to the favorable reviews *Nisei Daughter* received when it was originally published. Students might think about the timing of Sone's autobiography (published only eight years after the internment camps were closed), her likely audience and how it might partially determine her tone and use of humor, and her purposes for writing the book. Instructors should focus on the places where Sone is highly critical of white American racism, though in couched terms, as well as on passages in which she quickly alludes to intensely negative feelings before moving on.

To fully understand the issues of identity and assimilation that arise in Sone's narrative, groups of students can research the history of Japanese immigration in the context of earlier Chinese immigration, anti-Asian and anti-Japanese legislation, the racialized politics of the evacuation, the issues surrounding the loyalty questionnaire, and the postwar climate faced by the Nisei. Instructors may also find it helpful to tease out the relationship between racial or ethnic identity and national identity.

In addition, teachers might show students books such as Mine Okubo's *Citizen 13660* or Maisie Conrat and Richard Conrat's *Executive Order 9066*, which visually detail some of the living conditions in camp. Such tactics are crucial since many students unfamiliar with the facts of the internment frequently tend to conclude that it "wasn't that bad." Comparisons to the Nazi-run concentration camps in Europe are almost inevitable in such cases, often to disavow the ways in which the internment reveals the racism undergirding idealized notions of "American democracy." Several key points may help concretize the racist unconstitutionality of the internment, while disallowing the disrespectful use of the Holocaust as a way to shut down discussions about racial oppression in the United States: the unfounded accusations of subversive activity in the Nikkei community; the self-interested lobbying of anti-Japanese groups in favor of internment; the internment as an example of imprisonment without trial; and the fact that German and Italian Americans were not subject to mass incarceration.

Intertextual Linkages

With Richard Rodriguez's *Hunger of Memory: The Education of Richard Rodriguez*: strategies of assimilation, difference from immigrant parents, cultural conflict, representation of racial otherness.

With Jade Snow Wong's *Fifth Chinese Daughter*: expectations for female behavior, attitudes toward assimilation and the dominant white culture, the dichotomization of "Asian" and "American."

With Frederick Douglass's *Narrative of the Life of Frederick Douglass*: the didactic purpose of narrative, the uses of formal conventions to question the espousal of moral values by white Americans, the representation of an individual life to illustrate a communal experience.

Bibliographic Resources

Critical treatments of Sone's book may be found in the works by Elaine Kim, Sauling Cynthia Wong, Shirley Geok-lin Lim, Anne Rayson, Stephen H. Sumida, and Traise Yamamoto. Michi Weglyn's *Years of Infamy* remains one of the finest and most thoroughly researched studies of the internment. Those looking for a more concise account may refer to Roger Daniels's *Prisoners without Trial*. Richard Nishimoto offers both an account of daily camp life and a significant contrast to Sone's book. For more general accounts of Nikkei history, readers may wish to consult Daniels's *Asian America* or the works by Ronald Takaki and Sucheng Chan. Franklin Ng's six-volume *Asian American Encyclopedia* contains a wealth of information about Asians in the Americas.

Other Resources

Documentary films include Lise Yasui and Ann Tegnell's *Family Gathering*, Robert A. Nakamura's *Manzanar*, John de Graaf's *A Personal Matter: Gordon Hirabayashi v. the United States*, Steven Okazaki's *Unfinished Business*, Robert Nakamura's *Something Strong Within*, and Rea Tajiri's *History and Memory*. Instructors may also wish to contact the Hirasaki National Resource Center at the Japanese American National Museum in Los Angeles.

Note

1. Differences in terms relating to the internment may cause some confusion. The terms *assembly center* and *relocation center* are generally considered to be objectionable euphemisms employed by the government during the war. Some scholars consider *evacuation* and *evacuees* to be similarly euphemistic, preferring the terms *mass removal, mass incarceration*, and *prisoners*. Additionally, although the events relating to the imprisonment of the Nikkei are generally referred to as "the internment," the ten War Relocation Authority camps to which the majority of Nikkei were sent are technically referred to as "concentration camps." The four maximum-security camps run by the United States Department of Justice, which imprisoned a number of Japanese nationals, as well as some Germans and Italians, are technically referred to as "internment camps."

Bibliography

Chan, Jeffery Paul, et al., eds. *The Big Aiiieeeee! An Anthology of Chinese American and Japanese American Literature*. New York: Meridian, 1991.

Chan, Sucheng. *Asian Americans: An Interpretive History*. Boston: Twayne, 1991.

Conrat, Maisie, and Richard Conrat. *Executive Order 9066: The Internment of 110,000 Japanese Americans*. Los Angeles: UCLA Asian Amer. Studies Center, 1992.

Daniels, Roger. *Asian America: Chinese and Japanese in the United States since 1850*. Seattle: U of Washington P, 1988.

———. *Prisoners without Trial: Japanese Americans and World War II*. New York: Farrar, 1993.

Douglass, Frederick. *Narrative of the Life of Frederick Douglass, an American Slave*. 1845. Ed. and introd. Houston A. Baker, Jr. New York: Penguin, 1982.

Family Gathering. Dir. Lise Yasui and Ann Tegnell. Videocassette. NAATA, 1988.

History and Memory: For Akiko and Takashige. Dir. Rea Tajiri. Videocassette. Women Make Movies, 1991.

Kim, Elaine H. *Asian American Literature: An Introduction to the Writings and Their Social Context*. Philadelphia: Temple UP, 1982.

Lim, Shirley Geok-lin. "Japanese American Women's Life Stories: Maternality in Monica Sone's *Nisei Daughter* and Joy Kogawa's *Obasan*." *Feminist Studies* 16.2 (1990): 288–312.

Ling, Jinqi. *Narrating Nationalisms: Ideology and Form in Asian American Literature*. New York: Oxford UP, 1998.

Manzanar. Dir. Robert Nakamura. Videocassette. NAATA, 1971.

Ng, Franklin. *The Asian American Encyclopedia*. 6 vols. New York: Cavendish, 1995.

Rev. of *Nisei Daughter*, by Monica Sone. *Booklist* 1 Feb. 1953: 188.

Nishimoto, Richard S. *Inside an American Concentration Camp: Japanese American Resistance at Poston, Arizona*. Ed., introd., and afterword by Lane Ryo Hirabayashi. Tucson: U of Arizona P, 1995.

Oka, Takashi. Rev. of *Nisei Daughter*, by Monica Sone. *Christian Science Monitor* 26 Feb. 1953: 11.

Okubo, Mine. *Citizen 13660*. 1946. Seattle: U of Washington P, 1983.

A Personal Matter: Gordon Hirabayashi versus the United States. Dir. John de Graaf. Videocassette. NAATA, 1992.

Rayson, Anne. "Beneath the Mask: Autobiographies of Japanese-American Women." *MELUS* 14.1 (1987): 43–57.

Rodriguez, Richard. *Hunger of Memory: The Education of Richard Rodriguez*. New York: Bantam, 1983.

Scoggin, Margaret C. Rev. of *Nisei Daughter*, by Monica Sone. *Horn Book Magazine* June 1953: 231.

Something Strong Within. Dir. Robert Nakamura. Videocassette. Japanese Amer. Natl. Museum, 1994.

Sone, Monica. *Nisei Daughter*. 1953. Introd. S. Frank Miyamoto. Seattle: U of Washington P, 1979.

Sumida, Stephen H. "Protest and Accommodation, Self-Satire and Self-Effacement, and Monica Sone's *Nisei Daughter*." *Multicultural Autobiography: American Lives*. Ed. James Robert Payne. Knoxville: U of Tennessee P, 1992. 207–43.

Takaki, Ronald. *Strangers from a Different Shore*. Boston: Little, 1989.

Unfinished Business: The Japanese American Internment Cases. Dir. Steven Okazaki. Videocassette. NAATA, 1986.

Weglyn, Michi. *Years of Infamy: The Untold Story of America's Concentration Camps*. New York: Morrow, 1976.

Wong, Jade Snow. *Fifth Chinese Daughter*. 1950. Seattle: U of Washington P, 1989.

Wong, Sau-ling Cynthia. *Reading Asian American Literature: From Necessity to Extravagance*. Princeton: Princeton UP, 1993.

Yamamoto, Traise. *Masking Selves, Making Subjects: Japanese American Women, Identity, and the Body*. Berkeley: U of California P, 1999.

The Joy Luck Club
by Amy Tan

Leslie Bow

Publication Information

First published in hardcover by G. P. Putnam's Sons in 1989 and in paperback by Ivy Books (Ballantine) in June 1990. Was a Book-of-the-Month Club featured alternate and a Quality Paperback Book Club featured alternate, with magazine serial rights purchased by *Ladies' Home Journal* and the *Atlantic*. Translated into nineteen languages with foreign editions published in Britain, France, Italy, and the Netherlands.

Overview

Through sixteen interconnected stories, *The Joy Luck Club* narrates the lives of four Chinese immigrant women, Suyuan, An-mei, Lindo, and Ying-ying, and their relationships with their American-born daughters, Jing-mei, Rose, Waverly, and Lena. Jing-mei is asked to be the fourth seat at a mahjong table left vacant by the death of her mother, Suyuan. Her "aunties" reveal that they have contacted the two half-sisters that her mother had been forced to abandon in war-torn China. Despite Jing-mei's protests, the three women exact a promise that she will meet her half-sisters and tell them all about their mother's life. Jing-mei's impending responsibility and her hope that she can narrate her mother's life well enough to affirm a common familial connection frame the subsequent mother-daughter narratives. The stories of the mothers' experiences in prerevolutionary China seem to hold the key to resolving the problems of the upwardly mobile, divorce-prone, ethnically conflicted, Americanized daughters. Lindo's story of escaping an arranged marriage reveals that she has passed on her ambition and "deviousness" to her daughter, Waverly, in spite of the clashes of will that divide them. An-mei's story of her mother's degradation as a third concubine helps Rose find a sense of self-worth and the strength to fight for her own interests in her divorce. The lessons of Ying-ying's failed first marriage promise to be the catalyst for an alliance with her daughter, Lena. The novel ends with the completion of Suyuan's story of wartime sacrifice: Jing-mei's fulfillment of her mother's quest turns out to be a reconciliation with her mother's memory and legacy and grants her greater understanding of her own ethnic inheritance.

Reception

The Joy Luck Club has been a commercial as well as critical success. The novel spent nine months on the *New York Times* best-seller list with more than four million paperbacks in print (Epstein). The hardcover edition was reprinted twenty-seven times and sold 275,000 copies (Wong 174). The economic success of the work was anticipated by the publisher G. P. Putnam's Sons, who won the rights to the work in a bidding war with five other New York publishers (Kepner 58) and offered Tan a $50,000 advance, a sum five times more than the standard amount for a "literary first novel" (Woo). Hardcover editions of the novel had a higher list price than normal, prophesying good reviews (McDowell). Nine publishing houses participated in the auction for paperback rights in 1989, with a six-figure floor on the bidding (*"Joy Luck Club Rights"*) culminating in a $1.2 million paperback sale to Vintage–Random House (Lew). Publicity for the novel was later enhanced by the release of the 1993 film of the same name, directed by Wayne Wang with a screenplay coauthored by Tan and Ronald Bass.

   The Joy Luck Club's critical success was clear; it was a finalist for the 1989 National Book Award, the National Book Critics Circle Award, and the *Los Angeles Times* Book Prize and the recipient of the Commonwealth Gold Award and the Bay Area Book Reviewers Award in 1990. Reviewed by major publications following its release in March 1989, the novel garnered reviews that were not only positive but over the top in their use of superlatives. One critic noted, "The only negative thing I could ever say about this book is that I'll never again be able to read it for the first time" (See). Reviewers cited the universality of the experience depicted in *The Joy Luck Club*, often invoking such phrases as "the universal mother-daughter bond" or "the generation gap." While the reviewers no doubt found the novel's language, humor, and craft appealing, they consistently praised the ways in which the Chinese American experience depicted in the novel transcends its ethnic specificity. One critic wrote, "When I finished reading *The Joy Luck Club* and *Seventeen Syllables*, I found myself weeping about the chasm between my own immigrant mother and her lost ancestors and descendants" (Miner). In contrast, reception among Asian American literary critics and writers has been cautious as well as celebratory. The reception of Maxine Hong Kingston's *The Woman Warrior* and David Henry Hwang's *M. Butterfly* established a pattern of skepticism over issues of ethnic representation in regard to literary works with mainstream appeal. Writers and critics are particularly interested in investigating works that lend themselves to questionable clichés about East and West, such as the one offered by a reviewer who found *The Joy Luck Club* to be "snappy as a fortune cookie and much more nutritious" (Koenig 82).

Author's Biographical Background

Tan acknowledges that the four daughters in *The Joy Luck Club* are "fractured bits" of herself and her experience of growing up in Santa Clara, Santa Rosa, and Fresno, California. Tan notes that, like her characters, she "blamed everything on the fact that my mother was Chinese while I thought of myself as totally American" (Chatfield-Taylor). Yet Tan did not have a "totally American" experience. She was born in Oakland, California, in 1952, two and a half years after her parents' emigration from China. In a "one-in-a-million" coincidence, Amy's father, a former engineer turned Baptist minister, and her older brother died within six months of each other after developing brain tumors. Daisy Tan took her two surviving children to Switzerland to escape from what a geomancer verified was "a bad house, full of disease" (Kepner 160). For Tan, enrolling in a private girl's boarding school in Montreux at sixteen meant finishing high school while trying to fit into a landscape populated by the daughters of a European elite. Her adolescent rebellions included an attempted elopement with a German army deserter who turned out to be an escaped mental patient. Amy Tan returned with her family to the United States where she enrolled in Linfield College, a Baptist school in Oregon. When she transferred to San Jose State University to follow her Italian American boyfriend and changed her major from premed to English, her mother didn't speak to her for six months (Chatfield-Taylor; Lew). Tan earned a master's degree in linguistics, began a PhD program at the University of California, Berkeley, and worked for various periods as a switchboard operator, a carhop, a pizza maker, and a language development consultant to programs for developmentally disabled children. Like her fictional counterpart, Jingmei, Tan became a freelance business writer for companies like IBM ("Telecommunications and You"), Apple, and Bank of America under the pseudonym May Brown (Woo; Chatfield-Taylor). Tan found producing manuals that taught AT&T employees how to sell "Reach Out America" to be unrewarding; moreover, her success, while enabling her to persuade her mother that she could now provide for the family, made Tan a workaholic. After having her psychiatrist fall asleep on her after three sessions, she jokingly referred to her writing as "bad psychiatry" and turned to writing fiction and studying jazz piano as a means of curing work addiction. She lives in San Francisco's Presidio Heights with her husband, Lou DeMattei, a tax attorney (Woo; Somogyi and Stanton 27).

Although resisting readers' desire to see the novel as wholly biographical, Tan is nonetheless not shy about linking her own relationship with her mother, Daisy Tan, to the fictional relationships in *The Joy Luck Club*. She notes that fragments of the novel are true and come out of her family's history. Her mother's story forms the outline for her subsequent novel, *The Kitchen God's Wife*; in *The Joy Luck Club*, Daisy Tan "was the little girl watching her mother cut a piece of flesh from her arm to make soup, and she was the little girl watching her mother die when she took opium because she had become a third concubine" (Chatfield-Taylor). Daisy was an abused wife who procured a divorce in 1949. Custody of her three children from this first marriage automatically went to the father; the children were left behind despite Daisy's efforts to track them down after her immigration to the United States in 1949.

When Tan was twelve years old, her parents told her about these three half-sisters and a half-brother. Like Jing-mei who suffers from an implied comparison to the "lost" babies in China, Tan grew up with a sense of herself as "definitely the bad Chinese daughter" (Kepner 59). This pressure, in combination with the experience of growing up a racial outsider, caused her to comment, "Like a lot of Chinese-American children, I grew up with a lot of self-hate" (Woo). Yet she was able to reach a new understanding of her mother's ambitions for her, seeing that from her mother's point of view, her own privilege was that of choice, "the ultimate, incredible luxury of choices that we had in America" (Kepner 58).

Historical Context for the Narratives in *The Joy Luck Club*

The novel's historical context spans two generations and continents. Flashbacks of the mothers' experiences in China before the 1949 Communist Revolution led by Mao Tse-tung (Mao Zedong) highlight the Confucian households of their childhoods and the social upheaval of World War II caused by the Japanese invasion. The mothers' experiences as immigrants to San Francisco's Chinatown in the 1950s reference a particular moment in United States policy toward immigrants of Chinese ancestry. The childhoods of the second-generation daughters in the early 1960s lead into present-day narratives that reflect a mid-1980s concern with interracial relationships, upward mobility, and reconnecting with ethnic roots in the age of multiculturalism. While what is noticeable about the novel in comparison to works by other Asian American writers is its almost muted historical specificity, the events of the stories nonetheless take place within specific global-political movements and shifts in American perceptions of its ethnic populations.

Born in 1914, 1915, and 1918, not long after the 1911 Republican Revolution that overthrew the last imperial dynasty of the Manchus, the Joy Luck mothers share childhood and adolescent experiences grounded in what has been called the "golden age of the Chinese bourgeoise" (Bergere 1) and structured by the rites of Confucian domesticity. The portrayals of polygamy, exogamy, the separation of genders within the household, matchmaking, and ancestor worship in the mothers' narratives provide the backdrop for the novel's contrast to the seeming plethora of "choices" that American women possess a generation later. Yet the novel also anticipates the end of this era. In 1919, the May Fourth Movement put China on a course of antifeudalism, vernacular culture, and modernization of institutions with varying degrees of success. Set in Tietsin (Tianjin) in 1923, An-mei's story references the rise of a merchant class, the "newly rich Chinese people" who have taken up Western dress and furnishings (223); by the 1930s Lindo contests "stupid old-fashioned [marriage] customs" and comments on "how backward families in the country were" (51).

Suyuan's Kweilin (Guilin) story, set in 1944, portrays the apex of Japanese control of China during the Sino-Japanese War of 1931 to 1945, in which Japanese forces moving from the south and northwest eventually took control of Kweilin and marched toward Chungking (Chongqing). The rampant inflation, the rise of the black market, and the corruption depicted in the story prefigure the rise of the Communist Party and its skirmishes with the ruling Kuomintang or Nationalists in the years following the Japanese surrender in 1945. Yet the novel does not give the defeat of Chiang Kai-shek's Nationalist Army as the explicit reason for the emigration of any of the Joy Luck mothers, including Suyuan, the widow of a Kuomintang army officer. Canning and Suyuan Woo's emigration from Hong Kong to the United States is set in 1949, the year of Mao Tse-tung's victory over the Nationalists. The novel implies that there was "no time to pack" for travel to the United States, although the narrative also reveals that they left the mainland in 1947 (285). Instead, Lindo, Ying-ying, and Suyuan's stories reflect the desire to start anew as the chief reason for emigrating. It was not until 1953 and the "Red Scare" that Chinese immigrants were admissible as political refugees (Kitano and Daniels 45).

The mothers' stories do not necessarily reflect typical immigration patterns for Chinese women after 1943. The years following the repeal of the Chinese Exclusion Act did witness an influx of Chinese immigrant women to the United States because of a loophole in the quota system stipulating that Chinese alien women married to American citizens did not count toward the Chinese quota (Kitano and Daniels 24). The "smart girl's" advice to Lindo to have a baby in the United States reflects anti-naturalization laws in effect before 1943, although the novel places Lindo's immigration around 1949. Ying-ying's detainment at Angel Island would put her immigration before 1940, when the station burned down (Yung 279), while her classification choices reference the War Brides Act of 1945 and the Displaced Persons Act of 1948 (104). Although *The Joy Luck Club* offers suggestive snippets of Chinese immigration history, the dates do not line up exactly with the policies in force within the period following World War II.

Obliquely referencing the cold war, the novel notes the "closure" of China and its effect in breaking off communication between family members. The point at which "letters could be openly exchanged" (285) was enabled by the subsequent era of "Ping-Pong diplomacy" after President Nixon's trip to China in 1972. Beyond these hints, shifts in the political sphere in Sino–United States relations and their effect on the Chinatown community are not directly characterized as influences on the lives of the immigrant mothers.

Historical Context for the Writing of *The Joy Luck Club*

The historical context of the novel's writing coincides with its present-day narration ending with Jing-mei's trip to China in 1987. The mid-1980s California landscape informed by the civil rights and women's movement is evoked by the narrative's casual references to prenuptial agreements, community property, *Dynasty*, rent control, therapy, AIDS, "buying Suburu," Asian American studies, interracial marriage, and other evidence of Reagan-era American pop culture. *The Joy Luck Club* also came at a moment—and helped to produce a moment—of mainstream interest in literary treatments of the ethnic experience. Its success follows that of Maxine Hong Kingston's *The Woman Warrior* (1976) in Asian American literature and the success of other fiction by women of color, most notably Alice Walker's *The Color Purple* (1982) and *In Search of Our Mothers' Gardens* (1983) and Louise Erdrich's *Love Medicine* (1984), an acknowledged stylistic influence. In its potentially irresistible emphasis on family nostalgia culminating in a message of empowerment and reconciliation, the novel met what seemed to be the new criterion for ethnic best-sellers—as one New York editor put it, "Let's have more Grandma." (This anecdote appears in Richard Rodriguez's *Hunger of Memory* [7]; an editor urged him to drop discussion of political issues in his memoir, since "nobody is going to remember affirmative action in another twenty-five years" [6].) *The Joy Luck Club* served up, if not ethnic grandma, then ethnic matrilineal inheritance to feed the growing interest in stories about the lives of women of color for a general reading audience. The novel's thematic emphasis on the movement from silence to voice and the recognition of self-worth despite women's cultural conditioning reflects the motifs of foundational feminist criticism. The novel adds to these ideas a 1980s commentary on the ambivalent legacy of the women's movement: Lena's story in particular reveals the disjunction between the rhetoric of women's equality and the possibility of its fulfillment.

Begun in 1985, *The Joy Luck Club* was originally conceived as a collection of short stories (Somogyi and Stanton 26). Tan wrote "Endgame" (which later became the chapter "Rules of the Game") to enter a writing workshop run by Oakley Hall and Molly Giles (Woo). A member of the Squaw Valley Community of Writers, Tan eventually published the story, her first, in *Seventeen*, where it caught the eye of the agent Sandra Dijkstra. With Dijkstra's encouragement, Tan wrote two more chapters, "Waiting between the Trees" and "Scar," and an outline of the others (one of which merely stated, "A woman goes to China to meet her sisters with expectations and discovers something else") just before embarking on a trip to China with her mother to meet her half-sisters (Somogyi and Stanton 26). On returning to the United States, Tan found that she had offers on the yet unfinished book; she completed *The Joy Luck Club* within four months after the bid (Woo). Although she still thought of the work as a collection of stories "connected by theme or emotion or community," she compromised with her publisher, who labeled it a "first work of fiction" (Somogyi and Stanton 26).

The novel was written directly after a period in which Tan "connected" with her Chinese heritage in a tangible way: "When my feet touched China," she notes, "I became Chinese" (Lew). Such a sentiment reflects the *Roots* era of "rediscovered" ethnic pride or, as the critic Sau-ling Wong puts it, "post–civil rights ethnic soul-searching" combined with the literature of New Age self-healing (202). This shift in perception is the occasion for Lindo's ironic comment that Waverly now "wants to be Chinese, it is so fashionable" (253). The representation of ethnicity as mere "fashion" may reflect America's anxious self-representation as a multicultural nation. Tan's "China as motherland, America my fatherland" characterization plays to the current national rhetoric of diversity—America not as melting pot but as mosaic (Chatfield-Taylor). Yet it may be the novel's emphasis on family reconciliation that most resonates with its historical moment; Tan attributes the novel's success in part to its generational convergence. As a baby boomer, she has put her finger on an issue that might have special significance for women "whose mothers have either just recently died or may die in the near future" (Somogyi and Stanton 29).

The novel's release in the spring of 1989 came only a few months before an event that propelled images of China into every American living room—the massacre in Tiananmen Square on 4 June 1989. Ironically, this image of China seemed to bear little relation to the exotic representations of upper-class domesticity offered in Tan's work. On being asked to comment on the recent events in China, Tan said:

> The first thing I would like to emphasize—because these events are so sensitive—is that my feelings are strictly personal. My relatives represent all sides of the situation. My uncle is a high Communist official, and my sister is a member of the Communist party, which is a very small elite in China. I also have relatives who are students and professors. The media was so one-dimensional, the evil villains versus the noble student heroes. But this wasn't a football game, it was my family! (Chatfield-Taylor)

Major Themes

mother-daughter relationships
matrilineal inheritance
parental expectation
biculturalism
voice and storytelling
Chinatown immigrants
the acculturation experience
Confucian family structure
women's roles across cultures
class mobility within immigrant families
sentimentality
ethnic exoticism and orientalism
interracial marriage
Third World women's experiences
generational cultural conflict
familial reconciliation
reconnection with ethnic heritage

Critical Issues

A dominant narrative at work in the novel is one that coincides with Anglo-American feminist criticism. For the Joy Luck mothers, storytelling is a medium for understanding gender oppression in ways that can lead to self-affirmation; for the daughters, the mother-daughter relationship is the site for a reenvisioning of self based on a maternal legacy. Storytelling is represented as a form of self-help that culminates in ethnic reconciliation. Matrilineality both narrativizes the shared experience of women's oppression and represents a source of women's empowerment and connection. Because so many reviewers have praised the novel for representing ethnic experiences that "could belong to any immigrant group" (Lew), one critical issue that arises is whether the work presents an ahistorical feminism in its emphasis on the mother-daughter bond.

Beyond the novel's overt emphasis on women's self-actualization, critics have necessarily analyzed the ways in which *The Joy Luck Club* deviates from a singularly feminist message on the basis of its ethnic content. The conflicts between mothers and daughters are clearly located in differences of class, language, education, and degrees of acculturation, in addition to the conflicts that arise from mother-daughter embeddedness. One debated issue concerns the novel's representation of racial and ethnic difference—whether it reflects or dislodges an "orientalist" or exoticized projection of China and Chinese Americans and whether it relies on or counters a static East-West opposition. At stake is an analysis that links the novel to prevailing cultural representations of Asians—the daughters as model minorities, for example, or Chinese women as prefeminist. Such an inquiry necessarily locates the novel in its cultural context by suggesting a link between the novel's popularity and its ability to reflect mainstream American tastes and interests. *The Joy Luck Club*'s success in the market has raised concerns about canonicity and what type of works become representative of Asian American literature and experience. In the light of this attention to gender and racial representation, it is easy to overlook the form of the novel. A series of interconnected, first-person monologues, the novel's form complements its thematic emphasis on collectivity over individuality, and it joins a body of contemporary literature that represents a textual reality from multiple perspectives.

Pedagogical Issues and Suggestions

Students find *The Joy Luck Club* engaging though sometimes confusing at first, given its similarly voiced first-person narratives. The most salient issue that arises in teaching *The Joy Luck Club* seems to be that of identification. Students may respond to the book on the basis of whether or not they identify with the mother-daughter conflicts in the narrative, especially from the daughters' point of view. Students will often label the theme of parental conflict, particularly gendered conflict, "universal." This reaction is also reflected in Tan's book reviews; "universality" is what many reviewers find most appealing about the novel. While this response can give students a positive and productive "in" to the work, focusing simply on the gendered aspects of the narrative may preclude a more developed understanding of how race and ethnicity function in the text. The instructor might anticipate this response and use it as a springboard from which to situate these conflicts in relation to more historically specific circumstances, particularly in regard to the relation between immigrant acculturation and class expectation and conflict.

For example, students may read "Rules of the Game" as a typical instance of parent-child conflict about autonomy and individuation. Yet instructors might also show them the ways in which the story reveals Lindo's ambivalence about Waverly's increasing acculturation as she goes farther away from home in pursuit of winning at chess, a feeling in conflict with Lindo's initial desire to see Waverly's success as a means of overcoming the family's economic placement in a tourist ghetto. Similarly, the characters' comments may invite a simple comparison between the relative freedoms for women in China and the United States, the past and present. (Consider, for example, the statement, "That was China. That was what people did back then. They had no choice" [241].) An examination of the terms *fate* and *choice* can reveal an alignment of determinism and agency along national lines: Chinese fate versus American choice, for example. What idea of "America" circulates in the text, and what purpose does it serve in mediating the conflicts between mothers and daughters? The instructor might focus on passages that reflect the daughters' characterizations of "Chineseness" to explore the characters' attitudes toward their own ethnicity and to analyze how these attitudes become displaced onto their mothers.

The film is an obvious resource to teach with the novel. As readers and spectators, students generally enjoy both representations; the challenge is to encourage a critical perspective that will analyze how a text produces a specific message or effect. One strategy is to explore the film's sentimentality as an emotionally manipulative technique, how and where the film conditions cathartic responses from its audience. In exploring the differences between the textual and the visual, the instructor might pose questions about the film's aesthetics—the glamorous portrayals of characters and domestic spaces—and how it might challenge the images the students derive from the reading. Comparing the novel and the film may also provoke a discussion of the representation of Asian masculinity, particularly in the film's substitution of an Asian actor for his Caucasian counterpart in Lena's story.

The novel offers students accessible language, easily identifiable conflict, and a clear understanding of symbolism (a poorly balanced table indicates a marriage without foundation; the Moon Lady who turns into a man represents false dreams). This straightforwardness may lead to textual analysis that stops at the idea that meaning is produced through a series of simple oppositions or substitutions. Yet the multiple intertwinings of race, gender, class, nationality, and generation that undergird the narrative make teaching the novel potentially more rewarding than its overt emphasis on triumph, reconciliation, and healing may initially suggest.

Intertextual Linkages

With Denise Chong's *The Concubine's Children*: similar themes of women in
patriarchal families, the degraded position of the second wife, lost babies,
reconciliation with siblings, mother-daughter relations; contrasting realistic
treatment of how immigration laws, labor conditions, and political changes
influence generational conflict and connection.

With Velina Hasu Houston's *Tea*: war brides, four Asian women in America,
the legacy to American-born or multiracial daughters.

With Nora Okja Keller's *Comfort Woman*: the effect of discovering a mother's
secret on a daughter in America, a mother's past sufferings and
connections to spirituality.

With Frank Chin's *The Year of the Dragon*: father-son as opposed to mother-
daughter relationships in a Chinatown setting.

With Akemi Kikumura's *Through Harsh Winters* or Mary Paik Lee's *Quiet
Odyssey: A Pioneer Korean Woman in America*: Japanese and Korean
immigrant women's autobiographies focusing on Asian women in
agricultural labor.

With Louise Erdrich's *Love Medicine* (Tan's inspiration for writing *The Joy Luck
Club*): similarity in novelistic form, interlocking first-person narratives.

With Carol Edgarian's *Rise the Euphrates*: an Armenian American novel
contrasting three generations of women beginning with flashbacks to the
Armenian massacre.

Bibliographic Resources

For a first-person narrative on the role of women within the Confucian family structure,
see Su-ling Wong and E. H. Cressy. For an economic-political analysis of the era, see
Marie-Claire Bergere. For a discussion of Chinese immigration to the United States
in the twentieth century, see the works by Harry Kitano and Roger Daniels, Sucheng
Chan, and Judy Yung.

While Tan initially said that she did not want to write "son of *Joy Luck*" (Woo),
those drawn to the themes of *The Joy Luck Club* will not be disappointed with Tan's
subsequent work. *The Kitchen God's Wife* and *The Hundred Secret Senses* are based on
a similar narrative premise—that repressed family stories can help to mediate conflict
in the lives of following generations. She has written two children's books, *The Moon
Lady* and *The Chinese Siamese Cat*; the former is a retelling of a story that appears in
The Joy Luck Club. In addition to selected literary-critical sources, the novel may be
supplemented by a number of interviews with the author.

For fiction dealing with women's roles in China in the period after 1949, see
Anchee Min's *Red Azalea* or Wang Ping's *American Visa* (alphabetized under *Wang*).

Other Resources

Wayne Wang's film adaption of *The Joy Luck Club*, which features Asian American actors fairly well known to mainstream audiences and uses China as a backdrop for part of the dramatic action, may be contrasted with Wang's earlier film on the mother-daughter relationship, *Dim Sum* (1985), which is modestly budgeted and focuses on San Francisco's Chinatown.

Bibliography

"Amy Tan." *Writers Dreaming*. Ed. Naomi Epel. New York: Southern, 1993. 280–89.

Bergere, Marie-Claire. *The Golden Age of the Chinese Bourgeoise, 1911–1937*. Trans. Janet Lloyd. Cambridge: Cambridge UP, 1989.

Bow, Leslie. "Cultural Conflict/Feminist Resolution in Amy Tan's *The Joy Luck Club*." *New Visions in Asian American Studies: Diversity, Community, Power*. Ed. Franklin Eng, Judy Yung, Stephen Fugita, and Elaine Kim. Pullman: Washington State UP, 1994. 235–47.

Briggs, Tracey Wong. "Tan Transforms Family Rift into a Book of 'Joy.'" *USA Today* 24 Apr. 1989: n. pag.

Chan, Sucheng. *Asian Americans: An Interpretive History*. Boston: Twayne, 1991.

Chatfield-Taylor, Joan. "Cosmo Talks to Amy Tan." *Cosmopolitan* Nov. 1989: 178.

Chin, Frank. *The Year of the Dragon*. Seattle: U of Washington P, 1981.

Chong, Denise. *The Concubine's Children*. New York: Viking, 1995.

———. "Emotional Journeys through East and West." *Quill and Quire* 55.5 (1989): 23.

Dim Sum: A Little Bit of Heart. Dir. Wayne Wang. Perf. Victor Wong, Kim Chew, Laureen Chew, and Cora Miao. Orion, 1985.

Dorris, Michael. "Mothers and Daughters." *Chicago Tribune* 12 Mar. 1989: 1C.

Edgarian, Carol. *Rise the Euphrates*. New York: Random, 1995.

Epstein, Hillary. Personal communication. 13 Feb. 1996.

Erdrich, Louise. *Love Medicine*. New York: Holt, Rinehart, 1984.

Heller, Dana. "A Possible Sharing: Ethnicizing Mother-Daughter Romance in Amy Tan's *The Joy Luck Club*." *Family Plots: The De-Oedipalization of Popular Culture*. Philadelphia: U of Pennsylvania P, 1995. 113–28.

Heung, Marina. "Daughter-Text/Mother-Text: Matrilineage in Amy Tan's *Joy Luck Club*." *Feminist Studies* 19.3 (1993): 597–616.

Houston, Velina Hasu. *Tea. Unbroken Thread: An Anthology of Plays by Asian American Women*. Ed. Roberta Uno. Amherst: U of Massachusetts P, 1993. 155–200.

The Joy Luck Club. Screenplay by Amy Tan and Ronald Bass. Dir. Wayne Wang. Hollywood Pictures, 1993.

"*Joy Luck Club* Rights Acquired by Vintage." *New York Times* 15 Apr. 1989, sec. 1: 15.

Keller, Nora Okja. *Comfort Woman*. New York: Viking, 1998.

Kepner, Susan. "The Amazing Adventures of Amy Tan." *San Francisco Focus Magazine* 36.5 (1989): 58+.

Kikumura, Akemi. *Through Harsh Winters: The Life of a Japanese Immigrant Woman*. Novato: Chandler, 1981.

Kim, Elaine. "'Such Opposite Creatures': Men and Women in Asian American Literature." *Michigan Quarterly Review* 29.1 (1990): 68–93.

Kitano, Harry H. L., and Roger Daniels. *Asian Americans: Emerging Minorities.* 2nd ed. Englewood Cliffs: Prentice, 1995.

Koenig, Rhonda. "Heirloom China." *New York Magazine* 20 Mar. 1989: 82–83.

Lee, Mary Paik. *Quiet Odyssey: A Pioneer Korean Woman in America.* Seattle: U of Washington P, 1990.

Lew, Julie. "How Stories Written for Mother Became Amy Tan's Best Seller." *New York Times* 4 July 1989, sec. 1: 23.

Lim, Shirley Geok-lin. "Asian American Daughters Rewriting Asian Maternal Texts." *Asian Americans: Comparative and Global Perspectives.* Ed. Shirley Hune, Hyung-chan Kim, and Stephen Fugita. Pullman: Washington State UP, 1991. 239–48.

Ling, Amy. *Between Worlds: Women Writers of Chinese Ancestry.* New York: Pergamon, 1990.

Lowe, Lisa. "Heterogeneity, Hybridity, Multiplicity: Marking Asian American Difference." *Diaspora* 1.1 (1991): 24–44.

Marks-Frost, Marjorie. "1989 *Los Angeles Times* Book Prize Nominees." *Los Angeles Times* 3 Sept. 1989: 6.

McAllister, Melanie. "(Mis)Reading *The Joy Luck Club.*" *Asian America: Journal of Culture and the Arts* 1 (1992): 102–18.

McDowell, Edwin. "The Media Business: Publishers Experiment with Lower Prices." *New York Times* 8 May 1989: D10.

Min, Anchee. *Red Azalea.* New York: Berkley, 1999.

Miner, Valerie. "*The Joy Luck Club.*" *Nation* 24 Apr. 1989: 566.

Rodriguez, Richard. *Hunger of Memory: The Education of Richard Rodriguez: An Autobiography.* Boston: Godine, 1981.

Schueller, Malini Johar. "Theorizing Ethnicity and Subjectivity: Maxine Hong Kingston's *Tripmaster Monkey* and Amy Tan's *The Joy Luck Club.*" *Genders* 15 (1992): 72–85.

See, Carolyn. "Drowning in America, Starving for China: *The Joy Luck Club* by Amy Tan." *Los Angeles Times* 12 Mar. 1989: 1.

Somogyi, Barbara, and David Stanton. "Amy Tan: An Interview." *Poets and Writers Magazine* Sept.-Oct. 1991: 24–32.

Souris, Stephen. "Only Two Kinds of Daughters: Inter-Monologue Dialogicity in *The Joy Luck Club.*" *MELUS* 19.2 (1994): 99–123.

Tan, Amy. "Alien Relative." *Charlie Chan Is Dead: An Anthology of Contemporary Asian American Fiction.* Ed. Jessica Hagedorn. New York: Penguin, 1993. 450–61.

———. *The Chinese Siamese Cat.* New York: Macmillan, 1994.

———. *The Hundred Secret Senses.* New York: Putnam, 1995.

———. *The Joy Luck Club.* New York: Putnam, 1989.

———. *The Kitchen God's Wife.* New York: Putnam, 1991.

———. *The Moon Lady.* New York: Macmillan, 1992.

———. "Mother Tongue." *Under Western Eyes: Personal Essays from Asian America.* Ed. Garrett Hongo. New York: Anchor-Doubleday, 1995. 314–20.

———. "Young Girl's Wish." *New Yorker* 2 Oct. 1995: 80–89.

TuSmith, Bonnie. *All My Relatives: Community in Contemporary Ethnic American Literatures.* Ann Arbor: U of Michigan P, 1994.

Wang, Ping. *American Visa*. Minneapolis: Coffee House, 1994.

Wong, Sau-ling Cynthia. "'Sugar Sisterhood': Situating the Amy Tan Phenomenon." *The Ethnic Canon: Histories, Institutions, and Interventions*. Ed. David Palumbo-Liu. Minneapolis: U of Minnesota P, 1995. 174–210.

Wong, Su-ling, and E. H. Cressy. *Daughter of Confucius: A Personal History*. New York: Farrar, 1952.

Woo, Elaine. "Striking Cultural Sparks: Once Pained by Her Heritage, Amy Tan Has Tapped It for a Piercing First Novel." *Los Angeles Times* 12 Mar. 1989: 1.

Xu, Ben. "Memory and the Ethnic Self: Reading Amy Tan's *The Joy Luck Club*." *MELUS* 19.1 (1994): 3–18.

Yung, Judy. *Unbound Feet: A Social History of Chinese Women in San Francisco*. Berkeley: U of California P, 1995.

Drama

The Year of the Dragon
by Frank Chin

Cheng Lok Chua

Publication and Production Information

First stage production at the American Place Theatre, New York City, 22 May 1974. A television production for PBS was videotaped by WNET, New York, in 1975 for the series Theatre in America. Released in softcover book format in 1981 in The Chickencoop Chinaman *and* The Year of the Dragon: *Two Plays by Frank Chin*, edited by Dorothy Ritsuko McDonald and published by the University of Washington Press.

Overview

As the play begins, Pa Eng seems to have accomplished the American immigrant's dream of prosperity, posterity, and even celebrity. He is the proprietor of the successful Chinatown Tour and Travel agency, he has fathered three children, and he is the mayor of Chinatown. But Pa is elderly and ill, and he senses that his days are numbered. He wants to die surrounded by his family, so he has sent for his first wife, China Mama, without communicating his intent to the other family members. China Mama's unannounced arrival causes much consternation, and throughout her visit Pa Eng shows himself to be an inconsiderate, uncomprehending, and autocratic patriarch.

Indeed, Pa Eng's patriarchal dominance and his Chinese values have acted as long-standing denials of his eldest son Fred's sense of identity and self-worth. Fred, the protagonist of the play, loves and hates, respects and resents, obeys and rebels against his father. He has sacrificed his ambition to become a writer for the duties of running the family travel agency and providing his sister Sissy's college expenses (thus enabling her to start her food and cookbook business in Boston in partnership with her Caucasian husband, Ross). Fred nurses his father when he spits blood, wipes him

175

after he defecates. But because Fred is neither a doctor nor a lawyer (Chinese Americans' stereotypical icons of success), Pa considers him to be nothing at all. Fred is also aware that his younger brother, Johnny, is fast deteriorating into a pistol-wielding Chinatown mobster and wants him to leave his environment and go east to college. Johnny resists, but Fred knows that Johnny will comply if Pa Eng orders him to go. Pa refuses. Instead, he wants Fred to accompany him to his mayoral Chinese New Year address. In this speech, Pa plans to acknowledge Fred as his heir, but he will do so in such a way that Fred will always be saddled with the stereotypical identity of being his father's Number One Son (à la Charlie Chan's), a person whose worth derives only from his forebear. This is unacceptable to Fred, who refuses to accompany his father as long as his father refuses to order Johnny to leave Chinatown. Attempting to impose his will, Pa slaps Fred around. This exertion proves to be too much for the sick old man, and he dies in this pitiful moment of futile tyranny. Tragically, Pa Eng's death does not free his family. The final tableau of the play shows Fred congealed in his milieu as he slips into his spiel of a Chinatown tour guide pandering an exoticized glimpse of his people to a voyeuristic audience (whom he curses sotto voce). As Fred trots out his patter on a darkened stage, the theater's spotlight singles him out, a solitary figure garbed in glaring white, the Chinese color of death.

Reception

The Year of the Dragon opened on 22 May 1974 at the American Place Theatre in New York City with a cast of several fine Asian American artists led by the Shakespearean actor Randall Kim and the well-known Pat Suzuki. Reviews of Chin's theater have typically been mixed. On the one hand, the *New Yorker*'s Edith Oliver lauded Chin as a gifted creator of convincingly complex characters, and on the other hand, the *New York Daily News* reviewer could make no sense of Chin's work (Watt 238); meanwhile, striking a balance, Clive Barnes's notice in the *New York Times* was characteristic of the sympathetic but bemused reviewer. Most reviewers tended to appreciate the importance of Chin's intent and subject matter—a serious treatment of Chinese American life—but they also faulted such aspects as the play's discursiveness and its overly painful realism.

The play was sufficiently well regarded to be videotaped in 1975 by PBS for its Theatre in America series. A West Coast production of the play (with Frank Chin playing the role of Fred and designing the set) was staged in 1977 by the Asian American Theater Workshop in San Francisco, and although Bernard Weiner of the *San Francisco Chronicle* liked its powerhouse plot, he also thought that the play was grossly overwritten.

The Year of the Dragon was the second play by Chin to receive the recognition of a New York production. His first play to do so was *The Chickencoop Chinaman*, staged by the American Place Theatre in 1972. These two dramas place Chin as the first Chinese American playwright to have had serious drama produced on the New York stage. To be sure, C. Y. Lee's *Flower Drum Song* (adapted from his novel) had been immensely popular the decade before, but Lee's work was a determinedly cheerful comedy presenting an exoticized, sanitized, and, in Elaine Kim's phrase, "highly euphemized" (106) picture of Chinatown life. In Chin's plays, the humor when present is dark and angry, and his work has been compared with that of John Osborne (in the vein of Britain's angry young men) as well as with that of Clifford Odets. In their intellectual content and intent Chin's dramas resemble problem plays, turning on intertwining issues of identity—ethnic, gender, individual, and generational. They explode stereotypes of Chinese Americans as members of a model minority who are emasculated, who live happily together in hierarchical families in exotic ghettos, and who efface their individual selves in deference to community. On the contrary, Chin's dramas thrust into their spectators' faces painful truths about searing conflicts—familial, individual, and communal. These truths are told with exuberant verbal pyrotechnics, a trademark of Chin's writing, and Chin's language ranges from black ghetto dialect to hipster talk to authentic Chinatown Cantonese—not Hollywood's Charlie Chan–ese.

Frank Chin's pioneering work on the American stage has opened the door for serious Asian American dramatists who followed him, writers such as David Henry Hwang (with whom Chin disagrees about many things) and Philip Kan Gotanda. Chin's daring and verbally exuberant theater asserted the presence of the richly unique and deeply human complexity of Chinese American urban life, and his work brought this presence to the attention of the American public. He criticized the false myths and deadening stereotypes of self and ethnicity about Asian Americans held by Caucasians and Asians alike. At a time when it was ripe and necessary to do so, Chin proclaimed and demonstrated that there was such an entity as Asian American theater and literature—a claim that American literary history has to reckon with if it is to be true to itself.

Author's Biographical Background

By his own accounting Frank Chew Chin, Jr., is fifth-generation Chinese American, born on 25 February 1940 (a Year of the Dragon) in Berkeley, California, where his parents lived and worked. Through the World War II years he was raised in the Mother Lode country (i.e., the Sierras). He also spent several of his growing up years in the Chinatowns of Oakland and San Francisco where, according to Chin, his father became president of the Six Companies (a position equivalent to being the mayor of Chinatown). Frank Chin, therefore, writes about San Francisco's Chinatown from a store of personal knowledge and experience.

From 1958 to 1961, Chin attended the University of California, Berkeley, where he won several prizes for fiction writing. In 1961, he was awarded a fellowship at the writer's workshop at the University of Iowa, where he remained until 1963.

After leaving Iowa, Chin worked for the Southern Pacific Railroad, becoming the first Chinese American to be a brakeman on the rails laid by his forefathers. Chin eventually quit the railroad company to become a writer-producer for KING-TV in Seattle during the late 1960s, and several of his shows were aired by PBS and on *Sesame Street*. By this time, Chin was married and had become the father of two children.

Chin left Seattle to teach Asian American studies at San Francisco State University and the University of California, Davis, in 1969–70. With a group of other scholars, he organized the Combined Asian American Resources Project, which did important pioneering work in collecting and preserving the Asian American materials that are now housed in the Bancroft Library of the University of California, Berkeley. The group was also responsible for the republication of several key Asian American texts by the University of Washington Press. Chin and several of his collaborators edited *Aiiieeeee!*, an important if controversial anthology attempting to define present Asian American literature. In 1972, Chin founded the Asian American Theater Workshop in San Francisco with the support of the American Conservatory Theater (where he has been a writer in residence). That same year saw the production of Chin's first play, *The Chickencoop Chinaman*. Chin's work has received the recognition and support of many endowments, including the Rockefeller Foundation and the National Endowment for the Arts.

Since the 1980s Chin has located himself in Los Angeles and is in his third marriage. He has channeled his energies more toward the writing of fiction and children's literature rather than toward drama. Meanwhile, his continuing research in Asian American lore and history has also borne fruit in several significant exhibitions and another coedited anthology, *The Big Aiiieeeee!* (Chan et al.).

Historical Context for the Narratives in *The Year of the Dragon*

In Chin's drama, two relatively minor characters provide context and draw attention to two different yet related elements of Chinese American history. China Mama is an apparition of the Chinese American past; Ross is a harbinger of the Chinese American future.

China Mama appears on the stage like a malodorous breath of the Chinese American past. On the one hand, because of the insensitive manner in which Pa Eng foists China Mama on his second wife, China Mama is a reproachful reminder of the demeaning sexist Chinese system of polygamy and concubinage that was common practice in imperial China and through the earlier twentieth century. On the other hand, China Mama's presence and her former absence are emblematic of the dehumanizing and racist American immigration laws that were designed to exclude Chinese (and other Asians) from establishing themselves in the United States (Nee and Nee 409–10). Indeed, one such law, the Immigration Act of 1924, specifically excluded Chinese women, wives, and prostitutes from immigrating to the United States (see Kingston, *China Men* 156). Pa Eng came to the United States in 1935 and therefore had to leave

China Mama in China. Frank Chin puts an additional spin on this historical situation by having Pa Eng eventually marry Ma (Hyacinth), an American-born Chinese and thus an American citizen. By marrying Pa, Ma was breaching yet another American law intended to prevent Chinese from establishing themselves in the United States: citizens who married Chinese persons stood to lose their United States citizenship.

Contrasting and complementing China Mama, the character Ross is an ominous harbinger of the Chinese American future. Ross, a Caucasian, is married to Sis. Chin paints him with an unsympathetic brush, making him out to be a well-intentioned but bumbling sinophile—a cultural voyeur who has married into a Chinese family almost like a tourist seeking a privileged entrée to an exotic spot. Sis, like many Chinese Americans, married out of her race after the miscegenation laws were lifted by various states in the 1950s and 1960s. Indeed, exogamy for Asian Americans as a whole is becoming commonplace. As this trend continues, some observers (among them Chin) foresee an end to Chinese America as it now exists and regard Chinese Americans as a doomed breed of people.

Historical Context for the Writing of *The Year of the Dragon*

The 1970s, the decade in which Frank Chin brought this play to production, was the decade that followed the era of the civil rights movement and the anti–Vietnam War protests. It was, consequently, a time of heightened awareness of ethnic identity and an increased sense of ethnic pride. Ethnic minorities were not so eager to blend away their distinguishing ethnic traits and heritages into the mythical melting pot of America. Rather, many wanted to preserve and assert their ethnic differences and configure America as a plural rather than a homogenized society. Asian American consciousness of such ideals was undoubtedly heightened by upheavals such as the Third World student strikes at San Francisco State University (1968) and at the University of California, Berkeley (1969). In a development parallel to the black arts movement, Asian American writers and scholars (in whose vanguard was Frank Chin) began to do invaluable work in recuperating Asian American literary works from obscurity and in producing literary works that asserted and sought to define the Asian American identity and experience. This mood of assertive ethnicity is noticeably reflected in the in-your-face style of Chin's writing and in the themes that preoccupy him.

Readers will also notice that *The Year of the Dragon* presents a picture of a Chinatown that, like the Eng family, is disintegrating and dying and that is in danger of being peopled not by real human inhabitants but only by caricatural figments of the tourists' and the media's stereotypes. During the late 1960s and 1970s, San Francisco Chinatown was a bitterly contested site between forces of urban development and those wishing to preserve its identity as an ethnic community. Matters came to a head in the violent incidents surrounding the demolition of the International Hotel, which seemed to portend the eradication of an essential feature in San Francisco Chinatown's character (Nee and Nee 389–91), and the mood of mortality in Chin's play reflects the pessimism of certain Chinatown dwellers.

Major Themes

Asian American identity (including the myth of the model minority and the
    stereotype of the emasculated Chinese American male)
individual identity (including filial identity, patriarchal identity)
Homo ludens (artistic accomplishment vs. material success, extravagance vs.
    necessity)
the immigration experience
generational conflict (including immigrant vs. native-born generations)
dysfunctional families
the relationship between fathers and sons (including oedipal ramifications)
intermarriage and exogamy
Chinatown: moribund ghetto or model community?

Critical Issues

Unlike Chin's earlier, more surrealistic play, *The Year of the Dragon* is written in a realistic mode. Some might even term it naturalistic drama because of its insistence on the more unsavory aspects of life—for example, Fred's waving his feet in China Mama's face, Ma's hysterical hemorrhoids, and Pa's gargantuan defecation. Yet, despite the predominantly realistic mode that governs the scenes set inside the Engs' apartment, Chin broadens the conventional theater's suspension of disbelief with several scenes set in an abstract site outside the Engs' apartment. These exterior scenes all depict Fred Eng going through his tour guide's spiel. In fact, since the tour spiel both opens and closes the play, it becomes a framing device for the drama's action and signals the ironic and what Fred feels and thinks as a human being. This framing device is also perhaps intended to challenge and discomfit members of Chin's theater audience by putting them into the position of the gawking tourists listening.

    Chin's play puts the counterpoint of exterior-abstract and interior-concrete scenes to further use. For instance, in the play's climactic and catastrophic moment when Pa slaps Fred and then dies, the unseen exterior action represented by the jubilant sounds of the New Year's parade ironically punctuate the violent argument occurring in the interior of the apartment. The parade signaling the passing of the old year parallels the death of Pa Eng. This contrapuntal technique is more frequently seen in the montage sequences of film than it is on stage, though its provenance is the spatial form that Flaubert brought to perfection in his *Madame Bovary* (see Frank 14–16).

    Identity is a central theme of Chin's play. Around this thematic core revolve corollary questions and conflicts such as the stereotyping of identity (especially the stereotyping of Asian Americans as a model minority), the denial of identity (such as a father denying that his son can be an independent entity), and the creation of identify and self-worth (such as Fred's attempt to assert his ability and his worth as a writer). One of the especially ironic twists that Chin gives to this theme occurs when he shows how a member of a group can internalize a stereotyped identity put on him by a majority entity and then apply that stereotype to others of his own group: this colonized state of mind (Li 218) is illustrated by the way in which Pa Eng internalizes the stereotype of Charlie Chan and adopts it as a suitable model for his own behavior.

Another important theme related to that of identity is the conflict between the values of necessity and extravagance (S. Wong 175–86). One sees this conflict fueling the hostility between Pa (the champion of utilitarian values of material success) and Fred (an aspirant to the aesthetic values of self-actualization as a writer).

Pedagogical Issues and Suggestions

As with most plays, the best way to experience *The Year of the Dragon* is to view a performance of it. Revivals of this play are rare, however, and the videotaped performance recorded by WNET of New York and broadcast by PBS in 1975 is not easily available. It is always useful for readers of plays to visualize a production and its stage setting. The photographs included in Dorothy McDonald's edition of the play provide a useful starting point for class discussion—the characters begin to have faces, and the stage space starts to fill with furniture.

For student readers unfamiliar with the sound of the Cantonese dialect, Frank Chin's transcriptions of his Chinese characters' speech may appear daunting. But Chin either has parenthetical translations of these utterances in his text, or else he has slipped the meaning of the utterance into the text of the dialogue itself, so that the alert reader can be cued into Chin's meanings by these prompts. For the unaccustomed, Pa Eng's pronunciation of English may be difficult to unravel, but probably no more so than the southern speech and spelling of a writer like William Faulkner or Richard Wright. An exposure to speech patterns similar to Pa Eng's could be provided by watching and listening to the Chinese American actor Victor Wong in such films as *Eat a Bowl of Tea* or *Dim Sum*.

A topic that elicits the curiosity of students is the exclusionary immigration legislation erected by the United States against Chinese and other Asian immigrants. Background on this subject can be found in a readable, book-length treatment of Asian American immigration, Ronald Takaki's *Strangers from a Different Shore*. A brief enumeration of these laws is also set forth in the chapter entitled "The Laws" in Maxine Hong Kingston's *China Men*.

There is an abundance of writing on Asian Americans as the "model minority." An article popularizing this term during the 1960s is *U.S. News and World Report*'s "Success Story of One Minority Group in the U.S." In the 1980s, *Newsweek* trumpeted this construct with its report "Asian-Americans: A Model Minority" (Kasindorf and

Shapiro) and was echoed by articles in *Time* (Doerner), *Fortune* (Ramirez), and *New Republic* (Bell). The term may at first blush seem to have flattering connotations. But writers like Chin have strongly objected to it for its falsifications and invidiousness (see, e.g., Chin and Chan's "Racist Love").

Intertextual Linkages

With Louis Chu's *Eat a Bowl of Tea*: father-son relationships, the comparison between New York's and San Francisco's Chinatown.

With Milton Murayama's *All I Asking for Is My Body*: father-son relationships, family life in a Japanese American plantation community in Hawai'i and in a Chinatown community.

With Maxine Hong Kingston's *The Woman Warrior*: the mother-daughter relationship and the father-son relationship, polygamy (the wife from China—see Kingston's chapter "At the Western Palace").

With Jade Snow Wong's *Fifth Chinese Daughter*, Pardee Lowe's *Father and Glorious Descendant*, or Laurence Yep's *Dragonwings*: depictions of growing up in Chinatown and the parent-child relationship.

With Hisaye Yamamoto's "Seventeen Syllables": utilitarian values in conflict with aesthetic values.

With David Henry Hwang's *Family Devotions*: the suburban Chinese American family and the Chinatown family.

With Chinua Achebe's *Things Fall Apart*: the father-son antagonism and the differences between the values of the men—Okonkwo's utilitarian values of warrior and worker contrast with his father's aesthetic values of music and good will, as well as with his own son's Christian spiritual values; the sense of a society that is decaying and dying.

With Piri Thomas's *Down These Mean Streets*: father-son relationships, coming to terms with a racial identity.

Bibliographic Resources

Chin's other published play is *The Chickencoop Chinaman*; another play, *Gee, Pop*, has been circulated in manuscript form. Chin has also published several works of fiction—a collection of eight short stories entitled *The Chinaman Pacific and Frisco R.R. Co.*, and two novels, *Donald Duk* and *Gunga Din Highway*—as well as a volume of essays, *"Bulletproof Buddhists" and Other Essays*. Several of his short stories treat parent-child situations and Chinatown backgrounds similar to those dramatized in *The Year of the Dragon*. Worth noting are "Food for All His Dead" and "A Chinese Lady Dies." Chin has coedited two important anthologies of Asian American literature, *Aiiieeeee!* and

The Big Aiiieeeee! (Chan et al.), which feature bracing polemical introductions and an essay by Chin. Several of Chin's interviews give useful and revealing glimpses into his intentions and opinion; see "Frank Chin, 32," in Victor Nee and Brett de Bary Nee's *Longtime Californ'*, and Robert Murray Davis's "Frank Chin: An Interview." *Longtime Californ'* also contains many interesting and informative interviews with Chinatown dwellers of the 1960s.

Bibliography

Achebe, Chinua. *Things Fall Apart*. New York: Fawcett, 1959.

Barnes, Clive. "Theater: Culture Study." Rev. of *The Year of the Dragon*, by Frank Chin. *New York Times* 3 June 1974: 39.

Bell, David A. "The Triumph of Asian-Americans." *New Republic* 15–22 July 1985: 24–31.

Chan, Jeffery Paul, et al., eds. *The Big Aiiieeeee! An Anthology of Chinese American and Japanese American Literature*. New York: Meridian, 1991.

Chin, Frank. *"Bulletproof Buddhists" and Other Essays*. Honolulu: U of Hawai'i P; Los Angeles: UCLA Asian Amer. Studies Center, 1998.

———. The Chickencoop Chinaman *and* The Year of the Dragon: *Two Plays by Frank Chin*. Ed. Dorothy Ritsuko McDonald. Seattle: U of Washington P, 1981.

———. *The Chinaman Pacific and Frisco R.R. Co.* Minneapolis: Coffee House, 1988.

———. "A Chinese Lady Dies." Chin, *Chinaman Pacific* 109–30.

———. *Donald Duk*. Minneapolis: Coffee House, 1991.

———. "Food for All His Dead." *Asian-American Authors*. Ed. Kai-yu Hsu and Helen Palubinskas. Boston: Houghton, 1972. 47–61.

———. *Gunga Din Highway*. Minneapolis: Coffee House, 1994.

———. "I Am Talking to the Strategist, Sun Tzu, about Life When the Subject of War Comes Up." *Amerasia Journal* 17.1 (1991): 65–106.

Chin, Frank, and Jeffery Paul Chan. "Racist Love." *Seeing through Shuck*. Ed. Richard Kostelanetz. New York: Ballantine, 1972. 65–79.

Chin, Frank, et al., eds. *Aiiieeeee! An Anthology of Asian-American Writers*. Washington: Howard UP, 1974.

Chu, Louis. *Eat a Bowl of Tea*. New York: Stuart, 1961.

Davis, Robert Murray. "Frank Chin: An Interview." *Amerasia Journal* 14.2 (1988):81–95.

———. "West Meets East: A Conversation with Frank Chin." *Amerasia Journal* 24.1 (1998): 87–103.

Dim Sum: A Little Bit of Heart. Dir. Wayne Wang. Perf. Victor Wong, Kim Chew, Laureen Chew, and Cora Miao. Orion, 1985.

Doerner, William R. "To America with Skills." *Time* 8 July 1985: 44–46.

Eat a Bowl of Tea. Dir. Wayne Wang. Perf. Cora Miao, Russell Wong, and Victor Wong. Columbia, 1989.

Flaubert, Gustave. *Madame Bovary*. 1875. Paris: Garnier, 1958.

Frank, Joseph. "Spatial Form in Modern Literature." *The Widening Gyre*. New Brunswick: Rutgers UP, 1963. 3–62.

"Frank Chin, 32." *Longtime Californ': A Documentary Study of an American Chinatown.* Comp. Victor Nee and Brett de Bary Nee. Boston: Houghton, 1974. 377–89.

Gotanda, Philip Kan. *Yankee Dawg You Die.* New York: Dramatists Play Service, 1991.

Hwang, David Henry. *Family Devotions. FOB and Other Plays.* New York: Plume, 1990. 87–146.

———. *M. Butterfly.* New York: Plume, 1989.

Kasindorf, Martin, and Daniel Shapiro. "Asian-Americans: A Model Minority." *Newsweek* 6 Dec. 1982: 39–42.

Kim, Elaine. *Asian American Literature: An Introduction to the Writings and Their Social Context.* Philadelphia: Temple UP, 1982.

Kingston, Maxine Hong. *China Men.* New York: Knopf, 1980.

———. *The Woman Warrior: Memoirs of a Girlhood among Ghosts.* New York: Knopf, 1976.

Lau, Joseph S. M. "The Albatross Exorcised: The Rime of Frank Chin." *Tamkang Review* 12.1 (1981): 93–105.

Lee, C. Y. *Flower Drum Song.* New York: Farrar, 1957.

Lee, Josephine. *Performing Asian America: Race and Ethnicity on the Contemporary Stage.* Philadelphia: Temple UP, 1997.

Li, David Leiwei. "The Formation of Frank Chin and Formations of Chinese American Literature." *Asian Americans: Comparative and Global Perspectives.* Ed. Shirley Hune et al. Pullman: Washington State UP, 1991. 211–23.

Ling, Jinqi. *Narrating Nationalisms: Ideology and Form in Asian American Literature.* New York: Oxford UP, 1998.

Lowe, Pardee. *Father and Glorious Descendant.* Boston: Little, 1943.

McDonald, Dorthy Ritsuko. Introduction. Chin, Chickencoop Chinaman ix–xxix.

Murayama, Milton. *All I Asking for Is My Body.* San Francisco: Supa, 1975.

Nee, Victor G., and Brett de Bary Nee. *Longtime Californ': A Documentary Study of an American Chinatown.* Boston: Houghton, 1974.

Oliver, Edith. "Reunion." Rev. of *The Year of the Dragon,* by Frank Chin. *New Yorker* 10 June 1974: 64.

Ramirez, Anthony. "America's Super Minority." *Fortune* 24 Nov. 1986: 148–60.

"Success Story of One Minority Group in the U.S." *U.S. News and World Report* 26 Dec. 1966: 73–76.

Takaki, Ronald. *Strangers from a Different Shore: A History of Asian Americans.* Boston: Little, 1989.

Thomas, Piri. *Down These Mean Streets.* New York: Knopf, 1967.

Watt, Douglas. "Chicken Coop Chinaman Is No Fun to Be With." *New York Theatre Critics' Reviews* 33.15 (1972): 238.

Weiner, Bernard. "Overwritten Family Drama." Rev. of *The Year of the Dragon,* by Frank Chin. *San Francisco Chronicle* 19 Apr. 1977: 44.

Wong, Jade Snow. *Fifth Chinese Daughter.* New York: Harper, 1974.

Wong, Sau-ling Cynthia. *Reading Asian American Literature: From Necessity to Extravagance.* Princeton: Princeton UP, 1993.

Yamamoto, Hisaye. *"Seventeen Syllables" and Other Stories.* Latham: Kitchen Table, 1988.

Yep, Laurence. *Dragonwings.* New York: Harper, 1975.

Yankee Dawg You Die
by Philip Kan Gotanda

Nancy Cho

Production and Publication Information

Yankee Dawg You Die had its world premiere at the Berkeley Repertory Theatre in Berkeley, California, in February 1988 and was presented by Playwrights Horizons in New York City in April 1989. First published in 1991 by Dramatists Play Service, New York, it is now more widely available in Fish Head Soup *and Other Plays*, a collection of four plays by Gotanda with an introduction by Michael Omi, published in 1995 by the University of Washington Press.

Overview

Yankee Dawg You Die blends comedy and drama to depict the aspirations and frustrations of Asian American actors in the entertainment industry. The play centers on the relationship between two characters, a seasoned veteran of stage and screen named Vincent Chang and an idealistic, rising performer named Bradley Yamashita. While Vincent has made his career by never turning down a role, even those including throwaway lines like the one expressed by the play's title, Bradley claims that he would never stoop to playing ethnically stereotyped bit parts. Over the course of the play, the political tension and professional rivalry between them settles into an uneasy friendship, as they realize that they share common goals and experiences both as actors and as Asian American men.

Roughly employing a play-within-a-play structure, *Yankee Dawg You Die* uses conversations between Vincent and Bradley, dramatic monologues, and excerpts from performance pieces to convey the evolving relationship between the two characters and to explore the larger dynamic of Asian Americans in popular culture. Humorous allusions to figures such as Godzilla and Neil Sedaka counterpoint references to Asian

American performers as Vincent and Bradley discuss their lives and work. The play does not conform to one genre or tone but, rather, becomes a testing ground for various types of acting—naturalism, song and dance, abstract performance art—that mediate the representation of Asians on the stage and screen. In *Yankee Dawg You Die*, questions of cultural identity and personal growth are intimately linked to the professional choices made by the characters, so that the realm of acting and performance becomes a fluid medium through which to communicate ideas about race, ethnicity, gender, and sexuality, as well as about the craft of making plays and films.

Reception

Receiving both critical and popular acclaim in Berkeley and New York (see the reviews by Kramer and Hornby), *Yankee Dawg You Die* helped to broaden Gotanda's fame beyond the network of Asian American theaters where he honed his playwriting skills in the late 1970s and early 1980s. The play, along with David Henry Hwang's *M. Butterfly* and Velina Hasu Houston's *Tea*, is part of an ever-growing body of Asian American dramas that have been produced in regional theaters around the country and have drawn attention from the mainstream press. *Yankee Dawg You Die* and the play Gotanda wrote just before it, *The Wash* (1986), are his two best-known works. Gotanda received the 1989 Will Glickman Playwriting Award for *Yankee Dawg You Die*.

Author's Biographical Background

Gotanda is a Sansei, a third-generation Japanese American, who grew up in Stockton, California, during a time when Asian American consciousness was just taking root. His early years were shaped by exposure to both Japanese and American cultural influences, ranging from samurai movies and the Buddhist Church to the music of Bob Dylan and Miles Davis. On entering the University of Santa Cruz in 1969, Gotanda experimented with several paths of study and participated in the budding Asian American movement, while he also nurtured his love for music by playing in rock bands. In 1970 he traveled to Japan to study ceramics and returned with a determination to explore his creative interests and contribute to the making of Asian American culture. Gotanda wrote numerous songs about his experiences as an Asian American but could find no marketing niche for his work—a situation with parallels to the themes expressed in *Yankee Dawg You Die*. Gotanda also pursued a legal career as a means of both helping the Asian American community and securing a more stable professional life.

Gotanda's playwriting career began while he was still completing his legal studies and working for the North Beach–Chinatown Legal Aid in San Francisco. His first piece was a rock musical entitled *The Avocado Kid*, which was based on the Japanese folk tale "Momotaro." After the East West Players in Los Angeles produced the play in 1979, Gotanda turned to playwriting full time. In addition to *The Avocado Kid* and *Yankee Dawg You Die*, Gotanda's many works for the stage include *A Song for a Nisei Fisherman*, *The Dream of Kitamura*, *Bullet Headed Birds* (all first presented by the Asian American Theater Workshop), *The Wash*, *Fish Head Soup*, and *Day Standing on Its Head*.

Historical Context for the Narratives in *Yankee Dawg You Die*

Although the play is implicitly set in the present moment (no historical period is specified in the stage directions), *Yankee Dawg You Die* engages rather broadly with the entire history of Asian Americans in the entertainment industry. We are told that Vincent is a "former hoofer" (72) in his mid to late sixties, while Bradley is described as an actor in his mid to late twenties. Thus, the play's historical context includes the contemporary film and television arenas as well as the early days of the "Chop Suey Circuit," the avenue by which Asian American performers first took the stage as singers and dancers in nightclubs like the Forbidden City in San Francisco and the China Doll in New York City. From the dialogue in the play, we learn that Vincent was one of the pioneering Asian American performing artists, along with figures like Anna Mae Wong and Sessue Hayakawa.

Yankee Dawg You Die weighs the achievements of Vincent, who throughout his career has had little control over his roles, against the more politically aware choices of Bradley, who has come of age during a period of Asian American consciousness-raising. The character of Vincent serves as a reminder of the time when it was considered a major breakthrough for an Asian performer simply to be seen on the stage or screen, even if the role was demeaning or stereotypical. Bradley's character, by contrast, denotes the wider range of opportunities afforded by the contemporary theater and film world, particularly with the advent of Asian American writers creating works for Asian American performers and audiences. It is crucial, however, to avoid viewing the career histories of Vincent and Bradley as markers on an evolutionary path from objectification to empowerment. Even in the contemporary entertainment industry, as Bradley discovers, there is a dearth of roles available to Asian American actors and a tendency in the mainstream marketplace to associate Asian faces with the accents and appearances of ethnic caricatures. Furthermore, the play suggests that some of the bit parts and cardboard characters of Vincent's early career helped pave the way for subsequent Asian performers to take the stage, and Bradley himself admits that Vincent has served as an important role model. The historical context for the play is thus quite rich; it asks the audience to contemplate the interdependency of past and present and reveals the little-known participation of Asian Americans in the history of American popular culture.

Historical Context for the Writing of *Yankee Dawg You Die*

Gotanda wrote *Yankee Dawg You Die* at a significant moment in the evolution of Asian American theater and cultural production. During the mid-1980s when the play was being composed, Asian American studies was starting to expand beyond California institutions, and Maxine Hong Kingston's seminal work, *The Woman Warrior*, was fast becoming a staple in college and university courses. Meanwhile, the national visibility of Asian American theater received a huge boost with the Broadway success of David Henry Hwang's *M. Butterfly*. In keeping with this emergent mainstreaming of Asian American culture, *Yankee Dawg You Die* could be viewed as Gotanda's crossover work, in that it has played primarily not in Asian American theaters but in several major regional venues around the country. Within the context of Gotanda's career, *Yankee Dawg You Die* signals a departure from the intimate, family-centered drama of his earlier works by positioning Asian American experience within a wider social and political spectrum. The success of this play with mainstream audiences thus registers the increased national recognition of Asian American issues and suggests the play's ability to engage with this changing social context.

At the same time, however, the historical moment of the play's creation calls attention to the limitations surrounding the movement of Asian Americans into the public sphere. The premiere of *Yankee Dawg You Die* almost exactly coincided with the controversy over the casting of *Miss Saigon*, a British musical about the Vietnam War that was poised to make its Broadway debut in 1988. When Jonathan Pryce, an English actor, was cast to play the Eurasian role of the Engineer, vehement protest ensued from the Asian American theater community. Pryce had played the role to great success in London and had worn prosthetics on his eyelids to convey a Eurasian appearance. After much heated debate in the popular press, Actors Equity allowed Pryce to reprise the role on Broadway without the use of prosthetics. The *Miss Saigon* controversy thus highlighted the inequities of casting practices in the professional theater, as well as the dearth of substantive roles for Asian and Asian American actors.

Major Themes

the role of popular culture in Asian American experience
the history of racism in the entertainment industry
the internalization of stereotypes
the tension between artistic idealism and political realities
the price of assimilation
the use of performance to assert a cultural identity
intergenerational relationships among Asian Americans
masculinity and sexuality
the mutability of identity

Critical Issues

The play is at once a scathing satire of the entertainment industry's history of racial caricature and a thoughtful meditation on identity formation that uses the theater as a metaphor to explore the permutations of selfhood. In other words, the play's obvious political argument—that stereotypes are both omnipresent and deeply damaging—is complicated by a more questioning tone that asks the audience to think very carefully about what constitutes a stereotype in the first place and what defines a "good" role for an actor.

The play's central conflict resides in the tension between the pressures of the commercial marketplace and the idealism of artistic expression. Gotanda contemplates the vexing question of whether it is preferable to take any part in a mainstream project to gain national exposure or to work only in ethnic-specific productions in hopes of preserving personal integrity. Over the course of the play, the audience sees Bradley and Vincent switch positions on this matter, so that in the end Bradley chooses a bit part in a mainstream Hollywood project while Vincent accepts a low-paying part in a new work by an Asian American playwright. *Yankee Dawg You Die* suggests that there is no "correct" path to take and that Asian American performers must use a variety of tactics to gain experience and make their voices heard. Despite the play's subtlety and thoughtfulness, it has nonetheless drawn some criticism for being complicit in the very gestures that it seeks to subvert. Like David Henry Hwang's *M. Butterfly*, Amy Tan's *The Joy Luck Club*, and other commercially successful works, *Yankee Dawg You Die* has failed to escape accusations that it, too, has sold well to mainstream audiences precisely because it has "sold out" (see the works by Moy for a full account of this argument). Whether or not one reads the play as successful in its attempt to dismantle marketplace stereotypes, the central point remains that no artistic production is ever "free" from commercial concerns.

The play's resistance to generic classification is also worth discussing. Because the two main characters are also actors, *Yankee Dawg You Die* presents its audience with a lively collage of different acting techniques and theatrical genres. The play interposes naturalistic scenes with musical comedy, dramatic monologues, and dream sequences. Thus, the very form of the play is an embodiment of the search for belonging and appropriate self-expression undertaken by both Vincent and Bradley.

Pedagogical Issues and Suggestions

Yankee Dawg You Die would work well in a literature, drama, or Asian American studies course. Gotanda addresses urgent and accessible issues, such as the power of stereotypes and the role of material culture in disseminating these images. Students are likely to enjoy the humor of the play, and they will probably appreciate Gotanda's focus on masculinity, which contrasts with the focus of many of the most "canonical" works of contemporary Asian American literature.

Students who are not accustomed to reading plays might need some help imagining how the play would look and sound in performance, and any attempt to bring the work "off the page" would be extremely beneficial to classroom study. Teachers might suggest that students pair up to read particular scenes out loud or have them do creative projects in which they imagine costumes, props, or musical accompaniments for the piece. The goal with these tactics is to encourage students to "stage" the play in their heads, so that they understand the challenge of translating the written script into a piece for performance. Individual students are likely to interpret the stage directions and dialogue very differently, thereby enriching the classroom study of the play. To foreground the visual and aural impact of live performance, teachers might want to show videos that introduce students to the history of Asian Americans in theater and film (see Other Resources, below). Certainly the play also invites students to contemplate the current state of Asian Americans in film and television and to investigate whether progress has been made.

Intertextual Linkages

With David Henry Hwang's M. *Butterfly*: the play-within-a-play structure, the politics of stereotyping, the production of "orientalism" on the Broadway stage, the performance of gender and racial roles, the fluidity of identity.

With David Henry Hwang's *The Dance and the Railroad*: masculinity, the need for role models, the use of performance to assert a cultural identity, the tension between artistic idealism and political realities.

With Frank Chin's *Donald Duk*: masculinity, the need for role models, the role of popular culture images in defining an identity, the interdependency between the present and the past.

With George C. Wolfe's *The Colored Museum*: the humorous confrontation of racial and ethnic sterotypes, the cultural "ownership" of these stereotypes, the performance of ethnic identity.

With Luis Valdez's *Zoot Suit*: the performance of ethnic identity, the politics of stereotyping, the need for role models, the mixing of theatrical genres, masculinity, the price of assimilation.

Bibliographic Resources

The drama anthology edited by Misha Berson contains *The Wash*, as well as some brief biographical background on Gotanda; this text provides an opportunity to compare Gotanda with other contemporary Asian American playwrights. Two other anthologies, edited by Velina Houston and Roberta Uno, collect plays by Asian American women. Both these anthologies contain introductory essays that provide useful overviews of Asian American theater and help to place Gotanda's work in a historical continuum. For those wanting to situate *Yankee Dawg You Die* in the context of Gotanda's oeuvre, the play appears in Fish Head Soup *and Other Plays*, along with *The Wash, A Song for a Nisei Fisherman*, and the title work of the collection. Finally, the anthology *Playwrights of Color*, edited by Meg Swanson, includes *Yankee Dawg You Die* and an introductory essay to the play and author.

Few critical studies discuss *Yankee Dawg You Die*. The primary works to consult, which both compare the play with David Henry Hwang's *M. Butterfly*, are James Moy's argument in *Theatre Journal* (slightly modified in his *Marginal Sights*) and Josephine Lee's analysis of the power of stereotypes in chapter 4 of *Performing Asian America*. Lee's book, in addition to its specific discussion of Gotanda's play, provides an excellent examination of some of the larger critical issues informing the production and reception of Asian American drama. Moy's *Marginal Sights* is useful for tracing the historical development of the racial images that appear in *Yankee Dawg You Die*.

Other Resources

Deborah Gee's excellent documentary, *Slaying the Dragon*, provides a fine overview of the history of Asian Americans in theater and film, with particular emphasis on media depictions of women. The film includes interviews with prominent Asian American actors as well as clips from numerous films and performances. Another important video resource is Arthur Dong's documentary, *Forbidden City U.S.A.*, about the legendary San Francisco nightclub.

Bibliography

Berson, Misha, ed. *Between Worlds: Contemporary Asian-American Plays*. New York: Theatre Communications, 1990.

Chin, Frank. *Donald Duk*. Minneapolis: Coffee House, 1991.

Forbidden City U.S.A. Dir. Arthur Dong. Natl. Asian Amer. Telecommunications Assn., 1989.

Gotanda, Philip Kan. Fish Head Soup *and Other Plays*. Seattle: U of Washington P, 1995.

———. *Yankee Dawg You Die*. New York: Dramatists Play Service, 1991. Rpt. in Gotanda, Fish Head Soup 69–130, and in Swanson 129–57.

Hornby, Richard. Rev. of *Yankee Dawg You Die*, by Philip Kan Gotanda. *Hudson Review* 42 (1989): 463.

Houston, Velina Hasu, ed. *The Politics of Life: Four Plays by Asian American Women*. Philadelphia: Temple UP, 1993.

Hwang, David Henry. *The Dance and the Railroad*. FOB and Other Plays. New York: Penguin, 1990. 51–86.

———. *M. Butterfly*. New York: NAL, 1989.

Kramer, Mimi. Rev. of *Yankee Dawg You Die*, by Philip Kan Gotanda. Playwrights Horizon, New York. *New Yorker* 29 May 1989: 97–98.

Lee, Josephine. *Performing Asian America: Race and Ethnicity on the Contemporary Stage.* Philadelphia: Temple UP, 1997.

Moy, James. "David Henry Hwang's *M. Butterfly* and Philip Kan Gotanda's *Yankee Dawg You Die*: Repositioning Chinese American Marginality on the American Stage." *Theatre Journal* 42 (1990): 48–56.

———. *Marginal Sights: Staging the Chinese in America.* Iowa City: U of Iowa P, 1993.

Slaying the Dragon. Dir. Deborah Gee. Natl. Asian Amer. Telecommunications Assn., 1987.

Swanson, Meg, ed. *Playwrights of Color.* Yarmouth: Intercultural, 1999.

Uno, Roberta, ed. *Unbroken Thread: An Anthology of Plays by Asian American Women.* Amherst: U of Massachusetts P, 1993.

Valdez, Luis. *Zoot Suit and Other Plays.* Houston: Arte Publico, 1992.

Wolfe, George C. *The Colored Museum.* New York: Grove, 1985.

Tea

by Velina Hasu Houston

Roberta Uno

Production and Publication Information

Before its publication, *Tea* was produced many times, beginning with its professional premiere at the Manhattan Theatre Club in New York City in October 1987. It is one of the most widely produced Asian American plays in mainstream, Asian American, and college and university theaters. Notable productions include the Old Globe Theatre production in San Diego, California, in 1988; the Whole Theatre production in Montclair, New Jersey, in 1989; the Syracuse Stage production in 1991; the Mount Holyoke College Department of Theatre production in South Hadley, Massachusetts, in 1991; and the Theatre X production in Tokyo, Japan, in 1995. First collected in *Unbroken Thread: An Anthology of Plays by Asian American Women*, edited by Roberta Uno, it was published in 1993 in hardcover and softcover by the University of Massachusetts Press.

Overview

Set in 1968 in Junction City, Kansas, a community attached to the United States Army base at Fort Riley, *Tea* explores the lives of five Japanese "war brides," native Japanese women married to United States servicemen during the post–World War II American occupation of Japan. Following the suicide of Himiko, an alienated member of their isolated community, four women, Atsuko, Teruko, Setsuko, and Chizuye, gather to clean her house. While the spirit of Himiko lingers in a peripheral netherworld, the women begin by sitting down to tea. Almost immediately the tensions and differences within the group surface. Atsuko, married to a Japanese American, is snobbish and prejudiced, convinced that by marrying within the race, she is superior. Teruko, married to a white Texan, ignores Atsuko's cruel comments regarding Koreans,

193

black Americans, and Vietnamese and buoys the group with her good nature and naïveté. Chizuye, the most Americanized of the group and the widow of a Mexican American, cannot mask her contempt for Atsuko and seizes choice moments to provoke and confront her. Because of her patient, forgiving, and compassionate nature, Setsuko, the widow of an African American, serves as the peacemaker. As the women take their tea they reminisce about their homeland, how they fell in love, their families' reactions to their marriages, the hostility encountered on arriving in and adjusting to their new country, the attitudes of their husbands, the joys and struggles of raising children—always returning to thoughts of Himiko, the misfit of their community. As Himiko's spirit implores them for understanding, they begin to face the truths of a woman who experienced a life of pain at the hands of an abusive husband and unsupportive community.

The play's construction reflects the themes of dual identity, fragmentation, and the confluence of past and present through the use of actors playing multiple roles; the mixture of linear dialogue, expressionistic monologue, and nonlinear flashbacks; and the use of dual location.

Reception

Tea was favorably reviewed in the establishment and Japanese vernacular presses, receiving outstanding notices in *Variety*, *Drama-Logue*, the *Los Angeles Times*, the *Seattle Times*, the *San Diego Tribune*, the *Honolulu Star-Bulletin*, and the *Rafu Shimpo*. It was selected as the critics' choice by both the *Los Angeles Times* and *Drama-Logue* in 1991; cited as one of the best ten plays of 1988 by Sylvia Drake of the *Los Angeles Times* for the Old Globe Theatre production; given the San Diego Drama Critics Circle Award for the Old Globe Theatre production in 1988; awarded the Susan Smith Blackburn Prize of London in 1986 as one of the best ten plays by women worldwide; and awarded the National First Prize in the American Multicultural Playwright's Festival of the Group Theatre in Seattle, Washington.

The collection in which *Tea* is published, *Unbroken Thread* (Uno), received enthusiastic reviews from *Choice*, *Theatre Journal*, *Asian Theater Review*, *Feminist Collections*, and others. It was cowinner of the Popular Culture Association's Susan Koppelman Award.

Author's Biographical Background

Tea is the third play of an autobiographical trilogy. *Asa Ga Kimashita* [Morning Has Broken], written in 1980, is based on the difficult courtship of Velina Houston's native Japanese mother and her father, a United States Army MP of African American and Blackfoot Indian descent, during the American occupation of Japan. *American Dreams*, written in 1983, follows the young couple as they arrive in the United States to an uneasy reception in the African American community. *Tea* departs from immediate autobiography and expands to a larger community of women, although the character of Setsuko is based on Houston's mother.

Born in Tokyo, Japan, in 1958, Houston emigrated at the age of two, settling with her family in Junction City outside the Fort Riley, Kansas, army base. Largely rejected by both their Japanese and their African American family members, her parents raised her, her younger sister, and an older adopted brother with a strong sense of their multiple heritages. Houston experienced racial prejudice from both the larger Caucasian population of Kansas and the African American community, finding acceptance and support in the Amerasian community. As a member of that community, Houston was privileged to hear the stories of the Japanese international brides firsthand, interviewing some fifty women as research for *Tea*.

Houston was an honors student in journalism, mass communications, theater, and philosophy at Kansas State University; in 1981 she earned a master of fine arts degree in theater and playwriting at the University of California, Los Angeles. An associate professor at the University of Southern California School of Theater, Houston teaches modern dramatic literature and directs the playwriting program. She is also the cofounder and president of the Amerasian League, a not-for-profit organization dedicated to fostering awareness of Amerasian culture. She is proud to be raising her own two children, Kiyoshi Sean Shannen Kamehanaokala and Kuniko Leilani Marie.

A prolific writer and one of the most widely produced Asian American playwrights, Houston writes dramas and screenplays that consistently probe issues of culture, race, and gender, particularly as they affect interracial relations in America. She is especially concerned with what she terms "the Afro-Asian diaspora" (Uno 156) and is critical that the discourse on race is generally limited to black-white confrontations. She is the editor of *The Politics of Life: Four Plays by Asian American Women* and *But Still, Like Air, I'll Rise: New Asian American Plays*.

Historical Context for the Narratives in *Tea*

Following World War II, despite the United States Army policy warning against fraternization between army personnel and Japanese natives, some 100,000 Japanese women married United States servicemen and immigrated to the United States. Many factors contributed to these women's decisions to marry in the face of prejudice and even ostracism from their families and society. Postwar Japan was desperately poor, and it had suffered huge losses of marriage-age young men. The United States occupation of Japan offered opportunities for young Japanese women to encounter American men casually as well as in the workplace. Japanese women were eligible for interpreter, clerical, and other support jobs with the occupation administration; dance halls and bars also served as a place of employment and social contact. Commonly labeled war brides, the Japanese brides joined other international brides from European countries (and later from Korea and Vietnam), often resettling in communities adjacent to isolated army bases. Some three hundred Japanese women and their families were resettled in Junction City, Kansas, adjacent to the Fort Riley army base. In 1968, the setting for *Tea*, Junction City was also home to a large number of European, Korean, Vietnamese, and Thai international brides and their families.

Major Themes

the relation between ceremonial ritual and daily ritual
the coexistence of a physical and spiritual world
the role of ritual in healing
"doubleness," dual and multiple identities and perspectives
fragmentation, displacement, the sense of being in between countries, cultures,
     loyalties, identities
collective memory and history
assimilation and Americanization
racism toward Japanese war brides and their interracial children
prejudice within the Japanese community
silence and denial regarding domestic violence
the psychology of the victim of domestic violence
sexism in marriage and in intercultural relationships
intergenerational tension, attitudinal differences between immigrants and their
     American-born children
identifying sources and manifestations of female strength and power

Critical Issues

To understand *Tea*'s unique structure, fully appreciate its engrossing theatricality, and probe its complex themes, readers must engage the author's perspective and sensibility about her multiracial, multicultural, and binational identity. Historically, persons of bi- or multiracial identity have been described in negative terms, ranging from the subtle and racist, such as "halves" and "mixed," to the overt and racist, such as "half-breed," "mongrel," and "misfit." These terms support the notion that persons of dual and multiple heritages have no sense of belonging; indeed, the "tragic mulatto" has inspired an entire genre of literature.

In marked contrast, Houston embraces the metaphor of "doubleness" to describe her racial and cultural identity. It is a term that profoundly subverts and obliterates historical notions of fragmentation, impurity, and displacement. Doubleness enables a simultaneous occupation of more than one cultural space; similarly, an added lens sharpens, expands, and deepens vision. If we view *Tea* with this lens of doubleness, we begin to understand its structure, meaning, and sensibility. Structurally, it takes place in two initially estranged locations—a spiritual "netherworld" and the tea room of the deceased Himiko. At the play's end, the spiritual and material worlds are unified and revealed as temporally coexistent. Important characters who are referred to are enacted by the Japanese women themselves. Thus we see the women portraying their husbands and teenage daughters; we learn not only how these family members see the Japanese women but also how the Japanese women see themselves being seen. While many of the structural elements of *Tea* such as double casting, casting against gender or age, fluid use of time, and multiple settings are commonly employed playwriting devices, their use in *Tea* transcends clever theatricality, resulting in a sophisticated expression of social and political point of view through dramatic form.

Another aspect of this doubleness is the capacity of each character to embody or evoke more than one point of view. For example, Himiko's suicide is an act of surrender, as well as of defiance and active choice. Teruko's apparent passivity is revealed as an enduring strength.

Pedagogical Issues and Suggestions

Students respond extremely well to *Tea*, finding it emotionally moving and theatrically engaging. Although it is difficult to assign historical research because of the paucity of materials on Japanese war brides, this play lends itself well to a comparative examination of the media. It may be interesting, for example, to have students catalog images of Asian, or specifically Japanese, women in the media and compare these images with the characters in *Tea*. A useful video on images of Asian American women is Deborah Gee's *Slaying the Dragon*. For most students, this will be the first time they encounter race relations that include those between Asians and other people of color. Regge Life's video *Doubles* gives excellent background on relations between Japanese women and United States servicemen during the occupation era and focuses on interviews of their adult children both in Japan and in the United States. Excerpts of the film *Sayonara* not only address the issue of United States Army policy on marriages between Japanese women and United States servicemen but also, due to the liberalization of motion picture codes regarding miscegenation, show the first on-screen kiss between a Caucasian man and a Japanese woman.

Students will probably not have any knowledge of United States immigration policy toward Asians or the history of antimiscegenation laws and attitudes. Teachers may find it useful to provide them with a relevant overview.

Finally, the opportunity to dramatize the scenes either by reading them or by minimally staging them should not be missed. The multiple character work in *Tea* is particularly effective.

Intertextual Linkages

With Pearl Cleage's *Flyin' West*: emigration, displacement, resettlement, miscegenation, violence, women and healing.

With Migdalia Cruz's *Miriam's Flowers*: abuse, healing, mother-daughter relationships, spirituality, suicide.

With Louella Dizon's *Till Voices Wake Us*: spiritual and physical worlds, time fluidity, memory, silence.

With Velina Hasu Houston's *Asa Ga Kimashita* (in Houston, *Politics*): the contrasting attitudes of Japanese and African Americans on interracial marriage, the silence and voice of women characters.

With Nella Larsen's *Quicksand*: miscegenation, inside versus outside community, marriage, bonds between women.

With Ntozake Shange's *For Colored Girls Who Have Considered Suicide When the Rainbow Is Enuf*: multiple voice, collective memory, women's choices, bonds between women.

With Wakako Yamauchi's *And the Soul Shall Dance* or *The Music Lessons*: different women's responses to marriage, environmental circumstance, arranged marriage versus marriage by choice, choices, the expression of women's strength, the response of the community to domestic problems, mother-daughter relationships.

Bibliographic Resources

Houston's introductions to *The Politics of Life* and *But Still, Like Air, I'll Rise* are very useful, as is her introduction to *Asa Ga Kimashita*. The appendix to *Unbroken Thread* (Uno), an extensive listing of plays by Asian American women, includes production histories for many of Houston's works. Stephanie Arnold provides a flawed history of the Asian American theater but useful discussions of an early, unpublished version of *Tea* and plays by Wakako Yamauchi and Momoko Iko. Evelyn Glenn's volume contains interesting oral histories of Japanese international brides. Elfreida Shukert and Barbara Scibetta provide background on living conditions during the United States occupation of Japan.

Other Resources

Slaying the Dragon and *Doubles* are discussed above under "Pedagogical Issues and Suggestions." The Uno Archive of Plays by Asian American Women, housed in the special collections section of the W. E. B. Du Bois Library at the University of Massachusetts, contains most of Houston's scripts, some in various drafts, as well as video and audio interviews with the playwright and various reviews and articles.

Bibliography

Arnold, Stephanie. "Dissolving the Half Shadows: Japanese American Women Playwrights." *Making a Spectacle: Feminist Essays on Contemporary Women's Theatre*. Ed. Lynda Hart. Ann Arbor: U of Michigan P, 1989. 181–94.

Cleage, Pearl. *Flyin' West*. Perkins and Uno 46–78.

Cruz, Migdalia. *Miriam's Flowers*. *Shattering the Myth: Plays by Hispanic Women*. Ed. Linda Feyder. Houston: Arte Publico, 1992. 51–83.

Dizon, Louella. *Till Voices Wake Us*. Perkins and Uno 127–57.

Doubles. Dir. Regge Life. Film Lib., 1995.

Glenn, Evelyn. *Issei, Nisei, War Brides: Three Generations of Japanese American Women in Domestic Service*. Philadelphia: Temple UP, 1986.

Houston, Velina Hasu, ed. *But Still, Like Air, I'll Rise: New Asian American Plays*. Philadelphia: Temple UP, 1997.

———. "Home." *Homemaking: Women Writers and the Politics and Poetics of Home*. Ed. Barbara C. Bowen. New York: Garland, 1996. 277–81.

———, ed. *The Politics of Life: Four Plays by Asian American Women*. Philadelphia: Temple UP, 1993.

———. *Tea*. Uno 155–200.

Larsen, Nella. *Quicksand* and *Passing*. New Brunswick: Rutgers UP, 1986.

Perkins, Kathy A., and Roberta Uno, eds. *Contemporary Plays by Women of Color*. London: Routledge, 1996.

Sayonara. Dir. Joshua Logan. Goldwyn, 1957.

Shange, Ntozake. *For Colored Girls Who Have Considered Suicide When the Rainbow Is Enuf*. Old Tappan: Macmillan, 1977.

Shukert, Elfreida, and Barbara Scibetta. *War Brides of World War II*. Novato: Presidio, 1988.

Slaying the Dragon. Dir. Deborah Gee. Natl. Asian Amer. Telecommunications Assn., 1987.

Uno, Roberta. *Unbroken Thread: An Anthology of Plays by Asian American Women*. Amherst: U of Massachusetts P, 1993.

Yamauchi, Wakako. *And the Soul Shall Dance*. *Between Worlds: Contemporary Asian-American Plays*. Ed. Misha Berson. New York: Theatre Communications, 1990. 128–74.

———. *The Music Lessons*. Uno 59–104.

M. *Butterfly*
by David Henry Hwang

Angela Pao

Publication and Production Information

M. *Butterfly* premiered in Washington, DC, at the National Theatre on 10 February 1988 and opened in New York on Broadway at the Eugene O'Neill Theatre on 20 March 1988. The play was originally published by Dramatists Play Service in 1988. New American Library–Plume has published a paperback edition of the text since 1989.

Overview

M. *Butterfly* is a play in three acts and twenty-seven scenes that unfold in nonlinear sequence. The action begins in the Paris prison cell of René Gallimard, a French diplomat who has been convicted of spying for the People's Republic of China. Gallimard serves as narrator for the subsequent scenes as he recalls how his infatuation with a Chinese opera singer, Song Liling, led to his downfall. In flashback scenes, Gallimard recalls his social ineptitude as a younger man and his growing acquaintance with Song Liling, who flattered his masculinity. The episodes from Gallimard's past are interspersed with reenacted moments from Giacomo Puccini's opera *Madama Butterfly*.

By act 2, Gallimard and Song have become lovers. Their relationship appears idyllic to Gallimard, in contrast to his marriage with the outspoken Helga. Song, however, has been passing on information about United States troop movements in Vietnam gleaned from Gallimard to Comrade Chin, an agent of the Communist government. To ensure Gallimard's devotion and to counter his discontentment with the fact that Song will make love only in the dark, Chin agrees to supply a baby who Gallimard will be told is his and Song's child. Throughout the second act, in the course of exchanges between various characters, the politics of East-West relations are debated.

During the intermission between acts 2 and 3, the actor playing Song removes makeup, wig, and kimono to become a man in a fashionable suit. This transformation takes place onstage, in full view of the audience.

As act 3 begins, Song takes over the narrative as he tells a French judge how he followed Gallimard to Paris with "their" son and continued to engage in espionage. Song explains that he was able to manipulate Gallimard so easily because the latter was predisposed through various prejudices concerning both women and Asia to believe that he had indeed met his "fantasy woman." Song also suggests that the common Western perception of the West as dominant and masculine and the East as feminine and submissive would similarly lead to the defeat of Western imperialist and military enterprises in Asia. In a climactic confrontation between Song and Gallimard, Song strips completely, forcing Gallimard to confront the truth of his self-delusions. In a final act of acceptance and resistance, Gallimard dons the cast-off wig and kimono, applies women's makeup to his face, and then reenacts Madama Butterfly's ritual suicide to the "Love Duet" from Puccini's opera.

Reception

The first play by an Asian American playwright to reach a broad mainstream audience, M. Butterfly initially met with a mixed critical response. Many audience members and critics were confused about the protocols of interpretation to be applied to a play that did not fit into preconceived notions of a play with "oriental" subject matter. Other critics, however, recognized the originality and innovative aspects of Hwang's work and were receptive to his interrelated critiques of the stereotyping of Asians, social constructions of gender and sexuality, and the imperialist history of European and American foreign policy in Asia (Skloot). Some gay critics recognized the work as an exploration of the nature of masculinity and love. For others, the play's submersion of the issue of sexual preference raised the question of whether M. Butterfly was homophobic.

Opinion regarding the play's ultimate effect on how Asians are perceived has diverged widely. While many Asian Americans of all ethnicities celebrated the first international recognition accorded an American dramatist of Asian descent and the publicizing of views that had previously received little attention outside the Asian American community, others felt that Hwang ended up perpetuating the very stereotypes he intended to subvert (Moy, "M. Butterfly" and Sights; Wong). It has been argued, for instance, that M. Butterfly continues to promote an exoticized view of East Asia as well as the perception that Asians are devious, manipulative, and cunning. Reactions broke down to a large extent along gender lines. Women were inclined to appreciate the play for its overturning of long-standing stereotypes of the submissive "lotus blossom" (Kondo, About Face and "M. Butterfly"; Loo), while men were more likely to protest the continued effeminization of the Asian male (Moy, "M. Butterfly" and Sights). From an international perspective, the play has also been criticized for its superficial treatment of the Asian political situation, notably its cartoonish portrayal of Chinese communism, and for failing to remark that its account of East-West relations proceeds from a dominant Western positioning (Lye).

M. *Butterfly* received several major awards, including the 1988 Tony Award for the best play, the Outer Critics Circle Award for the best Broadway play, and the Drama Desk Award for the best new play. The play had a successful run in London, was taken on tour in the United States and translated for performance in about two dozen other countries in Asia and Europe, and continues to be regularly produced by regional theater companies.

Author's Biographical Background

David Henry Hwang, a second-generation Chinese American, was born in 1957. His father, who was from Shanghai, emigrated from China in 1948, moving first to Taiwan and then to the United States, where he went into banking. His mother, a pianist and music teacher, was from a Chinese family living in the Philippines. They met in the United States and raised their children, David and a younger sister, in San Gabriel, California. The community was predominantly Euro-American, and Hwang's main contacts with other Chinese came through the family's membership in a Chinese church. He received his BA from Stanford University in 1979, writing his first play, *FOB*, during his senior year. After graduation he attended the Yale School of Drama. His work attracted the attention of Joseph Papp, who mounted *FOB* for the Public Theatre in New York in 1980. The play, which portrays tensions between native-born Americans of Chinese descent and recent immigrants in a nonrealistic mode, won an Obie Award for best play of the 1980–81 season. Hwang's second drama, *The Dance and the Railroad*, inspired by the experiences of the Chinese workers who built the transcontinental railroad in 1867, was written and produced the following year. *Family Devotions*, an almost surrealistic farce that examined the unique chaos produced by Christian fundamentalism in a suburban Californian Chinese-American family, was also produced by the Public Theatre in 1981. The last two plays were nominated for Drama Desk Awards, and in 1982 Hwang was also honored with a Chinese American Cultural Council Award for his "Chinese-American trilogy."

In addition to works that deal directly with aspects of Chinese American experience, Hwang has written a pair of plays based on Japanese sources, *The House of Sleeping Beauties* (1983) and *The Sound of a Voice* (1983), both of which deal with relations between the sexes. A one-act play, *As the Crow Flies* (1986), explores the relationship of two older women, the one Chinese American and the other African American. Following the success of M. *Butterfly*, Hwang undertook a variety of creative projects, notably the book for *One Thousand Airplanes on the Roof* (1988); the libretto for Philip Glass's 1992 opera, *The Voyage*; and several screenplays, including *Golden Gate*. With *Bondage* (1992), Hwang returned to an examination of the power politics of race and sex in interracial relationships. A farce, *Face Values* (1993), attempted to use the issues arising from the *Miss Saigon* casting controversy to make audiences think about whether the notion of race is "real" or simply a form of mass delusion. Hwang's 1997 play *Golden Child*, set in China, examines the effect of early East-West encounters on Chinese social structures as a man decides to have his family, including his three wives, convert to Christianity.

Since 1980, Hwang has moved between New York and Los Angeles.

Historical Context for the Narratives in *M. Butterfly*

M. Butterfly is based on an actual affair that came to light in 1986. Bernard Boursicot was an accountant assigned to the French embassy in Beijing after France recognized the People's Republic of China in 1964. Within a few months of his arrival, he met Shi Pei-pu, a Chinese opera singer, at an embassy party. The two became lovers. They maintained sporadic contact over the next nineteen years, primarily because of the existence of a child, who Boursicot believed was his son by Shi. In 1983, French intelligence officials began investigating the relationship between Boursicot and Shi, who were now living in Paris. Boursicot admitted that to protect Shi from persecution during the Cultural Revolution, he had passed on confidential embassy documents to a Chinese contact. In the course of Boursicot's trial for espionage, it was revealed that Shi was a man—not a woman as Boursicot had believed. Boursicot maintained that he never realized that his lover was a man because he never saw Shi naked. He said he accepted her modesty as a "Chinese custom."

Whereas the most common public reaction was to see Boursicot's claim of ignorance regarding the true gender of his lover as a denial of his homosexuality, Hwang (as he explains in the afterword that accompanies the published play) concluded that the Frenchman was deceived because "he had fallen in love not with a person, but with a fantasy stereotype" of Asian women as "bowing, blushing flowers" (94). Hwang interpreted the situation as a reversal of the Madame Butterfly paradigm in which a naive Asian woman is deceived by a worldly Western man. Here, a clever Shi Pei-pu had apparently been able to turn the tables on a gullible Boursicot. In Hwang's estimation, the Frenchman must have fantasized that he was Pinkerton and that his "oriental" lover was Butterfly. By the end of the play, however, the Frenchman realizes that, as the dupe of love, he has been playing the part of Butterfly all along, while the Chinese spy who exploits that love has been the real Pinkerton.

The stereotype of the Asian female to which Hwang is referring can be traced to the late nineteenth century after the forced "opening" of Japan to trade with America and Europe. By the turn of the century, the figure of the Japanese geisha had entered Western popular culture. The narrative of Madame Butterfly, introduced in the United States in a novelette by John Luther Long (based on a French version by Pierre Loti), was first adapted for the stage as a one-act play by David Belasco (1900). It appeared in its most famous incarnation, Giacomo Puccini's opera *Madama Butterfly*, in 1904. The narrative of an attractive young Asian woman who rejects a suitor from her own culture (always portrayed as insensitive and tradition-bound) in favor of a European or Euro-American man, whom she continues to love even after he abandons her, would become one of the twentieth century's most common paradigms for representing Asian women (Marchetti; Pao, "Eyes").

Historical Context for the Writing of *M. Butterfly*

Hwang's deconstruction of the Madame Butterfly motif must be placed in the context of Asian American political and cultural awareness that emerged in the late 1960s and 1970s. One of the most significant aspects of this movement was the challenging of stereotypes of Asians that had been created and perpetuated by Western literature, theater, film, mass media, and popular culture during the nineteenth and twentieth centuries. Hwang himself acknowledges that he avoided inquiring into the details of the case so that this information would not interfere with his own speculations—speculations that proceeded from his positioning as an Asian American. This positioning is reflected in his deliberate conflation of various Asian national experiences or traditions (e.g., Chinese opera, Japanese geishas, the Vietnam War) in M. *Butterfly*. This conflation parallels the blurring of ethnic differences in favor of a common Asian American experience that has prevailed until recently.

The American experience in Vietnam during the 1960s and 1970s provided the most immediate context for Hwang's observations regarding the relation between United States foreign policy in Asia and popular perceptions of Asia and Asians.

Major Themes

stereotypes of Asian women and men
the exoticizing of Asia in general and Asian women in particular
the gendering of ethnicity
the relation between foreign policy or international relations and popular
    cultural representations
essentialist versus constructivist models of gender and race
the politics of sexuality and sexual preference
cross-dressing and gendered identities
performance and identity
gender as performance
the relation of the real and the imaginary

Critical Issues

The interest excited by M. *Butterfly* is due largely to its timely integration of themes involving the complex nature of gender and sexuality with the question of historical relations between East and West. The ambiguity of the title announces the destabilizing of gender distinctions that will take place during the course of the play. The action of the play is in effect an argument against essentialist notions of both gender and race and the concept of a unitary identity. Gender and race are shown to be as much the product of imaginary constructions and concrete social practices as they are the result of biological or genetic determinants (Butler; Garber; Kondo, *About Face* and "*M. Butterfly*"). Critics concerned with constructions of masculinity have found highly relevant material in *M. Butterfly* (Kehde; Q. Lee).

While the questions about constructions of gender hold relevance for all cultural groups, Hwang treats them from a specifically Asian American point of view. In *M. Butterfly*, issues of gendered identity are inseparable from the stereotyping of Asian women and men and the gendering of ethnicity that has taken place in American culture and society. While the play most overtly addresses the exoticizing of Asian women (Kim; Ling; Tajima), this phenomenon cannot be separated from the corresponding effeminization of Asian men (Chin and Chan; Kim; Moy, "*M. Butterfly*" and *Sights*). The play can be seen as a dramatization of Edward Said's arguments that the effeminization of the Orient and the Oriental through discursive and visual representations was integral to European and American colonialist and military activity in the Middle and Far East.

As Hwang notes in his afterword, the gendering of ethnicity figures in both heterosexual and homosexual relationships. *M. Butterfly* offers rich material for gay and lesbian studies in its revelation of the politics of sexual preference at work in Gallimard's denial or repression of the homosexual aspects of his attraction to Song (Eng; Q. Lee).

The eminently theatrical nature of *M. Butterfly* has drawn the attention of critics who note that Hwang's deconstructivist project cannot be discussed apart from the performance conventions and narrative structures used to present those arguments (Chang; Chen; Haedicke; Remen).

Pedagogical Issues and Suggestions

M. Butterfly offers challenging and intriguing material for students at all levels. In an introductory-level course, the question of gender formation consistently generates the most lively discussions. The essentialist versus constructivist debate can be approached by having students recall incidents where what was considered gender-appropriate behavior was rewarded and departures from that behavior were censured by figures of authority or by peer pressure. To address the specifically Asian and Asian American aspects of the play, instructors may find it helpful to show the class examples of the stereotypes Hwang was working against. In terms of supplementary readings, the works by Frank Chin and Jeffery Chan, Chalsa Loo, James Moy ("Hwang's *M. Butterfly*"), Robert Skloot, Renee Tajima, and William Wong provide the most accessible discussions of the critical issues. Although the film version of *M. Butterfly* departs considerably in mood and focus from the stage version, excerpts are useful for allowing students to observe the gender impersonation. For more advanced students who have some background in contemporary critical theory, the play can be read in conjunction with excerpts from Edward Said and Judith Butler to introduce the students to the fundamental concepts of orientalism and gender constitution as performance. The works by Marjorie Garber, Dorinne Kondo (*About Face* and "*M. Butterfly*") and James Moy (*Marginal Sights*) offer more theoretically informed treatments of the central issues of race, gender, sexuality, and representation in *M. Butterfly*.

Intertextual Linkages

With Frank Chin's *The Chickencoop Chinaman* and Philip Kan Gotanda's *Yankee Dawg You Die*: the construction of Asian American masculinity in the face of media and popular stereotypes.

With Velina Hasu Houston's *Tea*: interracial marriages between Japanese women and American servicemen that show Asian women as complex individuals.

With Caryl Churchill's *Cloud Nine*: the politics of gender, race, and sexuality; the acting out of essentialist, constructivist, and performative models of identity; the links between colonialism and sexism.

Bibliographic Resources

Although Hwang has distanced his work from the actual Boursicot-Shi incident, it may be of interest to students to examine the equally problematic questions of gender and sexuality in the real-life case as it has been documented by Joyce Wadler in *Liaison*. An extensive listing of critical reviews of *M. Butterfly* that appeared in American and British newspapers and magazines is included in an article by Angela Pao ("Critic"). Gina Marchetti provides one of the most complete filmographies to date of Hollywood movies representing Asians. Josephine Lee's book situates Hwang's work in the larger context of Asian American theater and drama.

Other Resources

Slaying the Dragon is a sixty-minute film available on videocassette that reviews the principal stereotypes of Asian women that have dominated American films and media.

Bibliography

Berson, Misha, ed. *Between Worlds: Contemporary Asian-American Plays*. New York: Theatre Communications, 1990.

Butler, Judith. "Performative Acts and Gender Constitution: An Essay in Phenomenology and Feminist Theory." *Performing Feminisms: Feminist Critical Theory and Theatre*. Ed. Sue-Ellen Case. Baltimore: Johns Hopkins UP, 1990. 270–82.

Chang, Hsiao-hung. "Cultural/Sexual/Theatrical Ambivalence in M. *Butterfly*." *Tamkang Review* 23 (1992): 735–55.

Chen, Tina. "Betrayed into Motion: The Seduction of Narrative Desire in M. *Butterfly*." *Hitting Critical Mass: A Journal of Asian American Cultural Criticism* 1.2 (1994): 129–54.

Chin, Frank. *The Chickencoop Chinaman*. Seattle: U of Washington P, 1981.

Chin, Frank, and Jeffery Paul Chan. "Racist Love." *Seeing through Shuck*. Ed. Richard Kostelanetz. New York: Ballantine, 1990. 65–79.

Churchill, Caryl. *Cloud Nine*. Rev. American ed. New York: Routledge, 1991.

Cody, Gabrielle. "David Hwang's M. *Butterfly*: Perpetuating the Misogynist Myth." *Theatre* 20.2 (1989): 24–27.

Cooperman, Robert. "Across the Boundaries of Cultural Identity: An Interview with David Henry Hwang." Maufort 365–73.

———. "New Theatrical Statements: Asian Western Mergers in the Plays of David Henry Hwang." Maufort 201–13.

Deeney, John J. "Of Monkeys and Butterflies: Transformation in M. H. Kingston's *Tripmaster Monkey* and D. H. Hwang's M. *Butterfly*." *MELUS* 18.4 (1993): 21–39.

DiGaetani, John Louis. "M. *Butterfly*: An Interview with David Henry Hwang." *TDR: The Drama Review* 33.3 (1989): 141–53.

Eng, David. "In the Shadows of a Diva: Committing Homosexuality in David Henry Hwang's M. *Butterfly*." *Amerasia Journal* 20.1 (1994): 93–116.

Garber, Marjorie. "The Occidental Tourist: M. *Butterfly* and the Scandal of Transvestitism." *Nationalisms and Sexualities*. Ed. Andrew Parker et al. New York: Routledge, 1992. 121–46.

Gerard, Jeremy. "David Hwang: Riding on the Hyphen." *New York Times Magazine* 13 Mar. 1988: 44+.

Gotanda, Philip Kan. *Yankee Dawg You Die*. Fish Head Soup *and Other Plays*. Seattle: U of Washington P, 1995. 69–130.

Haedicke, Janet. "David Henry Hwang's M. *Butterfly*: The Eye on the Wing." *Journal of Dramatic Theory and Criticism* 7.1 (1992): 27–44.

Houston, Velina Hasu, ed. *The Politics of Life: Four Plays by Asian American Women*. Philadelphia: Temple UP, 1993.

———. *Tea. Unbroken Thread: An Anthology of Plays by Asian American Women*. Ed. Roberta Uno. Amherst: U of Massachusetts P, 1993. 155–200.

Hwang, David Henry. *As the Crow Flies*. Berson 97–108.

———. *Broken Promises: Four Chinese American Plays* [FOB, *The Dance and the Railroad, Family Devotions, The House of Sleeping Beauties*]. New York: Avon, 1983.

———. *Golden Child*. New York: Theatre Communications Group, 1998.

———. M. *Butterfly*. New York: NAL-Plume, 1989.

———. M. *Butterfly*. Dir. David Cronenberg. Perf. John Lone and Jeremy Irons. Warner, 1994.

———. *The Sound of a Voice*. Berson 109–26.

———. *Trying to Find Chinatown and Bondage*. New York: Dramatist's Play Service, 1996.

Kehde, Suzanne. "Engendering the Imperial Subject: The (De)Construction of (Western) Masculinity in David Henry Hwang's *M. Butterfly* and Graham Greene's *The Quiet American*." *Fictions of Masculinity: Crossing Cultures, Crossing Sexualities*. New York: New York UP, 1994. 241–54.

Kim, Elaine H. *Asian American Literature: An Introduction to the Writings and Their Social Context*. Philadelphia: Temple UP, 1982.

Kondo, Dorinne K. *About Face: Performing Race in Fashion and Theater*. New York: Routledge, 1997.

———. "*M. Butterfly*: Orientalism, Gender, and a Critique of Essentialist Identity." *Cultural Critique* 16 (1990): 5–29.

Lee, Josephine. *Performing Asian America: Race and Ethnicity on the Contemporary Stage*. Philadelphia: Temple UP, 1997.

Lee, Quentin. "Between the Oriental and the Transvestite." *Found-Object* 8 (1993): 45–59.

Ling, Amy. *Between Worlds: Women Writers of Chinese Ancestry*. New York: Pergamon, 1990.

Loo, Chalsa. "*M. Butterfly*: A Feminist Perspective." *Bearing Dreams, Shaping Visions: Asian Pacific American Perspectives*. Ed. Linda A. Revilla, Gail M. Nomura, Shawn Wong, and Shirley Hune. Pullman: Washington State UP, 1993. 177–80.

Lye, Colleen. "*M. Butterfly* and the Rhetoric of Anti-essentialism: Minority Discourse in an International Frame." *The Ethnic Canon: Histories, Institutions, and Interventions*. Ed. David Palumbo-Liu. Minneapolis: U of Minnesota P, 1995. 260–89.

Marchetti, Gina. *Romance and the Yellow Peril: Race, Sex, and Discursive Strategies in Hollywood Fiction*. Berkeley: U of California P, 1993.

Maufort, Marc, ed. *Staging Difference: Cultural Pluralism in American Theatre and Drama*. New York: Lang, 1995.

Moy, James S. "David Henry Hwang's *M. Butterfly* and Philip Kan Gotanda's *Yankee Dawg You Die*: Repositioning Chinese American Marginality on the American Stage." *Theatre Journal* 42.1 (1990): 48–56.

———. *Marginal Sights: Staging the Chinese in America*. Iowa City: U of Iowa P, 1993.

Pao, Angela. "The Critic and the Butterfly: Sociocultural Contexts and the Reception of David Henry Hwang's *M. Butterfly*." *Amerasia Journal* 18.3 (1992): 1–16.

———. "The Eyes of the Storm: Gender, Genre, and Cross-casting in *Miss Saigon*." *Text and Performance Quarterly* 12.1 (1992): 21–39.

Remen, Kathryn. "The Theatre of Punishment: David Henry Hwang's *M. Butterfly* and Michel Foucault's *Discipline and Punish*." *Modern Drama* 37.3 (1994): 391–400.

Said, Edward. *Orientalism*. New York: Vintage, 1979.

Shimakawa, Karen. " 'Who's to Say?' or, Making Space for Gender and Ethnicity in *M. Butterfly*." *Theatre Journal* 45.3 (1993): 349–61.

Skloot, Robert. "Breaking the Butterfly: The Politics of David Henry Hwang." *Modern Drama* 33.1 (1990): 59–66.

Slaying the Dragon. Dir. Deborah Gee. Prod. Pacific Productions. CrossCurrent Media, 1987.

Tajima, Renee E. "Lotus Blossoms Don't Bleed: Images of Asian Women." *Making Waves: An Anthology of Writings by and about Asian American Women*. Ed. Asian Women United of California. Boston: Beacon, 1989. 308–17.

Wadler, Joyce. *Liaison*. New York: Bantam, 1993.

Wong, William. "*M. Butterfly*: A Symbol of Mainstream Success or Selling Out?" *East/West News* 4 Aug. 1988: 6–9.

Gold Watch

by Momoko Iko

Stephen H. Sumida

Publication and Production Information

Responding to a notice about a playwriting contest sponsored by the East West Players in Los Angeles, Momoko Iko began work on the two-act drama *Gold Watch* in 1970, basing it on an unpublished novel of hers (Uno 107, 318). It was first produced at the Inner City Cultural Center in Los Angeles in 1972. *Gold Watch* rose to prominence when it was adapted for broadcast on the Visions series of American dramas on PBS in 1975. A production by the Asian Exclusion Act of Seattle followed in 1977, and productions have been mounted at Stanford University in 1977, 1982, 1987, and 1988. The first act of *Gold Watch* was published in *Aiiieeeee! An Anthology of Asian-American Writers*, edited by Frank Chin et al. The full drama is published in *Unbroken Thread: An Anthology of Plays by Asian American Women*, edited by Roberta Uno.

Overview

Gold Watch takes place during the Labor Day weekend of 1941 and continues through the Japanese bombing of Pearl Harbor to the eve of the Japanese American community's mass uprooting from their homes to detention centers in the spring of 1942. The community is of the rural town and surrounding farms of Wapato in the Yakima Valley of central Washington.

The ostensible protagonist, Masu Murakami, is an Issei farmer who cultivates melons and vegetables. Playing equally strong roles in the drama are Masu's wife, Kimi Murakami; their fourteen-year-old Nisei son, Tadao; and Tanaka, the proprietor of a grocery and dry goods store in the town. While the play dramatizes differences and conflicts among these main characters and others, its collective "protagonist" is the ideologically and temperamentally heterogeneous Japanese American community. The

209

antagonists, then, are the United States society and government that remove them from their homes at Wapato in the late spring of 1942 with only the belongings they can carry in their hands.

Several important dramatic turns occur in act 1 of *Gold Watch*. Masu stands in rebellious distinction from the others in the Murakami family. Kimi has to negotiate, secure, and repay the annual farm loans with the bankers in town. Tadao and his four-year-old sister, Chieko (who is five in earlier scripts), have to deal every day during the school year with children among whom the Murakamis' race grows to be an issue. But Masu confines himself to the farm they lease, where under the big sky of the northern tier states he fancies being free. When Tadao prompts Masu to speak of this sense of freedom, Masu tells of how he wanted to escape from the strictures of a life in Japan, where he was supposed to become a Buddhist monk. Iko has commented that, in a sense, her play is a tragedy about a man who thinks that he can escape from history and society by secluding himself on his farm, and it is about how he has to awaken from that dream (Personal interview).

Masu's awakening comes with Japan's bombing of Pearl Harbor. Meanwhile, Tadao undergoes a reversal. At the beginning of the play, he is the all-American boy who asks Masu for a pair of football shoes (which Masu refuses). When Tadao's schoolmates turn against him after Pearl Harbor, however, he begins to be interested in the idea of the family "going back" to Japan, even though it has never been his home (134–37). In their "man-to-man" talk at the end of act 1, Masu not only states his refusal to return to Japan but also realizes that Tadao has "grown up [. . .] right here, in this house and [Masu] didn't even notice it" (134). Masu's sentiment and its occurrence at that moment in the play are inextricable from the sociohistorical context he must henceforth increasingly engage himself with: Pearl Harbor and its consequences for the Japanese Americans even in rural Wapato.

Tanaka, the merchant, originally of a lower class than Masu and lacking the high education of priests, is contrasted with Masu and with Setsuko Tanaka, his wife, who, unlike the other parents in the play, is a Nisei. At the holiday party three weeks after the attack on Pearl Harbor, it is the Tanakas' son, Hiroshi, who enters the play as an *eiron*, a character deeply critical of the actions, words, and attitudes he observes in the scene. Hiroshi has returned reluctantly from Japan. A kibei (born in America but educated in Japan), Hiroshi was recalled by his parents when the threat of war loomed large, and he remains devoted to the "Imperial way" of Japan. Impressing no one but Tadao with his talk of "Japanese pride," Hiroshi functions to support Tadao's thought of "going back" to Japan. Act 1 thus establishes the differences among the characters and yet their closeness as a family and a community. In the Murakami family, this closeness is enacted near the end of act 1. The Murakamis bathe together, Japanese family style, their tub now heated by a gas burner that Masu purchases as a Christmas gift for his wife.

In act 2, the historical process underway breaks apart the characters. Late in the spring of 1942 the Japanese American community of Wapato meets to discuss what is to happen to them, now that the implementation of President Franklin Delano Roosevelt's Executive Order 9066, of 19 February 1942, threatens the community with removal, imprisonment, and, some fear, worse. The people are full of rumors about acts of vandalism and assault against Japanese Americans. They meet in the basement of the Wapato Japanese Methodist Church to argue about the next step. Tanaka, grateful to America for his upward mobility, argues passionately for obeying government orders, while the rebellious Masu opposes him, and others get involved in the argument. The people in the crowd wonder what to do when two of their leaders, Tanaka and Masu, are in conflict. Methodists and Buddhists speculate about each other. Communications fail. Even the meeting of so many Japanese Americans is illegal at that time.

The conflicts flood into the Murakami home, between Kimi and Masu and between Tadao and his father. The play ends with echoes of its opening words: "Oki-nasai, Masu. Wake up. It's morning time" (153), Kimi sobs, while her husband lies in her arms, shot dead in a fight with night raiders on the eve of the departure for detention camps.

The play's title, *Gold Watch*, refers to Masu's whimsical Christmas gift to Tadao at the end of act 1. It is not an heirloom but an old watch that Masu bought in a pawnshop when he first landed at the docks in Seattle. He writes a note to go with it: "I am sorry about the football shoes. Take this watch instead. In Japan, if you go, it will be more useful" (137). Masu attempts to transmit something from father to son in this way and through the man-to-man talk that preceded this action. The attempt fails in act 2, except that the play leaves the watch and its possible meanings in Tadao's hands. Meanwhile, in act 2, the bond between Kimi and her son, Tadao, grows stronger. Kimi, too, transmits something to the boy (149–51). It is her narrative of how she and Masu were introduced to each other and how, when she shipped off to America, she was carrying in her the one who would be her firstborn, Tadao.

Reception

Iko's scripts *The Old Man* and *Gold Watch* won the East West Players playwriting contests of 1969 and 1970 (Chin et al. 89–114). The broadcast of *Gold Watch* on PBS in 1976 not only brought wide attention to the play but also helped explain its historical setting as the history of the Japanese American internment was rising out of the past in that decade. The Monte Carlo International Television Festival accepted the television production as one of the two entries from America in 1976.

Uno speculates about some Japanese Americans' responses to *Gold Watch*:

In investigating the particular dynamics between a man with a fiercely independent spirit in conflict with social forces that conspire to constrain him, Iko strikes a sensitive chord within the Japanese American community: exposing the tension between individualism and the dynamics of the group. In doing so she challenges the myth of Japanese American complacency in the face of the evacuation order, dramatizing the range of responses to that edict. (107–08)

In the 1970s Iko was considered a "young Nisei," because she is the same age as some members of the next generation, the Sansei (third-generation Japanese Americans). The Sansei generation generally came of age in the 1970s (as the Nisei had generally come of age during the internment and World War II), when the new realization that 120,000 Issei and Nisei had been victims of an unjust internment in concentration camps both baffled and angered the younger, largely post–World War II generation. Sansei asked how their parents, the Nisei, could have allowed such a thing to happen to them. Uno's observation that Iko "challenges the myth of Japanese American complacency" indicates one of the ways the play spoke to those who demanded an answer. Like John Okada's *No-No Boy* when it was revived in the 1970s, Iko's *Gold Watch* profoundly demonstrated that not all Japanese Americans quietly went along with their internment.

From the experience of one who acted in the 1977 Seattle production mounted by the Asian Exclusion Act (a forerunner of the Northwest Asian American Theatre), I can add that for some Nisei and Sansei members of the audience, *Gold Watch* served as a reminder or a revelation that the Issei had once been as they were on the stage. Masu in his forties, Kimi in her early thirties, and Tanaka in his forties are vigorous and mature, in their prime, verbally articulate and intellectually agile, young in comparison to the perceived images of the Issei, who by the 1970s were seen as old folks, grandparents, immigrant people marginal to American culture and language, no matter how revered. A theme in the play is the "transmission" of culture, the continuation of an awareness of history from one generation to the next, and *Gold Watch* embodies that transmission. It gave Nisei and Sansei viewers a glimpse of the Issei, and this very action countered another myth, that of cultural chasms preventing the generations from understanding one another. Iko offers a positive understanding of such a chasm and its current of time when Masu says that his and Tadao's "lives are different, must be different, if [they] are to survive" (136).

Author's Biographical Background

Momoko Iko was born in Wapato, in the Yakima Valley of Washington, in 1940; hence she was two when the evacuation occurred (for biographical details, see Uno 105–06; a résumé of Iko's has supplied some dates that differ from the ones Uno cites). The Japanese Americans of Wapato were assembled at a site in Portland, Oregon, and then sent to the concentration camp at Heart Mountain, Wyoming, a facility so new that the internees had to watch the barbed wire fences still being erected around them after their arrival (see Ehrlich's *Heart Mountain*). Iko's family of eight included an older brother who joined the United States Army Military Intelligence Service (like the authors John Okada and Milton Murayama), so the Ikos experienced the irony of having in their family a soldier serving the country that had imprisoned them because of "military necessity." But Momoko Iko has "scant recollection" of the three years she spent in the camp. Her family "relocated" from Heart Mountain to Seabury Farms,

New Jersey, to pursue migrant farm work there, and then moved to Chicago, where they settled and where "the Iko apartment became a gathering place for displaced Japanese Americans seeking to resettle following the war" (Uno 106). Here Iko heard what she had been too young to remember: "As I was growing up, our house was like a center for young Nisei [. . .] because after the war our home was one of the few where the family was together. [. . .] There were always people coming in and out. [. . .] I know a lot of stories come out of that period" (qtd. in Uno 106).

One of the youngest of that "young Nisei" generation, Iko evidently kept in touch with the older generation and their stories of the internment, the relocation, and the anomie of resettlement in the Midwest, stories that many Nisei remained silent about when raising their own Sansei children. Returning to Chicago and her expressed interests for a brief time later in life, Iko in 1975 served as project director of the Issei Gerontology Project of the Japanese American Service Committee of Chicago, where she wrote and produced, among other works, two thirty-minute films, *Social Services: Seeking a Human Dimension* and *Issei: A Quality for Survival*.

Iko attended Northern Illinois University in Chicago and majored in English at the University of Illinois, Urbana. She graduated in 1961. Iko's inspiration to try to write drama came when she saw Lorraine Hansberry's *A Raisin in the Sun* and "recognized the political potential of the theater." An artist of sharp insight, Iko recalls how in Hansberry's play she saw parallels with Japanese Americans (Uno 106).

After her success with *Gold Watch* Iko went on to work at the American Film Institute and other places as a director, documentary filmmaker, scriptwriter, teacher, and artist. Her career as a playwright also includes dramas that Uno cites (318–19): *When We Were Young* (1974), the play that inspired Wakako Yamauchi to adapt *And the Soul Shall Dance* to dramatic form; *Flowers and Household Gods* (1975); *Second City Flat* (1978); *Hollywood Mirrors* (1978); and *Boutique Living and Disposable Icons* (1987). Among the grants she has been awarded for her work are those from the Zellenbach and the Rockefeller Foundations and the National Endowment for the Arts.

Historical Context for the Narratives in *Gold Watch*

See the unit in this volume on Wakako Yamauchi's *And the Soul Shall Dance* for resources in the history and oral narratives of the Issei, particularly in rural areas of the United States; for studies of the "evacuation" and internment of Japanese Americans, see the units on John Okada's *No-No Boy* and Monica Sone's *Nisei Daughter*. According to Uno, Iko insists that the characters in *Gold Watch* are "neither prototypical nor symbolic"; rather, they "are specific people within a specific situation" (107).

The Japanese Americans of Wapato, Washington, have an interesting history. The first of the antialien land laws on the West Coast of the United States was inscribed in the 1889 constitution of Washington State. An attempt to restrict British incursions into the Northwest, the law forbade any aliens lacking a sincere intent to become citizens of the United States from owning real property in the new state. The

213

law applied to Asian immigrants as well, since by United States laws Asians were barred from naturalization and therefore could not claim to have a sincere intent to become citizens. At about the turn of the century, Issei in the environs of Seattle and Tacoma sought a way around the state law that was tightening to restrict even the rental of farm lands by Asians. Some found that they could move eastward over the Cascades to the Yakima Indian reservation, administered by the Bureau of Indian Affairs under federal and not state jurisdiction, and rent farmland there outside the reach of the state anti-Asian land laws. The Japanese American community surrounding Wapato, Washington, began in this way, with the Issei joining the Yakima Indians in negotiations for the rental of sagebrush-covered lands that would become farms. As soon as Nisei youths came of age, transactions having to do with land rental were put in their names, under which land ownership also became possible since, unlike their parents, the Nisei were United States citizens by birth. But with five-year leases for the most part, the Issei farmer could grow only annual truck crops. Orchards provided some people with work and wages, but growing fruit trees took too long for the Issei to be able to do it themselves on their leases.

In the early 1900s poets in the community established the Yakima Senryu, the first club in North America devoted to the writing of the seventeen-syllable satiric verses called senryu. These differ from haiku in being not about nature and the artist's perception of nature but about society and the artist's ironic observations about people. A Yakima poet using the pen name Koyo thus writes:

". . . and early to rise . . ."
No matter how early, though,
It don't make me rich! (qtd. in Sumida, "Hawai'i" 13)

In *Gold Watch*, Masu is a member of the Yakima Senryu (119). This affiliation is scarcely mentioned in the play, but like Masu, Iko's father "possessed [. . .] a poetic soul" (Uno 107). (For an account of the poetry and life of Teiko Tomita, an Issei woman writer of Wapato, see Nomura, "Tsugiki.")

The closeness between generations while the Nisei were growing up in Wapato is evident in the Issei support of the Wapato Nippons baseball team (see Nomura, "Playing Field"). This was part of the social and cultural context into which Iko was born and in which her *Gold Watch* begins. The argument between Tadao and his father over the football shoes notwithstanding, the continuity and agency the Wapato Japanese Americans had achieved—by dealing with the laws of the land (they were not ignorant foreigners), writing a new poetry of America, and participating in the sports of their American-born children—set the drama apart from narratives based on assimilation, intercultural conflicts between generations, and broken histories. (My source for this historical sketch is Nomura's research, both published and unpublished, on the Asian Americans of the Yakima Valley and on their interracial histories.)

Historical Context for the Writing of *Gold Watch*

At the time that Iko wrote *Gold Watch*, and to a considerable extent since then, a controversy was boiling up about the view that Asian Americans are marginal to both "Asian" and "American" cultures and norms. This widespread and disempowering discourse was countered by works such as Iko's, but not because her characters are without conflict over culture and nation (Tadao surely is conflicted). Rather than imply a view of Japanese American history as broken and thus powerless, *Gold Watch* demonstrates the struggle to live, whatever the conflicts, a continuing narrative going all the way back to Japan (in Masu's and Kimi's stories to Tadao) and stretching into the nighttime of the internment at the play's end. It is this narrative that constitutes what it means to be "American." Frank Chin and the other editors of *Aiiieeeee!* sought out writings such as Iko's because these works embodied what they and others went on to call the "heroic tradition" of Asian American literature, as opposed to a dominant assimilationist and intrinsically "racist" one (see Sumida, "Assimilation").

Moreover, while it seemed unprecedented in the early 1970s that a Japanese American was writing something good enough to be aired nationwide, Iko and her colleagues drew power from knowing that they stood on the shoulders of their forebears. Iko's father was a poet. The community where he settled and where Iko was born formed the first senryu poetry club in America. They brought their literary experience with them from Japan and used it to write poetry about Yakima, Washington, USA. Literary work was not new to Iko's Japanese American culture. In Asian American social history, the era of the early 1970s is marked by a resurgence of Asian American engagement with and against assimilationism, alienation, and the erasure of history. It may be especially fitting that the creator of *Gold Watch* is a Nisei writer whose family was living in Chicago, because the intent of their forced diaspora was to break up their community and cause the family to wither away. Compounding these difficulties was the intense alienation that the Nisei reportedly experienced in Chicago in the 1950s. It may well be that Iko's work is the stronger for her not falling victim to these pressures.

Major Themes

Issei and Nisei relations (especially father and son, mother and son)
the Japanese American internment; World War II
the transmission of culture from one generation to the next
political conflicts or heterogeneity within a Japanese American community
resistance against the internment
the kibei and their alleged Japanese nationalism
social stratification within the community
escapism versus social interaction
rural, agricultural Japanese American life

Critical Issues

Between the 1974 publication of act 1 in *Aiiieeeee!* and the 1993 publication of the full text of *Gold Watch* in *Unbroken Thread*, the work was accessible mainly through television and theater productions, and it has not been discussed much in critical studies. As I have suggested, a number of issues arise from the way the two generations of Japanese American characters regard nationalism and from the characters' responses to what the American nation has done to them.

Masu is a rare Issei character in the tradition of Japanese American literature. Rejecting nostalgia for Japan, he tells his son his own strongest reasons for venturing to and staying in America. He speaks like one who discovered America, and this inference may well raise issues, especially with respect to the Yakama Indians on whose land the play is set, about who "owns" America. Masu stayed because in America, he says,

> I was freer. I could see what it was like to be a lumberjack, a fisherman, and anything else that came my way. Try it out and forget it. Put a blanket on my shoulder and go where I wanted. This land was wide and boundless once. Every act still had no name, and every piece of land and sky was not spoken for. It's different for you. You were born here, and so, when other people tell you that you don't belong, it must hurt. That didn't hurt me. I knew I didn't come from this land. I knew what I came from. It can't be helped. We were born, Tadao, to different times, so our lives are different, must be different, if we are to survive. (136)

Tanaka, too, commits himself fully to America, but for reasons that lead him and Masu to fight each other, for America has made it possible, up to the war, for Tanaka to achieve the status he would have liked in Japan. But this status comes to nothing when the United States government strikes down the entire community, including Tanaka. And this very blow infuriates Masu (146). When we last see Tanaka in the play, by contrast, he is pleading for the community to bow to the authority of America, against which Masu has rebelled.

As a Nisei character, Tadao too is exceptional. In history and literature, Nisei since the war have generally been characterized as having proved themselves loyal to America by their cooperation with and sacrifice in their internment and, more powerfully mythical, by their service in the United States military during World War II. The internment was based in part on the assumption and divisive construct that the Issei were of Japan and thus tied to the enemy and that the Nisei by birth and upbringing were also tied to Japan because of their parents. This construct is the gist of the lecture that the Nisei sociologist, who is collaborating with the government, gives to the Issei in *No-No Boy* (Okada 124–25). The notion of inherited loyalty to Japan prompts the separation of Issei and Nisei, because the Nisei know they are not from or of Japan and now have to prove it through conflict with their parents. But Tadao goes in the other direction. He wants to go to Japan. In Japanese American literature Tadao resembles another character, who is never seen on the page but is talked about: Mike, the older brother of Emi's estranged husband, Ralph, in *No-No Boy*. A veteran of the United States Army in World War I, Mike left America for Japan to protest the internment (Okada 97–98). Ichiro, the title character of that novel, thinks he too has chosen loyalty to Japan and his Issei mother but has done so wrongly. Mrs. Yamada, Ichiro's mother, tragically enacts in *No-No Boy* the principle behind Tadao's change of loyalties in *Gold Watch*: If they insist on treating me as a Jap, I'll be a Jap!

Iko also characterizes Tadao as a naive bigot, as seen in a brief exchange with Masu in which Tadao adopts the racist term *nigger* (134–35). Elaine H. Kim quotes from Iko's "And There Are Stories, There Are Stories" to illustrate Iko's exploration of "the bonds between Black and Japanese Americans as adversaries of white racism" (235). This exchange hints at the coalitional theme that may indeed be germane to the play's setting: a gathering place of the indigenous Yakama people; of Mexicans with a long historical presence there; of European Americans who were once, on that same site, considered to be of highly distinct ethnicities; and of farm renters and workers of different colors and cultures, including Japanese and Filipinos.

This play deserves further critical attention to and analysis of something that becomes evident when actors and directors work on it. While in my view the protagonist of the play consists of the male and female Japanese American characters collectively, *Gold Watch* is, or appears to be, strongly male-centered, in the character Masu. If, however, Iko criticizes Masu's desire to be left alone on the farm and thus to be "free," then Kimi's daily interactions with the merchants, the bank (where her dealings over farm loans are utterly necessary to the survival of the family), the people at her children's schools, and the church (she belongs to Reverend Sugano's Methodist Church) are also heroic in Iko's conception. Her coming to America as a bride is symbolic of a heterosexual, dominant, Japanese American narrative of the establishment of families in the twentieth century up to 1941, whereas Chinese and Filipino Americans were largely inhabitants of bachelor societies. Kimi's story is nonetheless highly particularized. Her transmission of her story to Tadao, in act 2, is as important to the drama and its very title as is Masu's gift of his American gold watch and the stories behind it.

Pedagogical Issues and Suggestions

In the full two-act version published in *Unbroken Thread*, the text of *Gold Watch* is not divided into scenes. A useful exercise for introducing students to the structure of this drama and, in theory, others might be to analyze how act 1 proceeds from one grouping of characters and their dialogues to another. Readers of the play—and the act of reading a play can be difficult at first—may also perceive how attention to the set shifts around the stage, which may lead some to try to picture the set design they are beginning to imagine (see Iko 113 for a description of the set). The script springs some surprises. For instance, near the middle of the script, the directions call for "an old wooden Japanese-style tub with an aluminum corrugated roof siding" (not previously described) with the actors, nude, inside (131). How is the tub to get there? (This ofuro was a permanent fixture on the set in the 1977 production in Seattle.)

Such exercises introduce the idea that a drama is a work that continues to be under construction beyond the writing of it. Consequent questions about characters and how they think and feel have to do, therefore, with how they speak and act, and how they act and interact has to do with how they function in the drama. Even as readers we become involved in imaginatively acting, directing, and interpreting through our analyses. A good dramatic and thematic question to pursue involves each character's sense or claim of relationship with America and with Japan and the way those relationships are disclosed and acted on.

Because of its genre and Iko's use of that genre, *Gold Watch* depends less on a reader's study of its contexts through other sources than do many other fictive works about the internment and Japanese Americans in the first year of the war. Understanding *No-No Boy*, by contrast, strongly depends on information that is not explicit in its text. The stage directions for *Gold Watch* indicate places where historical documents are to be screened, literally to set contexts where needed. More thoroughly compelling, the characterizations all together tend to counteract, dramatically, certain prejudices about Japanese Americans (e.g., stereotypes about Issei being nostalgic for Japan and about Nisei hating their parents for not being American). But prejudices still die hard, and in teaching *Gold Watch*, one should be cautious that readers refrain from or question interpretive moves that assume the characters to be what dramatically they are not. None of them, for instance, is "Japanese," not even Hiroshi, if being Japanese means living the current history of the nation that bombed Pearl Harbor. Their being "Japanese" was the rationale for interning the Japanese Americans, something Iko certainly does not endorse. According to Iko's play, being in America makes the characters as American as Masu's senryu poetry.

Intertextual Linkages

With Monica Sone's *Nisei Daughter*, John Okada's *No-No Boy*, Wakako Yamauchi's *And the Soul Shall Dance*, Maxine Hong Kingston's *The Woman Warrior: Memoirs of a Girlhood among Ghosts* and *Tripmaster Monkey: His Fake Book*, Shawn Wong's *Homebase* and *American Knees*, Joy Kogawa's *Obasan*, and Frank Chin's *Donald Duk*: cultural transmission from immigrants to children or, sometimes, the failure of such attempts.

With Hisaye Yamamoto's "The Legend of Miss Sasagawara," Okada's *No-No Boy*, Kazuo Miyamoto's *Hawai'i: The End of the Rainbow*, and Chin's unpublished play "The Comic": resistance or a subversive, unsettling response to the internment of Japanese Americans.

With Milton Murayama's *All I Asking for Is My Body* and *Five Years on a Rock*, Yamauchi's *And the Soul Shall Dance*, and Akemi Kikumura's *Through Harsh Winters: The Life of a Japanese Immigrant Woman*: rural lives of Japanese immigrant families; isolation versus questions of larger social interactions.

With Yamamoto's "Seventeen Syllables" and Yamauchi's *And the Soul Shall Dance*: the Issei poet and artist.

Bibliographic Resources

See the units in this volume on Okada, Sone, and Yamauchi. See especially Kazuo Ito's *Issei*, a large volume containing a great number of haiku and senryu by Issei particularly of the Northwest. Ito tells the history of Japanese Americans through the "voices"—spoken and literary—of his subjects. Nomura's study of the poet Teiko Tomita ("Tsugiki") is also highly pertinent to seeing what Iko may mean by a specific person in the "specific situation," the historical time and place, of her characters (Uno 107).

Bibliography

Chin, Frank. *Donald Duk*. Minneapolis: Coffee House, 1991.
Chin, Frank, et al., eds. *Aiiieeeee! An Anthology of Asian-American Writers*. Washington: Howard UP, 1974.
Ehrlich, Gretel. *Heart Mountain*. New York: Penguin, 1988.
Iko, Momoko. *Gold Watch*. Uno 111–53.
———. *Gold Watch*. Visions. PBS. KCET, Los Angeles, 1975.
———. Personal interview. Feb. 1977.
Ito, Kazuo. *Issei: A History of Japanese Immigrants in North America*. Trans. Shinichiro Nakamura and Jean S. Gerard. Seattle: Executive Committee for Pub. of *Issei*, 1973.
Kikumura, Akemi. *Through Harsh Winters: The Life of a Japanese Immigrant Woman*. Novato: Chandler, 1981.
Kim, Elaine H. *Asian American Literature: An Introduction to the Writings and Their Social Context*. Philadelphia: Temple UP, 1982.
Kingston, Maxine Hong. *Tripmaster Monkey: His Fake Book*. New York: Knopf, 1989.
———. *The Woman Warrior: Memoirs of a Girlhood among Ghosts*. New York: Knopf, 1976.
Kogawa, Joy. *Obasan*. 1981. New York: Doubleday, 1994.
Miyamoto, Kazuo. *Hawai'i: The End of the Rainbow*. Rutland: Tuttle, 1964.
Murayama, Milton. *All I Asking for Is My Body*. 1975. Afterword by Franklin Odo. Honolulu: U of Hawai'i P, 1988.
———. *Five Years on a Rock*. Honolulu: U of Hawai'i P, 1994.
Nomura, Gail M. "Beyond a Level Playing Field: The Significance of Pre–World War II Japanese American Baseball in the Yakima Valley." *Bearing Dreams, Shaping Visions:*

Asian Pacific American Perspectives. Ed. Linda Revilla et al. Pullman: Washington State UP, 1993. 15–31.

———. "Tsugiki, a Grafting: A History of a Japanese Pioneer Woman in Washington State." *Women in Pacific Northwest History: An Anthology*. Ed. Karen J. Blair. Seattle: U of Washington P, 1988. 207–29.

———. "Washington's Asian/Pacific American Communities." *Peoples of Washington: Perspectives on Cultural Diversity*. Ed. Sid White and S. E. Solberg. Pullman: Washington State UP, 1989. 113–55.

———. "Within the Law: The Establishment of Filipino Leasing Rights on the Yakima Indian Reservation." *Amerasia Journal* 13.1 (1986–87): 99–117.

Okada, John. *No-No Boy*. 1957. Seattle: U of Washington P, 1979.

Sone, Monica. *Nisei Daughter*. 1953. Seattle: U of Washington P, 1979.

Sumida, Stephen H. "Assimilation." *A Companion to American Thought*. Ed. Richard Wightman Fox and James T. Kloppenberg. Cambridge: Blackwell, 1995. 44–48.

———. "Hawai'i, the Northwest, and Asia: Localism and Local Literary Developments in the Creation of an Asian Immigrants' Sensibility." *The Blue Funnel Line*. Spec. Asian Amer. lit. issue of *Seattle Review* 11 (1986): 9–18.

Uno, Roberta, ed. *Unbroken Thread: An Anthology of Plays by Asian American Women*. Amherst: U of Massachusetts P, 1993.

Wong, Shawn. *American Knees*. New York: Simon, 1995.

———. *Homebase*. New York: Reed, 1979.

Yamamoto, Hisaye. "The Legend of Miss Sasagawara." Yamamoto, *"Seventeen Syllables"* 20–33.

———. "Seventeen Syllables." Yamamoto, *"Seventeen Syllables"* 8–19.

———. *"Seventeen Syllables" and Other Stories*. Latham: Kitchen Table, 1988.

Yamauchi, Wakako. *And the Soul Shall Dance*. *West Coast Plays*. Vol. 11-12. Ed. Rick Foster. Los Angeles: California Theatre Council, 1982. 118–64. Rpt. in *Between Worlds: Contemporary Asian-American Plays*. Ed. Misha Berson. New York: Theater Communications, 1990. 128–74.

And the Soul Shall Dance
by Wakako Yamauchi

Stephen H. Sumida

Publication and Production Information

The short story "And the Soul Shall Dance," on which this two-act drama is based, was first published in *Rafu Shimpo*, the newspaper of the Japanese American community of Los Angeles, in 1966. It was included in *Aiiieeeee! An Anthology of Asian-American Writers*, edited by Frank Chin et al., in 1974. Interest in Yamauchi's story led to her winning a grant from the Rockefeller Foundation to develop it into a script for production at East West Players in Los Angeles. The Asian Exclusion Act, an Asian American theater company in Seattle, mounted a workshop production of "And the Soul Shall Dance" in March 1976. Yamauchi saw the production and went on to revise her script, which the East West Players performed in 1977, both in the theater and for broadcast on PBS. *And the Soul Shall Dance* won the Los Angeles Critics Circle Award for the best new play of 1977 and has since then been produced a number of times from Hawai'i to New York. In the early 1990s the Pan-Asian Repertory Company of New York took it on the road for a North American tour. The full script was published in *West Coast Plays* (ed. Foster) in 1982 and *Between Worlds* (ed. Berson) in 1990. Act 1 appeared in *The Big Aiiieeeee!*, edited by Jeffery Chan et al., in 1991. Meanwhile, the original short story has reappeared in a variety of anthologies.

Overview

And the Soul Shall Dance is set "on and between two small farms in Southern California's Imperial Valley" beginning in the summer of 1935 and ending the following spring (132).[1] An accidental bathhouse fire at the Murata farm brings the family members (Murata; his wife, Hana; and Masako, their eleven-year-old daughter) closer to their neighbor, Oka. Oka expresses his longing for a past family life the Muratas had not known he had, while at Oka's house the Muratas witness the wretchedness and abuse in his present life with Emiko, his wife.

The Muratas learn that Emiko is the sister of Oka's late first wife, Shizue, a hard-working woman who died never having left Japan for America. Oka discloses that he and Shizue had a daughter, Kiyoko, and that he wishes to bring the fourteen-year-old to join him in America so that he, too, can have a family like Murata—a family, however, that excludes Emiko and does so at her own expense. Profoundly affecting the bad relations between Emiko and Oka is the latter's inferior social status. Like Emiko, whom he tries to dominate, Oka was enlisted in service to a patriarchy. In Japan he had been apprenticed in hard labor to a blacksmith. Born with the family name of Sakakihara, he took on his employer's name (*yoshi*, the practice is called) and was married to the older daughter because the Okas had no sons.

The title of the play refers to Emiko and her ethereal and even bizarre desires to recover the life from which she was snatched, when, because of a scandal of hers in Japan, her parents forced her to marry by proxy her late sister's widower and exiled her to him in America. Emiko had been learning such arts as flower arranging, the tea ceremony, and dance. But in America she exists in a desert that the Issei are toiling to turn into farmland, with a man who himself is baffled about why her parents sent their "prize mare" to be the mate of a "plow horse" like him (151). For two years Emiko has been trying secretly to save money to return to Japan and escape from Oka. Emiko dreams of the arts and the illicit lover she has lost. Although in daily life she smokes, drinks, and otherwise acts in ways criticized by the Issei as unsuitable for a woman, she pursues a self-consciously feminine refinement in which she was groomed. In the course of the play, Oka finds Emiko's can of money and steals it to pay for bringing his daughter, Kiyoko, to him. Emiko in her distress begs the Muratas to buy her treasured kimonos, for Masako. But whatever Hana Murata may know of the finer fabrics and arts of the Japan she and her husband left behind, she has no money to afford the luxury of kimonos for her daughter.

Although she in effect is the title character, Emiko is not often seen in the play. Yet she is everywhere. The play's theme song is hers. Composed by Yamauchi, the lyrics of the song, "Kokoro ga Odoru" ("And the Soul Shall Dance"), express Emiko's suffering, her melancholy, indeed her depression:

Akai kuchibiru	Red lips
Cappu ni yosete	Press against a glass
Aoi sake nomya	Drink the green wine
Kokoro ga odoru	And the soul shall dance
Kurai yoru no yume	Dark night dreams
Setsu nasa yo	Are unbearable
Aoi sake nomya	Drink the green wine
Yume mo odoru	And the dreams will dance (*And the Soul* 164)

Reception

The editors of *The Big Aiiieeeee!* introduce their selection of act 1 of *And the Soul Shall Dance* with the judgment that it is "the most honored and celebrated work in Asian American Theater" (Chan et al. 193). Yamauchi's winning of the 1977 Los Angeles Critics Circle Award stands as one item of evidence for this estimation. The inclusion of the entire play in the anthology *West Coast Plays* is surely another. And still another way of judging the importance of Yamauchi's drama and its reception involves the circles and communities of people involved in Asian American literary work in the 1970s. *And the Soul Shall Dance* followed Frank Chin's *The Year of the Dragon* and Momoko Iko's *Gold Watch* in being broadcast nationally on PBS during the middle and late 1970s. These works had the distinction of being the first Asian American dramas to be viewed on television. It was certainly not the mere fact of national exposure that was valued in these cases (at a time when the much-produced *Flower Drum Song*, by C. Y. Lee, was criticized for trading in stereotypes of Chinese Americans). With Chin's and Iko's dramas, Yamauchi's *And the Soul Shall Dance* came to be considered a classic in Asian American drama. This judgment generally comes from critics and audiences who compare these dramas of the 1970s with the more numerous Asian American dramatic works of the 1980s and 1990s, some of which, such as David Henry Hwang's *M. Butterfly*, have been more widely seen and celebrated than the three classics of the 1970s. It may well be that performances in popular culture have influenced the writing of the plays. Radio shows of the 1940s and 1950s resound in *The Chickencoop Chinaman* and other works of Chin. For *And the Soul Shall Dance*, Yamauchi composed songs in the style she remembers from her youth ("Kago no Tori" and the title song of the play, "Kokoro no Odoru" [*And the Soul* 164]). She has them performed along with a historical example of such a song, "Tokyo Ondo," so that all the music in the play, in an understated way, suggests a historical depth (143). By contrast the generation of Asian American playwrights who have followed Yamauchi, Iko, and Chin has grown up with television, its dramatic performances, its reruns, and its sitcoms. These influences seem evident not only in the references to contemporary media but also in the structures of the newer plays—as well as in "mainstream" receptions of them. Philip Kan Gotanda's *Yankee Dawg You Die*, with its alternation of scenes and interludes, is a good example of his composing a structure that resembles the media of film and television that the play is about (in Gotanda 69–127).

Author's Biographical Background

Wakako Yamauchi (née Wakako Nakamura) was born in 1924 in Westmoreland, California, in the Imperial Valley where her play is set. Her departure in the drama from the more usual narrative of the injustices heaped on Japanese Americans during World War II by no means signals an avoidance of a critique of racism. Themes from her youth run through *And the Soul Shall Dance*, as if in writing the short story and drama she was finding a necessary vehicle for interpreting and presenting her own most significant memories of when she was eleven like the character Masako. According to Roberta Uno, Yamauchi's mother had a profound influence on her by instilling pride in being Japanese (54). Yamauchi attributes her own "sense of tragedy" in her writing to her mother's expressive nostalgia for Japan and a longing to return, enforced by her continually having to respond to racial discrimination in the United States (55).

When Wakako Yamauchi was a teenager her family moved to Oceanside, California, in search of better opportunities. There she met Hisaye Yamamoto, who became a lasting influence as a friend, mentor, and fellow writer. Like Yamamoto, she was later interned at Poston, Arizona, during World War II. "Relocated" to Chicago in 1944, Yamauchi found work in a candy factory and went to art school (Uno 55), but she returned to the Poston camp after learning of her father's death there, whereupon she and her surviving family members were relocated again while the war ended and the internment camps were vacated. In 1948 she married Chester Yamauchi (they were divorced in the 1970s), and she has a daughter, Joy.

Yamauchi wrote the short story "And the Soul Shall Dance" in 1959, but between 1959 and 1961 her writings were either rejected for publication or seemingly ignored by readers, even after she was published in *Rafu Shimpo*. Yamauchi turned again to her other art, painting, until the early 1970s when Hisaye Yamamoto put her in touch with Shawn Wong and the others researching and compiling the anthology *Aiiieeeee!* In 1974 she went, with Frank Chin and Shawn Wong, to see Momoko Iko's *When We Were Young* performed at East West Players, whose founder and artistic director, Mako, later worked with her to secure the Rockefeller grant that funded her work of turning the short story into the play. It was Yamauchi's first dramatic script, and it has been followed by *The Music Lessons* (1977), *Not a Through Street* (1981), *12-1-A* (1981), *The Memento* (1983), and *The Chairman's Wife (A Gang of One)* (1988), all of which have been produced. Several others are as yet unproduced (see Uno 327). Yamauchi has published a collection of her works, *Songs My Mother Taught Me: Stories, Plays, Memoir*, edited and introduced by Garrett Hongo, with an afterword by Valerie Miner. (For excellent biographical commentary on Yamauchi, see Uno 53–58.)

Historical Context for the Narratives in *And the Soul Shall Dance*

While studying *And the Soul Shall Dance* and other works about immigrants from Asia to the West Coast of the United States up through the first half of the twentieth century, readers should bear in mind the legal exclusions that generation faced. United States laws forbade them from becoming naturalized citizens of the United States. Hope was placed in their children, whose births on American soil made them citizens.

The immigrants faced antimiscegenation laws. But Japanese "picture brides" such as Emiko were allowed to enter the country until the total exclusion of Asians from immigration in 1924. California passed an antialien land law in 1913 and went on to tighten it thereafter, forbidding "aliens ineligible to citizenship" (i.e., Asians, since this group was distinctly ineligible) to own real estate (Takaki 203). The Muratas, the Okas, and the entire population of Issei farmers in the Imperial Valley of the play's setting could thus only rent the land they farmed. The short rental periods typically prevented the immigrants from planting orchards and long-term crops, so they specialized in truck farming (see also Momoko Iko's *Gold Watch*). If all else fails, Oka quips, as long as he remains in the country rather than moves to the city he will at least have carrots to eat. Murata laughingly responds, "All the carrots we been eating 'bout to turn me into a rabbit" (125). The laws relegate these immigrants to the status of aliens and short-term sojourners. But the characters in the play, as in many works of Japanese American literature, struggle to remain where they are, in America—with the exception of Emiko. Other characters' views of her emphasize her mad desire to return to a Japan that by now is a figment of her urgent nostalgia. But on the other side of Emiko's dream is her desperation to escape her present condition, from which the other characters, in their attempts to be sociable, try to avert their eyes. The causes for her dreadful condition extend beyond Oka, Emiko herself, her parents, and what they have done to her to include American measures for alienating the Issei, in the historical contexts surrounding the individual characters.

Historical Context for the Writing of *And the Soul Shall Dance*

Set in 1935, *And the Soul Shall Dance* is somewhat uncommon among Japanese American literary works: it is not about the bombing of Pearl Harbor and the injustice of the internment of Japanese Americans during World War II. Yamauchi's drama joins the company of several other exceptions to the Japanese American master narratives of "the war" (which in Nikkei, or Japanese American, idioms has specifically meant World War II). The Nisei fiction writer Toshio Mori wrote many of the stories in his *Yokohama, California* before World War II. Mori, Hisaye Yamamoto, and Wakako Yamauchi—major Nisei writers—have demonstrated that Nisei writers can (as who else can?) write powerful literature about Nikkei life before the war from vantage points after the war, their interpretations of the past filtered through their wartime experiences but without explicitly invoking Pearl Harbor and the camps. It may even be that not being about Pearl Harbor, the war, and the camps added to the appeal of *And the Soul Shall Dance*. The television version of Jeanne Wakatsuki Houston and James Houston's *Farewell to Manzanar* had aired in 1975. Iko's *Gold Watch* appeared on PBS in 1976. Both centered on the evacuation and internment of Nikkei of the West Coast. Yamauchi's difference from those newly recognized World War II and internment histories joined her with Yamamoto and Mori in finely evoking (as the character Masako does) the recollected sensibilities and private lives of Issei and Nisei from before the war. Whatever Issei and Nisei had lost in their outlooks because of their internment became all the more keenly comprehensible because Yamauchi and her Nisei colleagues were probing a time, before the war, that had become mythical to Japanese Americans. As noted above, Yamauchi's project of converting her short story into the two-act drama was supported by a grant from the Rockefeller Foundation to the East West Players. Perhaps during the early and middle 1970s a fuller, nation-wide presentation of Nikkei life than had ever appeared before was both desired and encouraged. This interest and the cultural productions it made possible contributed to the movement, during the next dozen years, for redress for former internees of the Japanese American concentration camps in World War II.

Major Themes

"necessity" and "extravagance" (in Sau-ling Wong's terms) in the presumed
    needs for ensuring the immigrants' survival in the Imperial Valley "desert"
    versus the seeming extravagance of what Emiko Oka has had and wants
a suppression of arts and artistry
gender relations complicated by class differences and custom
the expected and unexpected roles of women
the sexuality of Emiko and the violence of Oka's attempts to dominate her
the contrasts between a functioning and a dysfunctional family; themes of
    family and individual survival
rural Japanese American life before the war
the concept of literacy (here, the ability to read about a certain community) in
    Masako's question, "How come they don't write books about us . . . about
    Japanese people?" (141)
interracial tensions occurring at the margins of the characters' Japanese
    American family lives
the youthful observer (Masako), a witness to both tragedy and survival, as she
    comes of age and, by inference, goes on to become an artist and to "write
    books about us . . . about Japanese people" (141)

Critical Issues

Published critical commentary on *And the Soul Shall Dance* is as yet scarce despite the prominence of its author in Asian American literature. The comments are usually about the original short story with that title. Elaine H. Kim and Sau-ling Cynthia Wong each compare Yamauchi's Emiko with the "crazy lady" who dances wildly in Maxine Hong Kingston's *The Woman Warrior* (Kim 255; Wong 195). King-Kok Cheung may suggest a similar comparison with Hisaye Yamamoto's Miss Sasagawara.

Discussing "The Legend of Miss Sasagawara," Cheung notes that a "lost lover" motif occurs in Yamamoto's "Yoneko's Earthquake" and "Seventeen Syllables" as well as in two of Yamauchi's stories, "And the Soul Shall Dance" and "Songs My Mother Taught Me" (61). Connections between Yamauchi and Yamamoto are nearly always stated in studies of Yamauchi. See especially Stan Yogi's "Rebels and Heroines: Subversive Narratives in the Stories of Hisaye Yamamoto and Wakako Yamauchi." Yogi briefly includes discussion of And the Soul Shall Dance in his survey of Japanese American literature; he notes Yamauchi's recurrent themes of "the ambiguities of gender relationships, tensions between Issei and Nisei, and the confining lives of the Issei, in a desolate desert farming community" (139). Garrett Hongo's introduction to Yamauchi's collection, Songs My Mother Taught Me, places Yamauchi in a context of Japanese American literary history, where, Hongo asserts, her "work sets down the neglected social and emotional history of two entire generations of Japanese in this country" (16). In an afterword to that volume, Valerie Miner considers parameters of gender, class, setting, domesticity, and race in the works of Yamauchi. Miner describes the "rural existence" that Yamauchi dramatizes in And the Soul Shall Dance: "spare, arduous, lonely, monotonous. Disappointing" (250). A highly informative critical and biographical resource is Roberta Uno's treatment of Yamauchi in Unbroken Thread.

Uno takes her critical cues from the arts of drama, theater, and performance. In these genres, delineations and interactions among the characters are highly significant. In its simplicity, And the Soul Shall Dance enacts interesting, intriguing subtleties of character. Even while the violent relationship between Emiko and Oka spirals at the center of the play, And the Soul Shall Dance displays a fine and sensitive layering of relationships—of each character among the five others, of each character's interior complexities, and of the two families.

Yamauchi achieves a passionate elegance by her interplay of the characters and their evocation of themes. It would be entirely too simplistic to state that in Yamauchi's view of gender relations, men are farmers of the soil while women are artists of the sky. Hana Murata sympathizes to some degree with Emiko Oka; yet in the play it is Hana who is more "practical" and disciplined than any other character, including Oka, whereas Emiko is torn up by practicality, symbolized not only by her need for money to purchase her escape but also by her contrast with the characters surrounding her. Hana Murata is Emiko's foil. In another contrast to Hana, her husband, Murata, is a nonki-na kind of fellow, easygoing, whimsical, rather like Father in Murayama's All I Asking for Is My Body. The morning after a heavy rainstorm, Hana worries that the seeds they have just planted have washed away, while Murata is thankful that only some have been lost. Speaking of the storm, Hana comments on how painful life is for Kiyoko, who came from Japan only to live fearfully in a house where her father and stepmother drink homebrew and fight endlessly. "We're lucky, Mama, lucky," Murata simply replies. As for Oka, Yamauchi at first thought he was simply the cloddish villain of the piece, but the character's role, she soon saw, was to set plot and themes in motion as well as to stand in emotional, psychic, and physical conflict with Emiko (Personal interview). Unlike Murata, Oka is anything but easygoing. Yet Oka exits from the play self-satisfied, for with the money he has stolen from Emiko he has acquired not only a daughter but also, in her, an object for every impulse and desire he has ever had for loving someone. The two youngsters, Masako and Kiyoko, also differ from each other. Masako, in her first weeks as Kiyoko's neighbor, mocks and mimics their conversations and Kiyoko's mannerisms in order to understand their differences, while Kiyoko tries to bridge those differences by emulating her new American peers.

Although the play's central conflict has to do with gender, Yamauchi's characters complicate any abstracting of generalizations by gender. With her emphasis on individual characteristics and their effects, however, what does Yamauchi see as the social and structural causes for her characters' actions? The theme of functional and dysfunctional relations in the play questions how some families of Issei and Nisei managed at all to survive sometimes brutally divisive conditions. What conditions structure the conflicts they experience?

Oka and Emiko seem to be as able as the Muratas when it comes to farming and scraping money together—enough to enable Oka, with the money he steals from Emiko, to afford to bring Kiyoko from Japan and then to lavish her with the latest in schoolgirl fashions. Yamauchi focuses on the Okas' now-tragic histories almost as if the characters were ill-fated rather than inadequate to the social and environmental demands of being Japanese immigrant farmers. In two different worlds, Emiko and Oka want to live stories apart from each other, each with memories and dreams that exclude the other. Yamauchi's emphasis falls on the narrative of the individual more than it does on a critique of the social structures and strictures that she presents as givens.

Pedagogical Issues and Suggestions

And the Soul Shall Dance offers some clear openings for discussion. (Here and elsewhere in my discussion I am drawing from my experience of acting in the Seattle production in 1976.) Perhaps most immediately obvious are a comparison between the two families in it and questions about how and why, dramatically, information for that comparison is disclosed. The abuse Oka inflicts on Emiko can be distressing indeed to readers and viewers of the play. When Oka bellows in vulgar Japanese as he beats Emiko, the sound is more frightening than if he were yelling in English, some members of a theater audience remarked of the play's workshop performance in Seattle, 1976. That abuse is an issue that begs to be dealt with. At the same time, the complications of presumably conventional gender roles and attitudes raise interesting questions in the drama—questions about which of the characters dreams, and who dreams what and why, and about who remains down to earth, and how, when, and why they do so. These questions take us into the characters' motives, line by line, as the characters develop throughout the course of the play.

The drama also has contextual issues to deal with, and these can be nicely educational. The setting in 1935 is somewhat the result of coincidence, though that would roughly be the year that Yamauchi herself recalls observing and learning about a family like the Okas (Personal interview). In the workshop production in Seattle in 1976, music was needed for act 1, scene 2, where Hana plays for Oka "a *lively* ondo" (dance song) on a phonograph (143). A record of "Tokyo Ondo" turned up in Seattle. Although the record was new, the song was first released in 1935. It became part of the script. The setting also raises a perplexing question of how Kiyoko Oka, born a Japanese citizen in Japan, could enter the United States in about 1935, despite the legal proscription of all emigration from Asia by 1924. For that matter, when would Emiko have arrived in the United States and how? By Yamauchi's own experience and memory of the actual models for the Okas, those immigrations did occur. Constructing possible, fictive biographies for each character in just such historical circumstances, actors and directors—and certainly students—have learned considerably about the lengths to which immigrants (whether willing or not) and their families went in getting exceptions to the exclusion of Asians since 1924. These efforts and the motives, obligations, debts, troubles, and any benefits they incur should go into the makeup of each character's memory if the characters of the drama are to be intelligently conceived by those who read and perform them.

Intertextual Linkage

With Hisaye Yamamoto's "Seventeen Syllables" and "The Legend of Miss Sasagawara" and Maxine Hong Kingston's *The Woman Warrior: Memoirs of a Girlhood among Ghosts*: the frustration of artistic dreams; a madness associated with that frustration.

With Yamamoto's "Seventeen Syllables" and "Yoneko's Earthquake": lost love.

With the preceding stories by Yamamoto and with Eleanor Wong Telemaque's *It's Crazy to Stay Chinese in Minnesota*: Asian immigrant mothers and their daughters in rural life.

With some of Yamamoto's stories and with Toshio Mori's stories in *Yokohama, California*: works set before the war, by Nisei authors who grew up in that era; the attention of all three authors to the narratives of individuals and, often, their idiosyncracies.

With Akemi Kikumura's *Through Harsh Winters: The Life of a Japanese Immigrant Woman*: the first-person narrative of an Issei woman in an agricultural setting similar to the play's in place and time.

With Momoko Iko's *Gold Watch* and Milton Murayama's *All I Asking for Is My Body* and *Five Years on a Rock*: the rural life of Japanese immigrant families; themes of isolation, retreat from social concerns, and yet the impossibility of simple escape.

With Carlos Bulosan's *America Is in the Heart* and Kingston's *The Woman Warrior*: literacy in the need to read and write about communities from observation and experience despite a lack of written sources.

Bibliographic Resources

For backgrounds on Issei history, see Yuji Ichioka, *The Issei: The World of the First Generation Japanese Immigrants, 1885–1924*. Kazuo Ito's *Issei: A History of Japanese Immigrants in North America* contains poetry, writings by Issei, and transcriptions of oral narratives that present the subjects in their own voices. Studies of and contexts for Japanese American histories that include Issei agricultural work in the Imperial Valley of California are such interpretive surveys as Sucheng Chan's *Asian Americans: An Interpretive History*, Roger Daniels's *Asian America: Chinese and Japanese in the United States since 1850*, and Ronald Takaki's *Strangers from a Different Shore: A History of Asian Americans*. Valerie J. Matsumoto's *Farming the Home Place: A Japanese American Community in California, 1919–1982* is a strongly relevant historical resource, with its perspectives on family and gender.

Roberta Uno identifies and provides production histories for Yamauchi's plays. Yamauchi's *Songs My Mother Taught Me: Stories, Plays, and Memoir* includes a publication chronology that records all her published works, in the different genres, up to 1993.

Note

1. Quotations from *And the Soul Shall Dance* are taken from the anthology *Between Worlds: Contemporary Asian-American Plays*, edited by Misha Berson.

Bibliography

Bulosan, Carlos. *America Is in the Heart: A Personal History*. 1946. Seattle: U of Washington P, 1973.

Chan, Jeffery Paul, et al., eds. *The Big Aiiieeeee! An Anthology of Chinese American and Japanese American Literature*. New York: Meridian, 1991.

Chan, Sucheng. *Asian Americans: An Interpretive History*. Boston: Twayne, 1991.

Cheung, King-Kok. *Articulate Silences: Hisaye Yamamoto, Maxine Hong Kingston, Joy Kogawa*. Ithaca: Cornell UP, 1993.

Chin, Frank. The Chickencoop Chinaman *and* The Year of the Dragon. *Two Plays*. Seattle: U of Washington P, 1981.

Chin, Frank, et al., eds. *Aiiieeeee! An Anthology of Asian-American Writers*. Washington: Howard UP, 1974.

Daniels, Roger. *Asian America: Chinese and Japanese in the United States since 1850*. Seattle: U of Washington P, 1988.

Gotanda, Philip Kan. Fish Head Soup *and Other Plays*. Seattle: U of Washington P, 1995.

Hongo, Garrett. Introduction. Yamauchi, *Songs* 1–16.

Houston, Jeanne Wakatsuki, and James Houston. *Farewell to Manzanar*. Boston: Houghton, 1973.

Hwang, David Henry. M. Butterfly. New York: Penguin, 1989.

Ichioka, Yuji. The Issei: The World of the First Generation Japanese Immigrants, 1885–1924. New York: Macmillan, 1988.

Iko, Momoko. Gold Watch. Uno 111–53.

Ito, Kazuo. Issei: A History of Japanese Immigrants in North America. Trans. Shinichiro Nakamura and Jean S. Gerard. Seattle: Executive Committee for Pub. of Issei, 1973.

Kikumura, Akemi. Through Harsh Winters: The Life of a Japanese Immigrant Woman. Novato: Chandler, 1981.

Kim, Elaine H. Asian American Literature: An Introduction to the Writings and Their Social Context. Philadelphia: Temple UP, 1982.

Kingston, Maxine Hong. The Woman Warrior: Memoirs of a Girlhood among Ghosts. New York: Knopf, 1976.

Matsumoto, Valerie J. Farming the Home Place: A Japanese American Community in California, 1919–1982. Ithaca: Cornell UP, 1993.

Miner, Valerie. "Afterword: The Relocation of Identity." Yamauchi, Songs 245–54.

Mori, Toshio. "The Chauvinist" and Other Stories. Introd. Hisaye Yamamoto. Los Angeles: UCLA Asian Amer. Studies Center, 1979.

———. Woman from Hiroshima. San Francisco: Isthmus, 1979.

———. Yokohama, California. Introd. William Saroyan. Caldwell: Caxton, 1949. Introd. Lawson Fusao Inada. Seattle: U of Washington P, 1985.

Murayama, Milton. All I Asking for Is My Body. 1975. Afterword by Franklin Odo. Honolulu: U of Hawai'i P, 1988.

———. Five Years on a Rock. Honolulu: U of Hawai'i P, 1994.

Takaki, Ronald. Strangers from a Different Shore: A History of Asian Americans. Boston: Little, 1989.

Telemaque, Eleanor Wong. It's Crazy to Stay Chinese in Minnesota. Nashville: Nelson, 1978.

Uno, Roberta, ed. Unbroken Thread: An Anthology of Plays by Asian American Women. Amherst: U of Massachusetts P, 1993.

Wong, Sau-ling Cynthia. Reading Asian American Literature: From Necessity to Extravagance. Princeton: Princeton UP, 1993.

Yamamoto, Hisaye. "The Legend of Miss Sasagawara." Yamamoto, "Seventeen Syllables" 20–33.

———. "Seventeen Syllables." Yamamoto, "Seventeen Syllables" 8–19.

———. "Seventeen Syllables" and Other Stories. Introd. King-Kok Cheung. Latham: Kitchen Table, 1988.

———. "Yoneko's Earthquake." Yamamoto, "Seventeen Syllables" 46–56.

Yamauchi, Wakako. "And the Soul Shall Dance." Rafu Shimpo 19 Dec. 1966: 9+. Rpt. in Chin et al. 193–200.

———. And the Soul Shall Dance. West Coast Plays. Vol. 11-12. Ed. Rick Foster. Los Angeles: California Theatre Council, 1982. 118–64. Rpt. in Between Worlds: Contemporary Asian-American Plays. Ed. Misha Berson. New York: Theater Communications Group, 1990. 128–74.

———. The Music Lessons. Uno 59–104. Rpt. in Yamauchi, Songs 52–96.

———. Personal interview. Mar. 1976.

———. "Songs My Mother Taught Me." Amerasia Journal 3.2 (1976): 63–73.

————. *Songs My Mother Taught Me: Stories, Plays, and Memoir*. Ed. and introd. Garrett Hongo. Afterword by Valerie Miner. New York: Feminist, 1994.

Yogi, Stan. "Japanese American Literature." *An Interethnic Companion to Asian American Literature*. Ed. King-Kok Cheung. Cambridge: Cambridge UP, 1997. 125–55.

————. "Rebels and Heroines: Subversive Narratives in the Stories of Hisaye Yamamoto and Wakako Yamauchi." *Reading the Literatures of Asian America*. Ed. Shirley Geok-lin Lim and Amy Ling. Philadelphia: Temple UP, 1992. 131–50.

Other Genres

Navigating Asian American Panethnic Literary Anthologies

Sau-ling Cynthia Wong

Scope and Purpose

This essay provides information on selected panethnic Asian American literary anthologies for teachers—a need not served by the teaching units on individual titles. The number of anthologies relevant to Asian American literature is very large indeed (see, e.g., Cheung and Yogi); further, the number of new publications has been growing explosively in the last decade or so. Since exhaustiveness is impossible and in any case undesirable in a pedagogical aid, I have chosen to devote most of my attention to titles that are fairly readily available today (thus ruling out, for example, ephemeral campus publications); to panethnic rather than ethnic-specific anthologies; and to collections of primary texts rather than collections of literary or cultural criticism (such as Lim and Ling; Aguilar-San Juan; Omi and Takagi; and Eng and Hom; see Cheung, "Re-viewing," for an overview). To help teachers navigate the territory, I share my experience of sorting through the anthologies, explore various ways in which such anthologies can be grouped and compared, and provide brief notes on them. This way, teachers with specific needs in mind may have a better idea of where to start looking.

"Literariness" and Professionalization

I set myself the task of surveying literary anthologies, but this apparently self-explanatory term calls for clarification in the Asian American context. The conventional usage of the term *literary* is implicitly belletristic, referring to what is commonly known as "creative writing" in one or more established literary genres set off from "nonliterature." This type of text is familiar to literature students from anthologies of the traditional Anglo-American canon. However, many anthologies important in the development of Asian American literature, especially those based on emergent

235

identities, are deliberately multidisciplinary—what I call "mixed" for short, to differentiate them from traditional multigenre anthologies (in which *genre* refers to established literary genres like poetry, drama, short story, etc.).

"Creative writing" pieces may appear alongside sociological studies, historical accounts, political manifestos, activist agendas, literary analyses, interviews and oral histories, visual art, and so on; some anthologies have separate sections labeled "literature" while others do not. Moreover, the two groups that, for lack of better terms, might be called "professionals" (e.g., scholars, writers by vocation) and "community members" (e.g., activists, "ordinary people" deemed representative of certain conditions or sensibilities) are frequently presented as equal partners.[1] Examples include the works by Amy Tachiki et al. and Emma Gee et al., whose concerns are primarily panethnic; the feminist anthologies by Asian Women United of California, by Shirley Geok-lin Lim and Mayumi Tsutakawa,[2] and by Elaine Kim, Lilia Villanueva, and Asian Women United of California; the queer[3] anthologies by Cristy Chung, Alison Kim, and A. Kaweah Lemeshewsky, by Sharon Lim-Hing, and by Russell Leong; and the multiracial anthology by Velina Houston and Teresa Williams.[4]

Given the way that literature is taught in American academic institutions, most teachers using this resource guide will be familiar or comfortable with—and perhaps even required to implement—a belletristic approach. This is also the emphasis adopted in this volume by the coeditors, Stephen H. Sumida and myself, both university academics whose livelihood and interests are bound up with the institutionalization of literature. Yet while the existence of the "mixed" anthologies may, from one point of view, be said to create organizational problems for me as the author of this essay, from another it offers a most welcome opportunity to examine the nature and implications of anthologization.

The reasons that some anthologies refuse to conform to the established practice of isolating "creative writing" and according it a privileged venue are quite complex. Sometimes, when an emergent group seeks to be heard as well as to solidify its membership, the mixing of discipline and genre may be attributed to the relative paucity of available material and the desire to be welcoming to all constituents.[5] However, this tells only a small part of the story. Often the editors' design is to mount a deliberate challenge to the widespread bourgeois-romantic notion of literature as being above politics and of writers as a breed apart with extraordinary sensibilities and talents. The movements that birthed Asian American identity politics and Asian American studies have left a strong legacy of Marxist-influenced activism, among whose corollaries are a spurning of elitism, a high priority accorded to community building through practice (making a book together is one such effort), and close attention to the material conditions in which literature is produced, circulated, consumed, and institutionalized. Two key demands of the Asian American movement of the late 1960s and early 1970s were the establishment of Asian American studies and the inclusion of Asian American material in curricula, both of which have been achieved to some extent at the university level. Nevertheless, the resultant professionalization of Asian American literary studies has left many ambivalent. On the one hand, the recent surge in specialized

Asian American literary anthologies (by literary genre, theme, etc.) might be considered a measure of the field's professionalization. On the other hand, the production of "mixed" anthologies persists—perhaps a sign that professionalization continues to be contested.

Some of the dynamics of anthologization have been investigated by Te-hsing Shan, who analyzes Chinese American anthologies, and by both Cynthia Franklin and Young Mi Pak ("*Anthologizing*"; see also Pak, "Self" 185–215), who dissect the announced objectives, revealed assumptions, and sometimes the biases and contradictions of several recent "mixed" feminist Asian American anthologies. Pak considers *anthologizing* (her italicized term is meant to highlight her special usage) an apt metaphor for the mutually constituting relationship between individual voices and the community, and she stresses that the editorial structure of an anthology project is an integral part of its meaning. In other words, the product—the book in hand—and its content, which are conventional targets of critical attention, must be understood as the result of a material-social process rather than as the result of the unmediated playing out of some aesthetic Darwinism.

This sentiment contrasts markedly with that of an editor like Garrett Hongo (see *The Open Boat*), who is concerned with whether Asian American poets have gained recognition by already established (thus naturalized) gatekeeping institutions (e.g., major publishing houses, fellowship and award givers); who works alone as an arbiter of literary merit; and whose approach to anthologizing might be called taste making or enshrining.[6] Though single editorship is hardly an automatic indicator of such an approach,[7] the presence of an editorial collective with a relatively heterogeneous membership and egalitarian structure is almost a sure sign of the opposite—a community empowerment approach. Given the importance of mixed anthologies, in this essay I have chosen to eschew a mechanical application of the "literary anthology" criterion. Instead, to keep in view concepts of literature that are alternatives to the belletristic, as well as Asian American literature's history of constant struggle and negotiation, I have chosen to consider "mixed" anthologies to be literary anthologies in their own ways.

Navigating Anthologies by Panethnic Identity Concerns

Even without intending to give a historical survey, I still find it useful to begin with what is commonly known as the cultural nationalist period. But this so-called period is not enclosed by firm dates and, as Cheung reminds us ("Re-viewing"), should more accurately be regarded as a discourse whose dominance fluctuates at different times. Because the term is widely used, however, I will continue to use it here, but in highly selective ways. I mark it at one end, as many scholars do, with the Third World student strikes of 1968–69, around which Asian American activists rallied as part of a broad-based Asian American movement. Where the other end lies, if there is ever one, is a much less settled matter. Leaving this question open, I use the publication of Maxine

Hong Kingston's *The Woman Warrior* in 1976 to mark the end of the androcentric phase of cultural nationalism, since this event symbolically brought Asian American women's concerns to the forefront, eclipsing the masculinist assumptions of many earlier advocates of Asian American panethnicity. By this specification I hope to avoid implying that women played no part in defining cultural nationalism, that cultural nationalism is the monopoly of men, that feminism and cultural nationalism are incompatible, and so forth.

The androcentric cultural nationalist period saw the publication of such panethnic anthologies as Amy Tachiki, Eddie Wong, Franklin Odo, and Buck Wong's *Roots: An Asian American Reader* (mixed), Kai-yu Hsu and Helen Palubinskas's *Asian-American Authors* (multigenre), Frank Chin et al.'s *Aiiieeeee! An Anthology of Asian-American Writers* (multigenre), David Hsin-Fu Wand's *Asian-American Heritage: An Anthology of Prose and Poetry* (multigenre), Shawn Wong and Frank Chin's special Asian American issue of *Yardbird Reader* (multigenre), and Emma Gee et al.'s *Counterpoint: Perspectives on Asian America* (mixed), all of which played a significant role in solidifying the concepts of Asian American identity and community and all of which, because of the demographics of the time, were dominated by Chinese, Japanese, and Filipino authors. The works by Tachiki, Wong, Odo, and Wong and by Gee et al. are mixed anthologies; the others concentrate on literature.

Of this group of early panethnic anthologies, Chin et al.'s *Aiiieeeee!* continues to be widely read and remains readily available, not least because of its introduction, "Fifty Years of Our Whole Voice" (xxi–lxiv). Among other things, the introduction is a passionate manifesto of Asian American identity, and it has become an oft-cited document in Asian American culture. Many of the emphases expressed in that essay— antiracism, antiorientalism, American nativity, English monolingualism, ethnic communities in concentrated locales, working-class forebears, androcentrism, and heterosexism—have been influential in Asian American cultural criticism (though they certainly have been energetically challenged as well; see below).

Partly because these tenets have held such sway, David Wand's *Asian-American Heritage*, which shows greater inclusiveness than Chin et al.'s *Aiiieeeee!* on foreign-born writers, writers of Korean ancestry, and Polynesian oral literature, has fallen out of currency in the last quarter century. Ironically, recent critical attention on the Asian Pacific American concept, on the Asia-Pacific connection, and on the growing foreign-born composition of the Asian American population has enhanced Wand's contemporary relevance (see, e.g., Fujikane; Stillman, "History," "Nā Lei," and "Chants"; Sumida, *And the View* and "Postcolonialism").

Teachers interested in more recent Asian American cultural production might choose from among postandrocentric cultural nationalist anthologies, of which there are so many that further classification is necessary. One useful ad hoc category is panethnic anthologies that self-reflexively question the central place previously occupied by panethnic Asian American identity politics, that show a keen awareness of the group's internal diversity, and that valorize difference, ex-centricism, hybridity, fluidity, and indeterminacy, with or without acknowledging poststructuralist and postmodernist influences. Asian American panethnicity leaves a negative imprint, as it were, on these anthologies by serving as their unifying principle while being energetically disavowed as such. Shirley Lim and Mayumi Tsutakawa's *The Forbidden Stitch: An Asian American Women's Anthology* (mixed); Marilyn Chin, David Wong Louie, and Ken Weisner's *Dissident Song: A Contemporary Asian American Anthology* (multigenre); Jessica Hagedorn's *Charlie Chan Is Dead: An Anthology of Contemporary Asian American Fiction* (multigenre); and Garrett Hongo's *The Open Boat: Poems from Asian America* and *Under Western Eyes: Personal Essays from Asian America*, and possibly Walter Lew's *Premonitions: The Kaya Anthology of New Asian North American Poetry*—touched on in the introduction to this volume—fit this description. Of course, editors who question the meaningfulness of the Asian American label are caught in the contradiction of producing (and allowing to be marketed) books under precisely the same label.[8]

Overall, most recent anthologies are careful about going beyond the East Asian subgroups (Chinese, Japanese, Korean) that have come to stand for "Asian" in the American popular imagination. Inclusion of writers of Filipino, various South Asian, and Vietnamese descent is by now widespread, and writers of other backgrounds are increasingly, though still infrequently, represented (some of the rarer ones being Khmer, Laotian, Persian, Samoan, Thai, and Tibetan). Anthologies edited by college students are even more likely to features writings by previously underrepresented groups (e.g., Lee et al.; *Our Time*). Teachers focusing on Asian Americans' internal diversity or seeking material on specific subgroups would do better with recent anthologies than with those from the 1970s. However, in proportion to the representational diversity of an anthology and the editor's conviction about not imposing ordering principles (in order to avoid creating a master narrative), teachers would need to spend more time selecting pieces for course use and organizing a pedagogical framework for them.

Finally, another kind of challenge to panethnic Asian American identity politics is posed by Asian Americans of multiracial descent. Velina Hasu Houston and Teresa Williams's *No Passing Zone* is a mixed anthology of the "artistic and discursive voices of Asian-descent multiracials," in the words of the subtitle. The bulk of the volume is made up of expository essays, but there is a literature section as well. Note that the editors' preferred self-naming, "Asian-descent multiracials," reveals a refusal to privilege Asian ancestry (which I do as an Asian Americanist, treating multiracials as a subtype of Asian Americans for the purposes of this essay). Thus though this anthology is a special issue of an Asian American journal, *Amerasia*, the editors' and contributors' primary self-identification is not necessarily Asian American.

At this point, I am not aware of panethnic anthologies devised specifically to reflect geographical dispersal within North America (to the suburbs or to regions like the South that are not traditionally associated with Asian American concentrations), or else the multiple dislocations over the globe, of many contemporary Asian Americans. (Realuyo's *The NuyorAsian Anthology* focuses on New York City. The multiethnic "local" cultural production of Hawai'i, in which many Asian American writers participate, constitutes a unique case. See, for example, Chock and Lum.) Some anthologizers, however, do allude to these characteristics as complicating an ethnicity- and nation-based model of Asian American identity (see, e.g., Watanabe's introduction to Watanabe and Bruchac's *Into the Fire*), and the presence of "postcolonial" writers like Shirley Lim and Meena Alexander in some anthologies attests to the editors' awareness of the diasporic dimension of contemporary Asian American experiences. Roshni Rustomji-Kerns's *Encounters: People of Asian Descent in the Americas* (mixed), by encompassing diasporic Asian populations in South America, places Asian American (US) experiences in the context of the Americas.

Also absent are panethnic Asian American anthologies organized around class, despite a tradition of championing the socioeconomically underprivileged in the field.[9]

Navigating Anthologies by Gender and Sexuality Concerns

A second ad hoc way of navigating the profusion of recent anthologies is by gender and/or sexuality concerns. By this statement, I certainly do not mean to suggest that early anthologizers like Chin et al.; Wand; and Bruce Iwasaki, the editor of the literature section in Gee et al., are neutral to gender and sexuality issues. Quite the contrary. As Cheung notes, "From the beginning, race and gender have been intertwined in Asian American history and literature" ("Re-viewing" 10). While not excluding women writers, Chin et al. and Iwasaki are preoccupied with the emasculation of the Asian American male. They consider the rehabilitation of Asian American manhood the main mission of cultural projects, and they numerically favor male writers over female ones in their selections. Wand evidences his concern over emasculation in somewhat different ways (Fujikane 28–35). All share a heterosexist premise in their anxiety over being deemed insufficiently masculine by the conventional standards of Western culture. (Chin et al. and Iwasaki express this anxiety in openly homophobic terms.) Although these editors articulate and act on such beliefs in their anthologies, their concepts of gender and sexuality seem curiously "indirect"—that is, implicit in certain essentialist and static ways of conceptualizing whites, blacks, and Asians and women and men.

The very presence of Asian American women's anthologies brings gender to the forefront, by deploying gender as an explicit criterion of anthologization in addition to panethnicity. A similar situation obtains with queer interventions: what was previously elided, in the form of scattered adjectives and asides, is now rendered visible and is made into a cohering principle. Anthologies do differ from one another in terms of how consciously and elaborately they conceive of gender and/or sexuality as sites of identification and axes of mobilization. Some are celebratory; some are theoretically curious; yet others are motivated by a desire to address specific silences and injustices suffered by Asian American women or homosexuals.

Though I take the publication of Kingston's *The Woman Warrior* in 1976 as a convenient marker of the waning of androcentric cultural nationalism, the late 1970s and early 1980s were relatively quiet periods for the production of alternative anthologies. Beginning with the late 1980s, however, projects of feminist and/or queer intervention have led to a burgeoning of anthologies, many of which are panethnic. In 1987, Chung, Kim, and Lemeshewsky produced *Between the Lines: An Anthology by Pacific-Asian Lesbians of Santa Cruz, California*, the first Asian American lesbian anthology. In 1989 Asian Women United of California published *Making Waves: An Anthology of Writing by and about Asian American Women*, and Lim and Tsutakawa produced *The Forbidden Stitch*. Both works are mixed, both are based on open calls for submissions, and both are dedicated to illustrating the contemporary heterogeneity of Asian American women and defying stereotypical expectations on them. They differ, however, in editorial structure (two editors in one case, a collective in the other) and in formal structure (*Making Waves* is organized thematically around the water metaphor; *Forbidden Stitch* is resolutely unorganized). In content and tenor, especially in its commitment to panethnic alliance building, *Making Waves* is locatable in the cultural nationalist tradition, with the crucial difference, of course, that by its very design it seeks to counter the misogyny and American-nativity bias of a volume like *Aiiieeeee!* A sequel to *Making Waves, Making More Waves* (Kim, Villanueva, and Asian Women United of California) is similarly conceived, but the subsections, named after abstract nouns, are less evocative of a chronological narrative than their counterparts in the earlier volume were.

In 1990, Sylvia Watanabe and Carol Bruchac published *Home to Stay: Asian American Women's Fiction* (short stories and excerpts from longer works), organized loosely around women's life cycle. The impetus for this volume appears celebratory: to showcase the variety and range of Asian American experiences and to insist on "the normalcy of such diversity in a multicultural society." "It can reasonably be argued," the editors write, "that the stories in this book have arisen smack-dab out of the mainstream of American tradition" (xi).

In contrast to this sentiment, two anthologies of Asian American women's plays, both published in 1993—Velina Hasu Houston's *The Politics of Life: Four Plays by Asian American Women* and Roberta Uno's *Unbroken Thread: An Anthology of Plays by Asian American Women*—take a much less sanguine view of what the American mainstream is like. The introductions to both volumes recount the difficulties encountered by Asian American women playwrights in a theater world dominated by Euro-Americans and by men, "multiculturalism" notwithstanding; both argue for the vital necessity of community-based theater companies; both emphasize sociopolitical realities in the selected plays; and both pay tribute to the heroism of the women portrayed in them. Houston chose four plays by three playwrights with what she considers a feminist spirit (12). Uno conceives of her anthology as representing "some of the best dramatic literature written by Asian American women since the 1970s" (1).

Interestingly, an anthology that came out in 1991 seems impervious to the cultural changes outlined above. It is Jeffery Paul Chan et al.'s *The Big Aiiieeeee! An Anthology of Chinese American and Japanese American Literature* (multigenre), in some ways a sequel to the original *Aiiieeeee!* but in other ways not. Unlike its predecessor, it limits itself to Chinese American and Japanese American literature. This change may be read either as an indication of the editors' obduracy in the face of vast transformations in the Asian American population—that is, they shrink panethnic representation rather than expand it as other recent anthologizers do—or as part of the trend toward ethnic specialization (see below). On the other hand, the editors' persistence in androcentrism admits no alternative interpretation. In its Chinese American selections, *The Big Aiiieeeee!* is as close as anyone has come to assembling an Asian American men's anthology: among the nine pieces, only one woman, Sui Sin Far, long dead, is represented. (The Japanese American selections are more gender-balanced.) This imbalance may have resulted from applying the distinction between "real" and "fake" Asian American literature made in the introductory essay, "Come All Ye Asian American Writers of the Real and the Fake," signed by Frank Chin. Since, in his construction of "the real," "masculine" attributes feature heavily (for models of real Asian American manhood, Chin advocates returning to traditional Chinese heroic epics), it is not surprising to find female writers excluded. (A general introduction to the volume signed by all four editors is much shorter and somewhat more muted on this point.)

In addition to gender, sexuality, in the sense of sexual orientation, has been the focus of several recent panethnic Asian American anthologies.[10] *Witness Aloud*, a special issue of the *Asian Pacific American Journal*, covers lesbian, gay, and bisexual Asian Pacific American writing (in the subtitle's wording); there is no editorial statement or introduction. Sharon Lim-Hing's *The Very Inside: An Anthology of Writing by Asian and Pacific Islander Lesbian and Bisexual Women* (mixed), published in Canada, is much more substantial than its predecessor, *Between the Lines* (Chung, Kim, and Lemeshewsky); in addition, it includes bisexual women. In an account of her efforts to include Pacific Islander women and the obstacles she encountered, Lim-Hing concludes that celebration of diversity is more important than attempting to fully realize the "complex, perhaps impossible, promise of such a grouping" (introd., n. pag.). The volume has more contributors from various Southeast Asian groups than is usual in panethnic Asian American anthologies, in addition to South Asians and East Asians. The pieces are organized thematically to evoke an inspirational narrative.

Russell Leong's *Asian American Sexualities: Dimensions of the Gay and Lesbian Experience* (mixed) is built on a special issue of *Amerasia Journal* on the same topic. Unlike Lim-Hing's work, in which the liberation of lesbian and bisexual voices is the top priority, Leong's volume has a theoretical aim: "to explore linkages between race and same-sex sexuality" from an "interdisciplinary Asian American perspective" by bringing together "academics and artists who are mainly lesbian and gay, but also bisexual and heterosexual" (2). There is a separate literature section containing short stories and poems.

Recent anthologies, such as Song Cho's *Rice: Explorations into Gay Asian Culture and Politics* (multigenre) and Joel B. Tan's *Queer PAPI Porn: Gay Asian Erotica* (multigenre) have an explicit focus on libidinal expression and sexual transgressiveness.

Navigating Anthologies by "Specialization"

Finally, I deal with panethnic anthologies that are specialized in certain ways: for example, by ethnic subgroup membership, by traditional literary genre, or by the anthologies' projected usefulness for specific pedagogical situations. These groupings, intended for the benefit of teachers seeking to organize curricular material in particular ways, have relatively little bearing on the concepts of Asian American identity and community as set forth above.

Anthologies Organized by Specific Ethnic Subgroups

The following works are examples of ethnic specialization.

Cambodian American: Usha Welaratna, *Beyond the Killing Fields: Voices of Nine Cambodian Survivors in America* (oral histories). (Though not presented as anthologies, Joan D. Criddle and Teeda Butt Mam's *To Destroy You Is No Loss: The Odyssey of a Cambodian Family* and Joan D. Criddle's *Bamboo and Butterflies: From Refugee to Citizen* are also collections of oral histories.)

Chinese American: Eric Chock and Darrell H. Y. Lum, *Paké: Writings by Chinese in Hawai'i* (multigenre); Ling-Chi Wang and Henry Yiheng Zhao, *Chinese American Poetry: An Anthology* (poetry); Bennett Lee and Jim Wong-Chu, *Many-Mouthed Birds: Contemporary Writing by Chinese Canadians* (multigenre); The Women's Book Committee, Chinese Canadian National Council, *Jin Guo: Voices of Chinese Canadian Women* (oral histories).

Filipino American: Nick Carbo, *Returning a Borrowed Tongue: An Anthology of Filipino and Filipino American Poetry* (poetry); Luis Francia and Eric Gamalinda, *Flippin': Filipinos on America* (multigenre); Luis Francia, *Brown River, White Ocean: An Anthology of Twentieth-Century Philippine Literature in English* (multigenre; relevant in view of the porousness of the Philippine–Filipino American division); Yen Le Espiritu, *Filipino American Lives* (oral histories); Cecilia Brainard, *Contemporary Fiction by Filipinos in America* (fiction).

Hmong American: Sucheng Chan, *Hmong Means Free: Life in Laos and America* (oral histories).

Japanese American: Gerry Shikatani and David Aylward, *Paper Doors: An Anthology of Japanese-Canadian Poetry* (poetry); *Yoshi: An Anthology of the Japantown Arts and Media Workshop* (multigenre); *The Hawk's Well: A Collection of Japanese American Art and Literature* (multigenre).

Korean American: Maria Hong and David Kim, *Voices Stirring: An Anthology of Korean American Writing* (multigenre); Elaine Kim and Eui-Young Yu, *East to America: Korean American Life Stories* (oral histories).

Native Hawai'ian: Nathaniel B. Emerson, *Unwritten Literature of Hawai'i: The Sacred Songs of the Hula* (poetry); Samuel H. Elbert and Noelani Mahoe, *Nā Mele o Hawai'i Nei: A Hundred and One Hawai'ian Songs* (poetry); Mary Kawena Pukui and Alfons L. Korn, *The Echo of Our Song: Chants and Poems of Hawai'ians* (poetry); Mary Kawena Pukui, *Nā Mele Welo: Songs of Our Heritage* (poetry); Joseph P. Balaz, *Ho'omanoa: An Anthology of Contemporary Hawai'ian Literature* (multigenre); D. Mahealani Dudoit, *'Ōiwi: A Native Hawai'ian Journal* (multigenre).

South Asian American: Ketu Katrak and R. Radhakrishnan, *Desh-Videsh: South Asian Expatriate Writing and Art* (multigenre); Rakesh Ratti, *A Lotus of Another Color: An Unfolding of the South Asian Gay and Lesbian Experience* (mixed); Women of South Asian Descent Collective, *Our Feet Walk the Sky: Women of the South Asian Diaspora* (mixed); Sunaina Maira and Rajini Srikanth, *Contours of the Heart: South Asians Map North America* (mixed); Roshni Rustomji-Kerns, *Living in America: Poetry and Fiction by South Asian American Writers* (multigenre).

Southeast Asian American: Katsuyo Howard, *Passages: An Anthology of the Southeast Asian Refugee Experience* (multigenre).

Vietnamese American: James Freeman, *Hearts of Sorrow: Vietnamese-American Lives* (oral histories); De Tran, Andrew Lam, and Hai Dai Nguyen, *Once upon a Dream: The Vietnamese American Experience* (multigenre); *Viet Nam Forum* (multigenre; see also Viet Thanh Nguyen's essay on Le Ly Hayslip, this volume); Barbara Tran, Monique Truong, and Luu Truong Khoi, *Watermark: Vietnamese American Poetry and Prose* (multigenre).

Anthologies Organized by Specific Literary Genres

Prose narrative (short stories and excerpts from book-length publications) is the mainstay of most panethnic Asian American literary anthologies. Most editors do not make a rigid distinction between fiction and autobiography. Sylvia Watanabe and Carol Bruchac's *Home to Stay* and Jessica Hagedorn's *Charlie Chan Is Dead* feature fiction exclusively, as indicated in their subtitles. Maria Hong's *Growing Up Asian American: An Anthology*, because of its focus on coming-of-age narratives, contains a large number of autobiographical pieces, but it includes essays and fiction as well. Claire Chow's *Leaving Deep Water: The Lives of Asian American Women at the Crossroads of Two Cultures* is a collection of personal stories from a diverse group of women. Personal essays make up Garrett Hongo's *Under Western Eyes*. Watanable and Bruchac's *Into the Fire: Asian American Prose* is, as far as I know, the only panethnic Asian American anthology that uses *prose* in its title, although the editors' introductions do not discuss how this term is defined. The volume contains both fiction and nonfiction (personal essays, interviews or "conversations").

Anthologies devoted exclusively to poetry include Joseph Bruchac's *Breaking Silence: An Anthology of Contemporary Asian American Poets*, the first of its kind; Hongo's *The Open Boat*; Walter Lew's *Premonitions*; Juliana Chang's *Quiet Fire: A Historical*

Anthology of Asian American Poetry, 1892–1970, which is, as far as I know, the first to concentrate on the pre–cultural nationalist period; Cyril Dabydeen's *Another Way to Dance: Contemporary Asian Poetry from Canada and the United States*; and Eileen Tabios's *Black Lightning: Poetry in Progress*, which features discussions with the poets and includes drafts leading to the final version of a poem.

Native Hawai'ian poetry (*mele*) has been and continues to be passed on and developed in oral tradition and performance. Published anthologies of this literature began to appear in Hawai'i in the nineteenth century. Hawai'ian anthologies of poetry, with English translations, include Nathaniel Emerson's *Unwritten Literature of Hawai'i*, Samuel Elbert and Noelani Mahoe's *Nā Mele o Hawai'i Nei*, Mary Kawena Pukui and Alfons Korn's *The Echo of Our Song*, and Pukui's *Nā Mele Welo*. For a Web site with lyrics and translations see the *Huapala: Hawai'ian Music and Hula Archives*, compiled by Kaiulani Kanoa Martin (www.huapala.org).

Anthologies devoted to drama include Misha Berson's *Between Worlds: Contemporary Asian American Plays*, the first of its kind; Houston's *The Politics of Life* and Uno's *Unbroken Thread*, referred to above; and Brian Nelson's *Asian American Drama: Nine Plays from the Multiethnic Landscape*.

Other Anthologies

Though virtually all the anthologies are suitable for course adoption, the following might be of special interest to teachers in the multicultural classroom because of the works' design or additional background information provided:

Laurence Yep's *American Dragon: Twenty-Five Asian American Voices* (multigenre) is designed for young adult readers (age twelve and up); its short selections revolve around questions of identity faced by Asian American teenagers. It has a very short, one-page bibliography.

Maria Hong's *Growing Up Asian American: An Anthology* (multigenre), by virtue of its theme, is particularly suitable for both high school and beginning college students. It is organized loosely by the protagonists' age. It has a six-page bibliography of "prose writings about growing up and some stories about young adulthood by Asian American authors not included in this anthology" (406). Books intended for young people are so indicated.

Shawn Wong's *Asian American Literature: A Brief Introduction and Anthology* (multigenre), part of the HarperCollins Literary Mosaic Series edited by Ishmael Reed, is created as a textbook for the multicultural classroom at the college level. Wong's preface recounts his personal involvement in Asian American literature, while his introduction provides a brief literary history. The end of the volume features an "Alternate Table of Contents by Theme," a three-and-a-half-page selected bibliography of primary and secondary sources,[11] and an index by author name, title, and first line of poems.

In addition, Chung, Kim, and Lemeshewsky's *Between the Lines* has a five-page, annotated "Pacific-Asian Lesbian Bibliography," compiled by Alison Kim, who briefly discusses the difficulties of the undertaking. Hagedorn's *Charlie Chan Is Dead* contains a five-page section of selected readings that are "based on personal tastes," the editor emphasizes (563). Uno's *Unbroken Thread* has an appendix listing nearly two hundred works by Asian American women playwrights, including production histories. Chang's *Quiet Fire* contains a section entitled "Reminiscences: Asian North American Poetry Scenes" (from around 1970 to the mid-1980s), compiled by Walter K. Lew (106–37), and a twenty-one-page bibliography on Asian American poetry, organized into "single author volumes" and "anthologies."

Notes

1. I say *presented* because the "professionals" usually have closer ties to the publishing industry than the "community members" do. The dynamics involved are too complex to be analyzed in detail here, since they differ from anthology to anthology and from group to group.
2. This volume might prove an exception to the generalizations I make here about "mixed" anthologies; see the discussion later in the essay.
3. For the purposes of this essay, I have not made a distinction between the terms *gay* and *lesbian* (and *bisexual*) and *queer*, which some theorists (e.g., Eng and Hom) find important, since each term comes with a social history and theoretical implications. I use *queer* mainly for its brevity and inclusiveness.
4. Ethnic-specific collections that also deal with emergent identities, such as *Our Feet Walk the Sky* by the Women of South Asian Descent Collective, may also fit into this multidisciplinary, mixed-genre pattern.
5. Marketing demands regarding emergent topics—the convenience of covering varied ground in one volume, especially as a course text—might be a consideration as well when the publisher is commercially viable, but such concerns are unlikely when the anthology is self-published or published by a small press.
6. See Sunn Shelley Wong's essay on poetry in this volume for further analysis of Hongo.
7. Hagedorn's and Lew's anthologies, for example, stress both the political impetus and the aesthetic preoccupation of the project.
8. This contradiction is not addressed by Franklin, who considers Lim and Tsutakawa's self-reflexive rejection of the Asian American category a sign of a "more firmly feminist" (116) politics—a conclusion with which I do not agree.
9. Edna Bonacich cautions against treating class as a kind of cultural identity rather than as a structural issue, which, I suspect, an anthology organized by class status would be apt to do. Whether gender and sexuality are any less "structural" than class is another question to explore.
10. Sexuality, in the libidinal sense, is the focus of Geraldine Kudaka's *On a Bed of Rice*, a collection of erotica by women and men.
11. The use of the confusing identical subheadings for both sections of the bibliography (453) is apparently a typographical error.

Bibliography

Aguilar-San Juan, Karin. *The State of Asian America: Activism and Resistance in the 1990s.* Boston: South End, 1994.

Asian Women United of California, eds. *Making Waves: An Anthology of Writing by and about Asian American Women.* Boston: Beacon, 1989.

Balaz, Joseph P., ed. *Ho'omanoa: An Anthology of Contemporary Hawai'ian Literature.* Honolulu: Ku Pa'a, 1989.

Berson, Misha, ed. *Between Worlds: Contemporary Asian American Plays.* New York: Theatre Communications, 1990.

Bonacich, Edna. "The Site of Class." *Privileging Positions: The Sites of Asian American Studies.* Ed. Gray Y. Okihiro et al. Pullman: Washington State UP, 1995. 67–74.

Brainard, Cecilia Manguerra, ed. *Contemporary Fiction by Filipinos in America.* Pasig City, Philippines: Anvil, 1997.

Bruchac, Joseph, ed. *Breaking Silence: An Anthology of Contemporary Asian American Poets.* Greenfield Center: Greenfield Review, 1983.

Campomanes, Oscar V. "Filipinos in the United States and Their Literature of Exile." Lim and Ling 49–78.

Carbo, Nick, ed. *Returning a Borrowed Tongue: An Anthology of Filipino and Filipino American Poetry.* Minneapolis: Coffee House, 1995.

Chan, Jeffery Paul, et al., eds. *The Big Aiiieeeee! An Anthology of Chinese American and Japanese American Literature.* New York: Meridian, 1991.

Chan, Sucheng, ed. *Hmong Means Free: Life in Laos and America.* Philadelphia: Temple UP, 1994.

Chang, Juliana, ed. *Quiet Fire: A Historical Anthology of Asian American Poetry, 1892–1970.* New York: Asian Amer. Writers' Workshop, 1996.

Cheung, King-Kok, ed. *An Interethnic Companion to Asian American Literature.* New York: Cambridge UP, 1997.

———. "Re-viewing Asian American Literary Studies." Cheung, *Interethnic Companion* 1–36.

Cheung, King-Kok, and Stan Yogi. *Asian American Literature: An Annotated Bibliography.* New York: MLA, 1988.

Chin, Frank. "Come All Ye Asian American Writers of the Real and the Fake." Chan et al. 1–92.

Chin, Frank, et al., eds. *Aiiieeeee! An Anthology of Asian-American Writers.* Washington: Howard UP, 1974.

Chin, Marilyn, David Wong Louie, and Ken Weisner, eds. *Dissident Song: A Contemporary Asian American Anthology.* Spec. issue of *Quarry West* 29–30 (1991): 1–168.

Cho, Song, ed. *Rice: Explorations into Gay Asian Culture and Politics.* Toronto: Queer, 1998.

Chock, Eric, and Darrell H. Y. Lum, eds. *The Best of Bamboo Ridge: The Hawai'i Writers' Quarterly.* Honolulu: Bamboo Ridge, 1986.

———, eds. *Paké: Writings by Chinese in Hawai'i.* Honolulu: Bamboo Ridge, 1989.

Chow, Claire, ed. *Leaving Deep Water: The Lives of Asian American Women at the Crossroads of Two Cultures.* New York: NAL-Dutton, 1998.

Chung, Cristy, Alison Kim, and A. Kaweah Lemeshewsky, eds. *Between the Lines: An*

Anthology by Pacific-Asian Lesbians of Santa Cruz, California. Santa Cruz: Dancing Bird, 1987.

Criddle, Joan D. *Bamboo and Butterflies: From Refugee to Citizen*. Dixon: East/West, 1992.

Criddle, Joan D, and Teeda Butt Mam. *To Destroy You Is No Loss: The Odyssey of a Cambodian Family*. New York: Anchor-Doubleday, 1987.

Dabydeen, Cyril, ed. *Another Way to Dance: Contemporary Asian Poetry from Canada and the United States*. Toronto: TSAR, 1996.

Dudoit, D. Mahealani, ed. *'Ōiwi: A Native Hawai'ian Journal*. Vol. 1. Dec. 1998.

Elbert, Samuel H., and Noelani Mahoe, eds. *Nā Mele o Hawai'i Nei: A Hundred and One Hawai'ian Songs*. Honolulu: U of Hawai'i P, 1970.

Emerson, Nathaniel B., ed. and trans. *Unwritten Literature of Hawai'i: The Sacred Songs of the Hula*. Washington: Bureau of Amer. Ethnology, 1909. Rutland: Tuttle, 1965.

Eng, David L., and Alice Y. Hom, eds. *Q & A: Queer in Asian America*. Philadelphia: Temple UP, 1998.

Espiritu, Yen Le. *Filipino American Lives*. Philadelphia: Temple UP, 1995.

Francia, Luis H., ed. *Brown River, White Ocean: An Anthology of Twentieth-Century Philippine Literature in English*. New Brunswick: Rutgers UP, 1993.

Francia, Luis H., and Eric Gamalinda, eds. *Flippin': Filipinos on America*. New York: Asian Amer. Writers' Workshop, 1996.

Franklin, Cynthia. "The Making and Unmaking of Asian American Identity: *Making Waves* and *The Forbidden Stitch*." *Hitting Critical Mass: A Journal of Asian American Cultural Criticism* 3.1 (1995): 93–129.

Freeman, James M. *Hearts of Sorrow: Vietnamese-American Lives*. Stanford: Stanford UP, 1989.

Fujikane, Candace Lei. "Archipelagos of Resistance: Narrating Nation in Asian American, Native Hawai'ian, and Hawai'i's Local Literatures." Diss. U of California, Berkeley, 1996.

Gee, Emma, et al., eds. *Counterpoint: Perspectives on Asian America*. Los Angeles: Asian Amer. Studies Center, 1976.

Gonzalez, N. V. M., and Oscar V. Campomanes. "Filipino American Literature." Cheung, *Interethnic Companion* 62–124.

Hagedorn, Jessica. *Charlie Chan Is Dead: An Anthology of Contemporary Asian American Fiction*. New York: Penguin, 1993.

The Hawk's Well: A Collection of Japanese American Art and Literature. San Jose: Asian Amer. Art Projects, 1986.

Hong, Maria, ed. *Growing Up Asian American: An Anthology*. New York: Morrow, 1993.

Hong, Maria, and David D. Kim, eds. *Voices Stirring: An Anthology of Korean American Writing*. Spec. issue of *Asian Pacific American Journal* 1.2 (1992): 1–53.

Hongo, Garrett, ed. *The Open Boat: Poems from Asian America*. New York: Anchor-Doubleday, 1993.

———, ed. *Under Western Eyes: Personal Essays from Asian America*. New York: Anchor-Doubleday, 1995.

Houston, Velina Hasu, ed. *The Politics of Life: Four Plays by Asian American Women*. Philadelphia: Temple UP, 1993.

Houston, Velina Hasu, and Teresa K. Williams, eds. *No Passing Zone: The Artistic and Discursive Voices of Asian-Descent Multiracials*. Spec. issue of *Amerasia Journal* 23.1 (1997): 1–203.

Howard, Katsuyo K., comp. *Passages: An Anthology of the Southeast Asian Refugee Experience*. Fresno: California State U Southeast Asian Student Services, 1990.

Hsu, Kai-yu, and Helen Palubinskas, eds. *Asian-American Authors*. Boston: Houghton, 1972.

Katrak, Ketu H., and R. Radhakrishnan, eds. *Desh-Videsh: South Asian Expatriate Writing and Art*. Spec. issue of *Massachusetts Review* 29.4 (1998–99): 577–772.

Kim, Elaine H., Lilia V. Villanueva, and Asian Women United of California, eds. *Making More Waves: New Writing by Asian American Women*. Boston: Beacon, 1997.

Kim, Elaine H., and Eui-Young Yu. *East to America: Korean American Life Stories*. New York: New, 1996.

Kingston, Maxine Hong. *The Woman Warrior: Memoirs of a Girlhood among Ghosts*. New York: Knopf, 1976.

Kudaka, Geraldine, ed. *On a Bed of Rice: An Asian American Erotic Feast*. New York: Anchor-Doubleday, 1995.

Lee, Bennett, and Jim Wong-Chu, eds. *Many-Mouthed Birds: Contemporary Writing by Chinese Canadians*. Vancouver: Douglas, 1991.

Lee, James M., et al. *Burning Cane*. Spec. issue of *Amerasia Journal* 17.2 (1991): 1–132.

Leong, Russell, ed. *Dimensions of Desire: Other Asian and Pacific American Sexualities: Gay, Lesbian, and Bisexual Identities and Orientations*. Spec. issue of *Amerasia Journal* 20.1 (1994): 1–284.

———, ed. *Asian American Sexualities: Dimensions of the Gay and Lesbian Experience*. New York: Routledge, 1996.

Lew, Walter K. *Premonitions: The Kaya Anthology of New Asian North American Poetry*. New York: Kaya, 1995.

Lim, Shirley Geok-lin. "Always Already in Intersection: Feminist and Ethnic Literary Theories in the Quarrel of Asian American Writing." Fourth Annual *MELUS* Conf. U of Illinois, Chicago. 20 Apr. 1990.

Lim, Shirley Geok-lin, and Amy Ling, eds. *Reading the Literatures of Asian America*. Philadelphia: Temple UP, 1992.

Lim, Shirley Geok-lin, and Mayumi Tsutakawa, eds. *The Forbidden Stitch: An Asian American Women's Anthology*. Corvallis: Calyx, 1989.

Lim-Hing, Sharon, ed. *The Very Inside: An Anthology of Writing by Asian and Pacific Islander Lesbian and Bisexual Women*. Toronto: Sister Vision, 1994.

Maira, Sunaina, and Rajini Srikanth, eds. *Contours of the Heart: South Asians Map North America*. New York: Asian Amer. Writers' Workshop, 1996.

Mirikitani, Janice, et al., eds. *Time to Greez! Incantations from the Third World*. San Francisco: Glide–Third World, 1975.

Nelson, Brian, ed. *Asian American Drama: Nine Plays from the Multiethnic Landscape*. New York: Applause, 1997.

Omi, Michael, and Dana Takagi, eds. *Thinking Theory in Asian American Studies*. Spec. issue of *Amerasia Journal* 21.1-2 (1995): 1–200.

Our Time: An Anthology of Writings by Asian American Students from the University of Massachusetts, Boston, 1992–94. Boston: U of Massachusetts Inst. for Asian Amer. Studies, 1995.

Pak, Young Mi Angela. "*Anthologizing* by Asian American Women: Selves-in-Community and the Politics of Recognition." *The Brown Papers: A Monthly Essay of Reflection and Analysis from the Women's Theological Center* 2.10 (1996): 1–14.

————. "Self and Asian American Women: An Exploration in Feminist Ethics." Diss. Graduate Theological Union, 1999.

Pukui, Mary Kawena. *Nā Mele Welo: Songs of Our Heritage*. Arranged and ed. Patience Namaka Bacon and Nathan Napoka. Bishop Museum Spec. Pub. 88. Honolulu: Bishop Museum, 1995.

Pukui, Mary Kawena, and Alfons L. Korn. *The Echo of Our Song: Chants and Poems of the Hawai'ians*. Honolulu: U of Hawai'i P, 1973.

Ratti, Rakesh, ed. *A Lotus of Another Color: An Unfolding of the South Asian Gay and Lesbian Experience*. Boston: Alyson, 1993.

Realuyo, Bino A., ed. *The NuyorAsian Anthology: Asian American Writing in New York City*. Philadelphia: Temple UP, 1998.

Rustomji-Kerns, Roshni, ed. *Living in America: Poetry and Fiction by South Asian American Writers*. Boulder: Westview, 1995.

Rustomji-Kerns, Roshni, ed., with Rajini Srikanth and Leny Mendoza Strobel. *Encounters: People of Asian Descent in the Americas*. Lanham: Rowman, 1999.

Shan, Te-hsing. "The Invention of Tradition: Literary Anthologies and Chinese American Literature" [in Chinese]. Third Conf. on Chinese Amer. Lit., Inst. of European and Amer. Studies. Academia Sinica, Taipei. 11 Apr. 1997.

Shikatani, Gerry, and David Aylward, eds. *Paper Doors: An Anthology of Japanese-Canadian Poetry*. Toronto: Coach, 1981.

Stillman, Amy Ku'uleialoha. "History Reinterpreted in Song: The Case of the Hawai'ian Counterrevolution." *Hawaiian Journal of History* 23 (1989): 1–30.

————. "Nā Lei o Hawai'i: On Hula Songs, Floral Emblems, Island Princesses, and *Wahi Pana*." *Hawaiian Journal of History* 28 (1994): 87–108.

————. "Queen Kapi'olani's Lei Chants." *Hawaiian Journal of History* 30 (1996): 119–52.

Sumida, Stephen H. *And the View from the Shore: Literary Traditions of Hawai'i*. Seattle: U of Washington P, 1991.

————. "Postcolonialism, Nationalism, and the Emergence of Asian/Pacific American Literatures." Cheung, *Interethnic Companion* 274–88.

Tabios, Eileen, ed. *Black Lightning: Poetry in Progress*. New York: Asian Amer. Writers' Workshop, 1998.

Tachiki, Amy, Eddie Wong, Franklin Odo, and Buck Wong, eds. *Roots: An Asian American Reader*. Los Angeles: U of California Asian Amer. Studies Center, 1971.

Tan, Amy. *The Joy Luck Club*. New York: Putnam, 1989.

Tan, Joel B., ed. *Queer PAPI Porn: Gay Asian Erotica*. San Francisco: Cleis, 1998.

The Telling It Book Collective [Sky Lee, Lee Maracle, Daphne Marlatt, and Betsy Warland]. *Telling It: Women and Language across Cultures: The Transformation of a Conference*. Vancouver: Press Gang, 1990.

Tran, Barbara, Monique T. D. Truong, and Luu Truong Khoi, eds. *Watermark: Vietnamese American Poetry and Prose*. New York: Asian Amer. Writers' Workshop, 1998.

Tran, De, Andrew Lam, and Hai Dai Nguyen, eds. *Once upon a Dream: The Vietnamese American Experience*. Kansas City: Andrews, 1995.

Uno, Roberta, ed. *Unbroken Thread: An Anthology of Plays by Asian American Women*. Amherst: U of Massachusetts P, 1993.

Viet Nam Forum: A Review of Vietnamese Culture and Society 14 (1994): 7–358.

Wand, David Hsin-Fu, ed. *Asian-American Heritage: An Anthology of Prose and Poetry*. New York: Pocket–Washington Square, 1974.

Wang, L. Ling-Chi, and Henry Yiheng Zhao, eds. *Chinese American Poetry: An Anthology*. Santa Barbara: Asian Amer. Voices, 1991.

Watanabe, Sylvia, and Carol Bruchac, eds. *Home to Stay: Asian American Women's Fiction*. Greenfield Center: Greenfield Review, 1990.

———, eds. *Into the Fire: Asian American Prose*. Greenfield Center: Greenfield Review, 1996.

Welaratna, Usha. *Beyond the Killing Fields: Voices of Nine Cambodian Survivors in America*. Stanford: Stanford UP, 1993.

Witness Aloud: Lesbian, Gay, and Bisexual Asian Pacific American Writings. Spec. issue of *Asian Pacific American Journal* 2.1 (1993): 1–140.

Women of South Asian Descent Collective, eds. *Our Feet Walk the Sky: Women of the South Asian Diaspora*. San Francisco: Aunt Lute, 1993.

Women's Book Committee, Chinese Canadian National Council. *Jin Guo: Voices of Chinese Canadian Women*. Toronto: Women's, 1992.

Wong, Shawn, ed. *Asian American Literature: A Brief Introduction and Anthology*. New York: Harper, 1996.

Wong, Shawn, and Frank Chin, eds. Spec. Asian American issue of *Yardbird Reader* 3 (1974): 1–294.

Yep, Laurence, ed. *American Dragons: Twenty-Five Asian American Voices*. New York: Harper, 1993.

Yoisho: An Anthology of the Japantown Arts and Media Workshop. San Francisco: Japantown Arts and Media Workshop, 1983.

Asian American Short Fiction:
An Introduction and Critical Survey

Rachel Lee

This survey of Asian American short fiction focuses on one short story each from several writers and traces the intertextual coherence and divergence of the works. Teachers should note that the works presented here are not necessarily the most typical of each author's oeuvre. The primary emphasis is on the short stories rather than on the biographical personalities behind them.

These works are presented chronologically according to publication date. I would note, however, that the first appearance of many of these works does not necessarily correspond to the time in which they were incorporated into an Asian American canon. Several of these texts were written before the naming of a specifically Asian American political identity (see the sections on Sui Sin Far, Mori, Yamamoto, and Gonzalez). Others were neglected because their settings and topics were perceived to be beyond the scope of Asian American literature, which initially limited itself to analyzing the cultural artifacts of Chinese and Japanese Americans. Only recently have literary critics begun examining works by writers of South Asian and Southeast Asian ancestry (see the sections on Mukherjee, Gonzalez, and Santos). Moreover, the mutations in the term *Asian America* have not always promoted a widening of the field. For instance, many Hawai'ian and "local" writers reject the mainland designation Asian American, choosing to publish their works in journals specifically devoted to island traditions (see the section on Lum for a definition of "local").

As this cursory outline of Asian American literary studies suggests, each of the stories selected can be analyzed not only for its artistry and thematic content but also for its illumination of a series of Asian American political issues that have waxed and waned over the greater part of the twentieth century. To balance these two methods, I present the short stories in three broad movements, loosely corresponding to the chronological phases 1910–68, 1968–90, and 1990 and after. For ease of reference, I provide within these larger groupings self-contained readings of the individual short stories, reserving my comments on intertextual linkages until the end.

Critical Background on Short Fiction Forms

The short story is "a short, literary prose fiction" with affinities to the fable, anecdote, sketch, parable, fairy tale, ghost story, and folktale (Pasco 118).[1] Several characteristics of the short story distinguish it from longer forms. Much more so than the novel, the short story is expected to converge on some singular significance.[2] Whereas book-length fictional forms are rife with subplots and tangential description, conventional wisdom states that every detail in the short story must count.

Most definitions of the short story (such as that distilled above) focus on formal characteristics of the genre (e.g., brevity, tight structure, single effect) and emphasize the finer skills required of short story writers.[3] More recent accounts, however, probe the form's relation to subject matter as well as the short story's link to oral narrative traditions (two important points to underscore when teaching Asian American short fiction). For instance, Mary Louise Pratt argues that the short story—rather than the novel—allows the writer more freedom to experiment with taboo subjects such as sexuality and class (104), to which I would add race and racism. Because short stories take less time to write than book-length works, even those broaching heterodox topics pose fewer financial risks to the writer. Such material considerations partially account for the frequency with which short stories are used to introduce oftentimes stigmatized "submerged population groups" to a wider reading public (Pratt 106). According to Pratt, short story cycles break new ground, establishing a basic literary identity for a region or group, laying out descriptive parameters, character types, social and economic settings, and principal points of conflict for an audience unfamiliar either with the region itself or with seeing that region in print (105).

In this context, one comprehends the groundbreaking work of Asian American short stories that establish literary identities for ghettoized groups such as the Japanese in mobile farming communities and Filipinos working at United States Army camps in Luzon. Significantly, one of the first Asian American fiction writers to portray her subjects sympathetically was Sui Sin Far (Edith Eaton), an essayist and author of short stories (Ling 16).[4]

Another reason why Asian American authors may prefer short fiction lies in the form's historical connection to orality. Oscar Campomanes, for example, notes the decision by a Hawai'ian-based Ilokano literary group to write in forms, such as the drama and the sarita, that were accessible to a working-class community. He defines the sarita as "'talk' or story, not short story [. . .] because the emphasis is on the telling [rather than on] the genre" (Gonzalez and Campomanes 86). While Campomanes underscores the sarita's difference from the short story, I would argue that Asian American short fiction frequently alludes to its oral precursors: the ghost story, talk-story, and folktale. Instead of rejecting short stories wholesale—in effect ceding the genre to one of its variants, the canonized "modern short story"—it would be more valuable to insist on the multivalent, multicultural scope of short fiction. When introducing students to Asian American short stories, teachers may want to underscore the appropriateness of short fiction forms—expressly those rooted in oral traditions—to capture the marginalized sensibilities and hybrid identities of Asian Americans.

Short Stories, 1912–68: "The Very Best English"

In contrast to pieces published during and after the civil rights movement, early-twentieth-century short stories gained recognition by meeting rather than flouting the literary standards of their day. Though their subjects were not typical ones, the works of Sui Sin Far, Toshio Mori, Hisaye Yamamoto, and N. V. M. Gonzalez otherwise conform to the stylistic prescriptions of their times. Describing Mori's and her own use of language, Yamamoto writes, "Toshio, just as I, was trying to use the very best English of which he was capable" (Introduction 2). This statement likewise extends to the collection of short stories, Mrs. Spring Fragrance, in which the author, Sui Sin Far, favored a flowery prose style compliant with the formal diction of her times.

In a similar vein, Gonzalez chooses to write in the "school-learned language" of English rather than in his native Tagalog ("Workshop" 246).[5] His story "The Popcorn Man" expressly contemplates the Filipino's struggle with a mixed linguistic heritage that is due to multiple colonizations. Though dictional conformity proves common to these four writers, they otherwise engage very different issues, time periods, settings, and themes. Each responds to the particular circumstances that he or she knew best, with Sui Sin Far responding to the degrading stereotypes of the Chinese, Mori grappling with the growing enmity between the United States and Japan, Yamamoto focusing on a Japanese woman's artistic aspirations, and Gonzalez unearthing the peculiarities of (neo)colonial occupation.

"The Inferior Woman," by Sui Sin Far

Originally published in Hampton's (May 1910), "The Inferior Woman"—like its companion piece, "Mrs. Spring Fragrance"—uses a conventional tale of romantic tension and fulfillment to launch a complex critique of both Americans' racial antipathy toward the Chinese and middle-class women's bias against working-class women. The frame story of the short work focuses on a recent though Americanized Chinese immigrant, Mrs. Spring Fragrance, who decides to write a book about Americans: "the American woman writes books about the Chinese. Why not a Chinese woman write books about the Americans?" (41). Clearly, the author draws from the "Chinese as alien observer" subgenre—an account of the West told from the "upside-down" perspective of the Chinese.[6] Unlike other authors adept at this type of narrative, Sui Sin Far uses this reversal of perspectives not merely to entertain but to craft a political message as well.

Highlighting the question of authorship and the correlative notion of authority, the short story frames the vast business of writing and lecturing as based on book-learned opinions rather than first-hand experience. Initially, Mrs. Spring Fragrance concedes her lack of authority to write a book about Americans because "she lacks the divine right of learning." She declares, "Ah, these Americans! these mysterious, inscrutable, incomprehensible Americans! Had I the divine right of learning I would put them into an immortal book!" (30). The author slyly mocks those who have put "the Chinese" into books yet have not circulated among them. The "inscrutable" and "mysterious" caricature of the Chinese—or of any other group—derives in part from an insular book learning that cannot substitute for actually having lived among a people.

Mrs. Spring Fragrance contrasts the scholarly expositors of life with those who actually live it: "if the [Chinese scholars] had come to learn things in America, they, the merchants, had accomplished things. [. . .] As a boy [her husband] had come to the shores of America, worked his way up, and by dint of painstaking study after working hours acquired the Western language and Western business ideas" (31). In other words, Mrs. Spring Fragrance, having attended the "academy of life"—which includes her and her husband's close interaction with their American neighbors—has more authority to write about Americans than do the Chinese scholars who "have not time to read American poetry and American newspapers" because their heads are buried in classical texts (33).

This moral on book learning also proves important to the interior story: Mrs. Spring Fragrance's neighbor, Will Carman, loves a working-class girl, Alice Winthrop (the "inferior woman" of the title). Will's mother favors Miss Ethel Evebrook, a well-schooled and wealthy suffragette. The romantic plot serves as a platform to launch a political message regarding class, gender, and racial prejudices. Miss Evebrook writes an unoriginal tract on "the Opposite sex" culled from "one hundred books on the subject and [. . .] fifty lectures" (37). By contrast, her friend Alice Winthrop has worked as a secretary in an all-male law firm since the age of fourteen. She has a positive view of the opposite sex.[7] Through this comparison, Sui Sin Far critiques the lack of originality by scholarly authorities on subjects such as the "opposite sex" or "Chinese inscrutability" who make biased judgments born from a lack of direct association.

Will Carman's mother, who has never met the girl of whom she disapproves, similarly jumps to biased conclusions because of her lack of association with working-class women. By contrast, Mrs. Carman has no prejudices about the Chinese because she lived for a period in China. The story suggests that since prejudice is born of ignorance, it can be overcome through direct association with the groups or individuals who have been misjudged. Consequently, once Mrs. Carman realizes that she has acted out of prejudicial bias, she knocks on Alice Winthrop's door and invites her home.

It is important to frame this political message within the historical context in which it was written. Though politically conservative by today's standards, the notion that antipathy based on race, class, and gender could be overcome through desegregation appears a direct challenge to the ghettoization of the Chinese as well as to the domestic seclusion of middle-class women, both of which were standard practices in the early part of the twentieth century. As detailed in her autobiographical essay, "Leaves from the Mental Portfolio of an Eurasian," Sui Sin Far occupied a unique position as a Eurasian and as a working-class woman who could pass between these divided communities.[8] In her associations with whites (in which she was often assumed to be white rather than mixed-race), the author in effect carried out the further congress of white and Chinese by strategically announcing her Chinese nationality. By the same token, she was able to travel among the Chinese by virtue of her Chinese half.

As Mrs. Carman's feminist transformation at the conclusion of "The Inferior Woman" becomes a model for the reader's emulation, so does Sui Sin Far's tale of her own racial formation (presented in "Leaves") strive to reform her audience's biases. Sui Sin Far overcomes her initial revulsion at the sight of working-class Chinese through greater concourse with them. She converts from prejudice (and overidentification with her white half) to recognition of commonality, manifested in proclamations that she is "a Chinese" ("Leaves" 129). Her fiction and memoir thus operated on the premise that ideal turn-of-the-century readers of "The Inferior Woman" and "Leaves" would grow sympathetic with working-class women and with the Chinese through their vicarious association with them across these pages. Both the short works recount as well as invest in the salutary power of interclass and interracial association.

"The Brothers," by Toshio Mori

Introducing Toshio Mori's short stories, Hisaye Yamamoto emphasizes the author's accomplishment in having his first collection of short fiction slated for publication in 1942: "This was quite an achievement, because publishers are notoriously leery of short story collections" (8). Unfortunately, enmity between the United States and Japan during World War II delayed the publication of *Yokohama, California* for nearly eight years. It is this very conflict between Japan and the United States, as well as the effects of the rivalry on Japanese Americans, that becomes the subject of Mori's "The Brothers," first published in 1938. Appearing three years before the United States entered World War II, this allegorical tale forecasts an escalation in territorial skirmishes, be they between "brothers" or between nations. Interestingly, the topicality of "The Brothers," which prompted its initial recognition, now occasions its neglect. Unlike Mori's other short pieces, which limn the inner workings of Japanese American protagonists, this tale comments on a highly charged political situation. Moreover, "The Brothers" is overtly linked to a specific historical event, whereas the majority of Mori's short fiction tends toward timeless themes.[9]

Because of its historical specificity, "The Brothers" also opens a window onto an era not often examined from a Japanese American perspective: the 1930s, a period before the attack on Pearl Harbor, the internment of Japanese Americans, and the bombing of Hiroshima. According to Yamamoto, "The awareness of one's Japanese connections was omnipresent then as now [. . .] particularly in that time of tension in the thirties when Japan began to occupy Manchuria under the eyes of a disapproving world, and Japanese in the United States began to feel some of the backlash on top of the already existing prejudice" (Introduction 6).[10]

Mori's story unfolds against this historical backdrop. Peculiarly positioned as an American citizen with a Japanese heritage, Mori chose to craft a broad message about human folly rather than point an accusing finger solely at the Japanese. The story appears deceptively simple: a father tells a disinterested bystander about his two sons, George and Tsuneo, who are fighting over a desk that the father has handed down to the elder son. The story proceeds from the perspective of the disinterested bystander; thus the narrator—a curious yet dispassionate observer—acts as a model audience for the reader to emulate.

The tale begins with a denial of allegorical intent: "This is really about George and Tsuneo, two tiny Japanese boys who are brothers" (155), the effect of which is to disarm readers of their nationalist prejudices. The narrator details the several events leading up to the boys' current impasse. A year ago, the father gave an old desk to George. Once Tsuneo reached the age of three, he began to covet the desk. The father attempts to remedy the situation by having George "relinquish the lower drawer to Tsuneo so that the younger one, too, would have a part of the desk. Territory, he called it" (157). Making the connection between this small struggle occurring in the father's home and events in the larger world, Mori continues:

> At that time the Manchurian affair hogged the headlines and everywhere he went there was the talk of war and war clouds. So when we discussed the problem of George and Tsuneo and their struggle it was a timely one. The father had been aware of its relation long before this; that was why he spoke of his two tiny sons and shook his head and smiled. "What barbarians," he would say.
> "You have a bigger war right in your home than anywhere else," I said.
> (157)

The narrative leaves unclear whether the term "barbarians" alludes to the two boys or to the world powers fighting over territorial dominion. Drawer by drawer, Tsuneo takes over the desk, and soon all possessions come up for grabs: "George had three toy trains while Tsuneo had one. George had four color books and five boxes of crayons, and three brand new pencils. Tsuneo had one color book and two boxes of crayons, one new pencil and an old short piece" (159). The catalog of childhood playthings suggests the pettiness undergirding the rival claims. Both children are privileged in having trains, coloring books, and the promise of new tricycles, yet jealousy still besets them precisely because they look on these things as their sole possessions.

"The Brothers" ends with a tenuous détente. The father punishes his children, putting an end, temporarily, to their war. As the father watches his two boys quietly eating breakfast, however, "he knew that behind silence, behind little heads, their little eyes are for coveted things and their hands are to paw and smash, and the brewing trouble which is the worry and sadness of the earth is once again stirring" (161). Through the story, Mori attempts to make sense of the senselessness of war. He ends—perhaps as he only can—with a warning coupled with bewilderment.

The historical specificity of the "The Brothers," rather than limiting its appeal, renders it an excellent pedagogical tool. The story begs discussion on the relative merits of transcendent themes versus historical portraits. How does Mori negotiate between writing a polemic circumscribed by events particular to his time and crafting a message still relevant in other times? How does the allegorical structure make these two messages (one current for his time, the other transcending time) possible in a single narration? What difference does the Japanese American authorship of this story make in terms of its structure, its restrained language, and its use of microcosm? Students can fruitfully explore such questions by examining a narrative whose very articulation remains historically significant. Through "The Brothers," Mori suggests one example of how Japanese Americans came to terms with the growing enmity between their "mother country and their adopted land" (Mori, "Tomorrow" 20).

"Seventeen Syllables," by Hisaye Yamamoto

In 1974, the editors of *Aiiieeeee!* characterized Yamamoto's work generally as "technically and stylistically [. . .] among the most highly developed in Asian American writing" (Chin et al. 266). More recently, this short story has inspired a collection of critical articles attentive to Yamamoto's economy of style, manipulation of language, interweaving of plots, illuminations of character, and ironic and playful tones (see Yamamoto, *Seventeen Syllables* [ed. Cheung]). According to the author herself, "Seventeen Syllables," originally published in *Partisan Review* in 1949, is her most reprinted story (Cheung, Introduction 3).

Much of Yamamoto's short fiction portrays prewar rural Japanese American life. The Alien Land Law prevented Japanese immigrants from owning property in California. Thus, Japanese Americans were forced to migrate from site to site, tilling one plot of land and then moving on to the next. Anti-Asian sentiment also led Japanese Americans to settle in protective, racially homogeneous communities. In this regard, Yamamoto's description of fellow Nisei writer Toshio Mori's short fiction likewise pertains to her own work:

> In Toshio Mori's stories, it is the white who is marginal, only incidentally mentioned if he impinges on our daily lives, but in some of these pieces, we are made aware that he has been out there all the time, writing the rules of the game. Anti-Japanese discrimination in California is a fact of life which Toshio has accepted and taken in stride long since.   (Introduction 10)

In "Seventeen Syllables," Yamamoto similarly does not deal directly with "the white." Rather, she focuses on an adolescent narrator, Rosie Hayashi, who awakens to both the delicious possibilities and the perilous repercussions of sexuality. Rosie remains caught up in her own concerns, primarily her budding romance with Jesus Carrasco, a Mexican farmhand who works on the Hayashi farm. Rosie does not understand her mother's interest in writing haiku or her father's pent-up anger over her mother's literary aspirations. The narrative culminates in two earth-shattering events:

Rosie's father smashes a stylized Hiroshige print that Mrs. Hayashi has won in a poetry contest. His action precipitates the second climactic event: the revelation that Mrs. Hayashi married Rosie's father as an "alternative to suicide" (18). Rosie learns that her mother had an illegitimate, stillborn son while living in Japan. Her parents live in a partnership of convenience "devoid of romance or beauty" (Kim, *Asian American Literature* 115).

Thematically, "Seventeen Syllables" overtly explores the gap between Issei parents and their Nisei children—a generational difference compounded by cultural and linguistic estrangement. In the opening scene, Mrs. Hayashi tries to share with Rosie her newly penned haiku. Rosie, frightened that her poor Japanese language skills might be exposed, agrees that her mother's poem is very nice despite her inability to comprehend it. By contrast, she enjoys a haiku written in English—a spliced production of Japanese and American sensibilities. More subtly, the story illuminates the connections between mother and daughter: both hold secret loves, and Mrs. Hayashi rightly worries that Rosie will have a fate similar to her own. It is the contiguities between their situations as sexual subjects that Rosie tries to avoid seeing. Other themes explored in the tale include gender disparity—specifically, women negotiating between sexual and artistic freedoms and familial, patriarchal constraints—and silence as a communicative mode.

Yamamoto uses a limited point of view to temper a moralistic tone; in this sense, "Seventeen Syllables" remains in keeping with the modern short story's preferred distance from older short fictional forms such as the parable with its explicit moral. She disarms her reader with comic moments born from the juxtaposition of the narrator's naïveté and the depth of serious events around her (e.g., the discovery of her mother's "disgrace"). Moreover, the eponymous focus of "Seventeen Syllables" on a highly crafted poetic form rehearses Yamamoto's own stylistic feat. Through Yamamoto's craft, style becomes theme:

> The haikus that Rosie's mother writes become metaphors of both freedom and constraint. Writing allows Mrs. Hayashi to transcend her mundane and harsh existence and ponder higher ideas. The haiku form, in which "she must pack all her meaning into seventeen syllables," also becomes a metaphor for the constraints that force Mrs. Hayashi to find meaning in small ways.
>
> (Yogi 148)

Teachers might consider pairing a discussion of the short story with a screening of its film adaptation, Emiko Omori's *Hot Summer Winds*, originally broadcast in May 1991 on PBS's American Playhouse. The film consolidates two of Yamamoto's stories, "Seventeen Syllables" and "Yoneko's Earthquake" (the latter was selected for the collection *Best American Short Stories* in 1952). Robert Payne's critique of the film adaptation also provides an excellent starting point for class discussion on how genre and form (the cinematic medium versus the written short story) affect the political possibilities of the same story (see Payne).

"The Popcorn Man," by N. V. M. Gonzalez

Despite Gonzalez's canonical stature in the Philippines, his work has not been widely recognized in the United States.[11] Early accounts of Asian American literature do not include Gonzalez's fiction, perhaps because his chosen settings and topics were perceived to be outside the purview of the field. Only recently has the author's work garnered critical attention from Asian Americanists.[12] In 1993, the University of Washington Press issued a retrospective collection of several of Gonzalez's short stories, *"The Bread of Salt" and Other Short Stories*, making his corpus broadly available to a United States readership.

According to Mina Roces, Filipino literature in the prewar period was "more troubled by the question 'Is my English good enough?' than the problem of whether their writing was 'Filipino enough.'" This anxiety was a reflection of the prewar drive to show the Americans that the Filipinos had become westernized and ready for independence along western democratic lines. [. . .] After the war [and after independence in 1946] the second generation of Filipino writers in English had already mastered the language" and were now concerned with the opposition question: had Filipinos "become too westernized to the point of losing [themselves]?" (Roces 286, 279). In his postwar short story "The Popcorn Man," Gonzalez renders English the very battleground of nationalist struggle, reconfiguring the prewar concern with mastery of English as a postwar emergent consciousness of how English has mastered Filipinos. In its deft portrayal of a Filipino professor who teaches English at an American Air Force base in the Philippines, "The Popcorn Man" draws a parallel between the lingering effects of linguistic colonization and the continued American military occupation of the islands despite formal independence.

Crucial to contextualizing the short story is the background of its setting on the Sierra Madre Air Force Base outside San Miguel.[13] At the conclusion of the Spanish-American War (1898), the Philippine Islands were forcibly ceded to the United States, thus initiating over four decades of American colonization.[14] Though the Republic of the Philippines achieved formal independence in 1946, it remained a neocolony dominated by United States military and economic policies until the late 1980s. The Military Bases Agreement of 1947 permitted the United States "to retain control over twenty-three (large and small) land, sea, and airbases for [. . .] ninety-nine years" (Anderson 14).[15] Subic Naval Base and Clark Airforce Base—the largest installations—were to house "an array of nuclear-capable aircraft and vessels, as well as key military communications equipment" (Schirmer and Shalom 268).[16] By 1983, the removal of the bases had become a rallying point for Filipino groups protesting Ferdinand Marcos's dictatorship and United States support of his regime.

Though the eponymous protagonist of "The Popcorn Man" is Professor Leynes, Gonzalez begins his tale with the antagonist—the military base itself. The atmosphere of the base is incongruous and discomforting: a sign posted outside the officers' club announces an upcoming conference on guerrilla techniques. In barracks that double as classrooms, a huge map reminds students how far United States dominion extends.

Gonzalez immerses his reader in an atmosphere of sterility, formality, and military regulation.

Within this setting, Gonzalez stages Professor Leynes's struggle with English, his struggle with the colonial value system appended to the language.[17] Though Leynes knows the rules of English grammar backward and forward, he cannot command the respect of his American charges. One of his students, Jane Harris, belittles his lesson on the subjunctive mood, exclaiming, "Oh, well, you know the language better than we do!" (140). When Leynes encounters a former schoolmate who has made a career of denouncing the bases, the professor reassesses his situation. He begins to see himself as a "domestic" of the academic world, "bleaching the grammar of U.S. servicemen into presentable whiteness" (147). The subordinate status of the Filipino professors emerges through slight details: they are not permitted to purchase books, a privilege reserved for officers; though they dine at the officers' club, they eat at a separate hour from the United States servicemen. The popcorn—a culinary freebie at the club—symbolizes the light fare that Leynes accepts in lieu of demanding full recompense.

The story concludes with a group of professors seeking out "a real nice, heavy Filipino meal for a change" instead of eating the bland food at the base. They leave the military compound to return to the "open field [. . .] bamboo against the sky [. . .] a peninsula of rice [. . .] a grove of mango trees. His country, Leynes knew; and not that one back there" (150). Through details in setting and through the motifs of food and language, Gonzalez confirms Leynes's cultural affirmation. Thematically, the narrative emphasizes the convergence of linguistic and cultural displacement, the military occupation of the "postcolonial" Philippines, and the paradox of English literature as a vehicle for social protest as well as linguistic indoctrination.

American students may resist acknowledging the United States' history of imperialism. Teachers might consider handing out both the text of President William McKinley's speech that provided the "rationale" for territorial occupation and the history of subsequent Filipino resistance to the United States invasion (see McKinley; Francisco).[18]

To highlight the many levels on which the theme of language plays itself out, teachers might pose the question of intended audience and voice: Why does Gonzalez begin the narrative in the second person? Another way to approach the text is to have students trace the food and language motifs throughout the story. How do these motifs reflect on the larger themes of cultural alienation and cultural affirmation? Finally, students might want to reflect on the main character, Professor Leynes. Does Leynes achieve a certain self-knowledge by the story's conclusion? If not, how effective is Leynes as a protagonist, or how does the "anti-hero" relate to the historical and political contexts of the work?

1968–90: Ancestral Perspectives and Third World Identity

While the tales of Sui Sin Far, Mori, Yamamoto, and Gonzalez accomplish a "groundbreaking" in Asian American short fiction, the next set of works might be

261

considered the first Asian American short stories to be written after Asian America's emergence. In 1968, *Asian American* gained currency as a term under which various peoples of Asian descent began forming social, political, and cultural coalitions. Before this time, "ethnic disidentification"—or the distancing of one Asian group from another—predominated (Espiritu 34–35). The 1970s and 1980s saw a florescence of Asian American magazines, newspapers, collections, and anthologies designed to promote Asian American literature.[19] Also during this period, the Combined Asian Resources Project undertook archival work to uncover and revive literary texts by Asian Americans that either had gone out of print or had an international readership yet little or no American audience.

Many of the writers who came of age during this period are expressly committed to affirming and promoting the growth of Asian American literature (see the section on Chin). Others have more tenuous ties to this tradition, crafting stories under alternative rubrics such as Hawai'ian and "local" culture or the concept of a Third World identity in the United States (see the sections on Lum and Mukherjee). What is striking about all these selections, however, is their attention to those on the fringes of society. The stories of Darrell Lum, Bienvenido Santos, Frank Chin, and Bharati Mukherjee take the perspectives of outcasts, criminals, sociopaths, and illiterates, predominantly, to highlight the way in which racial and cultural norms of society render these subjects "outlaws." Santos, Lum, and Chin humanize their marginalized protagonists. Mukherjee, however, uses a violent first-person narrator to symbolize the murderous underbelly of American foreign policy that lumps together various dark-skinned people for random persecution.

"Primo Doesn't Take Back Bottles Anymore," by Darrell H. Y. Lum

The defining lines between "local" and "mainland" Asian American literary traditions have been the subject of considerable debate and probably will continue to be transformed under pressure from various writers and critics about what the terms signify and how they are intertwined. According to Stephen Sumida, " 'Local' (meaning here a certain kind of person) is usually thought of as nonwhite, for instance a native Hawai'ian, Asian American, Samoan, or Puerto Rican. [. . .] A *haole*, 'foreigner' in the Hawai'ian tongue and nowadays meaning Caucasian, is not usually assumed to be a local" (*View* xiv).

In 1986, Darrell Lum described local literature as having "a distinct sensitivity to ethnicity, the environment (in particular the land), a sense of personal lineage and family history, and the use of the sound, the languages, and the vocabulary of island people" (Chock and Lum 4).[20] Given this definition, local literature has affinities to texts written by Asian Americans (on the mainland) even as local literature remains distinct from both Asian American literature and Hawai'ian literature, the first being a mainland construction and the second referring to works by native Hawai'ians.[21] Local literature, then, derives from the sensibilities, connections, and codes among "local" peoples even as this cultural ethos "[undergoes] continual change" (Sumida, *View* xvi).

Because of Lum's pioneering role in developing a journal and anthologies specifically devoted to the literatures of Hawai'i,[22] one cannot but read his short fiction in
the context of an emergent and mutating local tradition. The five-page short story,
"Primo Doesn't Take Back Bottles Anymore," combines standard English narration
with pidgin dialogue and stream-of-consciousness sections. In this brief tale, Lum covers a wide range of issues, critiquing mainstream "family values" and the arbitrariness
of proprietary claims, while also leaving his readers with a deep sense of his protagonist,
Rosario (Rosa) Kamahele. During the course of the narrative, Rosa—a scruffy bottle
collector—loses his source of livelihood when the Primo Beer company phases out its
bottles for aluminum cans. Even more tragic, this loss of material support is paralleled
by a further deterioration in Rosa's social connections. Friendships are fleeting for
Rosa: family services separate him from his brother, who is "mahu" (homosexual),
and his affection for Harry—the bottle receiver at Primo—is stifled when the bottle-
recycling program shuts down. The story ends with Rosa's impotent rage at his world
gone awry. He paints "F-O-C-K" on Primo's company sign, but the paint is the same
color as the background. As the paint dries, the word disappears.

Lum's tale presents several perspectives on Rosa: the official criminal record of
Rosa as a petty thief of bottles; Harry's physical description of Rosa as a potbellied
bum; the perception of the lady at the welfare office, who sees Rosa as "a smart-ass
kid who beat up anybody who didn't pay protection money" (186); and Rosa's own
perspective, as both a boy and a man angry at the "haole" world that has failed him.
Through these multiple angles, Rosa comes to life as a local trying to make a living by
scrounging through garbage—an activity criminalized by an uncomprehending world.
Alternatively, one might view Rosa's recycling activities as an expression of an island
conservationist ethos that asserts that neither "resources [nor] disposal of wastes [can
be treated] as if they were unlimited and infinitely possible" (Sumida, *View* 105).

One way to approach the story is to ask students about the function of pidgin in
the narrative. Not only does it alert the reader to the jump into Rosa's perspective
but, more significantly, it also destablizes standard American English. Invisible quota-
tion marks exist around Miss Pate's speech about Rosa's need to develop a "healthy
family relationship and atta-tude" (as opposed to Rosa's own sense of responsibility
to protect his "bruddah" [186]). That Miss Pate separates Rosa from his only affection-
ate family relationship exposes the questionable character of the "healthy [. . .] relationship[s]" espoused by those from the mainland.

White readers must also confront Rosa's rage toward "haoles" who are associated
with arbitrary rules (e.g., the social worker who separates Rosa from his younger
brother) and notions of proprietorship that, for instance, render the garbage from an
apartment building someone's personal property ("Rosa figured that apartment building garbage was surely anybody's" [185]). "Haole" characters are reminders of foreign
(and sometimes militaristic) dominance: a new "haole" student from California is the
son of a marine. Rosa's anger at "all the haoles in the whole world" (187) bespeaks his
frustration at the mainlander's habit of pathologizing local customs and relationships.

One way for instructors to defuse some students' defensiveness about Rosa's rage is to pose the question of why Lum chooses this down-on-his-luck protagonist. What can the narrative reveal through a character like Rosa that it cannot through an "objective" narrative voice, for instance?[23]

Another strategy is to pair Lum's short story with popular images of Hawai'i as a paradise in advertisements, television shows, and fiction (from Melville to Michener). How does Lum's story respond to the idyllic images of Hawai'i represented in such texts?

"Immigration Blues," by Bienvenido Santos

A staple character in Bienvenido Santos's short stories is the Filipino old-timer who came to the United States during the 1920s and 1930s, often as a manual laborer. "Scent of Apples" depicts a moment of fellowship between one such Filipino farmer and a highly educated compatriot. "The Day the Dancers Came" conversely portrays an old-timer's rejected offer of hospitality by members of a Manila dance troupe.[24]

In "Immigration Blues," the author delves into some of the more current dilemmas facing a newer (post-1965) wave of immigrants. As Leonard Casper puts it, " 'Immigration Blues' describes the still precarious situation of aliens and permanent residents today" (Introduction xv). The story unfolds from the perspective of Alipio Palma, a widowed old-timer living in San Francisco. Quite by surprise, he is visited by two women: Mrs. Antonieta Zafra and her sister, Monica. Mrs. Zafra is married to an old acquaintance of Alipio's. During their visit, Mrs. Zafra tells the circumstances of her marriage: the immigration office threatened to deport her. Luckily, she found Carlito Zafra—"an elderly Filipino who was an American citizen" (13)—who agreed to wed her on short notice. Alipio shares a similar story regarding his own (now deceased) wife, Seniang. She, too, proposed marriage as an alternative to deportation. Finally, Mrs. Zafra and Monica admit that their visit was initiated by Monica's similar dilemma:

> Here's my sister, a teacher in the Philippines, never married, worried to death because she's being deported unless something turned up like she could marry a U.S. citizen, like I did, like your late wife Seniang, like many others have done, are doing in this exact moment, who can say? (19)

Not mere happenstance dictates the connection between these younger Filipina immigrants and the old-timers. The story probes not only the exigencies prompting these unions but also the chance blessings afforded by such marriages of convenience. Both Antonieta and Alipio frame their spousal commitments as godsends. Santos scrupulously depicts the affection emerging from these arranged partnerships. Alipio adored Seniang, and she returned his affection and care. Antonieta and Carlito Zafra, though childless, "live well and simply" (13).

Through this short tale, Santos suggests that "immigration blues" stretch across the twentieth century. The story provides teachers with the occasion to review the history of obstacles facing Asian immigrants to the United States, such as the Chinese Exclusion Act (1882), the Gentlemen's Agreement (1907) directed at the Japanese, the 1917 Immigration Act that effectively curtailed Asian Indian immigration to the United States, the Immigration Act of 1924, which barred entry to "aliens ineligible to citizenship," and the Tydings-McDuffie Act (1934), which reduced Filipino immigration to an annual quota of fifty persons.[25]

The story must also be placed within the context of the United States colonization of the Philippines (see the section on Gonzalez). Unlike other Asian immigrants, Filipinos were not considered "aliens" but "nationals" moving within the vast (overseas) territories of the United States. During World War II, thousands of Filipinos fought as part of United States regiments (see Quinsaat; Santos, "Filipinos"), and after the war, "Congress passed a law that extended citizenship to Filipino immigrants and permitted the entry of one hundred Filipino immigrants annually" (Takaki 362). Santos's story suggests that although Americans expressed goodwill to Filipinos immediately after the war, deportation once again looms large for more recent immigrants. Teachers might also want to emphasize Marcos's political dictatorship in the Philippines (supported by the United States government) as a primary cause of Filipino immigration to the United States in the 1970s.

Major themes of Santos's short story include the criminalization of the immigrant, the intersecting oppressions of gender and race for Filipinas, and the resilience of the old-timer generation.

"The Only Real Day," by Frank Chin

Frank Chin has taken many avenues toward reviving the cultural and historical traditions of Asian Americans. Not only is he a member of the Combined Asian Resources Project, which spearheaded the revival of long lost Asian American texts, but he also writes plays and short fiction, both of which are rooted in oral traditions.[26] In his short story "The Only Real Day" Chin once again has his eyes turned toward the past, specifically toward the "immigration blues" of Chinese old-timers.

"The Only Real Day" unfolds in Oakland and San Francisco during the late 1940s. As the title suggests, the lengthy story (running over thirty pages) captures one day in the life of its protagonist, Nelson Yuen Fong (called Yuen). The work might be considered a character sketch, providing its author the opportunity to eulogize an older generation of Chinese men who came to the United States in the late nineteenth and early twentieth centuries, often leaving their families behind. Most of them lived in Chinatowns, never learned English, and relied on Benevolent Associations to help them confront a hostile American society. Unlike Maxine Hong Kingston's China Men, which likewise portrays this generation, Chin's short story does not depict his protagonists' accomplishing grand feats (such as building the transcontinental railroad). Rather, "The Only Real Day" focuses on one old-timer just at the moment when he is being pushed aside by a younger generation.

The third-person narrative proceeds predominantly from Yuen's perspective. The reader learns that Yuen has lost contact with his wife and son in Hong Kong and that he has great affection for his boss's child, a boy named Dirigible. His affection, however, does not extend to his boss, Rose, whom Yuen characterizes as "one of these new-fashioned people giving up the old ways. She speaks nothing but American if she can help it, and has lo fan women working for her at her restaurant" (47). Within the story, Chin exposes the various strata of the Chinese American community: the old-timers like Yuen, the new-fashioned entrepreneurs like Rose, and the American-born generation represented by Dirigible. Rounding off the portrait is Jimmy Chan, a wealthy, soon-to-be naturalized Chinatown boss, who explicitly tells Yuen, "Your day is over" (69).

The narrative dwells on the quotidian details of Yuen's life: on Tuesdays, he commutes to San Francisco and spends the evening smoking and gambling with his old-timer friends; on Wednesdays, he returns to Oakland Chinatown where he works as a dishwasher. The narrative is imbued with a sense of repetition, daily routine, and unchanging surroundings. Two unusual occurrences interrupt the monotony of Yuen's life: one involves a "fangwai" (white) waitress at the restaurant where Yuen works; the other centers on a summons from immigration services. In the first instance, a lounging waitress trips Yuen as he attempts to pass by her in a narrow hallway. They end up limbs tangled, with Yuen pressed close again the waitress's wrinkled and decaying body. Yuen can only silently glare at the woman, unable to communicate his outrage and afraid that no one will believe his version of what happened: "'I guess I can't tell,' he thought. 'She'll say I kicked her'" (55–56). The encounter with the waitress reinforces Yuen's self-perception that "he had no right" (57)—a phrase initially used by his boss, Rose (who tells Yuen to mind his own business where Dirigible is concerned), but that evolves into a mantra encapsulating Yuen's frustration at having no privacy rights, no civil rights, and no right to be considered innocent until proven guilty. The second event only reinforces Yuen's sense of impotence: he cannot read the letter from the immigration department but instead must depend on Rose and her adolescent son to interpret its mandates and lead him through the American legal system. Moreover, the letter requires Yuen to have his fingerprints registered with the police and to testify that he has no criminal record.

Yuen disputes both Rose's and Jimmy Chan's assurances that if he does everything the legal authorities say, everything will be all right. Yuen's own experience has taught him that the United States treats Chinese as criminals, liars, and communist collaborators. Even if Yuen hasn't done anything wrong, he might still be charged with some crime: "Two and two don't make four in America, just because you're Chinese" (63).

Feeling helpless against a society that criminalizes his race, Yuen—like others before him—attempts suicide. Tragically, Rose's and Dirigible's efforts have largely erased the threat of deportation, yet the old man doesn't seem to care. The text suggests that Yuen wishes to kill himself because of the lack of virtue within the changing times. Yuen tells Dirigible about the heroes of Leongsahn Marsh, who "one by one [. . .] are accused of crimes by the government. They say he commit a crime he didn't and they make him run, see? And one by one, all the good guys made outlaw by the bad government come to Leongsahn Marsh and join the good guy, Soong Gong" (66–67). In the Chinese classic, the heroes are chosen because they refuse to lie, betray, steal, or sell out. But in these times, Yuen concludes, it is "too much to expect" (67) anyone to qualify as a hero. In the end, Yuen simply expires while taking a bath.[27]

The most daunting aspects of "The Only Real Day" are its length and pacing. One reviewer of Chin's collection suggests that the "sheer density of prose" might be attributable to these stories' function as preparatory pieces for Chin's "greater works, namely his plays" (Soo Hoo 177). Alternatively, the length of "The Only Real Day" could be interpreted as a deliberate stylistic choice relevant to the story's themes of decay, waste, and staying beyond one's time. The narrative illustrates Yuen's last day on earth not as a swift and decisive suicide but, rather, as a prolonged, Hamlet-like contemplation over one's lack of action. Teachers might pose the question of whether this is an effective stylistic strategy.

"The Only Real Day" also comments on the history of anti-Asian legislation in the United States. The 1892 Geary Act "required all Chinese in the United States to register. Thereafter, any Chinese in the country caught without a registration certificate was subject to immediate deportation" (Chan 91). Questions for analysis might focus on the potential abuses of such registration laws. How do these laws presume criminal behavior on behalf of immigrants? Why would immigrants rather than citizens be more apt to engage in illegal activity? Is registration merely a confirmation of illegal status under the pretenses of "legal" residence? Teachers might also pair "The Only Real Day" with articles and editorials about the more recent debates over undocumented workers.

"Loose Ends," by Bharati Mukherjee

Bharati Mukherjee's short story collection, "The Middleman" and Other Stories, won the National Book Critics Circle Award. Her commercially successful works have inspired both praise and criticism, with some reviewers heralding Mukherjee for broaching nontraditional perspectives and others faulting her for eliding the differences among her various ethnic minority subjects (See Nelson; Knippling). Unlike other short fiction examined in this essay, Mukherjee's stories feature a variety of Third World peoples, not only South Asians from Trinidad, Calcutta, and Uganda but also Afghanistanis, Filipinas, Chinese, and Vietnamese immigrants to the United States. Moreover, several works from "The Middleman" proceed from the perspective of non-Asians, such as the Italian American narrator of "Orbiting" and the white Vietnam veteran in "Fathering."

In "Loose Ends," Mukherjee likewise features a non-Asian as her protagonist. Her first-person narrator, Jeb Marshall, is a Vietnam veteran who now works as a contract killer for a drug smuggler based in Miami. Jeb dislikes immigrants, especially those wearing turbans: "'Who let these guys in?' I say [. . .] they come in with half a dozen kids and pay them nothing. We're coolie labor in our own country" (44). Though Jeb works for an immigrant (a Cuban American), he feels a spurious sense of power over Mr. Valesquez because he's "just another boat person" (47). In contrast to the antiheroes of the works by Lum, Chin, and Gonzalez, Jeb Marshall has few redeeming qualities, and he is defined mostly by his animosity toward minorities.

Through this murderous protagonist, "Loose Ends" details the type of racial hatred that is bred and maintained by the United States Department of State. During the narrative, Jeb repeats aphorisms from Doc Healy, presumably his former commanding officer in the war: "If you want to stay alive [. . .] just keep consuming and moving like a locust" (45) and "torch the whole hut [making] sure you get the kids, the grannies, cringing on the sleeping mat" (47). Jeb personifies the anti-Asian fury abetted in the Korean and Vietnam Wars. It is as if Mukherjee is proposing that the hostile "Nam Vet" is one kind of parameter for Third World identity.

After botching one of his "jobs," Jeb leaves town, finding his way to the Dunes Motel owned by the Patels. He storms their family dinner, surprised that "They look at [him . . .] like [he's] the freak." When the daughter of the motel owner, "one luscious jailbait in blue jeans" (52), escorts Jeb to his room, he attacks and rapes her. Through Jeb's multiple aggressions, "Loose Ends" forges a connection between anti-Asian violences enacted in one site (Vietnam) and the racist violences enacted against Asian minorities in other sites (the Patels live in the southern United States). The story proposes that anti-Asian violence in one place engenders anti-Asian violence in another. By doing so, the narrative creates a relation between Vietnamese and South Asians in the United States: both are sacrificed to the military's blood-hungry lust. Mukherjee's fiction also suggests that racism in America unites not just Asians in the United States but also various dark-skinned peoples across the globe. Jeb complains about the unwhitening of America, asking how is it that while "[he and his] buddies were barricading the front door [. . .] these guys [Cubans and South Asians] were sneaking in around the back?" (48, 53). Jeb becomes the story's device to link the racist dimensions of American foreign policy to the arbitrary violence directed against various dark-skinned immigrants—from Latinos to South Asians.

Students are probably familiar with the 1960s antiwar movement and the magnitude of the Vietnam War in changing the consciousness of Americans. They may be unfamiliar, however, with the way Vietnam crystallized Asian Americans' sense of racial injustice across the globe. According to Yen Le Espiritu, "For many Asian American activists, the American invasion of Vietnam involved more than the issues of national sovereignty or imperialism; it also raised questions of racism directed against Asian people" (42–43). In contrast to popular antiwar slogans like "Bring our boys home," Asian American protesters urged the United States, "Stop killing our Asian brothers and sisters" (Espiritu 43). In other words, many Asian Americans identified not so much with the American troops abroad as with the various people in Southeast Asia whose homes had become battlegrounds for cold war maneuvers.

Teachers might open discussion of "Loose Ends" by asking students to question the effectiveness of the dramatic monologue style of narration. Does this perspective mitigate as it personifies racist hatred? Students might also want to explore the reptilian motifs and gross images of eating associated with Jeb Marshall's murderous streak.

1990 and After: Generation Gaps, Ethnic Fragmentation, Territory

While Lum, Santos, Chin, and Mukherjee strive in various ways to forge as-yet-undefined Asian American, local, and Third World collective identifications, the authors presented in this last section focus more on the intergenerational tension and ethnic fragmentation within Asian America. Sylvia Watanabe explores the fractious opinions within a particular Hawai'ian village over island funeral rites, Gish Jen ponders divergences within Asian American notions of cultural-national affiliation, David Wong Louie focuses on the generation gap between a Chinese-speaking mother and her English-speaking son, and Gary Pak explores the conflicting territorial claims that not only pit mainland and Japanese investors against locals but also foment discord among local denizens.

Variety and internal conflict within Asian American literature is not a new phenomenon. Unlike the short fiction written in other time periods, however, the short fiction of the 1990s has had the benefit (or detriment, some might argue) of an audience desirous of "Asian American" writing yet also holding preconceived notions of what that writing should be. The emphasis in short fiction of the 1990s on internal differences takes on a more self-conscious edge, perhaps deliberately resisting the narrow ways "real" Asian American literature has been defined.[28]

The works in this section also animate discussions on the heterogeneity of Asian American cultures—not just in the traditional sense of ethnic disparity but with respect to regional and gendered differences as well. While Watanabe and Pak focus on the changing landscape of Hawai'i, Jen and Louie write about East Coast settings. In addition, Watanabe and Jen both craft sympathetic and oftentimes subversive portraits of female subjects, which partly accounts for their similar inclusion in *Home to Stay*, an anthology of Asian American women's fiction (Watanabe and Bruchac; selections from Mukherjee and Yamamoto are also included). The convergence of these writers' works around these alternative features of region and gender suggests other paradigms, overlapping with that of Asian America, that connect these short works to those of other ethnic writers.

"Talking to the Dead," by Sylvia Watanabe

In the author's note from *"Talking to the Dead" and Other Stories*, Watanabe describes the impetus behind her writing: "I wanted to record a way of life which I loved and which seemed in danger of dying away—as the value of island real estate rose, tourism prospered, and the prospect of unlimited development loomed in our future [. . .]. I wanted to save my parents' and grandparents' stories" (on the jacket). In her title piece, Watanabe generates concern over these passing generations and their way of life while also crafting a tale about the life choices open to women. The short story traverses the thematic terrain of both women's cultural practices and local literary traditions.

Yuri Shimabukuro, the first-person narrator of "Talking to the Dead," is eighteen years old at the story's outset (the narrative concludes twenty-five years later). Unlike other girls her age, Yuri does not get married, go off to school, or become a seamstress or a hairdresser—occupations deemed appropriate for girls. Instead, Yuri apprentices herself to Aunty Talking to the Dead, the village kahuna woman who prepares the deceased for their spiritual journey.

Yuri's rebellion, though directed against an older generation, registers more importantly as a rebellion against limited gender roles and the pettiness of public opinion. By aligning herself with Aunty Talking to the Dead, Yuri emulates a formidable woman in the village society. Part of Aunty's power derives from her association with a distasteful job: she attends to the deceased and communicates with the spirit world. Her occupation has little to do with good social standing in the community. Aunty Talking to the Dead's perspective stretches across a much larger horizon—one that includes the human and nonhuman worlds.

At the same time that Yuri resists her mother's efforts to marry her off, Aunty's son Clinton also breaks free from parental constraints. Through Clinton's character, Watanabe depicts the changes occurring in the Hawai'ian village due to a younger generation going to war, moving to the city, and returning with Western educations. Clinton enrolls in mortician's school on the GI Bill. When he returns, Clinton usurps his mother's authority over how to minister to the village's dead. Marketing his sanitized, "scientific" approach to the funeral trade, Clinton attends to the funerals of all the prominent villagers. However, the narrative frames Clinton's newfangled notions as a betrayal of Hawai'ian culture. Stressing "lifelike artistic techniques," Clinton concerns himself only with the exterior facade of the body rather than with the spirit that needs taking "home." While Clinton's primary concern is over the disposal of the corpse, Aunty Talking to the Dead understands the "wholeness of things" (317).

Watanabe uses comic effects to heighten the narrative tension and the dramatic staging of generational differences. While Clinton thrives in his new business, Yuri—who has replaced Clinton as Aunty's assistant—cannot get near a corpse without fainting. Yuri's indisposition seems to confirm both Mrs. Shimabukuro and Clinton's opinions that women should stick to marriage and that new and "better" customs from the mainland are displacing the old. The final scene of the short story reverses these "truths." At Aunty's funeral that Clinton has arranged, members of the wake notice that Aunty's eyes are open "because she is looking for someone." At that moment, Yuri realizes, "This was it: My moment had arrived. Aunty Talking to the Dead had come awake to bear me witness" (321). Yuri steals the body to take Aunty "home."

The last paragraphs of the story, relayed in chanting rhythms, perform both a spiritual and a narrative closure. Yuri cremates the body, the flames sending Aunty's spirit outward as "she sings, she sings, she sings" (321). The singing becomes an affirmation of Yuri's power. No longer the feeble assistant, Yuri prepares Aunty for her spiritual journey. Aunty's singing melds with Yuri's own naming and chanting, as the tale confirms that Aunty's powerful legacy has been passed on to Yuri.

On several levels, Watanabe's story relies on oral traditions such as the Hawai'ian oli.[29] Yuri's apprenticeship is constituted by listening to and learning Aunty's "naming chants" and "healing chants." The author herself comments on the story's inspiration in the "naming walks" Watanabe took with her father ("Talking" 310). Students may wish to explore the connections between "Talking to the Dead" and modern-day ghost stories (told around a campfire or at a slumber party) and between both of these and canonized American ghost stories such as Washington Irving's "The Legend of Sleepy Hollow." Why are ghost stories reserved for younger audiences? How might students argue the relevance of ghost stories to the adult, modern world? Other stylistic topics for discussion include the role of humor in the narrative and the reliance on sound and color symbolism. Thematically, students might explore "Talking to the Dead" within the context of women's writing, tracing the theme of female empowerment, and within local literary tradition, exploring the story's celebration of Hawai'ian value systems and cultural practices over and against their mainland counterparts.

"What Means Switch," by Gish Jen

Gish Jen is perhaps best known for her first novel, *Typical American* (1991), which was short-listed for the National Book Critics Circle Award. Her short fiction has also been well received. "The Water-Faucet Vision" was selected for *The Best American Short Stories, 1988* (Helprin and Ravenel), and many of her other short works have been anthologized. "What Means Switch," later expanded into the novel *Mona in the Promised Land*, features a Chinese American family living in the northeastern United States. In this tale, as in much of her fiction, Jen questions both the timelessness of cultural differences and the agency of Asian immigrants in determining their national identities.

"What Means Switch" centers on Mona Chang—the first-person narrator—whose family has recently moved from Yonkers to Scarsdale. Mona is a big talker; like Twain's Huckleberry Finn, she delights in telling tall tales. In typical high school fashion, Mona's concern is being popular with her friends. Her route to social acceptance involves her playing the role of the cunning Chinese: "I tell Barbara Gugelstein I know karate. [. . .] I rush on to tell her I know how to get pregnant with tea" (77). Giving a campy performance of Chinese expertise, Mona emerges the darling of her girlfriends' mothers. Mona becomes valued precisely for her racial difference even as she reveals that difference as a sham. Her actions ultimately destabilize essential, timeless notions of racial identity.

When another Asian student joins her high school, Mona fears she will be discovered. Sherman Matsumoto, however, is recently arrived from Japan and doesn't have either the English skills or the knowledge of Chinese culture to unmask Mona. Assuming that Sherman is, like herself, an American kid exoticized by others, Mona dispels the rumors about him circulating among her friends: "No, he doesn't eat raw fish. No, his father wasn't a kamikaze pilot. No, he can't do karate" (78). Ironically, Mona discovers that Sherman is more Japanese than Japanese American; he is "authentic" in ways that Mona doesn't anticipate (he practices Judo, has a Japanese understanding of gender roles, and feels national as well as cultural loyalty to Japan).

The story highlights Mona's and Sherman's differing perspectives even though both might be considered Asian Americans. Mona insists that anybody can "switch" national or religious identities. Sherman doesn't understand "what means switch." Instead, he illustrates his understanding of being Japanese by drawing a picture of a stick figure facing a Japanese flag. The potential rifts between Chinese and Japanese Americans are underscored through Mona's mother's outrage at seeing Sherman's drawing of the Japanese flag. She tries to tell Mona about the Rape of Nanking, which Mona misspeaks as "The Napkin Massacre."

As romance blooms between Mona and Sherman, each tries to get the other to switch perspectives. Mona thinks it's her duty to teach Sherman how to fit into an American setting; Sherman, soon returning to Japan, tells Mona she will need to study how to become Japanese. Their young love ends just before Sherman leaves for Japan. At an impasse over who will switch, Sherman suddenly flips Mona on her back with a Judo move. He literally turns her perspective upside down.

The short story also features a subplot wherein Mona's parents must decide whether to build a wall around their property. During the narrative, the family refrains from building the wall, suggesting the Changs' disposition of adjustment rather than confrontation or isolation. After having her perspective radically changed by Sherman, Mona comes to recognize the unique situation of her Asian American family: "we are the complete only family that has to worry about this. If I could, I'd switch everything to be different. But since I can't, I might as well sit here [and] nod and listen to the rest" (84). The passage can be read metaphorically: the Changs—unlike the other families in Scarsdale—are faced with the choice of putting up cultural walls or switching their ways. This conclusion also highlights Mona's more measured opinion of "switching." Perhaps it is not as easy as "learning some rules and speeches" but feels more like the painful disorientation of not knowing "where the ground [is], much less how hard it could be" (80, 84).

Embedded in this comic tale about adolescence is an interrogation of cultural, national, and racial identity—their convergences and divergences. The story also brings into relief the interethnic conflicts sometimes underlying pan-Asian identification. Because of its contemporary themes, vernacular narrative voice, and large doses of humor, students usually find "What Means Switch" an easy read. Teachers might want to have students explore what serious themes lie beneath the comic surface. How do the comic effects of the story enhance or detract from its interrogation of racial identity and sexual politics? Is Mona herself laughing in the end? In what ways are the readers' expectations turned upside down during the course of the narrative in the same way that Mona's perspective is flipped around? Teachers might also ask students whether the theme of sexual awakening is a salient motif or a mere premise for the story's contemplation of national and cultural identity. Is this practice—the working up of a manifest story line or premise to reveal a deeper, less localized meaning—typical of short story craft?

"Pangs of Love," by David Wong Louie

The title of David Wong Louie's "Pangs of Love" not only refers to its main character's last name but also evokes the story's major theme: the bittersweetness of affection (romantic, familial, and otherwise). Through a masterful interweaving of motifs, events, and carefully crafted characters, Louie leaves his reader with a sense of the tension between caring and pain, deception and hope. The first-person narrator (referred to by his mother as Ah-vee-ah) begins as a cynic who resents his mother's blissful ignorance of the world's tragedies: "What business do you have laughing, Mrs. Pang? [. . .] I roll my eyes. [. . .] The world's going through its usual contortions: bigger wars, emptier stomachs, more roofless lives; so many unhappy, complicated acres" (76). The narrator portrays his mother's concerns as parochial: she thinks only of putting food on the table; she laughs at the ridiculous shticks of Johnny Carson. He is the "responsible citizen of the planet," while she is a television junkie. For the narrator, his mother's enchantment with professional wrestling symbolizes her naïveté: "it's a big fake but my mother believes" (93).

Ironically, the narrator works for a manufacturer of synthetic fragrances—a company that specializes in fooling people's sense of smell. At an afternoon party, he sardonically quips that the corporation is "developing a spray for the homeless, a time-release formula that'll simulate, in succession, the smell of a living room in a Scarsdale Tudor, a regular coffee (cream and one sugar), a roast-beef dinner, and fresh sheets washed in Tide" (91). The narrator's "sick" joke is matched only by the policies of the mayor's office to put "prints of potted flowers [. . .] in the windows of abandoned buildings up in Harlem" (94). Rather than facing the problem head on, the city takes a cosmetic approach. In parallel fashion, the narrator simply waves his mother off with the words "Forget it" instead of trying to bridge their cultural, generational, and linguistic differences.

Part of the tension between mother and son stems from their inability to communicate. The narrator has a five-year-old's knowledge of Chinese, and his mother does not speak English. The misunderstandings multiply as the narrator cannot explain to his mother that the girlfriend she adored, Amanda Millstein, has left him for another man. The loss of Amanda becomes another grim truth that Mrs. Pang refuses to accept: "somewhere in that mind of hers she carries hope for the impossible. [. . .] Mandy back in our lives again. [. . .] the Communists [. . .] leaving China" (95).

Once the narrator crushes his mother's expectation for Amanda's return, he regrets the effect. She turns lifeless and somber, as she does only when describing the Japanese raids on her village during World War II. It is perhaps her firsthand experience with political upheaval and the violence of invasion that explains Mrs. Pang's holding out against all odds. The narrator begins to understand his mother's various hopes that her son will get married, that justice will prevail, that the American dream will come true. Thus, when his mother asks him why his brother, Bagel, doesn't have a girlfriend, the narrator lies and doesn't tell her that Bagel is gay. The story, on the one hand, suggests the difficulties gays and lesbians face in coming out to their parents and, on the other, recasts Mrs. Pang's deluded beliefs as necessary, hopeful illusions. "Pangs of Love" concludes with the narrator's slipping into the family's dinner a pill that sweetens bitterness.

In addition to the smell and flavor motifs, students might want to explore the multiple references to Japan. This latter motif highlights the ethnic fragmentation often glossed over in the term *Asian American*. In "Pangs of Love," the Japanese are the invaders, raiding China during World War II, taking over Hollywood industries in the 1990s, and moving in on the narrator's romantic terrain.[30] Though the narrative obliquely acknowledges that this "yellow peril" is an illusion, the short story nevertheless appears to abet the anti-Japanese sentiment in America that has had violent results, for instance, in the murder of Vincent Chin.[31] Teachers might ask students to discuss Louie's use of the "Japanese as bad guy" theme in the context of past anti-Asian movements in the United States as well as in relation to Japan's present status as an economic superpower.

Like Jen, Louie comments directly on the Americanness of his story. The narrative begins with the claim that Mrs. Pang is like "most Americans"—as if to say that her story is also an American one and not solely an ethnic or immigrant tale. Students might want to discuss the different insights gleaned when reading "Pangs of Love" for its ethnic themes or its "American" themes. As a follow-up question, teachers might ask, Are these two categories separable?

"The Watcher of Waipuna," by Gary Pak

In 1992, the editors of the literary journal *Bamboo Ridge* published a special double issue devoted to Gary Pak's short stories. This collection, entitled *"The Watcher of Waipuna" and Other Stories*, won the literary Book Award given by the Association for Asian American Studies. Buttressed by the combination of local publication venues and continental sources of critical validation, Pak's collection seems a testament to the productive alliances between local and Asian American constituencies.[32] Within his title piece, "The Watcher of Waipuna," Pak underscores the unhappy history of Hawai'i's invasion by various military and corporate institutions. In this work, somewhere between a short story and a novella in length, Pak uses comic effects and crisp dialogue to depict a village community's struggle for control over land, language, and culture.

The story features a naive protagonist, Gilbert Sanchez, who, despite or perhaps because of his "madness," protects the town of Waipuna from being overrun by a hotel conglomerate. Through crisscrossing narratives, the story comments on the correspondences among different forms of imperialism (e.g., militaristic, economic, territorial) and the effects of such territorial encroachments on island peoples. Two disparate story lines are woven together: the first focuses on Gilbert's sisters' scheming with a pair of haole hotel entrepreneurs to strip Gilbert of his claims to his parents' land. The second involves Gilbert's friendship with the "pupule-talk[ing]" (crazy talking) Nakakura-san, who is constantly on the watch for the invasion of "frogmen" (43). Gilbert's illiteracy and maddening ways collaborate to save him from his sister Lola's legal efforts to dispossess him. In addition, his taking over the responsibilities of the "lolo" (stupid; 39) Nakakura-san occasions his teaming up with his sister Lucy against the hotel developers. Through Lucy, Gilbert comprehends the changing face of the enemy "frogmen"—a symbol for the multiple invaders of Hawai'i.

Thematically, "The Watcher of Waipuna" explores the threat tourism poses to local and native Hawai'ian land rights. The Hawai'ian International Corporation wishes to buy the Sanchezes' "beach-front parcel" so that they can build another resort hotel. Representatives from the corporation tell the Sanchez sisters that their land is valuable property "but only valuable if it's put to the best use" (23, 39–40)—that is, the one that will make the developers the most money. By contrast, Gilbert views the land as a communal and family settlement; even though only his name appears on the deed, he perceives the house as belonging to his sisters as well.

As the short story illustrates, the issue of land rights in Hawai'i remains highly conflicted, often producing tensions among locals as well as between family members.[33] Gilbert's sister Lola wants to sell the land to the developers, while Gilbert—and, later, his sister Lucy—remembers their father's dictum, "No let no haole step on dah land" (64). The resistance to haole settlers remains especially acute given Hawai'ians' history of territorial dispossession. According to Candace Fujikane, "Half of all land in Hawai'i [. . .] was seized during the illegal overthrow of the Hawai'ian monarchy by American businessmen in 1893 and is currently leased by the U.S. military and private corporations" (30). A primary platform of the contemporary sovereignty movement in Hawai'i is to regain possession of these ceded lands.

"The Watcher of Waipuna" also dramatizes the theme of wisdom in madness. The story begins with the statement, "Gilbert Sanchez didn't know it, but he was going crazy" (21). The narrative suggests that craziness is an attribute assigned by others, having more to do with communal norms than with essential psychological dysfunction. Gilbert is deemed "lolo" because he talks to himself or talks nonsensically. Part of his mad ways are linked to his illiteracy: he cannot read the notes that his sisters leave for him and thus seems to act inappropriately (e.g., he thinks his mother's ghost has left him his favorite foods). Both Gilbert's madness and his illiteracy act as unwitting weapons against dispossession. Gilbert's conversations with his several selves distract him during the initial offer by the developers. Because he can't read, he fails to show up at an attorney's office as requested in a letter. Gilbert's illiterate madness acts as a strategic tool of resistance.

Though madness is a common literary theme across cultures, Pak links madness to Hawai'ian specifics by using the native words lōlō and pupule. Making a pun of lōlō, Pak suggests that sanity resides in Gilbert's respectful appreciation of the land and not in Lola's (crazy) collaboration with the developers.[34] In addition, "pupule talk" refers to Nakakura-san's efforts to alert the town of imminent invasion. The scheming of the Hawai'ian International Corporation to take away Gilbert's land reveals this "pupule talk" as not all that crazy.

The connection between past and current invasions of Hawai'i occurs through the central symbol of the "frogmen." Lucy warns Gilbert about the hotel developers: "Gilbert [. . .] dey coming to take dah land away from you." Gilbert responds, "Yeah. But I know dat already, dat dey coming here" (73). Lucy refers to the haole business-men, while Gilbert is talking about the frogmen. This connection between contemporary forms of economic imperialism (i.e., hotels) and residual forms of militaristic imperialism (i.e., invading soldiers) becomes more explicit as the narrative describes the Hawai'ian International Corporation's "large battalion of trucks and tractors and cranes, all methodically grinding and buzzing through the drowsy village [. . .] as if the construction company were an army of occupation" (81). Lucy clarifies for Gilbert that "Dah trucks and tractors like dat, das dah frogmen" (83). Through the several meanings of the "frogmen," Pak suggests that the invasion of Hawai'i takes multiple forms.

Teachers might wish to begin discussion of the story through its central symbol. What sorts of images do "frogmen" conjure up? If we take into account Nakakura-san's description that "dis is not dah first time dah frogmen wen come," to whom might the term *frogmen* refer? How does this vision of frogmen relate to Lucy's epiphany in her car surrounded by hundreds of frogs? How do the ambiguous meanings of the frogmen assist the story's themes? (On this latter point, teachers might want to remind students of the cloud Gilbert sees that changes size and shape.)

Other topics explored in "The Watcher of Waipuna" include the continuing need for watchdog activism and the history of militarism affecting Hawai'i (e.g., Gilbert is a Vietnam veteran, and Lola's husband was killed in the war). Students might also want to discuss the role of divine intervention in the narrative (the flood symbolism, the ghost seen marching down main street). On issues of genre and style, teachers might pose the question of how Pak's long story compares with a very short work, such as Lum's "Primo Doesn't Take Back Bottles Anymore." Does the method of the story's conveyance (dramatic unfolding, dialogue, stream-of-consciousness) reflect on both the length of the tale and its objective (e.g., character sketch, parable culminating in a moral)? Pak's use of local vernacular English also holds thematic significance (see the discussion of pidgin in the section on Lum). Standard and legalistic English emerge as the master's tools designed to dispossess locals and Hawai'ians of both land and culture. Fluency in English or "talk[ing] good" is associated with mainland chicanery—for instance, in the characterization of the haole attorney as "smart fo' talk" (52). Teachers might ask students to distinguish the use of vernacular in this story from its use in other works (to set a tone or to establish a child narrator, for instance).

Intertextual Linkages and Suggestions for Syllabus Organization

Several thematic and stylistic issues reverberate across these short stories. These topics also provide alternative ways to organize a syllabus.

Themes

language differences, communication gaps (Yamamoto, Chin, Louie, Pak)

criminalization of the immigrant (Sui Sin Far, Santos, Chin)

women's choices (Sui Sin Far, Yamamoto, Santos, Watanabe, Jen)

generation and the use of a child or adult narrator (Yamamoto, Chin, Watanabe, Jen, Louie)

interethnic coalitions: prospects and limitations (Mukherjee, Jen, Louie)

American imperialism (Gonzalez, Mukherjee, Pak)

East-West split: the older generation (Sui Sin Far, Mori); the younger generation emphasizing dual or multiple cultural heritage (Yamamoto, Chin, Watanabe, Jen, Louie)

Style

Standard English versus colloquial or vernacular English (Gonzalez, Lum, Mukherjee, Watanabe, Jen, Pak): Gonzalez thematically contemplates the burden of standard English; Lum, Watanabe, and Pak use pidgin dialogue combined with narration in standard English; Mukherjee and Jen write first-person narrations in slangy speech.

Mutation of perspectives (all the works): Contrast the semiomniscient narrators of Sui Sin Far and Pak; the objective narrator of Mori; the limited third-person perspectives of Yamamoto, Santos, and Chin; the second-person narrative voice at the onset of Gonzalez; the stream-of-consciousness in Lum; and the dramatic monologues of Mukherjee, Watanabe, Jen, and Louie.

Use of humor: How do the comic effects of Jen, Watanabe, Pak, and Yamamoto compare with one another? Is humor merely to entertain? Does humor disarm the reader to encourage acceptance of a sometimes bitter moral? Is humor linked to the oral dimension of short stories?

Another possibility for syllabus organization is for teachers to present the works according to the settings engaged in the tales (San Francisco: Sui Sin Far, Santos, and Chin; rural California: Mori and Yamamoto; Philippines: Gonzalez; Hawai'i: Lum, Watanabe, and Pak; southern United States: Mukherjee; northeastern United States: Jen and Louie). Finally, a more ambitious structure for organization would be for teachers to present the stories according to the specific issues that gained prominence in Asian American studies over time (e.g., recovering a lost history, the focus on the Chinese and Japanese, feminist critique, the diasporic turn, new ethnicities). The ordering and selection of the issues will vary according to the particular narrative of Asian American studies that the teacher wishes to emphasize.[35] It is possible, however, to suggest through the short stories a history of Asian America as an institution.

Notes

1. Not universally accepted as a genre in its own right, the short story remains loosely defined. I have appended a list of family resemblances to Pasco's definition.

2. Referred to as the "father of the American short story," Edgar Allan Poe insisted on the short story's having a "certain unique or single effect [. . .]. In the whole composition there should be no word written, of which the tendency, direct or indirect, is not to the one pre-established design" (47–48).

3. See May's introduction to *Short Story Theories* for a highly readable overview of short story criticism. His introduction to *New Short Story Theories* provides an updated revision; however, its emphasis on poststructuralist theories requires a sophisticated critical audience. Marler and Pratt each also offer accessible histories of the short story, while Pasco examines the difficulty of proposing definitions for the short story and for literary genres in general.

4. Ling attributes this pioneering authorial role to both Eaton sisters, Edith and Winnifred, the latter being a prolific novelist (16). Ling also notes, however, that "unlike the stories of Sui Sin Far, Onoto Watanna's [Winnifred Eaton's] novels do not so much challenge social myths as reinforce them" (52).

5. Gonzalez places that choice in a historical context, highlighting this experimentation in English as a reaction to the "commercialization" of the short story in *Pilipino* ("Workshop" 246). Paradoxically, English rendered these works inaccessible to "an audience beyond the university campus" at the same time that it enhanced the stories' status as part of a growing body of "world literature" ("Workshop" 249, 253).

6. According to Ling, such tales derive "their humor and charm from the unexpected and unfamiliar angle of vision given to things familiar to the readers themselves" (15). Ling further elaborates that since the time of Oliver Goldsmith's "Letters from a Citizen of the World" (1762), penned under the alias Lien Chi Altangi, the "Chinese have been asked so often to write their impressions of life in the West that we may call this form a subgenre" (15).

7. Ethel Evebrook concedes Alice's superior mettle: "It is women such as Alice Winthrop [. . .] who are the pride and glory of America [. . .] women who have been of service to others all their years and who have graduated from the university of life with honor" (Sui Sin Far, "Inferior Woman" 35–36). This description might be applied to Sui Sin Far herself, who could have moved in social circles other than the Chinese immigrant community. Instead, she devoted her life to the Chinese, forgoing more lucrative writing possibilities as well as romantic overtures (see "Leaves from a Mental Portfolio of an Eurasian").

8. See also the works by White-Parks; Ferens; Lee, "Images"; Ling; and Yin for autobiographical background and critical readings of Sui Sin Far's work.

9. In her survey of Asian American literature, Kim calls attention to Mori as a "Nisei universalist" who depicts the higher life of his subjects—the mental and spiritual cache of human existence hiding behind surfaces of silence and foolhardiness (*Asian American Literature* 163–72). Mori, furthermore, approaches these tales that depict "the bulldog tenacity of the human spirit" (Yamamoto, Introduction 12) by focusing entirely on Japanese American characters and settings. It is as if Mori responds to the narrow, exoticized images of the Japanese prevalent during his day by deliberately not dwelling on their racial distinctiveness.

10. Following the Mukden incident in 1931, Japan took complete control of Manchuria, installing a puppet government and declaring the independence of the newly named region, "Manchukuo." In 1933, the League of Nations refused to recognize Manchukuo, further straining relations between Japan and the United States. In 1937, full-scale war broke out between Chinese and Japanese forces in North China and thus began World War II. The United States did not enter the war until 7 December 1941, when Japan bombed Pearl Harbor.

11. Gonzalez has won every major literary award in the Philippines: the Commonwealth Literary Award (1941), the Republic Award of Merit (1954), the Republic Cultural Heritage Award (1960), and the Rizal Pro Patria Award (1961). According to Gertrude Ang, Gonzalez's works are required readings in any course on Filipino writing in English.

12. Campomanes explicates the ironies whereby the work of Filipino writers—more appropriately studied under the category of postcolonial literature—has been virtually ignored by critics of world literature; by contrast, the diasporic sensibilities of such fiction have been embraced by Asian Americanists (Gonzalez and Campomanes).

13. San Miguel was the site of a United States communications support station in close proximity to Subic Naval Base. Also, Casper remarks on the resemblance of Gonzalez's setting to Clark Field (New Writing 49).

14. From 1899 to 1902, the United States brutally suppressed Philippine independence movements (see Francisco). From 1942 through 1945, the Philippines were under Japanese occupation.

15. A revised agreement in 1966 set the lease on lands to expire in 1991.

16. According to an early and outspoken critic of the bases, Claro Recto, the military outposts in the Philippines were designed primarily "to act as magnets for enemy attacks" (qtd. in Schirmer and Shalom 153).

17. The formality of the setting is matched by the formality of English on which Leynes initially insists. He prefers the propriety of "Please pass the cream" to his colleague's playful phrase, "Hello, milk!" (Gonzalez, "Popcorn Man" 137).

18. An excerpt of Francisco's article also appears in Schirmer and Shalom.

19. Kim catalogs numerous venues devoted to Asian American literature (Asian American Literature 313).

20. Many of these themes are echoed in Sumida's study on the literary traditions of Hawai'i: "'local' is today's shorthand by which people in Hawai'i [. . .] label a culture, a sensibility, an identity, and [. . .] a personal, family, and community history" (View xvi).

21. Sensitivity to ethnicity, the environment, and family history seems a crucial part of Asian American literary traditions. What may be most distinctive about local writing, then, is the use of pidgin English and creole. Sumida calls the use of Hawai'i's pidgin English and creole "the hallmark of authenticity" in local literature ("Waiting" 312). See also Fujikane, who remarks on the strategic refusal of the name Asian American by many local Asians because of its continental origins and its failure "to recognize the anomalous status of Local Asians who are a part of a non-Native Hawai'ian, multiracial Local Movement asserting its own cultural identity" (24).

22. Along with Eric Chock, Lum founded Bamboo Ridge: The Hawai'i Writers' Quarterly and with several other editors issued Talk Story: An Anthology of Hawai'i's Local Writers (Chock et al.).

23. Sumida characterizes the story as providing "an 'underview' of life, from the bottom looking up, where sometimes we see more going on than we perceive from above" (Sumida, *View* 104).

24. See Kim, *Asian American Literature*, for concise readings of both "Scent of Apples" and "The Day the Dancers Came."

25. See Chan for a narrative account of these series of immigration acts (54–55). For a more thorough analysis of immigration laws as well as excerpts of selected laws and cases affecting Asian American immigration, see Hing.

26. Chin has also been an active storyteller, oftentimes revising or updating Chinese folklore for Chinese American audiences.

27. The perspective in the penultimate paragraph changes to Dirigible's viewpoint, with the young boy weeping because Yuen's story is his own. The narrative emphasizes the connection between this younger generation and the older one.

28. See the introductions to both *Aiiieeeee!* anthologies (Chan et al.; Chin et al.). See also critiques of the *Aiiieeeee!* editors' definitions: Cheung, "*Woman Warrior*"; Kim, Foreword; Lim; Wong; Campomanes; Lee, *Americas*.

29. While oli are a kind of mele, Sumida contrasts the lyric mele—often "mistaken for the whole of Hawaiian music and poetry"—with the more somber oli: "chants such as dirges, historical narratives, or epics, sacred chants, genealogical chants, genital and procreative chants" ("Sense" 224).

30. The narrator mentions the details of Sony's purchasing Columbia Pictures and identifies Amanda's new lover as a Japanese guy named Ito.

31. In 1982, Vincent Chin—mistaken for a Japanese—was beaten to death by two Euro-American men in Detroit, one of whom harbored anti-Japanese sentiments because of his close association with the American automobile industry, which at that time faced fierce competition from Japan. The Asian American community was shocked when the two men who murdered Chin—Ronald Ebens and Michael Nitz—were granted three years' probation and a fine of three thousand dollars each (Chan 176–78).

32. From another perspective, the volume's critical success with mainland readers raises the issue of Hawai'i's dependence on continental approval once again. Eric Chock voices this concern over mainland values as the standard that writers of Hawai'i are supposed to emulate: "We in Hawai'i are expected to believe that we are subordinate to the mainland. At best, we are expected to believe that we are really no different here and can even be like the mainland if we try hard enough. We are asked to reject the feeling that Hawai'i is special" (Chock and Lum 8). The award given by the Association for Asian American Studies signifies continental recognition of local literature, even as locals have resisted mainland scholars' attempt to plunder their cultural reserves (see Sumida, "Waiting" 318).

33. For instance, Fujikane remarks that the native Hawai'ian sovereignty movement, which focuses on the return of ceded lands, "has been a locus of anxieties for many Locals [who] are afraid that they will lose their own private property" (51).

34. On the one hand, Lola is correct in contesting the tradition of male primogeniture that confers proprietary rights solely on the son, Gilbert; on the other, greed undermines Lola as a voice of women's rights. Instead, Lola is portrayed as a lustful, selfish, and crazed sister.

35. Asian American critics are continually rewriting the history of Asian American stud-

ies. For a sampling of these contrasting institutional histories of the field, see Lim, Espiritu, and Omatsu.

Bibliography

Anderson, Benedict. "Cacique Democracy in the Philippines: Origins and Dreams." *New Left Review* 169 (1988): 3–31.

Ang, Gertrude. Rev. of *Mindoro and Beyond: Twenty-One Stories*, by N. V. M. Gonzalez. *Philippine Quarterly of Culture and Society* 8 (1980): 191–93.

Campomanes, Oscar. "New Formations of Asian American Studies and the Question of U.S. Imperialism." *Positions* 5 (1997): 523–50.

Casper, Leonard. Introduction. Santos, *Scent of Apples* ix–xvi.

———. *New Writing from the Philippines: A Critique and Anthology*. Syracuse: Syracuse UP, 1966.

Chan, Jeffery Paul, et al., eds. *The Big Aiiieeeee! An Anthology of Chinese American and Japanese American Literature*. New York: Meridian, 1991.

Chan, Sucheng. *Asian Americans: An Interpretive History*. Boston: Twayne, 1991.

Cheung, King-Kok, ed. *An Interethnic Companion to Asian American Literature*. New York: Cambridge UP, 1997.

———. Introduction. Yamamoto, *Seventeen Syllables* 3–16.

———. "*The Woman Warrior* versus *The Chinaman Pacific*: Must a Chinese American Critic Choose between Feminism and Heroism?" *Conflicts in Feminism*. Ed. Marianne Hirsch and Evelyn Fox Keller. New York: Routledge, 1990. 234–51.

Chin, Frank. "The Only Real Day." *The Chinaman Pacific and Frisco R.R. Co*. Minneapolis: Coffee House, 1988. 41–78.

Chin, Frank, et al., eds. *Aiiieeeee! An Anthology of Asian American Writers*. Washington: Howard UP, 1974.

Chock, Eric, and Darrell H. Y. Lum, eds. *The Best of Bamboo Ridge: The Hawai'i Writers' Quarterly*. Honolulu: Bamboo Ridge, 1986.

Chock, Eric, et al. *Talk Story: An Anthology of Hawai'i's Local Writers*. Honolulu: Petronium, 1978.

Davis, Rocío G. "Identity in Community in Chinese American Short Story Cycles: Sigrid Nunez's *A Feather on the Breath of God*." *Hitting Critical Mass* 3.2 (1996): 115–33.

Espiritu, Yen Le. *Asian American Panethnicity: Bridging Institutions and Identities*. Philadelphia: Temple UP, 1992.

Ferens, Dominka. "Tangled Kites: Sui Sin Far's Negotiations with Race and Readership." *Amerasia Journal* 25.2 (1999): 116–44.

Francisco, Luzviminda. "The First Vietnam—the Philippine-American War of 1899–1902." *Letters* 1–22.

Fujikane, Candace. "Between Nationalisms: Hawai'i's Local Nation and Its Troubled Racial Paradise." *Critical Mass* 1.2 (1994): 23–58.

Gonzalez, N. V. M. "In the Workshop of Time and Tide." Gonzalez, *Mindoro* 231–56.

———. *Mindoro and Beyond: Twenty-One Stories*. Quezon City: U of Philippines P, 1979.

———. "The Popcorn Man." *Look Stranger, on This Island Now*. Manila: Benipayo, 1963.

175–200. Rpt. in Gonzalez, *Mindoro* 181–92, and in *"The Bread of Salt" and Other Short Stories*. By Gonzalez. Seattle: U of Washington P, 1993. 136–50.

Gonzalez, N. V. M., and Oscar V. Campomanes. "Filipino American Literature." Cheung, *Interethnic Companion* 62–124.

Helprin, Mark, and Shannon Ravenel, eds. *The Best American Short Stories, 1988*. Boston: Houghton, 1988.

Hing, Bill Ong. *Making and Remaking Asian America through Immigration Policy, 1850–1990*. Stanford: Stanford UP, 1993.

Jen, Gish. *Mona in the Promised Land*. New York: Knopf, 1996.

———. *Typical American*. Boston: Houghton, 1991.

———. "What Means Switch." *Atlantic Monthly* May 1990: 76–85.

Kim, Elaine. *Asian American Literature: An Introduction to the Writings and Their Social Context*. Philadelphia: Temple UP, 1982.

———. Foreword. *Reading the Literatures of Asian America*. Ed. Shirley Geok-lin Lim and Amy Ling. Philadelphia: Temple UP, 1992. xi–xvii.

Knippling, Alpana Sharma. "Toward an Investigation of the Subaltern in Bharati Mukherjee's 'The Middleman' and Other Stories and Jasmine." Nelson 143–59.

Lee, Rachel C. *The Americas of Asian American Literature: Gendered Fictions of Nation and Transnation*. Princeton: Princeton UP, 1999.

———. "Journalistic Images and Literary Responses, 1910–20." Cheung, *Interethnic Companion* 249–73.

Letters in Exile: An Introductory Reader on the History of Pilipinos in America. Los Angeles: UCLA, Asian Amer. Studies Center, 1976.

Lim, Shirley. "Assaying the Gold: Contesting the Ground of Asian American Literature." *New Literary History* 24 (1993): 147–69.

Ling, Amy. *Between Worlds: Women Writers of Chinese Ancestry*. Elmsford: Pergamon, 1990.

Louie, David Wong. "Pangs of Love." *Pangs of Love*. New York: Plume, 1992. 75–98.

Lum, Darrell H. Y. "Primo Doesn't Take Back Bottles Anymore." 33–38. Chock and Lum 184–88.

Marler, Robert F. "From Tale to Short Story: The Emergence of a New Genre in the 1850's." May, *New Short Story* 165–81.

May, Charles E. Introduction. May, *New Short Story* xv–xxvi.

———. "Introduction: A Survey of Short Story Criticism in America." May, *Short Story* 3–12.

———, ed. *The New Short Story Theories*. Athens: Ohio UP, 1994.

———, ed. *Short Story Theories*. Athens: Ohio UP, 1976.

McKinley, William. "Remarks to Methodist Delegation." Schirmer and Shalom 22–23.

Mori, Toshio. "The Brothers." Mori, *Yokohama* 155–61.

———. "Tomorrow Is Coming, Children." Mori, *Yokohama* 14–21.

———. *Yokohama, California*. Caldwell: Caxton, 1949.

Mukherjee, Bharati. "Loose Ends." *"The Middleman" and Other Stories*. New York: Grove, 1988. 42–55.

Nelson, Emmanuel S., ed. *Bharati Mukherjee: Critical Perspectives*. New York: Garland, 1993.

Omatsu, Glenn. "The 'Four Prisons' and the Movements of Liberation: Asian American

Activism from the 1960s to the 1990s." *The State of Asian America: Activism and Resistance in the 1990s*. Ed. Karin Aguilar-San Juan. Boston: South End, 1994. 19–69.

Omori, Emiko. *Hot Summer Winds*. Amer. Playhouse. PBS, 1991.

Pak, Gary. "The Watcher of Waipuna." *"The Watcher of Waipuna" and Other Stories*. Spec. issue of *Bamboo Ridge* 55-56 (1992): 21–86.

Pasco, Allan H. "On Defining Short Stories." May, *New Short Story* 114–30.

Payne, Robert M. "Adapting (to) the Margins: *Hot Summer Winds* and the Stories of Hisaye Yamamoto." Yamamoto, *Seventeen Syllables* 203–18.

Poe, Edgar Allan. Rev. of *Twice Told Tales*, by Nathaniel Hawthorne. *Graham's Magazine* May 1842. Rpt. in May, *Short Story* 45–51.

Pratt, Mary Louise. "The Short Story: The Long and the Short of It." May, *New Short Story* 91–113.

Quinsaat, Jesse G. "How to Join the Navy and Still Not See the World." *Letters* 96–111.

Roces, Mina. "Filipino Identity in Fiction, 1945–1972." *Modern Asian Studies* 28.2 (1994): 279–315.

Santos, Bienvenido N. "The Day the Dancers Came." Santos, *Scent* 113–28.

———. "Filipinos at War." *Letters* 93–95.

———. "Immigration Blues." *New Letters* June 1997: 3–20. Rpt. in *Short Story International* Dec. 1979: 89–106 and in Santos, *Scent* 3–20.

———. "Scent of Apples." Santos, *Scent* 21–29.

———. *Scent of Apples: A Collection of Stories by Bienvenido N. Santos*. Introd. Leonard Casper. Seattle: U of Washington P, 1979.

Schirmer, Daniel B., and Stephen Rosskamm Shalom. *The Philippines Reader: A History of Colonialism, Neocolonialism, Dictatorship, and Resistance*. Boston: South End, 1987.

Soo Hoo, Michael. Rev. of *The Chinaman Pacific and Frisco R.R. Co.*, by Frank Chin. *Amerasia Journal* 19.1 (1993): 175–78.

Sui Sin Far [Edith Eaton]. "The Inferior Woman." *Mrs. Spring Fragrance*. Chicago: McClurg, 1912. 1–47.

———. "Leaves from the Mental Portfolio of an Eurasian." *Independent* 21 Jan. 1909: 125–32.

Sumida, Stephen H. *And the View from the Shore: Literary Traditions of Hawai'i*. Seattle: U of Washington P, 1991.

———. "Sense of Place, History, and the Concept of the 'Local' in Hawai'i's Asian/Pacific American Literatures." *Reading the Literatures of Asian America*. Ed. Shirley Geok-lin Lim and Amy Ling. Philadelphia: Temple UP, 1992. 215–37.

———. "Waiting for the Big Fish: Recent Research in the Asian American Literature of Hawai'i." Chock and Lum 302–21.

Takaki, Ronald. *Strangers from a Different Shore: A History of Asian Americans*. New York: Penguin, 1990.

Watanabe, Sylvia. "Talking to the Dead." Watanabe and Bruchac 310–21.

———. *"Talking to the Dead" and Other Stories*. New York: Doubleday, 1992.

Watanabe, Sylvia, and Carol Bruchac, eds. *Home to Stay: Asian American Women's Fiction*. Greenfield Center: Greenfield Review, 1990.

White-Parks, Annette. *Sui Sin Far / Edith Maude Eaton: A Literary Biography*. Urbana: U of Illinois P, 1995.

Wong, Sau-ling. "Denationalization Reconsidered: Asian American Cultural Criticism at a Theoretical Crossroads." *Amerasia Journal* 21.1-2 (1995): 1–27.

Yamamoto, Hisaye. Introduction. *"The Chauvinist" and Other Stories*. By Toshio Mori. Los Angeles: UCLA Asian Amer. Studies Center, 1979. 1–14.

———. *Seventeen Syllables*. Ed. and introd. King-Kok Cheung. New Brunswick: Rutgers UP, 1994.

———. "Seventeen Syllables." Yamamoto, *"Seventeen Syllables"* 8–19.

———. *"Seventeen Syllables" and Other Stories*. Latham: Kitchen Table, 1988.

———. "Yoneko's Earthquake." Yamamoto *"Seventeen Syllables"* 46–56.

Yin, Xiao-Huang. "Between the East and West: Sui Sin Far—the First Chinese-American Woman Writer." *Arizona Quarterly* 47.4 (1991): 49–84.

Yogi, Stan. "Legacies Revealed: Uncovering Buried Plots in the Stories of Hisaye Yamamoto." Yamamoto, *Seventeen Syllables* 143–60.

Sizing Up
Asian American Poetry

Sunn Shelley Wong

Taking Edmund Wilson's essay "Is Verse a Dying Technique?" (1934), Joseph Epstein's "Who Killed Poetry?" (1988), and Vernon Shetley's *After the Death of Poetry* (1993) as temporal coordinates for mapping the twentieth-century trajectory of poetry in the United States would generate a rather grim view of poetry's prospects. While some might argue that claims for the death of poetry are exaggerated at best and hyperbolic at worst, there has been, nonetheless, in recent years a heightened concern with the changing face and function of poetry at the closing of the twentieth century. What is poetry today? Who reads poetry? What is a poet? What is a poem? What is a reader?

Like American poetry as a whole, Asian American poetry has been subject to changing senses of what poetry is or does and what poets and readers are or do.[1] With an eye to identifying some of the ways that Asian American poetry might be taught in the literature classroom today, I offer here not a survey of twentieth-century Asian American poetry but, rather, a discussion of some of the difficulties the reading of this poetry is likely to entail and some of the critical debates it has generated. I begin by presenting a general typology of difficulties and then take up the more specific manifestations of these difficulties as presented by recent criticism of Asian American poetry.[2] Whether the context for that teaching is a course on American literature, American poetry, multiethnic literatures of the United States, or Asian American literature, an understanding of how poetry arrived at its present place in the world of letters will enable us to anticipate better the kinds of problems students might encounter in their study of Asian American poetry. For instance, given the nature and the sponsorship of this resource guide, can we avoid discussing the matter of the institutional training of readers? The very structure of this resource guide, with its emphasis on prose fiction, already tells us something about the status of poetry today and about the kinds of difficulties that we might encounter in the classroom when we propose to teach it. For example, if we concede that poetry has yielded generic preeminence to prose narrative over the past century, then we would need to think first about the reasons for that loss of preeminence and then about how that loss has conditioned our students' abilities or inclinations to engage with poetry.[3]

Poetry's ostensible fall from its Olympian heights can be looked at in terms of changing readerships and changing styles of poetry. For over a century now, poets and critics alike have lamented the demise of the "common reader." Critics working on a sociology of reading have pointed out some of the sociohistorical factors that may have contributed to this demise. For instance, the idea of a common reader calls up the idea of a common culture. In *The Making of the Reader*, David Trotter notes how critics have approached the issue of the shared grammar on which the notion of the common reader is predicated. He cites, for instance, F. R. Leavis's contention that "to be born into a homogeneous culture is to move among signals of limited variety, illustrating one predominant pervasive ethos, grammar and idiom [. . .] and to acquire discrimination as one moves" (2). For Leavis, it was the Industrial Revolution and the rise of mass society that destroyed a cohesive community of readers. The shift from gemeinschaft to gesellschaft meant that the socioeconomic basis for a "homogeneous culture " was no longer available. In the cultural sphere, a shared grammar, according to Leavis, had yielded to a Tower of Babel. In the wake of this loss of the common reader, poets were left to either hang up their pens or cultivate a new readership.

Critics such as Vernon Shetley have noted that a modernist emphasis on difficulty has helped to dispatch any vestige or trace of the common reader in this century. T. S. Eliot's assertion in 1921 that "poets, in our civilization [. . .] must be difficult" suggests that "poetry that fails to be difficult [. . .] either must be the product of an insufficiently 'refined' sensibility or must be failing in its job of giving comprehensive expression to contemporary life" (qtd. in Shetley 1–2). While many critics have pointed to modernism's emphasis on impersonality, allusiveness, obscurity of reference, and indirectness as possible factors in the demise of poetry's appeal to a general audience, still others note that even though the poetry of the last thirty or forty years has been considerably less "difficult" (in modernist terms), the readership for poetry has not rebounded. This observation has led critics to look for the difficulty of poetry not in the poems themselves but in the historical conditions of the act of reading. The way poetry has been taught and the kinds of writing that readers have come to identify as "poetry" have no doubt helped to shape a contemporary audience's response to the genre. Other shifts within American culture, including changing demographics, changing attitudes toward language and textuality, a new emphasis on visual and popular culture, and a resurgent anti-intellectualism that regards poetry as the preserve of a cultural elite, have led observers of the contemporary poetry scene to remark that "today poetry itself, any poetry, has become difficult for even the more ambitious general reader as the habits of thought and communication inculcated by contemporary life have grown to be increasingly at variance with those demanded for the reading of poetry" (Shetley 3). Even in this observation, however, we encounter again the problem of defining poetry—are we to include the spoken word, or rap for example, under the rubric of poetry?[4]

In teaching poetry, then, we need to think about not only the nature of the poetic work before us but also the historically shifting relations between poems and readers. Do the "difficulties" that students encounter in their reading of poetry stem from the nature of the work itself or from the nature of the interpretive equipment that those students, as well as their teachers, bring with them to the poetry classroom or from a combination of the two? How do race, class, gender, and sexuality condition that interpretive equipment? To these questions, we could also add the matter of canon formation: What poems do we bring into the literature classroom, and why these rather than others?

Clearly, at the end of the twentieth century in the United States, the cultural homogeneity that Leavis ascribed to preindustrial England (an arguable point in itself) is nonexistent. And what might it mean today to say that a reader's experience of difficulty with a poem stems from the lack of a shared cultural grammar? To put it another way (in a more positive register), what if the difficulty stems from a proliferation of cultural grammars as evidenced by the profusion of published work by minority writers over the past two decades? Are we to approach this current state of poetic affairs with a sense of nostalgia, resignation, relief, or celebration?

In relating these issues to Asian American poetry, I begin here with George Steiner's essay "On Difficulty" and go on to discuss, in the context of the typologies he offers, some of the major topoi in recent criticism of Asian American poetry.[5] Steiner proposes four types of difficulty that readers of Western post-Renaissance poetry are likely to encounter: contingent, modal, tactical, and ontological. Contingent difficulty is perhaps the most straightforward of the lot, encompassing problems of interpretation that arise when a given set of ideas, stock of allusions, or body of knowledge is superseded by another and subsequently disappears from the horizon of common knowledge. These problems of interpretation presumably could be solved by the recovery of that lost material or, as Steiner puts it, by readers doing their "homework" (29) and looking up the needed references. Modal difficulties are those that arise when "the tone, the manifest subject of the poem are such that we fail to see a justification for poetic form, [when] the root-occasion of the poem's composition eludes or repels our internalized sense of what poetry should or should not be about, of what are the intelligible, morally and aesthetically acceptable moments and motives for poetry" (28). Modal difficulties go beyond the matter of "taste" and present questions about that which is proper to a given genre. To address this class of difficulty, we would have to examine and readjust our evaluative mechanisms for deciding what makes a poem a poem. Whereas contingent and modal difficulties have to do with the reader's response to poetry, tactical difficulty "has its source in the writer's will or in the failure of adequacy between his intention and his performative means" (33). This failure of adequacy may be the result of political circumstances that necessitate coding and "allegoric indirection" or of the poet's recognition that the available language is "infinitely shop-worn" (34). The poet's various efforts to revitalize or reanimate the language generate a range of effects that generally estrange ready understandings, allowing the text's meaning to emerge only gradually. Shetley extends this notion in observing that tactical difficulty stems from the intractable problem "at the very root of the project of lyric, that of embodying subjectivity in the impersonal and resistant medium of language" (8). The final class of difficulties—the ontological—concerns the relation between being and language. More specifically, Steiner raises the issue of trying to represent authentic being in an "environment of eroded speech" (44). He offers the example of Paul Celan, who as "a survivor of the holocaust [was] writing poetry comparable in stature to Holderlin's and Rilke's, and poetry of the utmost personal compulsion, in the butcher's tongue" (44). While noting that his classificatory schema is "rough" and "preliminary," Steiner also suggests that "it would be unusual if any of the difficulties met with in poetry, and in literary texts as a whole, were irreducible to one of these four types or to the manifold combinations between them" (47). For my purposes here, Steiner's typology will serve as a rough and ready heuristic device that can open up some critical issues in the reading of Asian American poetry.

For Steiner, contingent and modal difficulties arise largely because of the passage of time. What was common knowledge in one period becomes a matter of obscurity in another. Similarly, the social and aesthetic forms of one era are frequently regarded by another era as either outmoded or repellent. To put it another way, we might say that literary forms—always bearing within themselves the ideological traces of their moment and place of origin—can outlast the social formations from which they emerged. This disjuncture across time, however, can also be a disjuncture across space, and a diachronic scheme can become a synchronic one; recent theories of reading and reception certainly testify to as much. Contingent and modal difficulties arise when works travel across time and also when works travel "across the boundaries of interpretive communities [. . .]. Different groups of readers have different skills and expectations; allusions familiar to one segment of an audience may be mysterious to another, and received conventions that structure the sense of what makes an utterance a poem may vary widely" (Shetley 9).

In the context of Asian American poetry, contingent difficulty stems less from readers who are confronting items that have passed from common knowledge than it does from readers who are confronting material that has yet to pass into common knowledge.[6] The contingencies here derive not only from historical shifts within a given culture but also from the historical encounter of different cultures. (Those contingent difficulties are compounded, too, when we take into consideration the specific developmental histories of a given group's encounter with, and ongoing relationship to, a dominant group.) For instance, allusions to a wide variety of Asian American cultural or historical phenomena or the inclusion of Asian American linguistic markers can create difficulties for readers not familiar with the phenomena or markers in question, difficulties that could be remedied by acquiring the necessary knowledge.

In "Reconstructing Asian-American Poetry: A Case for Ethnopoetics," Shirley Geok-lin Lim notes that the foregrounding of "ethnicity" in Asian American poetry "place[s] new demands on audience understanding. To answer even the most basic questions of the text—what's happening? why is it happening? what does it mean?— is to introduce conventionally non-literary materials more appropriately seen as sociological, anthropological, or political in nature" (55).[7] The need for readers of Asian

American poetry to do some extra legwork is part of the case that Lim makes for readings that accommodate what she calls (after Jerome Rothenberg) an "ethnopoetics." For Lim, an Asian American ethnopoetics operates on three primary "levels": the stylistic, the linguistic, and the contextual. All three levels fall largely within Steiner's category of contingent difficulties. "Style" here refers to "diction, figures of speech, imagery and turns of phrase which are identifiably Asian-American in association or origin." Lim points to Cathy Song's references to "dumplings," "wonton skins," and "bright quilted bundles" (in *Picture Bride*) as instances of such stylistic features (53). The "linguistic" level involves primarily "the incorporation of phrases or whole lines of the original language into the English text" (54). The "contextual" refers generally to the sociohistorical circumstances of a given writer. Lim illustrates the "contextual" with reference to the disparity between two assessments of John Yau's work. Lim observes that that disparity hinges on the respective critics' acknowledgment of, or failure to acknowledge, Yau's "ethnicity." "The ethnographic bent," writes Lim, "(which in its European manifestation is often elucidated and much appreciated in [canonical works such as Eliot's] 'The Wasteland') must first be acknowledged in Asian-American writing for full justice to be given to the literary merits of the work" (56).

In the course of arguing this case for contextualized readings of Asian American poetry that remain attentive to culturally diverse and dynamic referential fields, Lim also opens up a can of worms in relation to the idea of a distinct Asian American poetic voice or sensibility. Taking as her points of departure the observations that Asian American poetry is largely "non-European" in character and that Asian immigrants have largely staved off assimilation through their retention of their "first" languages, Lim remarks that a "stubborn residual identity which refuses oblivion characterizes much if not all of Asian-American writing today. Even an avant-garde third generation Chinese-American writer such as David Henry Hwang works and re-works elements of his original culture with the contemporary American aesthetic" (52). Since its inception in the 1960s, the term *Asian American*—with or without the hyphen—has proved a vexing issue. Here, Lim's assignment of ontological primacy to the first term (by way of a rhetoric of origins that speaks of "original cultures," "origins" (53), "first languages," and "residual identities") ends up privileging and hypostatizing "Asianness."[8] The two terms remain the two discrete poles of a split identity rather than the mutually constitutive aspects of a labile subjectivity.

While similarly asserting the existence of a distinct Japanese American literary sensibility, Richard Oyama locates that sensibility not in any "residual" Japanese identity but, rather, in the cumulative history of Japanese Americans. In "Ayumi: 'To Sing Our Connections,'" Oyama begins to make his claims for a Japanese American literary tradition by recalling one of the driving tenets of an Asian American literary manifesto—the introduction to *Aiiieeeee! An Anthology of Asian-American Writers*. There, the editors Frank Chin, Jeffery Paul Chan, Lawson Fusao Inada, and Shawn Hsu Wong speak of the Asian American writer's need to "legitimize the language, style and syntax of his people's experience, to codify the experiences common to his people into symbols, clichés, linguistic mannerisms, and a sense of humor that emerges from an organic familiarity with the experience" (xxxvii). For Oyama, the "experience" to be codified consists of the respective histories of four generations of Japanese Americans, histories that are variously marked by dislocation, racial oppression, gender inequality, internment, exile, and conflicted loyalties. In his article—devoted to elucidating a Japanese American "literary tradition" (250)—Oyama makes his case for a distinct Japanese American literary voice by tracing certain recurring codifications of that experience in the work of three generations of Japanese American writers. Other critics, such as John Crawford writing on Janice Mirikitani's work, have also noted how specific historical events are crucial to Mirikitani's poetry. Crawford notes how Japanese American internment, the bombing of Hiroshima, and the war in Vietnam variously inform Mirikitani's poetry of trauma. For both these critics, Japanese American identity is not "residual" but, rather, constituted through engagement with prevailing sociohistorical circumstances.[9]

In "Reading Asian American Poetry," Juliana Chang lends greater complexity to this notion of an Asian American voice:

> Poets like Kimiko Hahn, Marilyn Chin, Carolyn Lei-lanilau, and Arthur Sze are influenced by and incorporate Japanese and Chinese languages, literatures and philosophies in their work, but have a more complex and mediated relationship to them than one of simple cultural reproduction. As George Uba points out in his response to the introduction to *Chinese American Poetry: An Anthology*, "Situating a writer like Carolyn Lau [. . .] squarely within China's philosophical tradition may be true as far as it goes but undeniably devalues her powerful attraction to particular Western writers like Beckett, Woolf, and Kafka, as well as to postmodernism generally, while eliding the question of her precise relationship to Asian American cultural experiences." (90)

Both Chang and Uba proceed on the assumption that privileging any single constitutive factor would reduce and obscure the actual multiplicity of factors that mediate a given writer's work.

While clearly posing contingent difficulties, the incorporation of Asian linguistic elements or cultural referents in Asian American poetry can also pose modal difficulties if those incorporations are understood in some way to be extraliterary, that is, to be "sociological, anthropological, or political in nature" (Lim 55). In the absence of a stable referential field organized around a single "pervasive ethos, grammar and idiom," the presence of a far from "limited variety" of unfamiliar "signals" in a poem might well call into question the poem's status as poetry (Leavis qtd. in Trotter 2). Difficulties of this order can begin to be accounted for (though not necessarily relieved) by reexamining prevailing notions of what counts as a poem. A number of the debates on this issue can be organized under the heading of a broader argument over the relation between aesthetics and politics. Are poems marked by transcendence, timelessness, and universality or by immanence, historicity, and instrumentality? Are aesthetics and politics mutually exclusive categories? Is the "root-occasion" of the poem a heightened personal experience or a public polemic? Which occasion is deemed the legitimate province of poetry?

The question of what constitutes poetry can perhaps be illustrated by a look at the critical reception of Asian American poetry of the 1960s and 1970s. Variously characterized as "activist poetry," "populist poetry," or "protest poetry," the work of writers such as Janice Mirikitani, Merle Woo, and Al Robles was largely relegated by mainstream critics to the sidelines of the American poetry scene.[10] In this regard, they shared the fate of much protest poetry from other marginalized groups of the period. In the reductive either/or binarism of aesthetics versus politics (a binarism that privileges aesthetics as its primary term and that is frequently rendered as an opposition between elitism and populism), they were perceived to be squarely on the side of politics. Within the evaluative framework of official verse culture of the period, their work was deemed short on craft and long on identity politics. The status of their work as poetry was deemed questionable. Far from being difficult or elitist in the modernist mode, the work was more likely to be speech-centered, democratized in terms of subject matter, and characterized by informal diction and direct reference in the service of class-, race-, or gender-based oppositional politics. Much of the critics' reluctance to authorize this work as poetry may have stemmed both from an enduring modernist legacy that upheld complex formal structures, impersonality, irony, and intellect as the benchmarks of legitimate poetry and from the vestigial claims of a postwar aestheticism.

At the same time, to characterize Asian American production of the 1970s as largely an "activist" poetry would be doing a disservice to the variety of work published in that period. A brief perusal of a range of work from this period—including Lawson Fusao Inada's *Before the War* (1971); John Yau's *Crossing Canal Street* (1973) and *Sometimes* (1979); Wong May's *A Bad Girl's Book of Animals* (1969; alphabetized under *Wong*), *Reports* (1972), and *Superstitions* (1978); James Masao Mitsui's *Crossing the Phantom River* (1978); Ai's *Cruelty* (1973) and *Killing Floor* (1979); and Nellie Wong's *Dreams in Harrison Railroad Park* (1977)—clarifies how problematic the work of literary periodization and canon formation can be. From the jazz-inflected cadences of Inada's poems, to Yau's continual processing of identity through a poetics driven by jarring juxtapositions, chance association, and disjunctive narrative, to the prominent play and display of masks and personae in Ai's work, to the poetic line reminiscent of William Carlos Williams and Robert Creeley that surfaces frequently in Wong May's poems, to the local, minimalist details that inexorably add up to the weight of recognition in Mitsui's work, and to Wong's images of the ordinary that are pulled up short by ironic epiphanies, the range of poetic styles and themes here resist conflation. The characterization of the period's work as "activist," "populist," or "protest" poetry stemmed in part from social and political exigencies of the time. In the context of an emergent Asian American movement, literary work that foregrounded immediate social and political realities and that thus helped to galvanize this social movement was far more likely to receive attention—from Asian American and non–Asian American critics alike—than work that was less ostensibly driven by identity politics.

In "Versions of Identity in Post-activist Asian American Poetry," George Uba narrates a shift within Asian American poetry from an activist to a postactivist poetics. The impetus behind activist poetry of the late 1960s and early 1970s is to be found in "not only politics in the conventional sense but also the politics of poetry" (34). Uba identifies some possible sources of modal difficulties when he refers to Janice Mirikitani's "embracing [of] polemic" as a contestation of "standard Euro-American definitions of poetry" and to her reliance on "political slogans and the rhetoric of abstraction" as a "violat[ion of] the contemporary 'rules' of poetry" (34).[11] Mirikitani's work operates out of a " 'tribal' impulse common to poets of the late 1960s and early 1970s, an impulse that highlighted the 'shared experience[s] of subjugation' among people of color and that actively sought to 'unlock the [. . .] key to memory and to provide a base for unity' " (34–35). This tribalism, with its possibilities for contesting and resisting the normalizing imperatives of a dominant culture, proved to be a "common way of negotiating identity" (35). In part because of radical demographic changes within the Asian American population over the past two decades, the earlier base for unity could no longer function as a social adhesive. In the absence of that sense of a unified pan-Asian identity, more recent Asian American writers "have been thrust back upon their sense of an individual self. [. . .] Joined with a loss of faith in the efficacy of language as an agent of social reform and as a reliable tool of representation, this individualizing tendency has redirected poets toward Euro-American poetics" (35).[12] The "reification of the 'tribal' has become increasingly problematic" for postactivist poets who, in a postmodernist and deconstructivist turn, can no longer ratify the stability of identity. Instead, writers like Marilyn Chin, David Mura, and John Yau believe that "identity, whether tribal or otherwise, is always in doubt" (35). Uba is careful to note, however, that this new stance toward identity does not imply a lack of interest in questions of identity by these poets. Rather, "for Chin and Mura—although in different ways—conceiving identity is only possible by foregrounding its partialities, while for Yau every version of identity is radically contestable because of the unstable nature of the tools used to conceptualize it" (35–36).[13]

Even critics attuned to the aesthetic and political projects of Asian American poets of the 1970s, however, may find themselves on occasion representing those projects in ways that are at odds with their own critical intentions. The fulcrum of Uba's argument consists of the set of conditions that give rise to "postactivist" poetry—that is, the increasingly heterogeneous makeup of the Asian American population, "the absence of geographical centers" for Asian Americans, and a growing skepticism among poets concerning the "efficacy of language as an agent of social reform and as a reliable tool of representation" (35). The transition from a speech-based to a text-based poetry and poetics—that is, from one dominant version of Asian American identity to another—turns on this particular set of conditions. The implicit point in Uba's argument is that both activist and postactivist poetries are responses to their respective historical moments. However, because Uba does not make explicit the relation between a set of formal choices (whether the forms are polemical and performance-oriented or self-reflexive and text-oriented) and the sociohistorical formations within which those choices emerge, the reader is left to infer a developmental narrative line in that shift from activist to postactivist, an inference based not on Uba's implicit argument but on a rhetorical economy that sometimes shadows the main argument. The implied narrative line is generated out of a set of binary oppositions that set up a hierarchical progression from activist to postactivist status. A binary scheme that rhetorically lines up activist poetry with "raw energy" and "shock tactics" and postactivist poetry with "sophistication" and "finesse" lends itself to being read as a recapitulation of the politics-aesthetics divide, with the second term being privileged as developmental end point. Uba's characterization of the turn from an earlier politicized aesthetic whose procedural modes include "confront[ing]," "resist[ing]," and "violat[ing]" to a contemporary aestheticized politics whose procedural modes include "appropriat[ing]," "complicating," and "destabiliz[ing]" (34, 35, 37) recalibrates oppositionality and unwittingly traces out a coming-of-age narrative that can work to both naturalize processes of historical engagement and collapse the diversity of poetic production in these two periods.

The presence of this shadow narrative in Uba's article seems all the more unintended in the light of another essay, "The Representation of Asian American Poetry in *The Heath Anthology of American Literature*," where Uba critiques the shadowy presence of a related developmental narrative underlying the *Heath Anthology*'s selection of Asian American works:

> In one version of this narrative, the "development" of Asian American poetry begins with the oral poetry of the Angel Island Chinese, proceeds to the orally-based protest poetry of [Janice] Mirikitani, and "culminates" first in [Garrett] Hongo's efforts at cultural retrieval and then in [Cathy] Song's concentration on the family, in which the vexed process of assimilation continues. (192)

Uba reads these selections as the particular coordinates of a narrative of development, a narrative that enables this body of work's "assimilation into existing paradigms of American literature" (189). In this article, Uba questions the form and function of literary anthologies, especially teaching anthologies like the *Heath*. In pointing to this "hidden" narrative of development, Uba points out that marginalized literatures can easily become incorporated into "master narratives of American literature" (189). Incorporation of this sort leads not to "decanonization" but to "recanonization"— that is, the reconfirmation of an existing canonical "national literature" in which Asian American poetry figures as simply one more building block in the "fiction of inclusiveness" that underwrites the master narrative (189).[14] Uba's critical concerns here are twofold. First, teachers who use the *Heath Anthology* and who are unfamiliar with Asian American poetry may read these poets as "representative" of Asian American poetry or as the "touchstones" or "highwater marks" of Asian American poetry (188). Second, teachers and readers alike may read this particular grouping of selections as a narrative of historical eventuation whereby the story of Asian American poetry begins with the "non-professional" poets of the Angel Island immigration detention center, who wrote primarily to "bemoan" their plight, moves on to the polemic and didacticism of Janice Mirikitani's protest poetry, and finds its end point in Garrett Hongo, "who is 'concerned as much with his craft as with his message'" (187, 186), and in Cathy Song's private lyricism. These possibilities for "misreading" the work of individual poets as well as Asian American poetry as a whole have Uba asking how to "support and maintain the idea of a decanonical, or at least a perpetually negotiable, Asian American literature while still maintaining the currency of such literature in the marketplace of the university" (190).

Treating these problems of anthologizing as a particular kind of contingent difficulty, Uba speculates:

> Situated in a recognizable, if fluid, geographic, cultural and psychological locale, these writers necessarily will constitute diverse—and often oppositional—voices; they will be liberated from the shackles of a master narrative of American literature, yet at the same time be permitted their full range of differences not only from one another but from those who choose not to write at all. (191)

Here, Uba argues for the necessity of informed and contextualized readings if Asian American poets are to be relieved of the burden of "representativeness." This call for contextualized readings resonates with the point that David Mura makes in "The Margins at the Center, the Center at the Margins: Acknowledging the Diversity of Asian American Poetry" about the need to recognize the differing sets of expectations characterizing various interpretive communities (173) and the corresponding need to read Asian American poetry "against the backdrop of a multiplicity of contexts" (181). Mura's article discusses a variety of linguistic, cultural, institutional, and political circumstances that can limit readers' recognitions of the diversity or range of contemporary Asian American poetry. In the course of that discussion, Mura touches on different facets of each of Steiner's types of difficulty.

As a way of heading off contingent difficulties, Mura suggests that readers cultivate a variety of referential fields that would enable them to read Asian American poetry within the contexts of Asian American literature, American literature (or American literatures), and world literature. Given the "hybrid cultural history and experience" of many Asian American poets (173), this continual cross-referencing could richly complicate our understandings of the aesthetic and political dimensions of their work. One of the modal difficulties that Mura identifies concerns a particular manifestation of misreading Asian American poetry, one that returns us to the binary opposition between aesthetics and politics. In Mura's discussion, such a difficulty emerges when readers subscribe to an "ethnic studies model" that views Asian American poetry "solely from a social/historical" perspective. This perspective, according to Mura, requires Asian American poetry to "delineate a representative reality or experience" (172). In the introduction to *The Open Boat: Poems from Asian America*, Garrett Hongo spells out this ethnic studies model in greater detail by providing a caricatural "profile" of what he sees as an ethnic studies interpretive community's idea of an Asian American writer:

> Roughly, the profile was this: the Asian American writer was an urban, homophobic male educated at a California state university who identified with Black power and ethnic movements in general; he wrote from the perspective of a political and ethnic consciousness raised in the late sixties; he was macho; he was crusading; he professed community roots and allegiances; he mocked Eurocentrism and eschewed traditional literary forms and diction in favor of innovation and an exclusively colloquial style; his identity was stable and secure, a personification of a specific geographical region and an ethnic ethos; and, though celebrated in the Asian American "movement," his work was widely unrecognized by the "mainstream." (xxxi)

Mura finds in the anthology *Forbidden Stitch: An Asian-American Women's Anthology* an example of such misreading. There, the editors Shirley Geok-lin Lim and Mayumi Tsutakawa point out that in the process of assembling the anthology, they "had to by-pass some manuscripts reflecting experimental forms, some by very young writers, and some which did not carry a recognizable Asian voice." Responding to this editorial policy, Mura asks, "Why this prejudice against experimental poetics? How do we decide what is a 'recognizable Asian voice' and that this voice must somehow subscribe to certain aesthetic assumptions?" (172). To read Lim and Tsutakawa's statement of editorial principles as an example of the ethnic studies model of reading in action oversimplifies a complex of issues that takes in questions of identity politics, principles of editorial selection, and the role of literary anthologies in the processes of canon formation. To begin with, while an aversion to "experimental forms" might well mark the kind of writing favored by readers holding to the ethnic studies model (Hongo), as well as the kind of poetry featured in ethnic studies courses (Mura), might not this aversion equally be a defining feature of an anthology based on new formalist principles of selection? Similarly, unless we necessarily correlate "young writers" with "experimental forms," could we not equally plausibly attribute this principle of selection to matters of marketability, with the understanding that older, more established writers are likely to ring up more sales? The last principle of selection—"a recognizable Asian voice"—is the one most likely to secure Mura's point here. The criterion of a distinctive voice signals the anthology's concern with the politics and poetics of identity. My point here, though, in scrutinizing Mura's questions is neither to invalidate the questions per se nor to sanction a particular editorial practice but, rather, to try to recast and foreground a set of issues that is presently obscured by the demonizing of this ethnic studies model of literary production and consumption. These issues include the continuing recourse by both Asian American and non–Asian American critics to an opposition between aesthetics and politics, the politics of anthologizing, and the formation of literary canons.

Garrett Hongo's introduction to *The Open Boat*, with its more extended and more polemical critique of the ethnic studies model, provides a useful ground for recasting these issues. There, as in most other citings of this phenomenon, the model is constituted rhetorically rather than analytically. Invoked with all the ritual force of an intellectual bugaboo but displaying little of the analytical purchase of systematic critique, Hongo's notion of a hegemonic ethnic studies approach appears as a straw man in a miscast argument over literary authority; it is miscast in the sense that some of the principal actors in the struggle over literary authority fall outside the frame of intragroup conflict that Hongo dramatizes here. The specific event that catalyzed Hongo's public pronouncements on this issue was the 1991 Asian American Writers' Conference—"Shaping Our Legacy"—organized largely by students at the University of California, Berkeley. Hongo's main criticism of the event stemmed from his observation of a "troubling [. . .] interpretation that kept cropping up" throughout the conference. For Hongo, that interpretation produced a narrative that valorized a "politically radical, socially relevant, filially pietistic master writer" working in the service of "an idealized fiction called 'the community.'" This narrative essentially "flattened significant differences" among the writers in attendance (xxxiv). Hongo then names the three dominant critical assumptions maintained by an ethnic studies interpretive approach, assumptions that, taken together, add up to "fascism, intellectual bigotry and ethnic fundamentalism":

> 1) an unconscious assumption that what was *essentially* Asian American was a given work's overt political stance and conformity to sociological models of the Asian American experience, 2) the related notion that a writer writes from a primary loyalty to coherent communities, and 3) vehement castigation or rude, categorical dismissal for literary qualities deemed "assimilationist" or "commercial." It was, to me, significant that Bharati Mukherjee and Maxine Hong Kingston, members of the Berkeley faculty and writers of complicated fictions, were not invited to participate in the conference.   (xxxv)

From a pedagogical standpoint, what is of interest here in relation to Hongo's pronouncements is the effect of such polemics on what we come to regard as Asian American poetry and how we come to read it. The following discussion of Hongo's essay takes up three tasks: to identify the rhetorical strategies through which an ethnic studies straw man is constructed; to suggest some possible reasons for this particular demonization; and to note some of the possible effects of this demonization.

In "Hitting Critical Mass," Victor Bascara (one of the student organizers of the Berkeley conference) takes Hongo to task for misrepresenting the agendas of both the conference and its organizers. Bascara points out one of the main rhetorical strategies behind Hongo's "misrepresentations" when he asks, "Must we continually demonize, otherize and polarize to claim an exclusivity of insight?" (26). Behind Bascara's question is the recognition that "dichotomies are exercises in power and at the same time their disguise" (Sarap 101). Hongo does, indeed, set up rhetorical oppositions throughout his essay, oppositions that function largely to reinforce a base opposition between aesthetics and politics with the poets on the one side and the sociologically minded ethnic studies critics on the other side. In his staging of the confrontation between aesthetics and politics, Hongo marshalls dichotomies such as "art"/"social," "literary"/ "political," "delight" / "bitterness and anger," "complicated fictions" / "idealized fiction," "cosmopolitan"/"parochial," "individual"/"community," "unique"/"conformist," "bricolage"/"essentialism," and "new"/"outdated"—to cite just a few (xx, xxiii, xxx, xxxiii–viii, xl–xli). While Hongo generally privileges the first term of these pairings, his claim to "exclusivity of insight," or to literary authority, does not rest there. Authority is vested instead in the figure Hongo constructs who both emerges from and transcends these polar opposites, in the figure who is able to see the values and the shortcomings of both terms. In the essay, Hongo takes care to note his "movement roots" (xxxvi) in Asian American politics as well as his aesthetic roots in literature and creative writing departments. He takes equal care to note his resistance to the blandishments of an academic mainstream that patronizingly views his concern with identity politics as " 'going ethnic' on them," as well as to the "fascism" of an ethnic studies institution that views mainstream recognition of Asian American poets as a "sign of a given writer's personal assimilation of an insidious bourgeois culture and a corruption of that which is the 'authentic' literary culture of Asian America—something that stands defiantly and belligerently apart from the world of mainstream American letters" (xxi, xxxv).

This rhetorical balancing act enables Hongo to vest in himself, as the editor of a poetry anthology, the necessary authority to make particular selections and to define a canon. What remains unarticulated in Hongo's depiction of Asian American literary debates, however, is precisely this issue of literary authority. In the essay, he refers to a "kind of secondary system of literary authority *within* Asian America" constituted by the "ethnic presses, university ethnic studies programs, vanguard student groups, and community arts centers" (xxx–xxxi). What is left unstated is the location of a "primary" system of literary authority. At issue here is a larger debate within American poetry over who controls the formation of canons. In *From Outlaw to Classic: Canons in American Poetry*, Alan Golding suggests that recent thinking about canon formation in American poetry can be divided into two main schools of thought:

> One school holds that the process of canon formation, at least in this century, is governed by academic institutions. According to this view, teacher-critics shape canons through their criticism, reviewing, and teaching, while anthologies, the publishing industry generally, grant-giving agencies, and the structuring of English studies according to "field" all make up related parts of what one might call the institutional model for understanding canon formation. The other, which I shall call the aesthetic or poet-based model, holds that poetic canons are mainly the creation of poets themselves. (45)[15]

For Hongo, the primary system of literary authority left unstated earlier is finally named toward the end of the essay when he writes, "It is [. . .] left to us, as a new generation of writers, to provide cultural interpretations from a variety of perspectives" (xxxiii).

Given a long-standing suspicion of the academy by creative writers, we might be able to attribute the demonization of ethnic studies to its institutional location. However, that would not explain Hongo's embrace of other institutional sites such as the grant- or award-giving agencies, creative writing programs, and publishers he lists with approbation in his discussion of the recent spate of recognition accorded work by Asian American poets (xxxiii). Clearly, there must be differences among these different institutional sites—one of which is the kind and the degree of legitimacy it is within the power of each to confer. Bascara's speculation that Hongo's criticisms of the Berkeley conference stem from Hongo's "not wanting his sublime selections of poetry [in *The Open Boat*] to be read as academica and marginality[-]dependent Asian American protest literature" points toward these issues of legitimacy (27). It would seem that to be associated with the institutional site known as ethnic studies is to have one's poetry read primarily as a political or sociological artifact. Hongo's editorial mission is to ensure that Asian American poets be "collected together" and read in a "literary context" (xxx).[16] While sharing some of Hongo's apprehensions about the potential fallout from the association of Asian American poetry with ethnic studies, Mura gets closer to the provenance of the unease generated by this association when he remarks on "the ways certain white critics have characterized the aesthetics of poets of color as naive; in this way, postmodernist deconstructions of narrative or the lyric 'I' are often used as tools to silence or marginalize unruly voices, to keep the disenfranchised from speaking." Unlike Hongo, Mura acknowledges the presence of other "orthodoxies" that can be as limiting in their prescriptiveness as the ethnic studies model he identified earlier (173). The identification of ethnic poetry and ethnic studies programs with politics, aesthetic naïveté, and sociological-mindedness affords Asian American writing little literary purchase within the dominant strains of Anglo-American poetry. For example, we could look to some comments by Eliot Weinberger, the editor of *American Poetry since 1950: Innovators and Outsiders* (1993), as an instance of how ethnic poetry is received in some American poetry quarters today. In a discussion of the politics of both aesthetically revisionist anthologies and identity-based anthologies, Golding writes:

> Weinberger is the one editor of an aesthetically innovative anthology actively to dismiss the validity of identity-based selective criteria. In a surprising twist of logic (not to mention history), Weinberger argues that creative writing programs have produced a literary multiculturalism under which "poets, especially bad poets, tend to distinguish themselves from the mob not by aesthetic beliefs and practices, but according to extra-literary categories such as ethnic background and sexual preference" (405). [. . .] Weinberger's [. . .] suspicion of a poetic diversity "based on ethnicity, not poetry" (406) reaffirms the structural opposition of "ethnicity" and "poetry" and [. . .] leads him to repeat traditional defenses of a predominantly white male canon: "Those who count heads according to gender and race should first consider how many poets genuinely qualify within these chronological limits" [i.e., 1950–the present].
> (31)

In principle, few would object to Hongo's attacks on prescriptiveness or his efforts to unmask the sources of that prescriptiveness. His efforts become problematic, however, when they begin to obscure more than they reveal. In hailing the current spate of institutional recognition as "progress" and decrying the ethnic studies approach (as if ethnic studies were a univocal interpretive community) as the primary obstacle to the continued efflorescence of Asian American poetry, Hongo effectively mystifies the complex ways in which other critical "orthodoxies," institutional circumstances, socio-historical conditions, and his own institutional position function to determine what Asian American poetry is and how it is to be read.

While canonicity can condition readers' literary expectations, the normativity of language can condition the writer's available means of expression.[17] Mura opens his article by quoting James Baldwin's contention, "No true account really of black life can be held, can be contained in the American vocabulary" (171). For Mura, this statement encapsulates one of the major tactical difficulties encountered by Asian American as well as African American writers:

> Any poet who wants to describe that experience must somehow violate the accepted practice of the language, must bring into the language an alien vocabulary and syntax, rhythms that disrupt, images which jar, ideas which require totally new relationships to language and the reality it contains.
>
> (171–72)

In acknowledging that many, if not most, poets will of necessity confront the vexing problem of committing private being to public language, we cannot overlook the fact that the encounter will be inflected or conditioned by gender, race, class, nationality, and sexuality. How, then, might the conjunction of the writer's intention and the "impersonal and resistant medium of [the English] language" write itself out in the work of Asian American poets (Shetley 8)? In what ways might a given language or genre prove resistant?

A brief look at the lyric suggests something of that resistance. A growing skepticism over the referentiality of language and a reevaluation of the status of the lyric "I" have been critical commonplaces within recent poetry discussions. Norman Finkelstein has read some of the recent changes in the conception of a lyric "I" through Fredric Jameson's theory of the cultural logic of late capitalism—specifically, his observation that "one of the distinctions between the modern and the postmodern can be observed in 'the dynamics of cultural pathology,' which 'can be characterized as one in which the alienation of the subject is displaced by the fragmentation of the subject'" (4). But is the lyric "I" figured in the same way in all poetries? In relation to Asian American poetry, should we be asking whether or not the alienated "I" has been displaced by the fragmented "I"? Or should we be asking whether or not there was a lyric "I" to be alienated? That is, has the lyric "I" of Asian American poetry consistently been figured, or received, as a singular, unified, autonomous consciousness and identity? What are the aesthetic and sociopolitical ramifications of speaking from a unified or a fragmented "I"?

These questions very quickly reveal how tactical difficulty spills over into ontological difficulty. That is, in what way might the "American language" be the "butcher's tongue" or an "environment of eroded speech" for writers like Baldwin or Mura (Steiner 44)? What is the relation between being and performative means? Here, I propose two conceptual footings for thinking through these questions—one anecdotal, the other textual. The anecdote has to do with an elderly Chinese Canadian immigrant, an "old-timer," who tells the story of his learning to say "see you tomorrow." He observes that he taught himself to say "see you tomorrow" by intoning a homonymous phrase from his native Hoiping dialect, a phrase that might be rendered orthographically as something on the order of "si yiu doo maw la." The practice of substituting a set of sounds from one language for that of another is a common enough mnemonic device for those learning a new language, particularly for those not literate in the new language. Generally, the homonyms are selected almost exclusively on the basis of sound, with little regard for their semantic value. In this particular case, the sequence of homonyms "si yiu doo maw la" happened to form a coherent, meaningful utterance. It means "there's not even any soy sauce left." The paradoxical nature of this particular substitution is striking. In learning to say "see you tomorrow," one is learning to anticipate—in English—a future presence. In uttering "si yiu doo maw la," one learns to anticipate that future presence by acknowledging—in Chinese—a depletion, a present absence. What we see here is the operation of linguistic cleaving— or, one might even venture to say, ontological cleaving.[18]

The work of Li-young Lee and David Mura, for instance, can be viewed as working out of a poetics of cleaving or a poetics of negation. In Lee's work, for example, particularly in his second book, *The City in Which I Love You*, that cleaving is continually enacted in the action of what the Asian Canadian poet Fred Wah, in another context, calls a "synchronous axe" that simultaneously divides and binds father and son, past and present, Asia and the United States, self and other. In Lee's poems, the voice or voices emerge from the poems worn ragged by a dialectical tension and incapable of being dissolved or resolved in any final synthesis. The poetic utterance here is characterized by its ability and need simultaneously to say and not say.

The second footing comes by way of Franz Kafka's comments on the linguistic conundrum confronting the German Jewish writer. Kafka considered the German Jewish writer's use of the German language as the "overt or covert, or possibly self-tormenting usurpation of an alien property, which has not been acquired but stolen, (relatively) quickly picked up, and which remains someone else's possession even if not a single linguistic mistake can be pointed out" (qtd. in Arendt 31). While a certain degree or kind of linguistic alienation characterizes any writer's relation to an impersonal or public language, sociohistorical circumstances and specificities of race, class, gender, sexual orientation, and nationality affect that relation in particular ways. Within the context of Asian American writing, linguistic cleaving involves not only the ontologically intractable problem of rendering one's subjectivity in a largely imper-

300

sonal and public language but also the politically intractable problem of writing in a language that is not necessarily seen by the dominant group as the legitimate cultural property of Asian Americans. The ability to speak and write in English is not always accompanied by the cultural authority to do so. Perhaps for reasons as benign as the lack of a common alphabet or Indo-European root (though a number of other reasons having to do with the orientalist legacy of colonialism and imperialism also come to mind), Asian languages are generally seen as decidedly more foreign to English than, say, other European languages are. This attribution of a radical foreignness or otherness to Asian languages (and Asians or Asian Americans) can influence the way Asian American literature is received by a mainstream audience.

A certain degree of linguistic alienation is unavoidable if we concede the ever-present tension between the abstract dictionary definition of words and their actual day-to-day usage. This tension is further complicated or reconfigured when a particular language—such as English—is deemed the cultural territory of a dominant group in a given society. To the extent that an Asian American user of the language may be seen as an outsider within that cultural territory, we may characterize the Asian American poet's existence in the English language as one of estrangement. Far from being an isolated phenomenon, this sense of being estranged or alienated in language can be seen in poems as varied—thematically and stylistically—as Li-Young Lee's "Persimmons" (*Rose*), Wing Tek Lum's "Translation," Garrett Hongo's "Ninety-Six Tears" (*River*), Mei-mei Berssenbrugge's "Chronicle," Marilyn Chin's "Barbarian Suite," Timothy Liu's "Celan," and Jessica Hagedorn's "Song for My Father." For many Asian American poets, then, the performative means is inadequate to their intentions for reasons more specific than the "shopworn" nature of the English language.

At the end of his article, Mura returns art to the social when he makes a plea for poetry as "equipment for living" (182). The phrase, I gather, alludes to Kenneth Burke's essay "Literature as Equipment for Living."[19] For Burke, a literary work is the strategic naming of a social situation: "It singles out a pattern of experience that is sufficiently representative of our social structure, that recurs sufficiently often *mutatis mutandis*, for people to 'need a word for it,'" and "each work of art is the addition of a word to an informal dictionary" (259). The creation of the new word may necessitate the "chang[ing of] the rules of the game until they fit [the writer's] own necessities" (257). Mura's opening epigraph from which I drew the earlier Baldwin statement gains resonance here:

> You see, whites want black artists to mostly deliver something as if it were the official version of the black experience. But the vocabulary won't hold it, simply. No true account really of black life can be held, can be contained in the American vocabulary. As it is, the only way that you can deal with it is by doing great violence to the assumptions on which the vocabulary is based. But they won't let you do that. And when you go along, you find yourself very quickly painted into a corner; you've written yourself into a corner. (171; Baldwin 204)

For Burke, strategic naming involves fighting and writing oneself out of that corner: "The most highly alembicated and sophisticated work of art, arising in complex civilizations, could be considered as designed to organize and command the army of one's thoughts and images, and to so organize them that one 'imposes upon the enemy the time and place and conditions for fighting preferred by oneself'" (257). The matter of tactical difficulties raised by Mura finds a theorist in Burke.

The massive social, cultural, and political dislocations and realignments characterizing the end of the twentieth century call for new strategic namings, new "words" to enable us to see into the conditions of our own time and place and to clear the ground for future possibilities. The point of this essay is to size up the situation (as Burke would say) and to plot a few analytical coordinates for what to expect or what to look for when teaching Asian American poetry. This discussion of types of difficulties is by no means exhaustive, nor is it intended to be. It may be enough, though, if it can contribute in some measure to introducing students to Asian American poetry as "equipment for living."

Notes

I would like to thank Barry Maxwell for the numerous ways in which he has contributed to this article.

1. In saying this, I am not suggesting that the evolving fortunes of American poetry in this century function as a master narrative within which Asian American poetry appears as simply one of many seamlessly interwoven story lines. Clearly, the coordinates I have noted map out the contours of certain dominant schools of twentieth-century American poetry. Engaging in this kind of literary periodization would mask what could more accurately be described as the uneven development of a variety of alternative or countercanonical postwar poetries. The various ethnic and social movements of the 1960s and 1970s, for instance, can be seen as instrumental in the making of new poetry audiences and new poetic practices.

2. In the light of the function of a resource guide, some attention to problems one might encounter in the teaching of Asian American poetry and to some of the critical debates within Asian American poetry seems appropriate. The present discussion complements the survey of Asian American poetry that follows, by George Uba. Brief surveys of Asian American poetry can also be found in the essays by Chow and Chang. Chow's entry is organized around the principle of nationality, with separate sections devoted to Chinese American, Japanese American, Korean American, and Filipino American poets. The discussion elucidates common themes in these respective bodies of work. Chang includes a short narrative history of Asian American poetry. See also the essay by Lim for a selected bibliography of Asian American poetry. In choosing to discuss the broader contours of critical debates within Asian American poetry, I have not taken up all the existing scholarship on this body of work. Some of the work that is not directly discussed appears in the bibliography.

3. Chang notes, for instance, that in the 1960s and 1970s "poetry was considered an

important vehicle for expressing the politicization of race." She goes on to remark that by the late 1970s and early 1980s, poetry began to yield its preeminence "when prose fiction became a prevalent means of circulating narratives of racial difference among a larger audience" (81). Chang follows this observation with a short discussion of some of the social, cultural, and economic factors contributing to the popularization and promotion of certain prose forms by Asian American writers.

4. The complexity, not to mention ferocity, of current debates about canonicity would take me far afield of my more modest project here. As part of a discussion of contingent difficulties in the latter part of this article, however, I address the role of poetry anthologies and other institutional mechanisms in the making of canons.

5. Shetley's use of Steiner's essay in his study of the relation between contemporary poets and audiences has been very helpful for some of the early parts of this discussion.

6. Whether or not this material will ever pass into common knowledge is a question to be debated on at least two related fronts: in the politics of multiculturalism and the epistemological stakes of "common" knowledge.

7. In posing the issue of misunderstanding in terms of "literary" material needing to be supplemented by explanatory "non-literary materials" of a sociological, anthropological, or political nature, Lim sets up a binary opposition that the author herself, at different points in the article, finds dubious if not untenable. This inconsistency in the discussion undermines her efforts to argue for the equal merits of "ethnic" and "American" poetry (see, e.g., the reference to T. S. Eliot [56]). This binary opposition reveals another of its facets in Lim's subsequent distinction between "literary values" and "ideological values": "To say [that the Asian American referential field must be acknowledged if the literary merits of the work are to be recognized] is not to deny that literary values take precedence in a literary evaluation of a text, but it does bring to question the privileging of certain ideological values in literary criticism as it is practiced today; values which emphasize the European-based literary canon and debase and ignore literary effects and criteria which are non-European" (56). The article's implicit argument for contingent reading practices is frequently thwarted by a vestigial New Critical lexicon and practice that continue to naturalize and valorize the "literary" even as the article tries to argue for the opposite—that is, the contingency of literary evaluation.

8. Lim's discussion of "Asianness" in her article is marked by an ambivalence about the place of Asianness in a Euro-American context. At times, markers of Asianness are rendered as positives that enable Asian American writers to resist absorption by a dominant culture. At other times, the appearance of these markers are seen as "first language intrusions" (54–55) or as trafficking in "easy exoticism" (52) or "local color" (53). This ambivalence can be seen too in Lim's discussion of Cathy Song's and Charles Olson's respective poetic practices: "In Cathy Song's prize-winning first book of poems, Picture Bride, we find the attempt to reach for the tastes, smells, sounds, and colors of Asian-American experience expressing itself in images of Asian-American particulars: 'The children are the dumplings /[. . .] Wrap the children / in wonton skins, bright quilted bundles.' [. . .] The danger in this stylistic venture rises from an over-dependence on linguistic conventions; these ethnic images appear as isolated devices unrelated to the poems' integral unfolding. Jade, sour plums, mah-jongg [sic], tofu, and Buddha begin to attract too much self-conscious attention and to substitute for the poetic explosions of meaning found elsewhere in her work" (53). On the same page, Lim writes: "It is paradoxically only when the ethnic references in a work

become extra-local or when the force of that ethnocentred culture becomes a creative localism that the critic is compelled to pay mind to the presence of an underlying ethnopoetics. As Charles Olson, in a different context, put it, localism then becomes the new history and through it the writer rediscovers myth and rediscovers history" (53). My point here has less to do with Lim's particular assessments of Song's and Olson's works than with a problem that is left hidden, or unstated, in Lim's juxtaposing of these writers. What is left unstated, or is too hastily consigned to the realm of "paradox," is the question of how the "local" becomes, or takes on the force of, the "extra-local." How is it that Olson, in *The Maximus Poems*, can parlay the local color of Dogtown with its hogsheads, futtocks, bacalaos, gurry, cutwaters, and flake-racks into the "creative localism" of Gloucester and a "new history" of the United States writ large, while Cathy Song's localisms are more likely to remain "isolated devices unrelated to the poems' integral unfolding" and unable to achieve the force of the "extra-local"? What are the social and cultural conditions under which these respective writers are able, or unable, to move their localisms into universalisms? What part might race, class, or gender play in this process of representation?

9. The function of Oyama's article is primarily descriptive. In the absence of any sustained analysis of the issue of a "Japanese American" poetic voice or sensibility, Oyama's claims are supported largely by his description of thematic continuities in the body of work under discussion.

10. In the light of the by now familiar tripartite division of recent American poetry into the respective schools of language poetry, the new formalism, and the poetry of MFA or creative writing programs, I recognize the problems attending my usage of a conflationary term like *mainstream* to describe a significant bloc of producers and readers of American poetry. Each of these three groupings maintains a distinct relation to the idea of subjectivity. In an overly simplified formulation, language poetry is often said to be predicated on the deconstruction or erasure of subjectivity; the new formalism puts its poetic stock in the ability of traditional verse forms to adequately embody subjectivity; and the poetry of creative writing programs works from the assumption that subjectivity can still be embodied in meaningful ways, especially through the vehicle of the lyric or the "voice poem." In the context of continuing cultural fragmentation within the United States and of the sheer volume today of so-called marginalized poetries that question the organizing notion of "centers" and "margins," I use the term *mainstream* to designate the strains of Anglo-American poetry (whether contemporary or of an earlier period) whose dominance is reflected in their institutional preeminence.

11. Phrases like "standard Euro-American definitions of poetry," and "the contemporary 'rules' of poetry" could be construed as mere straw men, or empty counters, in an argument concerning the respective power of different groups to define the nature of poetry or literature. Commentators on twentieth-century American poetry could no doubt find common ground in assailing the idea of a standard definition of, or a set of rules governing, American poetry of that century. While I take it that their appearance here is largely in the service of a critical shorthand, it's useful to bear in mind that there are a variety of schools of poetry that make up the dominant "mainstream" of American poetry.

12. Another factor contributing to this redirection of poetics can be found in the proliferation, in the 1970s and 1980s, of MFA and creative writing programs across the country.

13. An extended discussion of Yau's poetics can be found in Wald's essay "Chaos Goes Uncourted." Wald takes up Yau's concern with subjectivity—more specifically, Yau's "ever-changing tale of a constructed subjectivity" (145). She notes that his poetry is characteristically "linked to a deferred narrative of identity," "a poetry committed to rewriting narrative coherence as an ever-changing tale" (146).

14. In a study of the processes of canon formation in American poetry, Golding discusses how teaching anthologies serve an affirmative function for dominant literary cultures: "The teacher-editor needs to accommodate extracanonical work if he or she is to represent the current state of poetry with any accuracy. When a textbook anthology such as *Norton Anthology of Poetry* canonizes poetic outsiders, however, it renders their work culturally and intellectually harmless. What one might call this detoxification of potent work has its sources in the interpretive community's survival instinct, and the fact that if a pluralist literature is to be taught, it must be systematized. The academy ensures its own survival and that of literature by adopting a more pluralist canon. A revised canon provides new texts for exegesis and helps keep alive the whole interpretive enterprise. The textbook anthology is one tool of systematization and of the literary academy's self-perpetuation" (36). To show how a dominant institution can use multiculturalism as a management strategy, Golding cites Cary Nelson's observation that "the dominant pattern for many years for general anthologies of American literature [and, I would add, poetry anthologies] has been to seek minority poems that can be read as affirming the poet's culture but not mounting major challenges to white readers" (38).

15. Golding goes on to argue for a model of canon formation that incorporates elements of both these models. He clarifies at the outset of his discussion that this formulation is specific to a discussion of twentieth-century American poetry and is not being offered as a general theory of canon formation.

16. Hongo's call for a "literary context" within which to read Asian American poetry needs to be set against a long history of conflicting standards and motives governing the process of making selections for anthologies. Nineteenth-century American poetry anthologies, as Golding observes, were motivated by matters of historical coverage, inspirational capacity, ability to advance the cause of a national literature, and comprehensiveness. The desire for historical coverage introduced its own conflicts in the debates over poetic breadth and poetic excellence. Whereas Rufus Griswold, the editor of *The Poets and Poetry of America* (1842), was concerned with displaying the historical range of American poetry—even when that meant including work "that was comparatively poor"—Conrad Aiken, in editing *Twentieth-Century American Poetry* (1944), "dismissed purely historical considerations and asserted that the aesthetic judgment [. . .] is the only sound basis for [editorial] procedure" (Golding 24). These conflicting motives could also be seen animating the production of nineteenth-century anthologies of African American poetry. Armand Lanusse's *Les Cenelles* (1845) "define[d] black poetry as any poetry written by blacks," whereas William G. Allen's *Wheatley, Banneker, and Horton* (1849) defined "black poetry by its racial themes" (Golding 27). These differences were compounded by another issue confronting anthologists of African American poetry. Arna Bontemps, in the preface to *American Negro Poetry* (1963), asks, "Is American Negro poetry a part of American literature or isn't it?" (qtd. in Golding 29). The desire to have a body of work read within a specified context carries with it a variety of assumptions that may take on the guise of universality but that remain historically specific in their evaluative

criteria. For an extended discussion of the history of American poetry anthologies, see Golding's opening chapter.

17. In *Legends from Camp* Inada remarks on his childhood experience of the tyranny of "Standard English" (what he refers to as "across town" or "Hit Parade English"): "We were all criticized, continually corrected and ridiculed in school for the way we talked—for having accents, dialects, for misusing, abusing the language" (57).

18. This moment of linguistic cleaving finds parallels in a number of conceptual venues. W. E. B. Du Bois's formulation of "double consciousness" comes to mind, as does Mikhail Bakhtin's notion of the dialogized utterance, where an utterance is seen as the locus of contending voices rather than as the single expression of a unitary authorial voice. The utterance as site of contending voices would seem to put any unified lyric "I" forever out of the minority writer's reach.

19. Burke describes the essay as a "statement in behalf of [. . .] a *sociological* criticism of literature" (254). He argues here for the need to break down invidious disciplinary boundaries, the old "division of faculties in our universities": "We have had the Philosophy of Being; and we have had the Philosophy of Becoming. In typical contemporary specialization, we have been getting the Philosophy of the Bin" (262). Literature is to be taken out of its bin and "reintegrated" into a "general sociological picture" (256).

Bibliography

Arendt, Hannah. Introduction. *Illuminations*. By Walter Benjamin. Trans. Harry Zohn. New York: Schocken, 1969. 1–55.

Baldwin, James. "The Last Interview." *James Baldwin: The Legacy*. Ed. Quincy Troupe. New York: Simon, 1989. 186–212.

Bascara, Victor. "Hitting Critical Mass (or, Do Your Parents Still Say 'Oriental,' Too?)." *Critical Mass: A Journal of Asian American Cultural Criticism* 1.1 (1993): 3–38.

Berssenbrugge, Mei-mei. *Summits Move with the Tides*. Greenfield Center: Greenfield Review, 1982.

Burke, Kenneth. "Literature as Equipment for Living." *The Philosophy of Literary Form/ Studies in Symbolic Action*. 1941. New York: Vintage, 1957. 253–62.

Chang, Juliana. "Reading Asian American Poetry." *MELUS* 21.1 (1996): 81–98.

Chin, Frank, et al., eds. *Aiiieeeee! An Anthology of Asian-American Writers*. Washington: Howard UP, 1974.

Chin, Marilyn. *The Phoenix Gone, the Terrace Empty*. Minneapolis: Milkweed, 1994.

Chow, Balance. "Asian-American Poetry: An Overview of a Pluralistic Tradition." *Critical Survey of Poetry: English Language Series*. Ed. Frank N. Magill. Pasadena: Salem, 1992. 3913–19.

Crawford, John. "Notes toward a New Multicultural Criticism: Three Works by Women of Color." Harris and Aguero 155–95.

Epstein, Joseph. "Who Killed Poetry?" *Commentary* 86.2 (1988): 13–20.

Finkelstein, Norman. *The Utopian Moment in Contemporary American Poetry*. Lewisburg: Bucknell UP, 1993.

Golding, Alan. *From Outlaw to Classic: Canons in American Poetry*. Madison: U of Wisconsin P, 1995.

Hagedorn, Jessica Tarahata. *Dangerous Music*. San Francisco: Momo's, 1975.

Harris, Marie, and Kathleen Aguero, eds. *A Gift of Tongues: Critical Challenges in Contemporary American Poetry*. Athens: U of Georgia P, 1987.

Hongo, Garrett. Introduction. *The Open Boat: Poems from Asian America*. Ed. Hongo. New York: Anchor, 1993. xvii–xlii.

———. *The River of Heaven*. New York: Knopf, 1988.

Inada, Lawson Fusao. *Legends from Camp*. Minneapolis: Coffee House, 1992.

Lee, Li-young. *The City in Which I Love You*. Brockport: BOA, 1991.

———. *Rose*. Brockport: BOA, 1986.

Lim, Shirley Geok-lin. "Reconstructing Asian-American Poetry: A Case for Ethnopoetics." *MELUS* 14.2 (1987): 51–63.

Lim, Shirley Geok-lin, and Mayumi Tsutakawa, eds. *Forbidden Stitch: An Asian-American Women's Anthology*. Corvallis: Calyx, 1989.

Liu, Timothy. *Burnt Offerings*. Port Townsend: Copper Canyon, 1995.

Lum, Wing Tek. *Expounding the Doubtful Points*. Honolulu: Bamboo Ridge, 1987.

Mura, David. "The Margins at the Center, the Center at the Margins: Acknowledging the Diversity of Asian American Poetry." Ng et al. 171–83.

———. "A Shift in Power, a Sea Change in the Arts." *The State of Asian America: Activism and Resistance in the 1990s*. Ed. Karin Aguilar–San Juan. Boston: South End, 1994. 183–204.

Ng, Wendy L., et al., eds. *Re-viewing Asian America: Locating Diversity*. Pullman: Washington State UP, 1995.

Oyama, Richard. "Ayumi: 'To Sing Our Connections.'" Harris and Aguero 249–56.

Sarap, Madan. "Home and Identity." *Travellers' Tales: Narratives of Home and Displacement*. Ed. George Robertson, Melinda Mash, Lisa Tickner, Jon Bird, Barry Curtis, and Tim Putnam. London: Routledge, 1994. 93–104.

Schweik, Susan. "The 'Pre-poetics' of Internment: The Example of Toyo Suyemoto." *American Literary History* 1.1 (1989): 89–109.

Shetley, Vernon. *After the Death of Poetry: Poet and Audience in Contemporary America*. Durham: Duke UP, 1993.

Song, Cathy. *Picture Bride*. New Haven: Yale UP, 1983.

Steiner, George. *"On Difficulty" and Other Essays*. New York: Oxford UP, 1978.

Trotter, David. *The Making of the Reader: Language and Subjectivity in Modern American, English, and Irish Poetry*. New York: St. Martin's, 1984.

Uba, George. "The Representation of Asian American Poetry in *The Heath Anthology of American Literature*." Ng et al. 185–93.

———. "Versions of Identity in Post-activist Asian American Poetry." *Reading the Literatures of Asian America*. Ed. Shirley Geok-lin Lim and Amy Ling. Philadelphia: Temple UP, 1992. 33–48.

Wah, Fred. *Breathin' My Name with a Sigh*. Vancouver: Talonbooks, 1981. N. pag.

Wald, Priscilla. " 'Chaos Goes Uncourted': John Yau's Dis(-)orienting Poetics." *Cohesion and Dissent in America*. Ed. Carol Colatrella and Joseph Alkana. Albany: State U of New York P, 1994. 133–58.

Wallace, Patricia. "Divided Loyalties: Literal and Literary in the Poetry of Lorna Dee Cervantes, Cathy Song, and Rita Dove." *MELUS* 18.3 (1993): 3–19.

Weinberger, Eliot, ed. *American Poetry since 1950: Innovators and Outsiders*. New York: Marsilio, 1993.

Wilson, Edmund. "Is Verse a Dying Technique?" *The Triple Thinkers*. New York: Oxford UP, 1948. 15–30.

Wong, May. *A Bad Girl's Book of Animals*. New York: Harcourt, 1969.

———. *Reports*. New York: Harcourt, 1970.

———. *Superstitions*. New York: Harcourt, 1978.

Yogi, Stan. "Yearning for the Past: The Dynamics of Memory in Sansei Internment Poetry." *Memory and Cultural Politics: New Approaches to American Ethnic Literatures*. Ed. Amritjit Singh, Joseph T. Skerrett, Jr., and Robert E. Hogan. Boston: Northeastern UP, 1996. 245–65.

Zhou, Xiaojing. "Inheritance and Invention in Li-Young Lee's Poetry." *MELUS* 21.1 (1996): 113–32.

Coordinates of Asian American Poetry: A Survey of the History and a Guide to Teaching

George Uba

Historical Overview

Asian American poetry constitutes a field of study marked by a wealth of materials and a diversity of aesthetic configurations. This essay surveys the historical production and conceptual frameworks of the poetry and provides the names of authors and titles that interested parties may wish to investigate further. The second half of the essay offers a guide to the teaching of this poetry.

Because the experience of Asian Americans and Asian Canadians in North America has been so diverse and because the literary expression can be traced back over a hundred years, Asian American poetry, like the term *Asian America* itself, eludes simple definition. Whether we speak of the different categories of nation and ethnicity that help particularize the histories of Asians in America, the different socioeconomic conditions for writing, or the different charges to which that writing responds or whether we speak of multiple physical and cultural geographies or multiple languages, generations, and audiences, we are speaking of a rich, multidimensional experience. As I employ the term, Asian American poetry is writing appearing in English by a person wholly or partially of Asian ancestry who self-defines the product as poetry or verse and who has inhabited the United States or Canada.[1] Because my definition prioritizes contact with a geographical and cultural site, poetry originally composed in an Asian language but subsequently translated into English may qualify under the rubric. Despite certain obvious problems with this definition—How long must the person have been an inhabitant? At what point is "partial Asian ancestry" constituted or deconstituted? To what extent can habitational site remain a vital criterion in an age of globalization?—I believe that it may prove useful in charting the poetry's history.

Literary repute alone is an unreliable index of that history. Nevertheless, a number of Asian-descent poets publishing in English (and living in the United States or Canada) gained recognition prior to about 1970. Writing in English at the turn of the nineteenth century and several decades into the next were the prolific Japanese writers Sadakichi Hartmann and Yone Noguchi. The half-German Hartmann published poetry, drama, and fiction, while producing volumes of critical work on Japanese art and on modern landscape, sculpture, painting, and photography. His early modernist poem "To the 'Flat-Iron'" (Chang 6) simultaneously glances back toward Whitman and anticipates Hart Crane. But in the first quarter of the twentieth century he also produced hybrid, Japanese-style syllabic verse, especially hokku (also called haiku or haikai) and tanka. Noguchi, a professor of English at Keio University in Tokyo, resided in America from 1893 to 1904 and from 1919 to 1920. Producing lush fin de siècle verse in an 1897 volume entitled *Seen and Unseen*, he had by 1903, in *From the Eastern Sea*, transformed his poetry with shorter lines, a tighter focus on nature, and the liberal importation of Japanese words and memories of Japan. Like Hartmann, Noguchi wrote original hokku and tanka in English. The emergence of Japanese verse in the West, as well as Noguchi's critical writing, likely influenced Pound's imagist movement (see Hakutani).

Emerging out of the neocolonial environment of the Philippines, Jose Garcia Villa gained considerable American and British acclaim with the 1942 publication of *Have Come, Am Here*, a volume of poetry steeped in paradox and in turbulent combinations of sensuality and reverence. Subsequent volumes in the same decade included the luxuriously romantic *Appassionata: Poems in Praise of Love* (1942) and the experimental *Volume Two* (1949), marked by its expressive use of commas to regulate tonal values. Many of Villa's favorite poems subsequently were collected in *Poems Fifty-Five: The Best Poems of Jose Garcia Villa* (1962). A fellow countryman to Villa but far removed from him in political sensibility, labor experience, and personal temperament, Carlos Bulosan published two individual volumes of poetry and appeared in two collections before the publication of his celebrated autobiographical fiction, *America Is in the Heart* (1946). In *The Voice of Bataan* (1943) and especially in *Letter from America* (1942), Bulosan displays an intense lyricism while grappling with inflammatory sociopolitical issues. By the mid to late 1960s, Asian Canadians were actively publishing volumes of poetry. Starting with *The Splintered Moon* (1968), Joy Kogawa produced a corpus of meditative yet highly accessible lyric poetry that attracted a following in both the United States and Canada well before the appearance of her breakthrough novel, *Obasan* (1982). Well-received by the avant-garde, the daring, experimental works of Fred Wah and Roy Kiyooka have in recent decades commanded critical and scholarly attention.

Literary repute always begs certain questions, such as what constitutes literary merit and who controls the institutional mechanisms that produce reputation. During the late 1960s scores of young Asian American writers, most of them unheralded, were writing poetry. But even earlier, as scholarship has since shown, Asians and Asian Americans were producing poetry in North America in amounts far in excess of what a few recognized names imply, while also bringing to the fore issues of race, class, and gender.[2] In 1980 in a noteworthy feat of historical retrieval, the editors and translators Him Mark Lai, Genny Lim, and Judy Yung produced *Island: Poetry and History of Chinese Immigrants on Angel Island, 1910 to 1940*, a bilingual volume of poems and self-narratives by otherwise "anonymous" Chinese arduously attempting to pass through the immigration station at Angel Island in San Francisco Bay. The editors translated 135 poems (of which 69 were finally chosen for publication), many of them copied from the walls of the decaying barracks, which were nearly demolished. The volume was important not only as a historical document but also as a literary resource. Whereas even the impoverished, self-educated Bulosan immersed himself in American and English literature and produced poetry in various ways linked to prevailing literary traditions in English, the Angel Island poets in effect imposed a different sensibility on poetry itself: a sensibility committed neither to Western aesthetics nor to cross-cultural aesthetic exchange. While they were not necessarily uninterested in aesthetic possibilities, these writers naturalized poetry as an appropriate medium of response to conditions of exclusion and marginalization.

Another notable contribution to the literary history was the bilingual *Ayumi: A Japanese American Anthology* (1980; Mirikitani et al.), which built on what was previously known about literary activities supported by newspapers such as *Pacific Citizen* and *Rafu Shimpo*, Nisei literary magazines such as *Reimei* and *Leaves*, and internment camp publications such as the *Poston Chronicle*, *Topaz Trek*, and *All Aboard*. Demonstrating the range of pre- and postwar writings in prose and poetry, *Ayumi* focused special attention on Issei and Nisei (first- and second-generation Japanese in America) writers, including Karl Yoneda, Yuriko Takahashi, Hiroshi Kashiwagi, Toyo Suyemoto, and Iwao Kawakami. Kawakami's book *"The Parents" and Other Poems* had received newspaper-sponsored publication in 1947. Some of the poets had enjoyed prewar publication in newspapers such as New York's *Nichibei* and San Francisco's *Nichibei Times*, several had been published in Japan, and others hitherto had gone unpublished.

In 1987 Marlon K. Hom's bilingual volume *Songs of Gold Mountain: Cantonese Rhymes from San Francisco Chinatown* continued and extended the landmark efforts of literary recovery and redefinition. So too did *Poets behind Barbed Wire* (1983), Jiro Nakano and Kay Nakano's selection and translation of tanka poems written by four Hawai'i Issei interned on the mainland during the war. More recently, Juliana Chang's valuable compilation *Quiet Fire* (1996) provided further evidence of a long-standing tradition of poetic production. Subtitled *A Historical Anthology of Asian American Poetry, 1892–1970*, *Quiet Fire* reproduces the work of twenty-nine writers, nearly two-thirds of whom were writing before the end of World War II, and ranges from the imagistic lyrics of Jun Fujita to the proletarian-inflected verse of H. T. Tsiang. Implicitly, these publications proclaim several vital points: that Asian American poetry draws from a variety of cultural and linguistic traditions; that its practices often range outside the conventions established by a professionalized literary regime; and that its history frequently recounts experiences of oppression and marginalization, though they may have occurred at different moments and in different ways.

The 1970s: Claiming a Tradition

The 1970s were significant both for the acceleration of literary production and for the efforts to define an Asian American literature. In some ways the problems were compounded for poetry, since its generic attributes especially lent themselves to what readers traditionally referred to as "universality." Nevertheless, the attempts to claim a tradition of Asian American writing attested to the fact that Eurocentric standards had ceased to successfully disguise themselves as universal. The last gasps of New Critical formalism could not help but reveal the political postulates, cultural biases, and racial assumptions that had always underlain its theoretical framework. The development of a pan-Asian, Third World consciousness was the ground from which an Asian American literature was to emerge.

Fueled by the social upheavals of the late 1960s and early 1970s, including the black power and antiwar movements, nascent efforts were undertaken not merely to identify Asian American literary works but also to name an actual literary tradition. The best-known expression of these efforts came with the 1974 publication of *Aiiieeeee! An Anthology of Asian-American Writers*, edited by Frank Chin, Jeffery Paul Chan, Lawson Fusao Inada, and Shawn Hsu Wong. Although the anthology limited itself to prose fiction and dramatic excerpts and additionally confined itself to writings by Chinese Americans, Japanese Americans, and Filipino Americans, it proved instrumental in constructing a national profile for an Asian American literature. Arguing at once for an Asian American "sensibility" and an Asian American "language" differentiated equally from the Euro-American and the Asian, the anthology claimed to represent "fifty years of our whole voice" (viii).[3] The statement's significance lies less in its strict accuracy than in its resolve to contribute to the building of a coalitional literary tradition. Two of the salutary effects of this anthology and others of the era were that they promoted literary-historical scholarship and stimulated new literary production. Also appearing in 1974 was a special issue of *Yardbird Reader* devoted to multiethnic, multigeneric writing (Wong and Chin) and a literary collection entitled *Asian-American Heritage: An Anthology of Poetry and Prose* (Wand). Two years earlier, Kai-yu Hsu and Helen Palubinskas had edited the literary anthology *Asian-American Authors* as a component of a multiethnic literature series. Also featuring both prose and poetry, this anthology agreed with *Aiiieeeee!* in declaring that an "Asian-American language" was a distinguishing element of the literature (5). While neither set of editors offered a sustained analysis of the components of this putative "language," both effectively signaled the importance of orality or aurality in general, and of vernacular traditions in particular, in the production of this literature, an imputation that was to be felt with particular intensity by many of the poets who found themselves gaining "voice" in the 1970s. Thus, for example, the 1975 anthology *Time to Greez!* (Mirikitani et al.) carried the subtitle "incantations," and the 1978 anthology *The Buddha Bandits down Highway 99* (Hongo, Lau, and Inada) acknowledged in its introduction its performative features and connections with Asian American musicians.

In actuality, no set of literary conventions or identified linguistic features accommodates the full range of Asian American literature. The editors of *Aiiieeeee!*, *Asian-American Authors*, and *Asian-American Heritage* nearly conceded as much by acknowledging the different circumstances and struggles confronting Filipinos in America. The *Aiiieeeee!* staff invited Oscar Penaranda, Serafin Syquia, and Sam Tagatac to write a separate introduction for the section "Filipino-American Literature" under the premise that "only a Filipino-American can write adequately about the Filipino-American experience" (lxiii). The production staff of *Liwanag: Literary and Graphic Expressions by Filipinos in America* (1975) likewise emphasized the "distinct differences in style and content within the particular socio-cultural values and attitudes" of Filipino Americans (Cachapero et al. 9). Even in *Talk Story: An Anthology of Hawai'i's Local Writers* (Chock et al.), a poet's location within the nonmainland locale rather than, say, the use of vernacular or allegiance to a particular oral aesthetics proved paramount in determining inclusion. The publication of *Green Snow: An Anthology of Canadian Poets of Asian Origin* (1976), a book whose contributors came mainly from India, Ceylon, and Sri Lanka and whose only Asian Pacific contributor was Joy Kogawa, served as a reminder that both heritage and literary practices differ widely. Indeed, editor Stephen Gill, in sharp contrast to his counterparts in the United States, sentimentally echoed the call for universality by insisting that poets "represent humanity at large and as such they are above any age or race" and by claiming that "writing is the one field in the world where racial and colour prejudices exist the least" (10).

Obstacles notwithstanding, the effort to subsume differences under a common experience of suffering, oppression, prejudice, and discrimination and to synthesize literature as a collection of vernaculars and an instrument of critique helped galvanize an emerging sense of a coalitional literary tradition. The respective critical essays preceding the literary selections included in the interdisciplinary anthologies *Roots: An Asian American Reader* (1971; Tachiki et al.) and *Counterpoint: Perspectives on Asian America* (1976; Gee et al.) conflated description and prescription in calling for "the merging of political action and literature" as the distinguishing mark of an Asian American literature (Tachiki et al. 98). While eschewing "crude didacticism," Bruce Iwasaki, the literature editor of *Roots*, declared that Asian American literature constituted a "vigorous confrontation" between "Asian American writers and their oppressive social-literary experience," a confrontation that could ignite "qualitative social change" (Tachiki et al. 94, 95, 98). In *Counterpoint*, the same editor again identified Asian American literature with Third World "struggle," imposing on writers a "duty" to make responsible "social choices" (Gee et al. 453). Among all the earlier theorists, Iwasaki in particular viewed poetry as a principal agent of change. A spirit of coalition actuates the 1972 anthology *Third World Women*, which, in linking itself to Third World race, class, and gender struggles, sought to overcome divisions caused by "cultural nationalism" and to stimulate cooperative efforts toward liberation and self-determination (see the volume's "Editorial" section). So too with the aforementioned multicultural poetry anthology *Time to Greez! Incantations from the Third World*, which defined itself as "a coalition of Black, Raza, Asian, American Indian, and Native Island people" (Mirikitani et al. v). Two politically engaged periodicals, *Bridge Magazine*, a product of New York's Basement Workshop, and *Amerasia Journal*, eventually housed permanently at the University of California, Los Angeles, also actively promoted the concept of Asian American literature. By the end of the decade, older and newer writers' workshops had flourished or had begun flourishing across the continent and in Hawai'i. In 1979 *American Born and Foreign*, a special Asian American issue of *Sunbury: A Poetry Magazine*, appeared, offering poetry as an instrument of self-definition, while attacking the "literary establishment" and "its token system regarding 'minority' writers" (Chiang et al. xiv).

Individual poets who came to prominence in the 1970s within the emergent field of Asian American poetry included Lawson Fusao Inada, whose first book of poetry, *Before the War* (1971), was hailed for its daring fusion of Western and non-Western poetic elements. Subtitled *Poems As They Happened*, Inada's book was marked by orality and an aura of spontaneity that subverted the traditional faith in poetry's monumentalism yet also allowed Inada sufficient latitude to exploit formal possibilities inherent in the traditions of Euro-American writing. His was not the first work of poetry by an Asian American to enjoy national distribution, but it was the first to do so as serious discussions about the nature of Asian American literature were beginning to take place. His triumph became a rallying point for the genre and provided further evidence of a flourishing literature.

Among the poets who gained wider readership through "movement" literary anthologies were Mei-mei Berssenbrugge, Janice Mirikitani, Al Robles, Jessica Hagedorn, Lonny Kaneko, Ron Tanaka, Diana Chang, Wing Tek Lum, and the aforementioned Penaranda, Syquia, and Tagatac, to name a few. But the literary anthologies and Inada tell only a partial story. Berssenbrugge, for example, had published her first volume of poetry, *Fish Souls*, as early as 1971. Hagedorn was highlighted in Kenneth Rexroth's chapbook, *Four Young Women: Poems* (1973), and subsequently gained readership for individually authored collections of prose and poetry entitled *Dangerous Music* (1975) and *Pet Food and Tropical Apparitions* (1981). Mirikitani was a literary icon to many younger activists by the time her first individually authored book, *Awake in the River*, appeared in 1978.

Other Asian American poets were publishing and claiming readerships during the 1970s. The first volume of poetry by Ai (Ai Ogawa), entitled *Cruelty*, appeared in 1973, followed by *Killing Floor* in 1979, which won the Lamont Poetry Prize (awarded to a distinguished second book of poetry), and other volumes. Indian-born Meena Alexander published her first book of poetry, *The Bird's Bright Ring*, in 1976. Cyril Dabydeen published several volumes during the decade. James Masao Mitsui's first two poetry books appeared in the decade, as did Arthur Sze's first, along with Nellie Wong's *Dreams in Harrison Railroad Park* (1977) and Mitsuye Yamada's *"Camp Notes" and Other Poems* (1976).

Poetry since 1980: Present Latitudes

While many poets claimed followings during the 1970s, from the perspective of Asian American poetry's gaining a material presence among a wide general readership of non–Asian Americans, the publication of Garrett Hongo's *Yellow Light* (1982), Cathy Song's *Picture Bride* (1983), and Joseph Bruchac's *Breaking Silence: An Anthology of Contemporary Asian American Poets* marked significant moments in the literary history. In the 1980s Asian Americans began to accumulate high-profile poetry prizes in substantial numbers. Hongo had earlier won the Discovery–The Nation Prize, and Song was selected by Richard Hugo as the winner of the Yale Series of Younger Poets Award. *Breaking Silence* won an American Book Award and by its very title seemed to unsettle the binaries of silence/speech, past/present, gestation/birth that orientalism had depended on. The cluster of publications and prizes marked a convenient way of suggesting that an incipient Asian American poetry had come fully of age. At times the official sanction implied by the poetry awards encompassed volumes that differed in pronounced ways from each other, as with John Yau's *Corpse and Mirror* (1983; Yau had begun publishing poetry in the mid 1970s) and David Mura's *After We Lost Our Way* (1989), both winners in the National Poetry Series, and Hongo's *River of Heaven* (1988) and Li-Young Lee's *The City in Which I Love You* (1990), both recipients of the Lamont Award. An abbreviated list of poets publishing first volumes of poetry (many of them award-winning) since 1980 might include Agha Shahid Ali, Marilyn Chin, Sesshu Foster, Vince Gotera, Kimiko Hahn, Alan Chong Lau, Carolyn Lau (now publishing as Carolyn Lei-Lanilau), Evelyn Lau, Russell Leong, Stephen Shu-Ning Liu, Timothy Liu, Kyoko Mori, Dwight Okita, Jeff Tagami, Lois-Ann Yamanaka, and cyn. zarco.

But while the awards attest to a certain type of recognition, a brief list of anthologies appearing since 1980 conveys more of the actual latitude of Asian American poetry: *Chinese American Poetry: An Anthology* (Wang and Zhao); *Dissident Song: A Contemporary Asian American Anthology* (Chin, Louie, and Weisner); *The Forbidden Stitch: An Asian-American Women's Anthology* (Lim and Tsutakawa); *Ho'omanoa: An Anthology of Contemporary Hawai'ian Literature* (Balaz); *Living in America: Poetry and Fiction by South Asian American Writers* (Rustomji-Kerns); *On a Bed of Rice: An Asian American Erotic Feast* (Kudaka); *Paper Doors: An Anthology of Japanese Canadian Poetry* (Shikatani and Aylward); *Passages: An Anthology of the Southeast Asian Refugee Experience* (Howard); *The Very Inside: An Anthology of Writings by Asian and Pacific Islander Lesbian and Bisexual Women* (Lim-Hing); and *Without Names: A Collection of Poems* (Bay Area Pilipino American Writers). The Hawai'i-based Bamboo Ridge Press continued its impressive publication record with such collections as *The Best of Bamboo Ridge* (1986; Chock and Lum), *Paké: Writings by Chinese in Hawai'i* (1989; Chock and Lum), and *Sister Stew: Fiction and Poetry by Women* (1991; Kono and Song).

Two anthologies of the 1990s especially help to reveal the range of contemporary Asian American poetry and the different ideas governing canon formation. Both *The*

Open Boat: Poems from Asian America (1993), edited by Garrett Hongo, and *Premonitions: The Kaya Anthology of New Asian North American Poetry* (1995), edited by Walter K. Lew, feature a variety of well-known and lesser-known poets. *The Open Boat* offers a generous sampling of the work of thirty-one poets, while *Premonitions* contains the work of seventy-three (remarkably, the anthologies share only ten poets). While both works contribute to the reconsideration of the term *Asian America* in the light of literary production in English from South Asians and others, Hongo circulates familiar geographic, ethnic, and cultural markers in identifying the poets and highlights their literary awards and placement in established (sometimes well-heeled) publications. His strategy derives not from a naive desire to achieve mainstream recognition or from an inherent opposition to institutional critique as a form of literary activity but from his belief that poetry as a mode of cultural production must not be limited by its ideological alignments. Hongo's idea of an "open boat" is one whose sources lie in a wide range of cultural nationalities, whose political affiliations are various, and whose self-evident ability to exploit a primarily Western aesthetic is finally paramount. Lew, meanwhile, serves as an avant-garde editor, with his anthology featuring experimental writings and cross-disciplinary forms. Lew also includes many more names unfamiliar to readers of Asian American literature in general. Perhaps the most telling difference between the two editors is that Hongo is guided by his firm belief in each poet's individual achievement, a belief sometimes inflected by a neoromantic yearning for a transcendent lyric, while Lew attempts to fashion a postmodern field of interpenetrating, overlapping, or coalitional discourses.

Amid the swirl of contemporary publication activity, it is well to recall that the literary recovery efforts discussed in the first part of this essay have produced their greatest yield during this same period of time. The invaluable longitudinal studies, along with the persistence of a movement-era sensibility in some older and younger poets, continue to play a vital role in determining the position of Asian American poetry. From a longitudinal perspective, Asian American poetry was not absorbed into an institutional marketplace of awards and prizes, dominant poetic practices and conventions, after about 1980 but instead accelerated its efforts to reveal its range and diversity and persisted in its determination to connect poetry to history and to change. In this light we should approach the teaching of Asian American poetry as simultaneously offering a wealth of opportunity and a cautionary tale.

Teaching the Multiples of Theme and Form

In the following sections I discuss the teaching of Asian American poetry. Implicitly, I attempt to reshape some of the reading practices that bear directly on that teaching. Because of space limitations, I restrict my discussion to individual poems rather than focus on entire books. Naturally, more poets merit attention than the space here permits. Although any one poem should not be seen as representative of an entire oeuvre,

I attempt to select works that at least exemplify some of the common writing practices of a particular poet and that seem to me instructive for pedagogy.

For various reasons, teaching Asian American poetry from a thematic perspective has proved a durable approach. Elaine H. Kim's landmark critical study, *Asian American Literature: An Introduction to the Writings and Their Social Context* (1982), identifies several "recurrent theme[s]" (221) in a lengthy final chapter devoted mainly to poetry: the Vietnam War; racism, assimilation, and interminority relationships; self-definition and Third World identity; restoring foundations, intergenerational connections, and cross-national links; Asian American women's perspectives; and the cultural displacements recorded in "recent immigrant literature" (272). Kim's work offers one rearrangement of earlier thematizations, such as that employed in *American Born and Foreign: An Anthology of Asian American Poetry* (1979; Chiang et al.): working mothers and fathers, rituals, Chinatown, alienation, relationships, passion, visions. The anthology *On a Bed of Rice: An Asian American Erotic Feast* (1995; Kudaka), fashions such themes as sexual awakening, embracing the female body, the size of it, colors of love, betrayals and infidelities, and mind sex. Thematic constructions, it is well to remember, are protean by nature, necessarily shifting, retreating, expanding, and changing even as they accommodate a variety of critical modalities. In its effort to meet the dangers residing in fixed categories, the anthology *Premonitions* organizes itself around "zones" rather than themes, with each zone, according to Walter K. Lew, constituting a "discourse" initiated by brief lines or "pulses" drawn from one of the poems to follow (e.g., "sculpted / in a vertiginous light" or "my hand that close to the unconscious"). Lew maintains that the "zones are meant to bring into successive, sometimes overlapping focus a wide range of geographies, histories, genres, languages, literary networks, and ethnic or erotic subcultures, without depending on restrictive labels." Within the zones, lines from or between texts may "dissolve, echo, or crest against the entrance of the next," thereby creating a postmodern field of interpenetration, overlap, or conjunction (577).

However one may adjust such a strategy for different audiences of students, teachers would do well to think in terms of multiplying existing or familiar themes. The works of, say, Agha Shahid Ali readily embody such themes as (to borrow Kim's categories) self-definition, restoring foundations, intergenerational connections, cross-national links, and cultural displacement, but also, as the cultural production of a poet originally from Kashmir, they present these "Asian American" themes in fascinating recombinations. Conversely, a multitude of authors can converge and articulate a "new" theme. For example, many poems by Asian American male writers focus on a father or father figure. A random, highly abbreviated list might include Eric Chock's "Poem for My Father," Stephen Liu's "My Father's Martial Art," Vince Gotera's "Dance of the Letters," Li-Young Lee's "The Gift," Wing Tek Lum's "I Caught Him Once," Garrett Hongo's "Winnings," and Timothy Liu's "Men Without." Other poems, such as Oscar Penaranda's "Lakai" and "Birthday Child / Innercity Queen," Luis Syquia's "Piano Lessons," Agha Shahid Ali's "Homage to Faiz Ahmen Faiz," Hongo's "The Unreal Dwelling: My Years in Volcano," and Lawson Fusao Inada's "The

Grand Silos of the Sacramento" examine the father figure in its multiple incarnations.[4] To view such poems as a staple of poetry written by men everywhere is to misapprehend the special role they play in an Asian American history marked by culturally specific legacies of patriarchalism on the one hand and, on the other, a plague of demeaning stereotypes and discriminatory practices directed toward men of Asian ancestry. Additionally, as an internal thematic within Asian American literary history, such constructions of the father figure pose a response to the *Aiiieeeee!* editors' erstwhile charge that Asian American literature is marked by "the failure of Asian-American manhood to express itself in its simplest form: fathers and sons" (Chin et al. xlvi).

As well as exploring multiples of theme, teachers need to consider what might be called in(ter)ventions of form. Because Asian American poetry has emerged from both institutional and noninstitutional literary sites, readers must be prepared to deal with a variety of formal practices. Janice Mirikitani's poems generally preserve the spirit and performative elements of a type of movement poetics, while eschewing unnecessary verbal complexity and "difficulty." Because they communicate her political philosophy clearly and unambiguously and because Mirikitani understands poetry as essentially an oral or aural practice (frequently augmented with music or other performative elements), her poems can prove important, entertaining, and accessible or else heavy-handed and didactic to different sets of readers. Paying close attention to form not only as a derivation of a theoretical position but as a writing element that swerves both in and out of the author's control can reopen the poetic text in a variety of ways. Such a strategy can promote a reading of Mirikitani's well-known poem "Breaking Silence" (*Shedding Silence* 33–36), for example, as a type of spatial discourse. In the poem the author juxtaposes the history of labor, imposed silence, and ultimately the incarceration of the Japanese in America, given on one side of each page, with excerpts from her mother's 1981 testimony to the Commission on the Wartime Relocation and Internment of Japanese American Civilians, given on the other. In part such spacing—especially with the government announcements occupying the "dominant" upper left margin space and the mother's testimony occupying a "subordinate" lower right-hand side—effects a visualization both of the racist binary that led to the internment and of the painful but necessary commission proceedings that solicited testimony from surviving internees. The use of the mother's quotes on one side of the page serves as a counter to the official internment discourse but additionally conveys her status as a spatial claimant in America. The poem is, as its title implies, about "breaking silence," but it is also about losing and finding space. As the mother's quotes gradually merge with the words of her daughter, they shoulder their way onto the left-hand side of the page, in effect dissolving the poem's visual segregation.

Jessica Hagedorn shares Mirikitani's political consciousness and commitment to performance but more frequently and perhaps more purposefully engages in a cross-disciplinarity that destabilizes meaning and unsettles mere language as the presumptive center of poetry. Such titles as "Filipino Boogie," "Latin Music in New York," "Canto Negro," and "The Woman Who Thought She Was More than a Samba" (all in *Danger and Beauty*) suggest a complex interaction among linguistic and nonlinguistic modes of expression. In the latter poem, for example, the samba serves superficially as a meta-phor for an objectified woman but resonates more deeply as one of the biorhythms constituting the dance. Samba consists of a series of steps involving pelvic tilts and a series of syncopated pushes with the foot, as if into the earth or the molten core of existence, the earth's center being the locus of creation according to numerous tribal myths. As a type of rhythm, the poem pulls against the static notion of art-as-monument and reconnects the woman to movement, creation, and life. In effect, she is simultaneously more than and no more than a samba. Hagedorn also experi-ments with visual phenomena. Extracted from her video *Words in Your Face*, her work "Lullaby" deploys a medley of photographs, iconic images, allusions to music and dream, and words spread over five pages (Lew 141–45). While the idea that "Lullaby" pays tribute to her child Paloma's powers of renewal is readily discernible, the words are not privileged over other forms of expression. Ultimately, the poem does not allego-rize its images and words; they do not come together to form a meaning. Instead, it honors the mystery of the lullaby and the inchoate nature of sleep.

A poet more reared in academic convention, Cathy Song also benefits from a close scrutiny of form. In the title poem "Picture Bride" (3–4) from Song's first book, the speaker, the granddaughter of a picture bride from Korea, tries to conjure an image of her grandmother standing on her wedding night before a stranger on a volcanic island in which the dry winds and cane fires evoke Dantean tortures of hell rather than the tourists' vision of a honeymooners' paradise. Founded on the idea of family history, the poem alludes simultaneously to class and race factors that historically gov-erned the "development" of the Hawaiian Islands. The poem depends in part on the power of contrast among sensory images, especially those of soft and hard, fine and rough, as in the "silk bow" of the bridal jacket against the "dry wind" (4) relentlessly insinuating itself beneath the folds of the elegant Korean hanbok. The unspoken ques-tion is, What can be given birth to under such violative circumstances? The first three lines of the poem are strikingly flat: "She was a year younger / than I, / twenty-three when she left Korea" (3). Constituting the only declarative sentence in the poem, these lines are followed by a series of four interrogative sentences of varying length and grammatical complexity. The poem is about searching, asking, and not knowing. It is about feeling cut off generationally and culturally. In effect, it declares that we cannot adequately recover history but nevertheless are compelled to engage in its search. While such a warning can be usefully sounded in every historical quarter, it resounds with particular poignancy among those, like Asian Americans, for whom histories have been suppressed, disallowed, and erased. It is a poem that unifies Asian American constituencies around a historical—and grammatical—configuration of unanswered questions.

It is entirely possible that Song intended the final image of her poem to be a static (though emotionally resonant) one—the kind of powerful tableau that characterizes many of the endings of her poetry and that once may have reflected dominant teaching practices in creative writing programs (see Altieri). But the form of this particular poem contains both a spatial trajectory and a temporal momentum that carry us to the point of unspoken consummation—and beyond. For if the poem leaves us with an unasked question, the fact remains that a consummation did take place and that this consummation ultimately produced a yield—in the form of the granddaughter who now attempts to produce the history of her ancestor. This attempt at inscription and preservation in turn marks another sort of violation, a violation of the dominant historical narratives of America and of the various acts of legislation that attempted to suppress the capacities for Asians to reproduce in America. Thus, by using the poem's own formal properties as a fulcrum, teachers can read beyond any limits of authorial intention and reconstruct the picture bride phenomenon as a trade practice designed to circumvent Asian extinction.

The possibilities of rethinking themes through a close consideration of forms have yet to be thoroughly pursued by critics and scholars. Yet these possibilities are legion. In concentrating on poetic form, we also may be teaching how writing practices inter-sect. The poet Mitsuye Yamada often seeks to recover local historical fragments of the Japanese American past, most notably life in the internment camps. In her poem "Desert Storm," she experiments with short, fractionalized lines: "This was not / im / prison / ment. / This was / re / location" ("*Camp Notes*" 19). Along with suggesting the awkward compression of people into minimalistic spaces, the fragmentation recalls the work of the poet and pacifist E. E. Cummings, whom Yamada, as a Nisei, probably read during the course of her schooling in America. Yet the brevity also reminds us of compressed, syllabic, sharply imagistic Japanese verse (which Yamada's Issei father wrote). At what point do the respective writing practices meet and depart? How do the formal conventions associated with each practice yield variant interpretations? And how does such a poem inform divergent literary histories? These questions and others show how the intersecting of multiple literary practices at the juncture of form deepens and enriches analytic possibilities.

The Effect of Audience

Audience is a vital yet often overlooked element in teaching poetry of any kind. But emphasizing the multiple coordinates of audience in Asian American poetry can help students rethink facile generalizations about poetry's universality. I have already im-plied aspects of audience in discussing works by the writers Janice Mirikitani and Jessica Hagedorn, but it may be instructive to consider further its conceptual functions. For Mirikitani there often exist at least two separable audiences. In one way she writes history for a readership outside Asian America, and in another she seeks to stimulate a sense of shared consciousness, mutual goals, and progressive social possibilities within an audience of Asian (or more broadly minoritized) Americans themselves. In the first instance she opens a distance between writer and audience by reformulating racial binaries in terms of knowledge/ignorance and experience/inexperience. The audience that lacks experience and knowledge is the one that must suspend judgment and (for once) maintain silence. In the second case, Mirikitani closes the distance between writer and audience by eschewing the kinds of poetic practices that might loosen her ties with a community of nonspecialist readers. Among her two audiences, then, one serves more as an abstraction, while the other enjoys a presence to which the language, rhythm, and sometimes interdisciplinarity of the poetry attempt to respond and in some sense inspire.

Clearly audience can serve as an instrument of inclusion or exclusion. Jessica Hagedorn's "Motown/Smokey Robinson" (Bruchac, *Breaking Silence* 45) directly addresses a young Filipina growing up in inner-city San Francisco in the 1960s. The young woman's fate—she's a runaway whose father may have dangled her as marriage bait to an Old-Timer; she eventually becomes pregnant and "give[s] up harmonizing"—is seen as a product of social and economic circumstances that she neither controls nor apparently understands. But while the socioeconomic critique remains firmly embedded in the poem, Hagedorn also wishes to celebrate the cultural vibrancy of the minoritized, nonsuburban space. To have experienced the inner-city "Motown" of the 1960s was to know that in a certain way "Life's never been so fine!" Twice near the end of the poem, the lyrics from a Smokey Robinson tune materialize on the page. If you know the tunes, you can sing along; if you don't, you can't, the poem seems to say. But the auditory registers of the poem also imply an exclusion: only those who lived the inner-city life can now hear, sing, or experience these songs in the "right" way. Thus, the net effect is not to reenfold a general audience (of a certain age) in nostalgia but to minoritize that experience by linking it to an expressly inner-city ethos. Coming at exclusion from a different direction, Garrett Hongo's subversively witty poem "Who among You Knows the Essence of Garlic" addresses an audience of amateurs (orientalists) who attempt to know (Asian) cultures by claiming to know their cuisines (*Yellow Light* 42). The poem mocks such superficial knowledge, along with the attendant trope of cultural consumption, by suggesting that the nonlocal (or non-Asian) audience members must always remain culinary outsiders. The poem's feat is that it manages to stimulate our senses of taste, even as it argues for an exclusivity of knowledge. Its inside joke is that its array of foods, as it turns out, cannot be linked to any single ethnic culture.

Teaching Asian American poetry through concepts of audience can also amplify and redirect existing interpretations. Marilyn Chin has won considerable critical acclaim for her linguistic inventiveness and stylistic agility—traits traditionally well received in American verse. But with her alinear, associational practices and her wealth of supposedly exotic images (cangue, mugwort, congee, kapok) that derive perhaps in equal parts from her studies in classical Chinese literature, her early childhood in Hong Kong, and her personal iconoclasm, Chin poses difficulties for many readers. Her poem "We Are Americans Now, We Live in the Tundra" seems invitingly clear, then, in telling how even a "Chinese girl [living in San Francisco] gets the blues" as she ponders an American environment ("the zoo!") that continuously compromises her sense of connection with China, a nation reduced on maps to "a giant begonia" (*Dwarf Bamboo* 28). The poem laments that, like the "giant Pandas," the speaker faces extinction, in her case because of the inexorable pull of assimilation. But to teach the poem in terms of its internal audience of Asian Americans alters and deepens the interpretation. The "we" of the title and of the poem refers to a specific ethnic cohort within America, a cohort that probably could be expanded to encompass other Asian Americans but certainly does not mean everyone in the United States. The "we" is an echo of an implied set of earlier "we's": the "we," for example, of Chinese railroad builders whose contributions to making America "a sea of cities, a wood of cars" were erased from national histories and from the visual maps constituted by government-approved photographs of the railroad workers; and the "we" of the activists in the Asian American movement who, influenced by the "blues song" of African Americans, initiated the sustained critique of Americanization from an Asian American perspective. The "we" of Chin's poem "live in the tundra / Of the logical"; its "we" do not inhabit the center of American culture but instead occupy the wild, uncultivated perimeters of its logic. The poem is not just about the pull of assimilation, then, but also about the pull of assimilation on an ultimately unassimilable audience. Teaching audience allows us to see that the "we" of Asian America remain confined to a territory outside America's central logic but at the same time occupy a region of encroachment, eruption, and critique. The poem bears affinities with writings of the early 1970s, even as it pursues its own highly idiosyncratic course.

While individual poems may envision a fixed internal audience of Asian Americans, audience alignments inevitably prove provisional. Asian America itself constitutes a multiple audience, as the critical reception of the novelist and poet Lois-Ann Yamanaka amply demonstrates. Yamanaka's book of poetry *Saturday Night at the Pahala Theatre* (1993) received widespread critical acclaim for its originality and skillful use of language, including pidgin. While she is only one of many Hawai'i-born writers who have responded to the beauty and demonstrable resources of the vernacular, readers were drawn as well to her powerful depictions of ethnic, class, and gender differentials and to her efforts at sweeping away the manicured image of Hawai'i as an exotic paradise, an image that has always depended in part on the exoticization of pidgin and the suppression of the islands' native speakers. Other readers recognized as legacies of Western imperialism the physical savagery, racism, sexism, class barriers, social oppression, and emotional deprivation observable in the attitudes and behaviors of the characters who populate her poems. Yet these same poems and her prose fiction, most notably the novel *Blu's Hanging*, so well received among non–Asian American (as well as among many Asian American) readers, have generated a firestorm within the field of Asian American studies itself.

The poem "Kala Gave Me Anykine Advice Especially about Filipinos When I Moved to Pahala" (Yamanaka 15–16) was sharply criticized, for example, for its negative depictions of a Filipino man. While the young Kala (in the next poem we learn that she is only in the seventh grade) serves as a distinctly unreliable narrator who parrots dire warnings and recycles racial stereotypes imposed from without, Yamanaka as a Japanese American stands in a historically privileged socioeconomic position relative to Filipinos in Hawai'i and in a shadowy relationship to the wartime presence of Japan in the Philippines. Thus, she occupies a morally ambiguous relationship to the

Filipino image being repropagated here and even more invidiously—and without a countervailing image—in *Blu's Hanging*, according to her detractors, who, like her supporters, comprise both Filipino Americans and non–Filipino Americans. While my reading of the poem differs from its critics' reading and although I believe that Yamanaka is a superb, and superbly ironic, writer, I can appreciate the fact that from the perspective of Asian American history and literary history, freedom of expression will be answerable at some point—at least to some among the hybrid and multiple Asian American audiences—to the unsatisfied moral claims of those histories. While I believe that freedom of speech tilts the issue decidedly in Yamanaka's favor, it never-theless remains vital to teach this conflict—as vital as it is to dissect the interior workings of the text or to demonstrate its aesthetic kinships with other poetry.

Preserving Difference

While diversity remains one of the particular strengths of Asian American poetry, teaching parameters threaten to narrow as more poets gain institutional recognition, whether in the form of honors and awards or access to high-profile publishers. I refer here not to an actual narrowing of range or shrinking of the quantity of poets but to the possibility that the teaching may fall prey to the process of homogenization that underwrites many of the awards and much of the publication in the first place. Such rewards attest to excellence—but frequently (not always) to the same type of excel-lence, one valorizing dominant writing practices within the academy. Such a statement in no way diminishes the importance of these poets or the value of these awards. Personally, I find many of these writers among the most compelling and rewarding that I teach, but I would never claim that they constitute the field of Asian American poetry. Literature teachers must guard against teaching only from a narrow, though comfortable, range of poets. They should guard too against drawing on traditional humanist notions that prematurely dissolve racial and ethnic differences in the name of universality, a particular temptation at a time when ethnographic signifiers, once seemingly ubiquitous, have ceased to be the sine qua non of Asian American poetry. I am not arguing that we must discover in every poem some feature that declares it either by design or by interpretation to be "Asian American." Rather, I am suggesting that we start by assuming the potential for difference rather than by assuming the reverse. Interpretive possibilities tend to contract when we expect to find the universal within a text; they expand when we scour it for the particular.

Sometimes the differences are readily apparent. Poets like David Mura and Mari-lyn Chin assume an active stance of resistance to assimilation, which they regard as an unnatural and abnormal process. To try too hard "to be white," as Mura suggests in his poem "A Nisei Picnic," is to pursue imposture and to run the risk of becoming grotesque like the "uncle," "aunt," and "father" he describes (*After We Lost Our Way* 14). Reading such writers, we are from the start alerted to the fact that no matter how skillfully they exploit the aesthetic possibilities of poetry as it is practiced (and rewarded) in America, they still seek to preserve a difference. Lawson Fusao Inada also has resisted the absorption of his poetry into a dominant Euro-American poetics, in part by experimenting with rhythm. His early poem "Blues for Dan Morin" not only pays homage to the African American blues and jazz greats that a West Fresno Sansei learned to appreciate but also depends on an improvisational rhythm that, like a jam session, draws bodies (in this case cultures) together: "Might as well / sing something / softly to myself, some / Bird thing tripped / quickly off the tongue" (*Before the War* 78). A much later poem, "Kicking the Habit," describes a self-professed "Angloholic" who one day decides to "stop using English"—permanently. Pulling "onto a dark country road," he "emerge[s] in another nation," a nation of insects and animals, a "greater world" in which he utters the words "Chemawa? Chinook?" and the pines answer "Clackamas, Siskiyou" (*Drawing* 48–51). As the Indian words are uttered, the shape of the poem gains elasticity, with the words seeming to circulate more freely across the page. The poem's aesthetic proclivities and jocular tone undergo a simultaneous transformation. By the end the poem expresses the Native American view of the interactivity of humans and the natural world, with the "yellow / sun" turned into the veritable source of language and enunciating the poet's own name—"Fusao. Inada" (*Drawing* 51).

Inada's two poems are perhaps obvious examples of the poet's circumventing dominant writing practices by linking sensibility to that of other minoritized peoples. But racial and ethnic difference also can serve as an interpretive starting point with poets who seem to locate their difference outside such categories. A poet who has gained an impressive critical following in a short period of time, Timothy Liu alludes to his Chinese ancestry or to intergenerational conflicts stemming from variant cultural practices only sparingly. The father appears as a figure weak, passive, decent but ineffectual, while the mother, suffering from a profound psychological disorder, exhibits the wrath of a Fury. Neither parent's behavior is readily traceable to cross-cultural factors or ethnic traits. Clearly foregrounded, however, are the poet's sexual activities, spiritual yearnings, and the joys and pains of human connection. Thus, the temptation sets in to view the work as a manifestation of racial and cultural transcendence and to revive the notion of poetry as a universal language.

The locus of Liu's difference, it seems, is his sexual orientation. Classified under the double rubric "Poetry Gay Studies," his second book of poems, *Burnt Offerings* (1995), boasts a back cover containing a black-and-white photo of the youthful, bespectacled, and apparently long-haired poet, along with a dose of generous praise from three venerable European American poets: Richard Howard, Marilyn Hacker, and Gerald Stern. Missing from these testimonials, however, is any mention of Liu as an Asian American or of his poetry as relating in any way to Asian American literary practices. The tension between the photograph and the testimonials goes unremarked except in the thumbnail biography's richly ambiguous declaration that "since serving a Mormon mission in Hong Kong from 1984 to 1986, he has devoted his life to poetry." Liu, it would seem, has been purified of such categories as race, ethnicity, and religious affiliation (and perhaps sexuality too) by becoming a votary at the shrine of Art.

Yet the relative absence of ethnographic signs speaks directly to the experience of being Asian American under specific conditions of class, locale, educational environment, and so forth in the 1990s. Such absence figures meaningfully into Asian American literary history too. In this light Liu's sexual orientation is not dominant over but instead inseparable from his race and ethnicity. In alluding to the one characteristic, his poetry automatically alludes to the other. In contrast to the poet, the teacher can effect a separation, analytically. When Liu describes two lovers' breakup in the poem "Winter" (*Burnt Offerings* 17), we should feel free to pose the question, Why (if we didn't know the poet by his name and photograph) would we tend to assume that both men in the poem are white? And how does it alter our interpretation to suppose that the speaker is Asian American? In addition, if we are versed in Asian Americana, we might show how Liu necessarily addresses the issue of Asian American masculinity, expanding it beyond both the historical stereotypes of the "effeminate" or nonsexual Asian American man and the cartoonlike images of machismo that sometimes serve as a retaliatory response. In renorming Asian American masculinity by refusing to equate "gay" with "effeminate," Liu has effectively signed into an existing debate within Asian American literary studies. Gayness for Liu is merely a different border for masculinity.

At the same time, to view Liu as a "queer" poet allows us to see how his sexual difference recoordinates the concept of Asian America. As a trope for difference, "queerness" can be paired—and is nearly historically synchronous—with the term "Asian America." In his article "Queer / Asian American / Canons," David L. Eng points out that both terms are "traditional" insofar as they have been "canonized by the mainstream through repetition and over time as a locus of absence—as dismissible and unimportant, for instance, in the consideration of American identity and nation formation" (16) From this historical perspective, "queer" does not merely expand definitions of Asian America but virtually overtakes it, renaming and renorming as it goes along. What, after all, were the immigrants at Angel Island if not subjects arbitrarily detained, inspected, isolated—in a word, "queered"—by American authorities? Their bodies subjected to humiliating medical examination, their language mocked, their customs declared undesirable, the poets of Angel Island consistently broached issues of normality. Their poems declare at once the historical imposition of queerness as a category and the constant act of self-reconstruction that the Asian of any generation in America is called on to engage in. Similarly, the obsession in some of David Mura's poetry with the white female body as constructed through pornography attests to a status historically "queered" in American culture even when heterosexual. In "The Colors of Desire," the title poem of his second book of poetry, Mura's speaker recalls observing a black man and a white woman engaging in sex in a porno film and wondering "(where am I, / the missing third?)" (5). As an Asian racial body, the speaker finds himself permanently trapped in the position of sexual voyeur, arbitrarily excluded from the position of sexual participation and literally parenthesized—acutely aware, however, of the queerness or absurdity of the marginalized (and darkened) Asian body observing the black and white bodies of America enacting what amounts to a social parody of interracial love.

While I do not argue that every poem by an Asian American manifests evidence of difference, I do maintain that being alert to it can reshape our teaching practices and oftentimes alter our interpretations. I take as a final example the poet Adrienne Su, the author of *Middle Kingdom* (1997). Raised in the American suburbs, far removed from movement politics in both age and locale and by training partial to certain formalistic conventions, including rhyme, Su is a poet who for all her apparent assimilation retains a self-conscious reservoir of difference. To read a poem like "Elegy" (31–32), a sestina leaving no racial or ethnic markers, is to be tempted to see a writer not only inhabiting a Western poetic tradition but also accepting uncritically the universalistic assumptions that frequently accompany it. In fact, however, her volume's initial poem, "Address" (not to mention her book's title), tells us otherwise. The poem's title refers both to the speaker's address ("Eldorado Drive / in the suburbs") and to the forms of address that ultimately unsettle ideas of universality. Beginning with the line, "There are many ways of saying Chinese / in American," the poem informs us that to use the wrong tonal element is to alter the meaning of the word completely: "One [tone] means restaurant. / Others mean comprador, coolie, green army" (3). For all her familiarity with suburbia ("slumber party," "swimming pool"), the speaker knows that "America bursts with things it was never meant / to have," including "a new crop of names, / like mine." Then, in a clever turn, the poem tells us that what is "different" is her first name rather than her surname: "because it is Adrienne. / It's French. / It means *artful*" (4). The obvious suggestion is that the artist is different, but the poem encodes a second message. Pretending not to understand that her real difference in America is not her first name (which has lost its etymological traces anyway) but her second, the speaker in effect warns us against ignoring other categories of difference. The absence of the word "Su" is part of the poet's artfulness here and elsewhere. She suggests that she will leave artful traces or subtle tones of her "Su" even in poems from which it is apparently altogether absent.

———

Asian American poetry has a rich and diverse history, its origins located in a variety of literary, cultural, and linguistic traditions, its production marked by multiple writing practices and theories. Its history does not compose a seamless narrative, but notions of critique and coalition recur with frequency, and points of connection arise even in unlikely places and among unlikely candidates. While increasing numbers of Asian American poets have established high-profile reputations, the field is equally constituted by the lesser known. For pedagogical purposes we should be prepared to investigate the multiples of theme and the variables of form, to explore the complex yet vital effect of audience, and to pursue the interpretive possibilities embedded in concepts of difference. Students and teachers are apt to find all this a most challenging task—but one that amply repays every expenditure of effort.

Notes

1. I follow critical tradition by including the works of Asian Canadians under the rubric *Asian American*.
2. Elaine H. Kim has observed that poems by Issei (first-generation Japanese in America) appeared in earlier though less widely known works, including Nixon and Tama's *Sounds from the Unknown* and Ito's *Issei*.
3. Because of their insistence that a particular Asian American sensibility and language characterize the literature, the *Aiiieeeee!* editors defined Hartmann as "Asian" rather than "Asian American." Similarly, Elaine Kim has viewed Villa as a colonially educated Filipino whose poetry "has little to identify it as the work of anyone other than an avant-garde American writer" (288).
4. These poems may be found in the following works: Chock, in *Talk Story* (Chock et al.); S. Liu, in *Breaking Silence* (Bruchac); Gotera, Hongo, and Ali, in *The Open Boat* (Hongo); Lee, in his collection *Rose*; Lum, in *Chinese American Poetry* (Wang and Zhao); T. Liu, in his *Burnt Offerings*; Penaranda and Syquia, in *Liwanag* (Cachapero et al.); and Inada, in his *Drawing the Line*.

Bibliography

Ai [Ogawa]. *Cruelty*. Boston: Houghton, 1973.

———. *Killing Floor*. Boston: Houghton, 1979.

———. *Sin*. Boston: Houghton, 1986.

Alexander, Meena. *The Bird's Bright Ring*. Calcutta: Writers Workshop, 1976.

———. *House of a Thousand Doors*. Washington: Three Continents, 1988.

———. *Without Place*. Calcutta: Writers Workshop, 1977.

Ali, Agha Shahid. *The Beloved Witness: Selected Poems*. New York: Viking, 1992.

———. *The Half-Inch Himalayas*. Middletown: Wesleyan UP, 1987.

———. *A Nostalgist's Map of America*. New York: Norton, 1991.

Altieri, Charles. *Self and Sensibility in Contemporary American Poetry*. New York: Cambridge UP, 1984.

Balaz, Joseph P., ed. *Ho'omanoa: An Anthology of Contemporary Hawai'ian Literature*. Honolulu: Ku Pa'a, 1989.

Bay Area Pilipino American Writers. *Without Names: A Collection of Poems*. San Francisco: Kearny Street Workshop, 1985.

Berssenbrugge, Mei-mei. *Fish Souls*. New York: Greenwood, 1971.

———. *The Heat Bird*. Providence: Burning Deck, 1983.

———. *Random Possession*. New York: Reed, 1979.

———. *Summits Move with the Tide*. Greenfield Center: Greenfield Review, 1974.

Bruchac, Joseph, ed. *Breaking Silence: An Anthology of Contemporary Asian American Poets*. Greenfield Center: Greenfield Review, 1983.

Bulosan, Carlos. *Letter from America*. Prairie City: Decker, 1942.

———. *The Voice of Bataan*. New York: McCann, 1943.

Cachapero, Emily, et al., eds. *Liwanag: Literary and Graphic Expressions by Filipinos in America*. [San Francisco]: Liwanag, 1975.

Cha, Theresa Hak Kyung. *Dictee*. New York: Tanam, 1982.

Chan, Jeffery, et al., eds. *The Big Aiiieeeee! An Anthology of Chinese American and Japanese American Literature*. New York: Meridian, 1991.

Chang, Juliana, ed. *Quiet Fire: A Historical Anthology of Asian American Poetry, 1892–1970*. New York: Asian Amer. Writers' Workshop, 1996.

Chiang, Fay, et al., eds. *American Born and Foreign: An Anthology of Asian American Poetry*. Spec. issue of *Sunbury: A Poetry Magazine* 7-8 (1979): 1–152.

Chin, Frank, et al., eds. *Aiiieeeee! An Anthology of Asian-American Writers*. Washington: Howard UP, 1974.

Chin, Marilyn. *Dwarf Bamboo*. Greenfield Center: Greenfield Review, 1987.

———. *The Phoenix Gone, the Terrace Empty*. Minneapolis: Milkweed, 1994.

Chin, Marilyn, David Wong Louie, and Ken Weisner, eds. *Dissident Song: A Contemporary Asian American Anthology*. Spec. issue of *Quarry West* 29-30 (1991): 1–168.

Chock, Eric. *Last Days Here*. Honolulu: Bamboo Ridge, 1990.

Chock, Eric, et al., eds. *Talk Story: An Anthology of Hawai'i's Local Writers*. Honolulu: Petronium–Talk Story, 1978.

Chock, Eric, and Darrell H. Y. Lum, eds. *The Best of Bamboo Ridge: The Hawai'i Writers' Quarterly*. Honolulu: Bamboo Ridge, 1986.

———, eds. *Paké: Writings by Chinese in Hawai'i*. Honolulu: Bamboo Ridge, 1989.

Dabydeen, Cyril, ed. *Another Way to Dance: Contemporary Asian Poetry from Canada and the United States*. Toronto: TSAR, 1996.

———. *Distances*. Vancouver: Fiddlehead, 1977.

Divakaruni, Chitra Banerjee. *Arranged Marriage*. New York: Anchor, 1995.

———. *Leaving Yuba City*. New York: Anchor, 1997.

Eng, David L. "Queer/Asian American/Canons." *Teaching Asian America: Diversity and the Problem of Community*. Ed. Lane Ryo Hirabayashi. Lanham: Rowman, 1998. 13–23.

Foster, Sesshu. *Angry Days*. Los Angeles: West End, 1987.

Francia, Luis H., and Eric Gamalinda, eds. *Flippin': Filipinos on America*. New York: Asian Amer. Writers' Workshop, 1996.

Fujita, Jun. *Tanka: Poems in Exile*. Chicago: Covici-McGee, 1923.

Gee, Emma, et al., eds. *Counterpoint: Perspectives on Asian America*. Los Angeles: UCLA Asian Amer. Studies Center, 1976.

Gill, Stephen, ed. *Green Snow: An Anthology of Canadian Poets of Asian Origin*. Cornwall, ON: Vesta, 1976.

Gotera, Vince. *Dragonfly*. San Antonio: Pecan Grove, 1994.

Hagedorn, Jessica. *Danger and Beauty*. New York: Penguin, 1993.

———. *Dangerous Music*. San Francisco: Momo's, 1975.

———. *Pet Food and Tropical Apparitions*. San Francisco: Momo's, 1981.

Hahn, Kimiko. *Air Pocket*. New York: Hanging Loose, 1992.

———. *Earshot*. New York: Hanging Loose, 1992.

———. *Mosquito and Ant*. New York: Norton, 1999.

Hakutani, Yoshinobu, ed. *Prose*. Cranbury: Assoc. UP, 1992. Vol. 2 of *Selected English Writings of Yone Noguchi: An East-West Literary Assimilation*.

Han, Stephanie. *L.A. (Lovers Anonymous)*. Venice: LALA, 1995.

Hartmann, Sadakichi. *"Drifting Flowers of the Sea" and Other Poems*. [New York]: [Hartmann], 1904.

———. *Japanese Rhythms: Tanka, Haikai, and Dodoitsu Form*. N.p.: n.p., 1926.

———. *Tanka and Haikai: Fourteen Japanese Rhythms*. New York: Bruno, 1915.

———. *White Chrysanthemums: Literary Fragments and Pronouncements*. Ed. George Knox and Harry Lawton. New York: Herder, 1971.

Hom, Marlon K., ed. and trans. *Songs of Gold Mountain: Cantonese Rhymes from San Francisco Chinatown*. Berkeley: U of California P, 1987.

Hongo, Garrett, ed. *The Open Boat: Poems from Asian America*. New York: Anchor, 1993.

———. *River of Heaven*. New York: Knopf, 1988.

———. *Yellow Light*. Middletown: Wesleyan UP, 1982.

Hongo, Garrett, Alan Chong Lau, and Lawson Fusao Inada, eds. *The Buddha Bandits down Highway 99*. Mountain View: Buddhahead, 1978.

Howard, Katsuyo K., ed. *Passages: An Anthology of the Southeast Asian Refugee Experience*. Fresno: Southeast Asian Student Services, California State U, 1990.

Hsu, Kai-yu, and Helen Palubinskas, eds. *Asian-American Authors*. Boston: Houghton, 1972.

Ikeda, Patricia. *House of Wood, House of Salt*. Cleveland: Cleveland State UP, 1978.

Inada, Lawson Fusao. *Before the War: Poems As They Happened*. New York: Morrow, 1971.

———. *Drawing the Line*. Minneapolis: Coffee House, 1997.

———. *Legends from Camp*. Minneapolis: Coffee House, 1992.

Ito, Kazuo. *Issei: A History of Japanese Immigrants in North America*. Trans. Shinichiro Nakamura and Jean S. Gerard. Seattle: Executive Committee for Pub. of *Issei*, 1973.

Jacinto, Jaime. *Heaven Is Just Another Country*. San Francisco: Kearny Street Workshop, 1996.

Kawakami, Iwao. *"The Parents" and Other Poems*. San Francisco: Nichibei Times, 1947.

Kim, Elaine H. *Asian American Literature: An Introduction to the Writings and Their Social Context*. Philadelphia: Temple UP, 1982.

Kim, Willyce. *Eating Artichokes*. Oakland: Women's Press Collective, 1972.

Kiyooka, Roy. *Kyoto Airs*. Vancouver: Periwinkle, 1964.

———. *Nevertheless These Eyes*. Toronto: Coach House, 1967.

———. *Pacific Windows: Collected Poems of Roy K. Kiyooka*. Burnaby, BC: Talonbooks, 1997.

———. *Wheels*. Toronto: Coach House, 1982.

Kogawa, Joy. *A Choice of Dreams*. Toronto: McClelland, 1974.

———. *The Splintered Moon*. Fredericton, NB: Fiddlehead, 1968.

Kono, Juliet S. *Hilo Rains*. Honolulu: Bamboo Ridge, 1988.

Kono, Juliet S., and Cathy Song, eds. *Sister Stew: Fiction and Poetry by Women*. Honolulu: Bamboo Ridge, 1991.

Kudaka, Geraldine, ed. *On a Bed of Rice: An Asian American Erotic Feast*. New York: Anchor, 1995.

Lai, Him Mark, Genny Lim, and Judy Yung, eds. *Island: Poetry and History of Chinese Immigrants on Angel Island, 1910 to 1940*. San Francisco: San Francisco Study Center, 1980.

Larsen, Wendy Wilder, and Tran Thi Nga. *Shallow Graves: Two Women and Vietnam*. New York: Random, 1986.

Lau, Alan Chong. *Songs for Jadina*. Greenfield Center: Greenfield Review, 1980.

Lau, Carolyn. *Wode Shuofa*. Santa Fe: Tooth of Time, 1988.

Lau, Evelyn. *Oedipal Dreams*. Victoria: Beach Holme, 1992.

Lee, Li-Young. *The City in Which I Love You*. Brockport: BOA, 1990.

———. *Rose*. Brockport: BOA, 1986.

Leong, Russell. *The Country of Dreams and Dust*. Albuquerque: West End, 1993.

Lew, Walter K, ed. *Premonitions: The Kaya Anthology of New Asian North American Poetry*. New York: Kaya, 1995.

Lim, Shirley Geok-lin. *Crossing the Peninsula*. Kuala Lumpur: Heinemann, 1980.

Lim, Shirley Geok-lin, and Mayumi Tsutakawa, eds. *The Forbidden Stitch: An Asian American Women's Anthology*. Corvallis: Calyx, 1989.

Lim-Hing, Sharon, ed. *The Very Inside: An Anthology of Writings by Asian and Pacific Islander Lesbian and Bisexual Women*. Toronto: Sister Vision, 1994.

Liu, Stephen Shu-Ning. *Dream Journeys to China*. Beijing: New World, 1982.

Liu, Timothy. *Burnt Offerings*. Port Townsend: Copper Canyon, 1995.

———. *Vox Angelica*. Cambridge: James, 1992.

Lum, Wing Tek. *Expounding the Doubtful Points*. Honolulu: Bamboo Ridge, 1987.

Maira, Sunaina, and Rajini Srikanth, eds. *Contours of the Heart: South Asians Map North America*. New Brunswick: Rutgers UP, 1996.

Mar, Laureen. *Living Furniture*. San Francisco: Noro, 1982.

Mirikitani, Janice. *Awake in the River*. San Francisco: Isthmus, 1978.

———. *Shedding Silence*. Berkeley: Celestial Arts, 1987.

———. *We, the Dangerous: New and Selected Poems*. Berkeley: Celestial Arts, 1995.

Mirikitani, Janice, et al., eds. *Ayumi: A Japanese American Anthology*. San Francisco: Japanese Amer. Anthology Committee, 1980.

———, eds. *Time to Greez! Incantations from the Third World*. San Francisco: Glide–Third World, 1975.

Mitsui, James Masao. *From a Three-Cornered World: New and Selected Poems*. Seattle: U of Washington P, 1997.

Mori, Kyoko. *Fallout*. Chicago: Tia Chucha, 1994.

Mura, David. *After We Lost Our Way*. New York: Dutton, 1989.

———. *The Colors of Desire*. New York: Anchor, 1995.

Nakano, Jiro, and Kay Nakano, eds. *Poets behind Barbed Wire*. Honolulu: Bamboo Ridge, 1983.

Nixon, Lucille M., and Tomoe Tama. *Sounds from the Unknown*. Denver: Swallow, 1963.

Noguchi, Rick. *The Ocean inside Kenji Takezo*. Pittsburgh: U of Pittsburgh P, 1995.

Noguchi, Yone. *From the Eastern Sea*. London: Unicorn, 1903.

———. *Japanese Hokkus*. Boston: Four Seas, 1920.

———. *Seen and Unseen; or, Monologues of a Homeless Snail*. San Francisco: Burgess, 1897.

———. *Selected Poems*. Boston: Four Seas, 1921.

Okita, Dwight. *Crossing with the Light*. Chicago: Tia Chucha, 1992.

Rexroth, Kenneth, ed. *Four Young Women: Poems*. New York: McGraw, 1973.

Robles, Al. *Kayaomunggi Vision of a Wandering Carabao*. San Francisco: Isthmus, 1983.

Roripaugh, Lee Ann. *Beyond Heart Mountain*. New York: Penguin, 1999.

Rustomji-Kerns, Roshni, ed. *Living in America: Poetry and Fiction by South Asian American Writers*. Boulder: Westview, 1995.

Saijo, Albert. *Outspeaks: A Rhapsody*. Honolulu: Bamboo Ridge, 1997.

Shikatani, Gerry. *Barking of Dog*. Toronto: Missing Link, 1973.

Shikatani, Gerry, and David Aylward, eds. *Paper Doors: An Anthology of Japanese Canadian Poetry*. Toronto: Coach House, 1981.

Song, Cathy. *Frameless Windows, Squares of Light*. New York: Norton, 1988.

———. *Picture Bride*. New Haven: Yale UP, 1983.

———. *School Figures*. Pittsburgh: U of Pittsburgh P, 1994.

Su, Adrienne. *Middle Kingdom*. Farmington: James, 1997.

Sunoo, Brenda Paik, ed. *Korean American Writings*. New York: Insight, 1975.

Sze, Arthur. *Archipelago*. Port Townsend: Copper Canyon, 1995.

———. *Dazzled*. Point Reyes Station: Floating Island, 1982.

Tabios, Eileen, ed. *Black Lightning: Poetry-in-Progress*. New York: Asian Amer. Writers' Workshop, 1998.

Tachiki, Amy, et al., eds. *Roots: An Asian American Reader*. Los Angeles: Continental, 1971.

Tagami, Jeff. *October Light*. San Francisco: Kearny Street Workshop, 1987.

Tham, Hilary. *Men and Other Strange Myths: Poems and Art*. Colorado Springs: Three Continents, 1994.

Third World Women. San Francisco: Third World, 1972.

Uyematsu, Amy. *Nights of Fire, Nights of Rain*. Ashland: Story Line, 1998.

———. *Thirty Miles from J-Town*. Brownsville: Story Line, 1992.

Villa, Jose Garcia. *Appassionata: Poems in Praise of Love*. 1942. New York: King, 1979.

———. *Have Come, Am Here*. New York: Viking, 1942.

———. *Poems Fifty-Five: The Best Poems of Jose Garcia Villa*. Manila: Florentino, 1962.

———. *Volume Two*. [New York]: New Directions, 1949.

Wah, Fred. *Among*. Toronto: Coach House, 1972.

———. *Loki Is Buried at Smokey Creek: Selected Poems*. Vancouver: Talonbooks, 1980.

———. *Mountain*. Buffalo: Audit, 1967.

Wand, David Hsin-Fu, ed. *Asian-American Heritage: An Anthology of Prose and Poetry*. New York: Washington Square, 1974.

Wang, L. Ling-Chi, and Henry Yiheng Zhao, eds. *Chinese American Poetry: An Anthology*. Santa Barbara: Asian Amer. Voices, 1991.

Wong, Nellie. *The Death of a Long Steam Lady*. Los Angeles: West End, 1986.

———. *Dreams in Harrison Railroad Park*. Berkeley: Kelsey Street, 1977.

Wong, Shawn, ed. *Asian American Literature: A Brief Introduction and Anthology*. New York: Harper, 1996.

Wong, Shawn, and Frank Chin, eds. Spec. issue of *Yardbird Reader* 3 (1974): 1–294.

Yamada, Mitsuye. *"Camp Notes" and Other Poems*. San Francisco: Shameless Hussy, 1976.

Yamanaka, Lois-Ann. *Blu's Hanging*. New York: Farrar, 1997.

———. *Saturday Night at the Pahala Theatre*. Honolulu: Bamboo Ridge, 1993.

Yau, John. *Corpse and Mirror*. New York: Holt, Rinehart, 1983.

———. *Radiant Silhouette: New and Selected Work, 1974–1988*. Santa Rosa: Black Sparrow, 1989.

zarco, cyn. *Cir'cum.nav'i.ga'tion*. Santa Fe: Tooth of Time, 1986.

Notes on Contributors

Nerissa S. Balce is a PhD candidate in ethnic studies at the University of California, Berkeley. She coauthored an essay on Filipino American literature with Jean Vengua Gier in the anthology *New Immigrant Literatures in the United States*. Her research focuses on the way Filipinos were racially imagined at the turn of the century and the way these representations can be traced in Asian American literature, historical texts, and popular culture. She was born and raised in Manila.

Leslie Bow is an assistant professor of English at the University of Miami, where she specializes in Asian American literature, ethnic autobiography, and writing by women of color. Her book *Betrayal and Other Acts of Subversion: Feminism, Sexual Politics, Asian American Women's Literature* is forthcoming from Princeton University Press. Her work has appeared in the journals *Cultural Critique, Profession, Prose Studies, Dispositio: American Journal of Comparative and Cultural Studies,* and *Forkroads: A Journal of Ethnic-American Literatures* as well as in several books, including *Who Can Speak? Authority and Critical Identity*.

Nancy Cho is an assistant professor of English at Carleton College, where she teaches courses in Asian American literature, American literature, and American studies. Her primary research interests include race and ethnicity theory, comparative American identities, and the history of racialized minorities in American theater. She is currently working on a manuscript entitled *Staging Ethnicity in Contemporary American Drama*.

Patricia P. Chu is an associate professor of English at George Washington University, where she teaches courses in American and Asian American literature. Her articles have appeared in *Arizona Quarterly, Asian Pacific American Heritage: A Companion to Literature and Arts,* and *Diaspora: A Journal of Transnational Studies*. Her forthcoming book, *Assimilating Asians: Gendered Strategies of Authorship in Asian America*, explores the cultural politics of gender and assimilation in Asian American coming-of-age narratives.

Cheng Lok Chua is a professor of English at California State University, Fresno; he has also taught at Moorhead State University and at the National University of Singapore. His research interests include Asian American literature and twentieth-century French fiction, on which he has published in *MELUS, Ethnic Groups* (London), *Modern Language Quarterly, Symposium,* and *Revue des lettres modernes*.

Shilpa Davé is a visiting assistant professor in the Asian American Studies Program and the English department at the University of Wisconsin, Madison. Her current research examines the development and representation in contemporary Asian American literature of the fetish for political and cultural citizenship. She also works on themes of community development in South Asian American women writers and writes about representations and theories of race and gender in Asian American popular culture and discourse.

Tamara C. Ho holds an MA and is completing her PhD work in comparative literature at the University of California, Los Angeles. Her other work on Wendy Law-Yone appears in *Amerasia Journal* and *Words Matter: Interviews with Asian American Writers* (2000). Her research focuses on Third World women, Asian American literature, and transnational and diasporic identities.

Laura Hyun Yi Kang is an assistant professor of women's studies and English and comparative literature at the University of California, Irvine. Her critical essays are included in *Writing Self, Writing Nation: Essays on Theresa Hak Kyung Cha's* Dictee and *Dangerous Women: Korean Women and Nationalism*. A book-length study, *Compositional Subjects: Enfiguring Asian/American Women*, is forthcoming.

Susan Koshy is an assistant professor in the Asian American Studies Department at the University of California, Santa Barbara. She has published articles on ethnicity, feminism and diasporic narratives, Asian American literature, whiteness and Asian American identity, and neocolonialism and human rights in *Diaspora, Social Text*, and the *Yale Journal of Criticism*. She is currently working on a book-length project on Asian American literature.

Rachel Lee is an assistant professor in the Departments of English and Women's Studies at the University of California, Los Angeles. She has held a National Endowment for the Humanities Fellowship and a Chancellor's Postdoctoral Fellowship at the University of California, Berkeley. She is the author of *The Americas of Asian American Literature: Gendered Fictions of Nation and Transnation* (1999). Her published articles appear in *African American Review, Cultural Critique, Boundary 2*, and various anthologies. Her work spans the fields of twentieth-century American literature, feminist theory, ethnic studies, and cultural studies.

Tim Libretti is an assistant professor of English and women's studies at Northeastern Illinois University. His essays on Chicana/Chicano, Asian American, and multiethnic literature and theory, United States proletarian literature, Marxism, cultural studies, and the intersection of working-class and racial and ethnic studies have been published in such journals as *MELUS, Race, Gender, and Class, Women's Studies Quarterly, Post Identity, Radical Teacher, Amerasia Journal*, and *Against the Current* and in several books.

Jinqi Ling is an associate professor of English and Asian American studies at the University of California, Los Angeles. He is the author of *Narrating Nationalisms: Ideology and Form in Asian American Literature* (1998). His articles have appeared in journals such as *American Literature* and *MELUS* and in critical collections of Asian American literature.

Marie Lo is a PhD candidate in rhetoric at the University of California, Berkeley. Her dissertation, "National Borders and Multicultural Citizens: Reading Asian American and Asian Canadian Literature," examines the effect of the United States–Canadian border on the internationalization of Asian American cultural criticism, reframing issues of globalization, nationalism, and multiculturalism in the context of an emerging body of Asian Canadian literature.

Viet Thanh Nguyen is an assistant professor of English and Asian American studies at the University of Southern California. His essays on Asian American literature have appeared in *Positions: East Asia Cultures Critique* and *American Literary History*, and he is working on a book about the representations of the body in Asian American literature.

Angela Pao is an associate professor of comparative literature at Indiana University, Bloomington. She is the author of *The Orient of the Boulevards: Exoticism, Empire, and*

Nineteenth-Century French Theater (1998) and articles on race and ethnicity in twentieth-century American theater that have appeared in *Amerasia Journal, Text and Performance Quarterly*, and *Theatre Survey*. She is currently working on a study of nontraditional casting practices and theories of race, ethnicity, and nationality.

David Shih is an assistant professor of English at the University of Wisconsin, Eau Claire. His primary research interests include Asian American autobiography and the ethnic canon, particularly its place and function within contemporary university curricula. His article "The Seduction of Origins: Sui Sin Far and the Race for Tradition" is forthcoming in the collection *Asian American Literature: Formations and Transformations*.

Stephen H. Sumida is a professor of American ethnic studies at the University of Washington, Seattle, where he researches and teaches in Asian Pacific American literature, including drama and theater, and in multicultural, interdisciplinary American studies. His work and interests currently involve him in international dimensions of American studies as well. He is the author of two volumes that have influenced the development of Asian Pacific American literary studies at large: *Asian American Literature: An Annotated Bibliography* (with Arnold T. Hiura, 1979) and *And the View from the Shore: Literary Traditions of Hawai'i* (1991).

George Uba is a professor of English and the acting chair of the Department of Asian American Studies at California State University, Northridge. His recent research includes essays on Jessica Hagedorn and Garrett Hongo, forthcoming in *The Reference Guide to American Literature*, and a study of innovative community teaching as a form of rewardable scholarship.

Roberta Uno is the artistic director of the New WORLD Theater, in residence at the Fine Arts Center at the University of Massachusetts, Amherst, and a professor in the university's Department of Theater. She has extensive directing credits in the Asian American canon and has lectured in the United States and abroad. The editor of *Unbroken Thread: An Anthology of Plays by Asian American Women* (1993) and a coeditor of *Contemporary Plays by Women of Color* (1996), she is also the author of *Monologues for Actors of Color* (1999) and articles in the *Dramatist's Quarterly, Parabasis, Theatre Topics*, and *International Theatre Forum*.

Sau-ling Cynthia Wong is a professor in the Asian American Studies Program, Department of Ethnic Studies, at the University of California, Berkeley. She is the author of *Reading Asian American Literature: From Necessity to Extravagance* (1993); the editor of *Maxine Hong Kingston's The Woman Warrior: A Casebook* (1998); and a founding coeditor of *Hitting Critical Mass: A Journal of Asian American Cultural Criticism* (since 1993). She has published extensively on Asian American autobiography, gender and sexuality, Chinese immigrant literature, and community and diasporic identity.

Sunn Shelley Wong is an associate professor in Cornell University's Department of English and Asian American Studies Program. She is also the director of the Asian American Studies Program. She has written articles on Mina Loy, Charles Olson, Toni Morrison, and Theresa Hak Kyung Cha.

Traise Yamamoto is an associate professor of English at the University of California, Riverside. She is the author of *Masking Selves, Making Subjects: Japanese American Women, Identity, and the Body* (1999). Her poetry has appeared in several anthologies and journals. She is currently working on a book of essays on Asian American feminism.

Chung-Hei Yun, a retired professor at Shawnee State University, is currently teaching as an adjunct professor of English at Central Michigan University. A former executive committee member of the MLA's Division on East Asian Languages and Literatures, she has presented extensively at conferences, translated Korean literature into English, and authored a critical study of Ronyoung Kim's *Clay Walls* in the anthology *Reading the Literatures of Asian America.*

Index